The History of
SCOTTISH LITERATURE

Volume 4

THE HISTORY OF SCOTTISH LITERATURE
general editor Cairns Craig

Volume 1 Medieval and Renaissance *editor R D S Jack*
Volume 2 1660 to 1800 *editor Andrew Hook*
Volume 3 Nineteenth Century *editor Douglas Gifford*
Volume 4 Twentieth Century *editor Cairns Craig*

DICTIONARIES from AUP

THE SCOTTISH NATIONAL DICTIONARY
(18th century to the present day)
in ten volumes

THE COMPACT SCOTTISH NATIONAL DICTIONARY
in two volumes

A DICTIONARY OF THE OLDER SCOTTISH TONGUE
From the twelfth century to the end of the seventeenth
Volumes 1 to 6 (and continuing)

THE CONCISE SCOTS DICTIONARY
editor-in-chief Mairi Robinson

GAELIC DICTIONARY
Malcolm MacLennan

i

The History of
SCOTTISH LITERATURE

Volume 4

Twentieth Century

edited by Cairns Craig

general editor Cairns Craig

ABERDEEN UNIVERSITY PRESS

First published 1987
This edition 1989
Aberdeen University Press
A member of the Pergamon Group

The publisher acknowledges subsidy from the Scottish Arts Council towards the publication of this volume.

British Library Cataloguing in Publication Data

The History of Scottish literature.
  Vol. 4: The twentieth century
  1. English literature—Scottish authors
  —History and criticism 2. Scottish
  literature—History and criticism
  I. Craig, Cairns
  820.9'9411   PR8511
  ISBN 0-08-035057-7
  ISBN 0-08-037728-9

Printed in Great Britain
The University Press
Aberdeen

For all who worked in and for *Cencrastus*, but especially for

Geoff Parker, whose idea this History was,
Craig Beveridge, who knew what it ought to be,
and Angus Calder, on whose knowledge our ideas were
honed.

Contents

Acknowledgements

My thanks to Colin MacLean and Marjorie Leith of Aberdeen University Press for their patience during this project, and in particular to my post-graduate student, Tom Nairn, without whose proofreading assistance the whole thing would have taken much longer. Our thanks to publishers who have allowed us to quote from published works, and to the many among them without whose endeavour to make Scottish writing available our culture would be much poorer.

List of Contributors

CRAIG BEVERIDGE studied and pursued research in history and psychology at Edinburgh University before taking up a career in the Health Service. He is now Deputy General Manager of the Edinburgh Mental Health Service. He has continued to research and write in the fields of Scottish history, historiography and the history of ideas and is co-author with Ronald Turnbull of the forthcoming book *The Eclipse of Scottish Culture: Inferiorism and the Intellectuals*.

RONALD I M BLACK is lecturer in Celtic at the University of Edinburgh. He is the author of *Mac Mhaighstir Alasdair: The Ardnamurchan Years* (1986) and of many articles on Gaelic literature. Gaelic editor to *The Scotsman* from 1977–85, he now contributes to a column on Gaelic matters called *Seall Seo* under his Gaelic name Raghnall Mac Ille Dhuibh.

CAIRNS CRAIG is a lecturer at Edinburgh University specialising in twentieth century poetry. He is the author of *Yeats, Eliot, Pound and the Politics of Poetry* (1982) and the forthcoming *Out of History*, and is a frequent contributor to the *Times Literary Supplement*.

BETH DICKSON is currently researching the modern Scottish novel at the University of Strathclyde.

FRANCIS HART teaches in Boston. He is the author of *The Scottish Novel* and, with J B Pick, of *A Biography of Neil M Gunn*. He has also written on American Literature and on the theory of fiction.

JOY HENDRY is the editor of *Chapman*. She is a freelance writer, broadcaster and poet, contributing to *The Scotsman* and *Glasgow Herald* as well as to the BBC, and has also worked extensively on Scottish women's writing. With Raymond J Ross she edited *Sorley MacLean: Critical Essays*.

TOM HUBBARD is the Librarian of the Scottish Poetry Library. A graduate of Aberdeen and Strathclyde, he formerly worked in Edinburgh University Library where he catalogued a portion of Hugh MacDiarmid's personal library. His poems (in Scots), essays, articles and reviews have appeared in various books and magazines. He serves on the editorial board of the Fife literary magazine *Scrievins*, which he founded.

DAVID HUTCHISON is Senior Lecturer in Communication Studies at Glasgow College of Technology. He is the author of *The Modern Scottish Theatre*

(1977) and editor of *Headlines: the Media in Scotland* (1978) and has published numerous articles and essays on aspects of theatre and media. He is currently working on a comparative study of the media in Scotland and Canada.

CATHERINE KERRIGAN has studied and worked in the Universities of Toronto, Edinburgh and Guelph. She is the author of *Whaur Extremes Meet* a study of Hugh MacDiarmid's earlier work. A further book on the later MacDiarmid is in preparation, as well as a study of Scottish women writers.

TERENCE McCAUGHEY. Since 1964 he has taught in the Irish Department of Trinity College, Dublin, and more recently has worked in its School of Biblical and Theological Studies. His essay 'Continuity and Transportation of Symbols' appeared in *Sorley MacLean: Critical Essays*.

MARGERY McCULLOCH is a graduate of the University of London and was awarded her doctorate in Scottish Literature by the University of Glasgow. She has written extensively on twentieth century Scottish Literature and is the author of a critical study of the novels of Neil M Gunn (1987). She is currently researching Scottish literary periodicals of the early twentieth century. She is a literature tutor with the Open University and in 1986 was *Glasgow Herald* Fellow in Scottish Literature at the University of Glasgow.

DONALD JOHN MACLEOD is currently Developments Officer with Commun na Gaidhlig (CNAG) in Inverness. He is the author of *Twentieth Century Publications in Scottish Gaelic* and has also contributed to *Gaelic in Scotland* edited by Derick Thomson.

MANFRED MALZAHN is a Foreign Language assistant in the Department of German at Edinburgh University. He studied English, American and German literature and linguistics at the University of Ruhr in Bochum and is the author of *Aspects of Identity. The Contemporary Scottish Novel (1978–1981) as National Self-Expression* (1985).

COLIN MILTON is a lecturer in English literature at the University of Aberdeen. His main interests are literature of the last two centuries in Britain and Europe, Scottish literature (particularly writing in the vernacular), language variety and change and their relation to the literary tradition—particularly in Scotland, and the inter-relations between culture and politics. He is the author of *Lawrence and Nietzsche: a study in influence* (1987) and of substantial essays on the relations between the late nineteenth century vernacular revival and MacDiarmid's 'Scottish Renaissance' movement.

ISOBEL MURRAY is a Senior Lecturer in the English Department at Aberdeen University. She has edited various works of Oscar Wilde and is currently completing the Oxford Authors Wilde. With her husband Bob Tait she wrote *Ten Modern Scottish Novels* (1984) and a new introduction for *Gillespie* (1979). She edited *Beyond This Limit: Selected Shorter Fiction of Naomi*

Mitchison (1986). Under the auspices of Aberdeen University Development Trust she is engaged on a series of indepth interviews with Scottish writers.

GLENDA NORQUAY is a lecturer in English at Liverpool Polytechnic. Her research interests are in nineteenth and twentieth century Scottish fiction and in women and literature.

IAN A OLSON is Clinical lecturer in Mental Health, University of Aberdeen. His principal literary research is into Scottish traditional culture, especially of the North East, and he has published extensively on the *Greig-Duncan Folk Song Collection*. He is editor of the *Aberdeen University Review*.

ALAN RIACH, a graduate of Cambridge and Glasgow, is a Fellow at the University of Waikato, New Zealand. He has contributed to magazines such as *Cencrastus* and *Edinburgh Review* (in Scotland) and *Landfall* (in New Zealand), and to the forthcoming book *Hugh MacDiarmid: Man and Poet* edited by Nancy Gish.

RITCHIE N N ROBERTSON is a graduate of Edinburgh University and Lincoln College, Oxford. He is presently Fellow in German and Director of Studies in Modern Languages at Downing College, Cambridge. His publications include *Kafka: Judaism, Politics, and Literature* (1985) and, forthcoming, *Heine*. He is a frequent contributor to various journals including *Modern Language Review*, *Oxford German Studies* and *Studies in Scottish Literature*.

VALERIE SHAW, a graduate of Edinburgh and Yale, is a lecturer in English literature at the University of Edinburgh. She is the author of *The Short Story: A Critical Introduction*.

RANDALL STEVENSON is a lecturer in English Literature at Edinburgh University. His publications include *The British Novel Since the Thirties: An Introduction* (1986). He reviews Scottish drama for *Times Literary Supplement* and BBC Radio, and is currently Vice-Chairman of the Royal Lyceum Theatre Club and a member of the Traverse Script Assessment Panel.

RONALD TURNBULL is currently on secondment from Edinburgh Language Foundation to St Andrews University where he teaches English as a foreign language. He is concerned to relate modern European thought to the work of major Scottish thinkers of the nineteenth and twentieth centuries. Co-author with Craig Beveridge of the forthcoming book *The Eclipse of Scottish Culture: Inferiorism and the Intellectuals*.

GAVIN WALLACE currently works with the Institute for Applied Language Studies at Edinburgh University, and is also a freelance lecturer. He is Reviews editor of *Cencrastus*.

RODERICK WATSON lecturers in English Studies at the University of Stirling. His publications include numerous critical articles and essays, as well as *True History on the Walls* (poetry); *The Penguin Book of the Bicycle* (with Martin Gray); *MacDiarmid* (1985) and *The Literature of Scotland* (1984), a literary history.

BARRY WOOD is Senior Lecturer in Literature at Bolton Institute of Higher Education. His publications include numerous articles and reviews in such journals as *Akros*, *PN Review*, *Stand* and *Edinburgh Review*.

Twentieth Century Scottish Literature: An Introduction

CAIRNS CRAIG

When T S Eliot, in a review in 1919, asked, 'Was There a Scottish Literature?', the past tense perspective seemed all too appropriate to the possibilities of Scottish literature surviving into the twentieth century as an independent cultural force. Scotland, politically more integrated into British society by the efforts of the First World War than it had ever been before, and seemingly culturally absorbed into English values by its participation in the previous century's imperial ambitions, had to look back to the era of Scott for a time when a writer's presentation of Scotland and the Scots had received international attention and literary recognition. By comparison, all that had followed had seemed a decline, and when a twentieth-century writer as eminent as Edwin Muir wanted to analyse the plight of modern Scottish writing, it was to Scott and Scotland that he turned for an explanation.

The expectation of an end was written into the very forms that had dominated Scottish writing in the period between 1880 and 1914. So-called 'Kailyard' novels were located in communities that were recalled nostalgically from the past, and recalled because they had passed out of any continuing contemporary existence or relevance; and the writers of the Celtic Twilight wrote in the lachrimose awareness of the death of the culture they sought to celebrate before the darkness finally descended. That the country's major writer of the second half of the nineteenth century, Robert Louis Stevenson, should have expended his energies on 'boy's fiction', and left his masterpiece, *Weir of Hermiston*, unfinished, pointed symbolically towards the flawed nature of the culture and its incapacity to fulfil itself any longer in literature. The continally anticipated extinction of both Gaelic and Scots pointed, it seemed, to an end to Scottish Literature which would not be much delayed after its linguistic bases had been eroded and Scotland had become just another part of the English speaking world.

That sense of impending extinction has never been far from the awareness of Scottish writers in the twentieth century. Behind them is a tradition which many assumed to have died; before them the apparent inevitability of absorption into English—or American—culture. Looking back to what they saw as the failure of an independent tradition, Scottish writers might locate the break differently—the Reformation and the acceptance of English as the language of religion, the removal of the Court to London in 1603, the dissolution of the Scottish parliament in 1707, the end of Scotland's intellectual golden age with

1

Carlyle's departure to London in 1832—but the finality of the rupture seemed inescapable. Even past cultural success, therefore, had to be seen, from the totality of Scottish life, as a defeat: the success of the Reformation, for instance, dooming Scots as the language of intellectual exchange, and the success of the Enlightenment being built upon conceptions of a 'universal' culture to which specifically Scottish experience was irrelevant. In a context where the prevailing critical orthodoxy—as expounded by critics like T S Eliot and F R Leavis—emphasised the central importance of 'tradition' to the continuing creativity of the present, the failure of the tradition implied inevitably that Scottish writing would not be able to regenerate itself or to retain any significant contemporary vitality.

Changes in the 'economy' of literature also had the effect of projecting an end to specifically Scottish writing. By the 1920s there remained only the vestiges of the once powerful Scottish publishing industry, and by the 1930s many of the small magazines and journals which had supported the work of new writers in the 1920s had disappeared. In the 1960s and 1970s the position improved dramatically as a result of the intervention of government patronage through the Scottish Arts Council, but through most of the century Scottish writers—and particularly, of course, those writing in Gaelic or in Scots—have struggled to find sustained outlets for their work. In the 1980s, the whole infrastructure of Scottish literature—the publishing channels, the theatres, the reviews—remains fragile, and after the political collapse of the movement for devolution in the Referendum of 1979, talk of 'the end' was as potent as its expectation had been at the beginning of the century in the debates that Ian Olson charts in relation to the publication of the Greig-Duncan collection in Chapter 3.

A crucial part of that literary infrastructure is, of course, the educational system. Literature in every country in the twentieth century has developed a symbiotic relationship with the universities and schools in which it is taught and studied and in which, increasingly, it is created. In Scotland, though, literature has had to operate without those educational supports: 'literature' in Scottish educational establishments, as in English ones, is taught under the title of 'English', and the Scottish literary inheritance has been only a marginal component of the subject where it has not been ignored entirely. It is only since the 1960s that there have been departments in Scottish universities devoted to Scottish studies, and even these are few and small in scale. The teaching of literature in Scotland has not taken place in a neutral environment in which the object of study is writing in English: it has taken place under the aegis of a subject which came into existence and defined itself in relation to requirements specific to English culture in the nineteenth century. Specifically, the study of English Literature was designed to promote class harmony in a divided society by offering a 'national' identity to which all could subscribe, and to promote an ideal of English civilisation which the peoples of the Empire would accept as representing the highest values to which they could aspire. The value systems which made of English culture an ideal model for human and humane development were propagated with enthusiasm in the universities and schools in Scotland, with a consequent neglect, not to say contempt, for the native traditions of the country. Where Scottish literature and history were taught, they were taught as subsidiaries to the 'mainstream' of English literature, and when the pattern of Scottish literature failed to conform to that of English literature it was regarded as a deviant or deformed version of the true shape of literary development.

The pressure of such forces should not be underestimated: until recently, few university students were introduced to Scottish literature and fewer had the opportunity to study it; few academics made it a subject of special study and most writers had to discover for themselves the traditions and precedents which would help them express the nature of their own culture. And yet, not only has 'the end' not come, Scottish writing in the twentieth century has flourished, and flourished in all three of the country's living languages. In defiance of critical theories that assert otherwise, the apparent lack of a coherent tradition, the lack of a coherent national culture, far from impeding development have been major stimuli to creativity. Scottish writers have been inspired by the condition of being between cultures rather than within a culture, and although it is too soon to pass final judgement, it seems that both the 1920s and the period of the 1970s and 1980s will go down as major contributions to the total literary achievement of Scottish culture.

Why then should Scottish Literature have retained and indeed asserted its independence in a context where the Scottish people—unlike the Irish, for instance—have seemed deeply resistant or apathetic about other forms of independence? In part, it is that Scotland has, despite both internal and external pressures, never been integrated into the culture values of the British state. The texture of Scottish life, in its religious, educational, legal, linguistic forms, remains distinct from that of England to an extent which is little recognised in England, let alone the outside world.

More importantly, however, the balance of the cultural organisation of the society is quite different. To the extent that much of Scottish middle class society models itself on English values, distinctively Scottish culture has more affinity with the working classes than English culture, is more imbued with a continuing sense of a living 'folk' culture. And to the extent that the element of the middle classes who are active in Scottish culture are professionals—legal, religious, educational—the tonality of Scottish culture is much more abstract and philosophical than in England. As Craig Beveridge and Ronald Turnbull point out, Scotland has retained links with the traditions of European intellectual debate in a way that England, locked into a conception of philosophy as description rather than criticism, has not. The fact that Scots law has a European basis, and Scottish religion takes its impetus from European centres, encourages an outwardness and a level of abstract engagement that is quite untypical of English culture in the twentieth century. Scottish writers are both more working class and more philosophical than is normal in English culture; their engagement is with a continuing 'folk' history and with absolutist values that do not fit into the comfortable ethics of Anglicanism and the English spirit of compromise.

And, of course, for all Scottish writers, as for few English writers until recently, the issue of language has an overwhelming significance that sets their writing quite different problems from those posed to the English writer. Few Scottish writers are not bilingual and few have not experimented in writing in two of the country's languages. The language of literature, for every Scottish writer, is a matter of choice, and those choices form an integral part of the act of the writing. In some cases this can be a powerful limitation, a fissure in the web of imagination which the writer cannot overcome; but in others it is the source of a linguistic vitality which has become the hallmark of much contemporary Scottish writing. For convenience, many chapters of this volume have been organised around linguistic divisions, but it is often from the interaction of different linguistic traditions that the creativity of Scotland's writers springs. As Catherine Kerrigan and Alan Riach point out, language itself was MacDiarmid's major theme as his poetry developed, and it is, equally, both content and form in writers as diverse in their linguistic choices as Edwin Morgan, Tom Leonard and Iain Crichton Smith.

Two consequences flow from this. The first is that many Scottish writers write in a language which is spoken by few even in Scotland, or which is unreadable without considerable difficulty by English speakers in the rest of the English speaking world. The foundation of their creativity is therefore a medium which severely limits their potential audience and their international recognition. However significant their contribution, they may fail to attract the attention of writers and critics from outside their own specific environment. Sorley MacLean, as Terence McCaughey demonstrates in Chapter 9, is a noble exception, but many other accomplished writers in Gaelic and in Scots have not received anything like their due. Alternatively, where the chosen language is English—or what appears on the page to be English—writers are assimilated into the development of English literature as though they were an integral part of *its* creativity rather than Scotland's. Muriel Spark is a prime example here: a writer who, as Valerie Shaw shows in Chapter 18, has been able to be at the forefront of international developments in English writing precisely because she is working out of the traditions of Scottish fiction, but whom critics often fail to acknowledge as having any significant connection with Scottish literature at all. The lack of recognition for some Scottish writers and the annexing of others to English literature encourages the often asserted view that Scottish literature is either parochial (only minor writers and writers in minority languages are Scottish) or frail (major Scottish writers are really part of English literature); while the lack of a strong educational foundation for the criticism of Scottish literature has allowed both of these perspectives to go largely unchallenged.

Such conceptions of modern Scottish literature as either a minor tributary of English literature, or a rather insignificant national tradition soon to disappear, are deeply at odds with the reality of its development. Not only because of the significance of individual writers and individual works, but because such conceptions continue to regard Scottish literature primarily in relation to English literature: however much Scottish writing has to live with the pressure of English culture, the development of twentieth-century Scottish literature has been synchronised not to the progress of literature in England, but to international changes, and especially to changes taking place in the wider English-speaking world. Scottish literature has always been responsive to international developments, but its peculiar position has made it even more so in the twentieth century—peculiar because Scotland was an active partner in the extension of the Empire that made of English a world language, while at the same time, in its own linguistic experience, it shared the experience of the colonised. To understand the pattern of the development of Scottish literature in the twentieth century we have to see it in relation to the world-wide assertion of cultural independence by peoples who have or have had English as their (imposed) official language.

The great wave of Scottish literary reassertion in the 1920s which we now call the Scottish Literary Renaissance took both name and some of its impetus from the more politically focused Irish movement of the previous decade. Though based on a century of political and cultural opposition to integration of the Irish into English culture, the flowering of the Irish Revival could only come at the moment when English culture collapsed exhausted from the effects of the First World War. That exhaustion was also the moment for writers in North America, in Australasia and in the non-English parts of the United Kingdom to make declarations of cultural independence. Writers in all these cultures recognised and asserted that English cultural traditions had both become a restriction on their own native forms of speech and were exhausted as vehicles for the expression of twentieth-century life. Whether it is Ezra Pound, contemplating the emptiness of post-war London, or Yeats constructing his Tower on Irish soil, or William Carlos Williams listening to the speech of his patients in industrial America, or MacDiarmid having returned to his small nation after fighting for the rights of other small nations; each discovers that the English on which they have fed is, as a literary language, dead: its accretions of past forms have made it unusable for contemporary speech and contemporary experience.

Each of these masters of the modernist poem began an exploration which had the same impulse whether it turned outward, in the attempt to graft on to English traditions from other European cultures, or whether they turned inwards and sought in local speech and dialect a language that had the power and the flexibility required to create a twentieth-century idiom. In Scotland, MacDiarmid 'discovered' Scots and brought it into this modernist application, but could do so only—as Colin Milton makes clear in Chapter 1—because others had been developing the capacities of a vernacular literature over a considerable period for reasons of regional commitment. The underlying and continuing development of a local literature intersected with the requirements of an international perception of changed literary requirements and the two fused into a single development. Similarly, in dealing with the development of the modern industrial world and its political consequences, Lewis Grassic Gibbon was able to combine uniquely the voice of the peasantry and the proletariat with the vision of world history as class conflict. Traditions of writing in Scots provided a medium for expressing international political and social concerns in a way which was impossible to writers in England, where traditions of dialect writing had neither the flexibility nor the status that they have in Scotland.

In Scotland the conjunction of international 'modernism' with vernacular revival gave the movement of the Renaissance its particular character: unlike the modernism of Joyce or Eliot, the modernism of the Scottish writers was not focused on the city and the effort to see in this new environment buried continuities with the creative potentialities of the past. In Joyce's *Ulysses*, for instance, the presentation of Leopold Bloom, advertising salesman, as a new version of the epic hero is a juxtaposition made possible only by the art itself. In Scotland there seemed to remain the possibility of a real continuity between present and Scottish past, so that such artistically forced continuities were unnecessary. In Neil Gunn's *The Silver Darlings*, for instance, the hero fulfils himself by becoming the reincarnation of the Finn of epic legend, proving in his own deeds the continuity of Gaelic culture in a fashion which the exiled Joyce would never have implied about his native Ireland.

The particular conjunction of the international and the national which lay behind the Scottish Renaissance has led certain critics—Tom Nairn, in particular, in *The Break-Up of Britain*—to view Scotland's literary revival in the twentieth century as a 'belated' version of the nineteenth-century European nationalisms which had themselves taken much of their original impetus from Scottish works like *Ossian* and the Waverley Novels. And the search by most of the writers of the Renaissance for a lost cultural continuity, a shared myth of the true Scot and the real Scotland, points in that direction. What, though, was to represent the true Scot and the true line of descent from past to present? Gaelic culture had clear claims and MacDiarmid came to see them as having priority, but most Scots had long since turned their backs on Gaelic culture and were not going to identify with it except in its most sentimentalised forms. Calvinism also had clear claims, since it had represented the backbone of political and theological power in the society for 400 years. Most writers, however, rejected Calvinism and all its works both because it was identified with nineteenth century Victorian values which, as good twentieth-century citizens, they were bent on overthrowing, and also because of Calvinism's apparent rejection of literature itself, as 'lies' concealing the true word of the Lord. The Enlightenment, too, represented a model on which modern Scottish writers could have drawn; but the Enlightenment was regarded as the period in which Scottish writers, however internationally famous, had rejected the Scottish tradition and so severed continuity with the past; Catholicism, too, had its proponents, many of whom looked to Scotland's pre-Reformation past as the real Scotland which was rural, Catholic and creative as compared with the dour, guilt-ridden, inhibited Scotland of the Reformation and after. But Catholicism was not only deeply antagonistic to many Scots because of the long and maintained traditions of Covenanting struggles for the national church; it was also feared by many because of the pressure of Catholic immigration from Ireland and the threat it posed to the local communities and traditions. And in the cities, many Scots saw the real Scotland in terms of a proletariat whose identity was with other proletarians around the world, rather than with a 'people' or a nation in which the industrial city happened to be situated.

Scotland's history was too complex for easy identification with some element of the national past, and what characterises the writers of the Renaissance, and distinguishes them from merely belated 'nationalists', is the restlessness of their search for a stable identity to the Scotland they were trying to express. There was no easy route towards a nationally acceptable conception of Scottish 'identity', and no political centre from which it could be imposed: Scotland was an agricultural country from which people had been forced into emigration for centuries; it was also a modern industrial country into which new people were migrating for work. In the industrial areas people drawn from the Scottish countryside moved out to escape the poverty of the industrial city as new people from Ireland, from the Baltic, from central Europe, moved in. Scots in Canada, the United States, Africa and Australia looked back to their homeland in nostalgic reminiscence of lost community; at the same time Glasgow in particular, but Dundee and even Edinburgh as well, burgeoned with immigrant communities with their own reminiscence of lost homelands and broken cultural traditions. In many respects, modern Scotland was a crossroads between the New World's melting pot cities and the decay of the old world's traditional rural communities.

The 'real' Scot, the 'true identity' was entirely unstable: it was an instability which, in comparison with the surety of other cultures' certainties—and particularly England's—gave rise to the conception of the Scot as, in some sense, schizophrenic, self-divided. The motif had been powerful in nineteenth-century Scottish literature—as a result no doubt of the conflict between Scottish and 'British' identities in Scotland—and was to maintain its apparent significance in modern Scottish literature not only in the presentation of character but in the penchant among Scottish writers for developing alternative personalities for themselves under their *nom de plumes*. In effect, however, Scotland's 'abnormality' in this respect was abnormal only in relation to assumed norms derived from the few modern nations—England and France are perhaps the only actual examples—where political, cultural and linguistic boundaries were—or had been enforced into being—co-extensive with each other. As the sweep of modernisation took in more and more of the world, and as the wars of the twentieth century broke down and reconstructed the 'nations' of the world, that model of a homogeneous nation shaped within a homogeneous cultural and linguistic tradition became more and more irrelevant not only to the reality of people's experience, but to any possible projection of what nations were ever likely to be. The fragmentation and division which made Scotland seem abnormal to an earlier part of the twentieth century came to be the norm for much of the world's population. Bilingualism, biculturalism, and the inheritance of a diversity of fragmented traditions were to be the source of creativity rather than its inhibition in the second half of the twentieth century and Scotland ceased to have to measure itself against the false 'norm', psychological as well as cultural, of the unified national tradition.

The second major wave of Scottish creativity in the twentieth century, spanning the period from the late 1950s to the 1970s, coincided therefore with the explosion of alternative 'Englishes' around the world in the wake of Britain's final retreat from Empire. Scottish writers worked between the rich vein of the national linguistic traditions and the explosive possibilities of an English which had ceased to be founded on the traditions of England's national literature. They turned increasingly to American exemplars, not as models to be imitated, but as the foremost exponents of an English no longer tied to sounds of English speech even if still working within the norms of English grammar. The liberation of the voice into the varieties of accent and dialect and alternative language which the collapse of the English literary imperium made possible has provided Scottish writers with renewed energies deriving from the actual linguistic possibilities of their situation. At the same time, the rapidly changing nature of Scotland's social experience—focused principally around the decline of the traditional industries which were the foundation of the world's first industrial economy—has given them themes whose significance is far from merely local.

The richness of the Scottish achievement in the twentieth century, in three languages, and the need to do justice to the varieties of forms in modern literature, has meant that even in a volume of this scale, choices have had to be made between comprehensiveness and depth. This volume makes no pretence, therefore, to comprehensiveness: it is a critical history and not an encyclopaedia. There are writers who are not mentioned not because they are not important in themselves, but because they could not be fitted in without reducing them to a mere mention which would have done neither them nor the history of Scottish literature any good. The contributors have been asked to attempt to draw out the major lines of development and to place individual authors within those, so that the reader can generalise in relation to other writers not specifically treated here. There are several guides to Scottish literature and culture in which such information can be found. Particularly in relation to this volume of our History, I have not asked the contributors to refrain from polemic, however polite. And even though we have taken the mid seventies as a rough cut-off point, the map is not fixed: the essays are intended to stimulate exploration rather than to end it. I have therefore also invited the contributions primarily from younger critics and writers whose perceptions may not fit easily with existing stereotypes. I trust that this is the best testimony to the vitality of the culture that we are charting, and to the expectation that the next year's creativity and the next decade's criticism will not only add to the creative wealth of the century's achievement in Scotland, but challenge and extend the perceptions which we have gathered here.

FURTHER READING

Bold, Alan, *Modern Scottish Literature* (London, 1983)

Davie, George Elder, *The Crisis of the Democratic Intellect* (Edinburgh, 1986)

Hart, Francis Russell, *The Scottish Novel* (London, 1978)

Harvie, Christopher, *No gods and precious few heroes:* Scotland 1914–18 (London, 1981)

Nairn, Tom, *The Break-Up of Britain: Crisis and Neo-Nationalism* (London, 1977)

Smout, T C, *A Century of the Scottish People* (London, 1986)

Watson, Roderick, *The Literature of Scotland* (London, 1984)

Chapter 1

Modern Poetry in Scots Before MacDiarmid

COLIN MILTON

Twentieth-century poetry in Scots is a vigorous and various growth, yet to knowledgeable observers like T F Henderson and J H Millar, who were writing major literary histories of Scotland at the turn of the century, it seemed unlikely that the vernacular would have any significant future, or indeed any future at all, as a medium for verse. At the end of his survey of Scottish vernacular literature, Henderson presents the history of poetry in Scots since the death of Burns as one of steady decline; Burns's stature as a vernacular poet has meant that subsequent verse in Scots has been completely overshadowed by his achievement and has dwindled into mere imitation of a feeble and predictable kind. Henderson ends his book with a vision of the final demise of the long and distinguished Scots poetic tradition which has a kind of melancholy grandeur; feeling that the final triumph of English is imminent and that no major writing in Scots is now possible, he looks back on the death of Burns as 'really the setting of the sun', after which 'the twilight deepened very quickly; and such twinkling lights as from time to time appear only serve to disclose the darkness of the all-encompassing night.'[1] Writing only a little later, Millar thought that there might still be a future for Scots in prose fiction, though there it would probably fill the subordinate role as the medium for dialogue in an essentially English narrative: on the future of vernacular verse, he shared Henderson's deep pessimism. Millar, too, felt that most recent verse in Scots was derivative and had 'the air of a more or less—and generally a less—skilful imitation of Burns', a situation which suggested that the poetic resources of Scots were exhausted. Like C M Grieve at the beginning of his literary career, Millar does not seem unduly disturbed at the prospect of Scots disappearing as a medium for the Scots writer, remarking that there have been a number of cultural situations in which literature has continued to flourish despite 'a clearly marked separation between the current spoken and written dialect.'[2] Clearly he assumed that the majority of Scots would continue to use one of the varieties of the vernacular, but that Scots writers would employ English in their work. Although it was not something which would have occurred to Millar himself, his observation does suggest one way in which vernacular poetry might be renewed: instead of continuing to imitate Burns, or turning to English, Scots poets might be able to tap the energy and inventiveness of spoken Scots by bringing the language of poetry into closer relationship with the living vernacular around them. If Scots dialect continued to be the primary means of expression of most Scots it would continue to develop and be a vigorous, versatile medium, well-suited to many of the needs of the contemporary Scots poet. Though neither Millar nor Henderson show any sign of being aware of the fact, just such a realignment of poetic language was going on in the last quarter of the nineteenth century (not only in Scots) and was to lead to the remarkable flowering of vernacular verse which preceded—and in many ways provided the foundation and impetus for—MacDiarmid's 'renaissance' achievements of the 1920s and 1930s.

Why, with the first glimmerings of the 'new day . . . indisputably dawning' around them, did capable observers like Henderson and Millar mistake 'the nightfall [for] the end of the world',[3] as C M Grieve put it? The fact is that watchers of the cultural skies, they were gazing steadily in the wrong direction both linguistically and geographically; their perspective was largely a metropolitan one and so they were mainly aware of what was going on in the south of Scotland, particularly in Edinburgh, while their pessimism about the future of vernacular poetry was based on what they saw as the exhaustion of literary Scots. When new energy came into Scots poetry in the last decades of the nineteenth century its main source was the popular vernacular of the day; younger poets began to draw increasingly on the resources of contemporary spoken Scots and by the end of the first quarter of the twentieth century it was clear that a renewal had indeed taken place. Even C M Grieve, who disagreed strongly with the direction it had taken, was in no doubt that (as he quoted approvingly from an article in the *Times Literary Supplement* in 1926) 'the present century [has] witnessed a remarkable revival of interest in the Scots Vernacular, which has taken several forms, lexical, dramatic and poetic.'[4] And—despite his deep dislike for the language and culture of the region—he was quite clear that the main centre of this renewed vernacular activity was the North-East of Scotland; indeed, in a letter to the *Scottish Educational Journal* in 1925 he refers to 'what may be termed the North-East revival.'[5] While he recognised that there was a vigorous interest in Scots and conceded the importance of the vernacular movement in halting, or at least slowing down, that 'complete assimilation to England [which] seemed a few years ago only a matter of time,'[6] he was also convinced that the current emphasis of the vernacularists on regional culture and speech was divisive and weakened the struggle to re-establish a confident Scottish cultural identity independent of England. He believed, too, that the current dominance of the North-East in vernacular activity meant that much of the writing in Scots was being done in a dialect which was undeveloped for literary purposes, which was inconsistent and debased and which, furthermore, was linguistically remote from most other Scots dialects. If Grieve was particularly scornful about the dialect of the North-East and largely contemptuous of the poetry written in it by Charles Murray, the best-known vernacular poet of the time, his opinion of the literary potential of the rest of the regional Scots dialects was not much higher. The current dialects were all unsuitable for 'major expressive purposes' as against 'homely local uses'[7] because the educated part of the Scottish population had largely abandoned the vernacular to the common people several centuries ago and in their mouths it had (naturally) deteriorated until it could no longer be put to serious literary use. In Grieve's view, the enthusiasts of the Vernacular Circle of the London Burns Club and their allies were engaged in a perverse effort to preserve the present debased and fragmentary varieties of Scots, the direct descendants of those 'gutter dialects employed by Burns and his imitators.'[8]

When, in 1887, Joseph Knight reviewed Stevenson's *Underwoods*, a volume which contained poems in both English and Scots, he devoted the main part of his discussion to the work in English, clearly feeling that it was the more interesting and original side of Stevenson's collection. He goes on to say that 'The Scottish poems may be more rapidly dismissed', since they are essentially derivative, following, for the most part, 'the method of Burns in his satirical pieces.' Knight does concede a certain energy to the Scots poems, referring to their 'ripe, broad humour' and adding that in the vernacular 'a man may venture upon freedom of expression which is denied the chaster Southern muse.'[9] There is a distinct ambivalence here, with notions of correctness and refinement struggling with a slightly uneasy admiration for the directness and even coarseness of Scots. It is as if Knight recognises and responds to the popular and colloquial affiliations of Stevenson's Scots idiom, even though his conscious affections are bestowed on the 'chaster Southern Muse.' While Knight saw the Scots poems in *Underwoods* as largely derivative in spirit from Burns, J M Bulloch, looking back on their appearance in 1918 and considering them rather from a linguistic point of view, saw them as representing something new. In an introduction written in that year for an undistinguished collection of verse in North-East dialect entitled *Bydand*, by one John Mitchell, he refers to the practice, established in every region of Scotland, but particularly strong in the North-East, of writing verse in the local dialect. It is clear from what Bulloch says about the language of Mitchell's own verse that he is not thinking of the familiar business of writing in a literary Scots largely derived from Burns, but of something altogether more local and less 'literary'—in fact of verse which is a written representation of the current popular speech of the region. Verse like Mitchell's reflects a 'spoken rather than a written language' and differs from the standard written form, 'classic Scots', which belongs to a different period and region; such verse therefore 'admits words that would shock a literary purist', but this is because such Scots is a 'living language' and therefore constantly changing and showing 'all the power of assimilation that belongs to life.'[10] Naturally the standard written forms cannot represent this kind of Scots and Mitchell therefore renders his dialect 'phonetically'. This kind of written Scots, which represents a current regional vernacular, developed most fully in the North-East because of just those characteristics of North-East Scots which Grieve emphasises in his hostile account of Charles Murray: North-East Scots is highly distinctive and sharply different from the Central Scots on which standard written Scots is based. Precisely because it was a spoken medium rather than a written one, this kind of regional Scots tended to be regarded as 'vulgar' and essentially 'unliterary', and as a result rarely found its way into print except as a 'harmless and subsidised hobby'. Such volumes would have had only a limited, local circulation. For Bulloch, it was largely Stevenson's work in Scots which was responsible for transforming this kind of idiom from a subliterary to a literary medium—he says of it 'As a literary and successful venture it did not reach the outside world till Stevenson took it in hand.' By the time *Underwoods* was published in 1887, Stevenson had already made his name as a writer, and his inclusion of poems in a contemporary Scots idiom in a volume intended for a general English-speaking market rather than for a purely Scottish audience undoubtedly helped to raise the literary status and cultural visibility of Scots dialect writing.

There is clear evidence, from the period before the appearance of *Underwoods*, of a general uncertainty about the literary status of writing based on spoken Scots dialect. William Alexander originally published *Johnny Gibb o' Gushetneuk* as a series of 'sketches' in the *Aberdeen Free Press* in 1869–70 and was only persuaded to publish the work in book form by the unexpected amount of interest the serialisation had aroused and by—in his own words— 'the direct request of certain persons whose judgement the writer felt bound to respect.'[11] The uncertainty evident here reflects doubts about the very high proportion of dense North-East dialect Scots in *Johnny Gibb*. The same unsureness about the literary acceptability of a written Scots founded on a current spoken dialect is reflected in the title James Logie Robertson chose for his 1886 collection of vernacular poems, *Horace in Homespun* (purportedly the work of 'Hugh Haliburton', shepherd of the Ochils). In the preface to his later collection *Ochil Idylls* (1891), Logie Robertson speculated about how much the gratifying 'measure of approval' accorded to the earlier volume was the result of the Scots being dignified by the association with the classics and how much to the fact that interest in and respect for the vernacular was greater than might have been expected. Although he says he would prefer to think he owes his success to the latter, Logie Robertson is not entirely confident about the matter and will again invoke the classical tradition to lend support to his Scots pieces:

> In this state of indecision the author . . . continues . . . the custom of a Latin text with which to introduce a few of his further efforts as a maker of Scots verse.[12]

Stevenson published his Scots poems at a favourable moment: in his note about them in *Underwoods*, he complains, half tongue-in-cheek, about what he feels is a current obsession with the clear discrimination and accurate recording of local dialect varieties among 'our new dialecticians.' The scholarly investigation of Scots (and English) dialects with which this 'pedantic' concern with linguistic accuracy was associated is an indication of the intense interest at the time in regional speech in all its forms. Stevenson is probably referring to the kind of investigation of Scots dialects which began with Sir James Murray's pioneering monograph on *The Dialect of the Southern Counties of Scotland* which appeared in 1873. Murray was one of the first to realise that, in his own words, 'colloquial, so-called illiterate forms of speech [are] as important to the science of comparative historical philology as the study of dead and existing literate languages . . .'[13] and while previous studies of dialect had tended to focus on lexis, Murray also investigated grammar, syntax and phonology. Greeted at first with 'amused contempt' by many, Murray's study provided the stimulus for further work on Scots dialect and this scholarly investigation was accompanied by widespread interest in the literary exploitation of regional dialects, particularly in prose.

Like many of his contemporaries, Stevenson was convinced that Scots, in all its various forms, was doomed to vanish in the fairly near future, when 'this illustrious and malleable tongue will be quite forgotten'. Under the circumstances, the ambition to compose in vernacular verse is largely prompted by nostalgia: it is a belated participation in a once-great, but now dying tradition: 'Till then I would love to have my hour as a native Maker and be read by my own country-folk in our own dying language.'[14] Given this conviction that Scots would disappear in the very near future, it was natural that Stevenson, despite his desire to have his 'hour as a native Maker', should have devoted his main poetic energies to his work in English, rather than to his efforts in the vernacular. Lacking deep roots in a dialect community and living for much of his life outside Scotland, he felt that dialect was more immediately and seriously threatened than it actually was. His Scots poet in 'The Maker to Posterity', looking back on his own time from far in the future, says of the vernacular, 'Few spak it then . . .' It is a claim often made then (and since) by Scottish intellectuals and literary men, but then—as now—the great majority of ordinary Scots spoke and will continue to speak in one of the regional varieties of the vernacular. The persistence of the idea that Scots was being rapidly abandoned by the younger generation and was spoken only by a diminishing older generation (Alexander Ross deplored this 'tendency' in *Helenore* in 1768) partly reflects the lack of contact with ordinary men and women among those who advanced it—partly, too, it was an understandable if mistaken reaction to the fact of language change—which tends to be seen as a process of dilution, impoverishment and decay. Like many others who wrote about the present state and future prospects of Scots from the mid-nineteenth century on, Stevenson may have felt that Scots was in danger of turning into a purely literary dialect, kept alive by writers, rather than in the mouths of the population as a whole. As eminent an authority as William Craigie speculated in 1923 that Scots might already be in this state. His argument is that while there was 'a remarkably widespread knowledge of lowland speech and a deeply-rooted attachment to it' which is reflected in the writing of the time, nevertheless 'all this literature has not availed either to restore the spoken tongue to a stronger position than it had in the eighteenth century, or even to prevent it from falling still further into disuse.'[15] The emergence in recent writing in Scots of books which 'owe not a little to closer imitation of the older writers and even a diligent use of the Scottish dictionary' seems to offer further evidence of the decline in spoken Scots; lacking the stimulus of a vigorous spoken medium, writers have been forced back on entirely literary sources of inspiration.

Those in closer and more continuous touch with the classes and communities in Scotland in which local dialect had always been—and continued to be—the general and habitual means of communication—were aware that its integrity, vitality and perhaps even its survival were menaced by increasingly powerful forces, but they were also conscious of the fact that local speech was by no means moribund. In his comments on Mitchell's use of North-East speech in *Bydand*, Bulloch had remarked on the resilience of the local vernacular and on the way in which it has continued to develop, evolving beyond the 'classic' Scots which has been fixed in written form. Mitchell's phonetic spelling reflects a distinctively regional phonology, while the fact that his poetic vocabulary 'sometimes admits words that might shock a literary purist in "classic" Scots'[16] is further evidence that regional varieties of Scots have continued to develop. Vernacular writers who used Scots more consistently than Stevenson, and felt more confidence in its durability, often came from social and economic circumstances in which Scots was still a natural and vigorous means of expression in all situations—except, perhaps, the class-room; Stevenson's middle-class Edinburgh background contrasts with the rural artisan origins which North-East poets like Charles Murray, Mary Symon and Helen Cruickshank share with Thomas Hardy. Though the vernacular was something he partly absorbed in his childhood from family servants (the young Violet Jacob, *née* Kennedy-Erskine, acquired her Scots in the same way), his use of Scots is also linked with the self-conscious adoption, during his student days at Edinburgh University, of a comic vernacular persona. In her note on one of his Scots poems, 'The Scotsman's Return from Abroad', in her edition of the *Collected Poems*, Janet Adam Smith comments that 'Mr Thomson', the supposed writer of the verse epistle and 'Mr Johnstone', to whom it is addressed, were 'roles invented for themselves in their student days by Stevenson and his friend and lawyer Charles Baxter.'[17] Stevenson and Baxter wrote letters to each other in character and, of course, in Scots.

Like C M Grieve at the beginning of his literary career, Stevenson saw Scots as having only limited possibilities: for both writers it seemed essentially 'the special preserve of the tour de force and the jeu d'esprit'[18] rather than a medium suitable for the more serious and ambitious kinds of utterance (most of Stevenson's work in Scots could be described quite fairly as 'light' or 'occasional' verse). Nevertheless, the Scots poems in *Underwoods* have a verve, fluency and humour which sets them above the work of most of his nineteenth-century vernacular predecessors and despite the fact that he often uses traditional forms (the Burns stanza, the verse-epistle in rhyming couplets) and tackles familiar subjects like the Scottish landscape and Scottish weather, as well as those interdependent features of Scottish life, 'Scotch drink and Scotch religion', his poems get much of their energy by drawing on the vitality of current spoken Scots. His predecessors, in contrast, tended to base the language of their verse on a dilute and old-fashioned Scots which derived largely from the lyric side of Burns. But despite the attempt by Kurt Wittig and others—including C M Grieve—to see Stevenson as a pioneer in the effort to create a 'synthetic', generalised literary Scots, drawing on the vernacular of different regions and periods, he really belongs more to the regional tradition which was responsible for the renewal of Scots verse in the late nineteenth century and the early part of the twentieth. Because, despite his impatience with what he saw as a pedantic concern for accuracy, it is clear that Stevenson did think of the Scots of his vernacular poems as being firmly based on a contemporary Scots regional dialect—that of the Lothians, where he had grown up. He is quite specific, for instance, about the phonology of his Scots:

> I am from the Lothians myself; it is there I heard the language spoken about [me] in my childhood; and it is the drawling Lothian voice that I repeat it to myself.[19]

And despite his rejection of the dialect precisians, he includes in his note in *Underwoods*, a table of spellings for vowel sounds which modifies standard Scots orthography so as to reflect that 'drawling Lothian voice' more accurately. The grammatical and syntactical features of the Scots he employs also reflect its local origins and despite Knight's reference to his debt to Burns in spirit, Stevenson insists that the actual language used by his great predecessor 'has always sounded in my ear like something partly foreign.' So for all his confession that he is a rootless cosmopolitan as far as lexis is concerned ('I simply wrote my Scots as well as I was able, not caring if it hailed from Lauderdale or Angus, from the Mearns or Galloway . . .'), it is clear that far from being a new, composite idiom, 'almost the "synthetic Scots" of the modern school' in Wittig's phrase, the language of Stevenson's Scots verse has its roots in the speech of the area he grew up in. In fact, it is clear from what Stevenson says about Scots in *Underwoods* that he would not have sympathised with the idea of deliberately creating a generalised linguistic medium or with the idea that lay behind Grieve's project, that the present Scots dialects represented the disintegrated fragments of a once unified and comprehensive Scots 'language'. Stevenson feels sad at the prospect of Scots dying precisely because of the variety of expressive possibilities which its different regional forms and traditions offer; if Scots were to disappear, not one, but many possible kinds of utterance will vanish:

> The day draws near when this illustrious and malleable tongue shall be quite forgotten: and Burns's Ayrshire, and Dr Macdonald's Aberdeen-awa', and Scott's brave, metropolitan utterance will be all equally the ghosts of speech.[20]

Stevenson's comment on the (mildly) mixed character of his poetic language has nothing to do with defying dominant regional trends in literary language and setting out in a new 'synthetic' direction; they are intended to underline, humorously, the fact that his poems are literary productions rather than examples of dialect usage. Essentially he is making the same point as Logie Robertson in his note on the language of *Horace in Homespun*: the dialect of 'these pastorals' Logie Robertson says, 'is that variety of the Scottish language which is still in vigorous use among the regular inhabitants of the Ochils', though it contains 'words and phrases, which are commonly regarded as peculiar to other districts of the country',[21] since even in rural areas where communities are settled, dialects interact with those of adjacent areas. Stevenson does of course draw on the literary models of his eighteenth-century predecessors, but the modern reader who is familiar with Scots dialect will find the language of his verse readily comprehensible and, within the limits of the verse-forms used, convincingly 'natural' in its movement; far from being an anachronistic and thoroughly literary medium, it is immediately recognisable as a modern and idiomatic one.

This is hardly surprising because much of the vernacular verse in *Underwoods* is dramatic in character and is intended to give the impression of relatively spontaneous and informal speech—indeed, Janet Adam Smith suggests that it was in some of his vernacular verse that Stevenson came nearest to tapping the intense dramatic imagination that is his power as a novelist. Often, as in 'Embro High Kirk' or 'The Scotsman's Return from Abroad', he creates a familiar kind of Scots-speaking persona which goes back to Burns's satires on the 'unco guid'; his speakers are hypocritical, narrow-minded, self-righteous, confident of their own salvation and the damnation of virtually everyone else. Like John Buchan's 'Midian's Evil Day', a verse-epistle from a Free Kirk elder to his minister written in the Burns stanza, 'Embro High Kirk' is not a mere exercise in pastiche, symptomatic of the poet's reluctance to confront the modern world, but a poem suggested by a contemporary controversy. Buchan's note to his poem outlines the legal struggle between presbyterian factions over church property which suggested it; the stimulus for Stevenson's poem came from the controversy over a proposal to instal an organ in the High Kirk of Edinburgh. For the speaker of 'Embro High Kirk', the proposal represents the final betrayal of reformation principles in their last surviving bastion and he comments, with true Calvinist relish, on the general decline and degeneracy of the age. Like many Scots poets who have portrayed Calvinism, Stevenson is ambivalent about the Scots religious tradition—like Burns in 'The Holy Fair' or MacDiarmid in 'Crowdieknowe', he simultaneously mocks the narrow legalism, the arrogance and self-righteousness of the Calvinist tradition while, at the same time, registering with a kind of admiration, through the concreteness, coarseness and vigorous movement of his speaker's Scots, the prodigious (and popular) energies he represents. The mood and idiom of the last part of the poem, where the speaker incites the leaders of the opposition to the organ, Begg and Niven, to emulate the feats of their reformation forebears, are a very long way from the rarefied 'poetic' English and hushed dream-like quality of much of Stevenson's English verse and the final stanzas have something of the energy—even violence—to be found in Medieval Scots poetry:

> Noo choose ye out a walie hammer;
> About the knottit butress clam'er;
> Alang the steep roof stoyt an' stammer,
> A gate mischancy;
> On the aul' spire, the bells' hie cha'mer,
> Dance your bit dancie.

Ding, devel, dunt, destroy, an' ruin,
Wi' carnal stanes the square bestrewin',
Till your loud chaps frae Kyle to Fruin,
Frae Hell to Heaven
Tell the guid wark that baith are doin'—
Baith Begg and Niven.

The same vernacular energy is tapped even more effectively in an untitled poem in *Underwoods* which expresses, in intimate and familiar Scots, the thoughts of a wealthy man as he lies in bed listening to a violent gale raging outside:

The masoned house it dinled through;
It dung the ship, it cowped the coo';
The rankit aiks it overthrew,
Had braved a' weathers;
The strang sea-gleds it took an' blew
Awa' like feathers.

Then, in a striking change of viewpoint, reminiscent of MacDiarmid, Stevenson moves from a local to a cosmic perspective; hearing 'in the pit-mirk on hie/ The brangled collieshangie flie', people are alarmed:

The warl', they thocht, wi' land and sea,
Itsel' wad cowpit;
An' for auld airn, the smashed debris
By God be rowpit.

The images, apocalyptic and comic at the same time point forward to the Scottish renaissance, particularly in the stanza which follows, where the viewpoint is reversed and the earth is now seen from an extra-terrestrial vantage-point:

Meanwhile frae far Aldeboran
To folks wi' telescope in han',
O' ships that cowpit, winds that ran,
Nae sign was seen,
But the wee warl' in sunshine span
As bricht's a preen.

In the next section of the poem the striking—and strikingly modern—image of the earth seen through a far-distant telescope, even its greatest catastrophes no longer visible, becomes a metaphor for the speaker's view of his own moral and spiritual situation. Secure at first in his conviction that he belongs to the Elect, he feels utterly remote from and unmoved by the struggles and misfortunes of those around him. But then, like the speaker in MacDiarmid's 'The Bonnie Broukit Bairn', his essential humanity asserts itself and he finds it impossible to maintain his serene 'cosmic' outlook in the face of human misery or to remain securely enclosed within his Calvinist creed. Stevenson is portraying and satirising here a kind of character who is a familiar target in Scottish literature, someone who thinks himself spiritually superior, a member of the Elect, but the characterisation is more complex than it is in, for example, 'Holy Willie'. In the contemporary world Calvinism has lost much of its old confidence and authority and its adherents experience doubts and hesitations. Their godly sense of separation from and superiority to the unregenerate majority is more fragile, as is their confidence in predestinate salvation and damnation. Calvinism is now an anachronism, belonging to a period in which the cosmos was seen as intimate, human-centred and governed by providence—it cannot survive unchanged in the universe of modern science, with its vast stretches of time and space and its dependence on physical rather than metaphysical laws, a universe in which the earth is just one among a multitude of heavenly bodies, many of which may support intelligent life.

This modern world-view is amusingly presented in the lively, idiomatic Scots of 'The Maker to Posterity', the introductory poem of the Lallans section of *Underwoods*. The speaker, a vernacular version of the poet himself, begins by stressing the universality of the principle of evolution, which affects things like languages and moral codes just as much as the physical world; in the far future the poem looks forward to the poet reflects, 'what was richt and wrang for me' will lie 'mangled throu'ther.' Moral codes do not enshrine timeless absolutes, eternally opposed metaphysical principles of right and wrong, but are historical and social creations, subject to time and change— 'good' and 'evil' have a genealogy and are notions generated by particular societies or social groups at particular times and for particular purposes. Languages, too, have their own periodicities, in which they rise, come to maturity, then weaken and die—like Scots, which is now on the verge of extinction. By linking the state of Scots with evolutionary processes, Stevenson seems to be accepting that its decline is inevitable, part of an irreversible natural cycle, which will leave it as incomprehensible to the reader of the far future as the inscriptions left by the earliest inhabitants of Scotland, the 'runes upon a standin' stane/Among the heather' are to us. Then, in a manoeuvre used by a number of writers in the period, Stevenson juxtaposes two kinds of time-scale, challenging the complacency of his imagined future speaker, proud of his 'braw new tongue', by reminding him that the cultural achievements of which he is so proud will be less lasting than those of his predecessors, since by his time most of the history of the earth and even of the cosmos, will have passed. The poem ends with a vision of the end of time, but while the traditional religious image of that event is of a final spiritual arranging and tidying, which leaves a simpler, more orderly and lasting state of things, Stevenson offers instead a comic vision of the apocalypse of contemporary science; the world ends not with a bang but a whimper, in the triumph of the second law of thermodynamics and the principle of entropy, as a state of maximum cosmic disorder is reached. The unfortunate citizen of the future has 'the hale planet's guts . . . dung/About [his] ears:

An' you, sair gruppin', tae a spar
Or whammeled wi' some bleezin' star,
Cryin', to ken whaur deil ye are,
Hame, France, or Flanders—
Whang sindry like a railway car
An' flie in danders.

The serious use of this kind of alternation between a human and a cosmic time scale is central to in the narrative strategy employed in two important near-contemporary works—Wells's *The Time Machine* and Conrad's *Heart of Darkness*, both of which reflect the greatly extended sense of time and space which educated people come to have in the nineteenth century as a result of developments in contemporary science. On the human and historical level, the actions of people or nations are seen as important and meaningful and they arouse an emotional response in us; in terms of cosmic or even geological time, even the most lasting human achievements dwindle into insignificance, particularly since the scientific view is that life is a chance occurrence in a meaningless universe. MacDiarmid's work, too, reflects this double perspective and often expresses the tension which it creates in the modern consciousness.

Fewer signs of distinctively modern sensibility are to be found in the work of Logie Robertson, whose vernacular verse is often linked with that of Stevenson in accounts of the pre-history of the Scottish renaissance—nor is the language of his poetry as close as that of Stevenson to popular Scots speech. He did claim that the Scots used in *Horace in Homespun* was based on the current speech of the Ochils, which was his own 'mother tongue and everyday speech',[22] though in fact one doubts whether Logie Robertson used Scots very much, in the classroom at least, during his years teaching English in the Merchant Company schools. The regional character of Logie Robertson's poetic language is often evident, even though it is sometimes obscured, as he points out himself, by the unsatisfactory state of Scots orthography. The regional character of his work is also made less evident by the dependence of many of his poems on Horatian originals, though he often changes the original Latin poem considerably or uses it largely as a stimulus or starting point for a poem in Scots. However, in his 'editorial' preface to *Horace in Homespun*, Logie Robertson refers to the 'remarkable correspondence' between the life of Hugh Haliburton, shepherd of the Ochils and that of Horace 'twenty centuries ago in ancient Rome'. This suggests that he is more interested in writing about what the present and the past have in common than in portraying what is distinctive about a particular part of present-day rural Scotland.

More often than not in Logie Robertson's poetry the scenes and circumstances of Scottish rural life are less important in themselves than as starting points for moralising reflections; landscape, weather, tasks, social customs are often little more than pretexts for the enunciation of some general truth, as titles like 'Anni Fugaces' or 'Comites Parati' indicate. This way of seeing things suggests the detached, contemplative perspective of the intellectual or the country gentleman of literary tastes; we would expect someone who worked on the land to have a more particular and intimate feeling for it. Logie Robertson only occasionally refers to the constraints and hardships of ordinary country life, although a number of his poems deal with the lack of opportunities in Scotland for the enterprising rural labourer. In 'Hughie at the Smiddy', the 'dramatic idyll' which concludes *Horace in Homespun*, a successful emigrant, who has made his fortune sheep-farming in Australia, returns to the Ochils and urges his stay-at-home compatriots to follow his example; despite his glowing report of the opportunities available in the antipodes, Hugh is too attached to his native place to consider leaving it. Again, in 'In Praise of the Ochils', the speaker celebrates the hills as being the last free places in a countryside which is increasingly being taken into private ownership, and fenced off from general access. You can still 'streek oot you shanks at lairge' among the Ochils where, as yet

> There's no a buird to stay ye
> Nor menace o' a trespass charge,
> Nor upstart to nay-say ye.

One of the English poems in *Ochil Idylls* has an opening section entitled 'The Country Fenced and Forbidden'. But it is only rarely that Logie Robertson's poems reflect the radical changes in the area he grew up in and in the Scottish country-side in general. These contemporary developments are documented more fully in a series of articles he contributed to the Edinburgh-based *Scots Observer* in 1888–89, under the title 'The Revolution in the Rural Districts'. In the first, in the issue of 22 December 1888, he deals with the depopulation of his native region, following the social and economic changes which have taken place there since the beginning of the century. Part of the account is in a vigorous, colloquial Scots, supposed to be spoken to the writer by one 'Gibbie Doss', a returned wanderer who is reduced to stone-breaking near the once thriving but now near-moribund village where he grew up. For Gibbie—and presumably for Logie Robertson—rural communities have been weakened not so much by the magnetism exercised by the developing industrial areas, as by forces operating from within, particularly the concentration of holdings into larger units (Gibbie has no doubt that 'The muckle-farm system did a' the mischief . . .') the enclosing of common land and the erosion of cottar's rights. The articles help to explain why so much of Logie Robertson's verse has an elegaic quality, but they also make it clear that the thin and scattered population and the almost exclusive dependence on sheep-farming in the community described in *Horace in Homespun* are not permanent features of the area. Till comparatively recently it has supported a vigorous spinning and weaving industry and was dotted with small but flourishing communities, centered on the mill and the inn.

However, it is a mistake to condemn Logie Robertson's verse for its lack of 'realism' or its 'kailyard' character because he is not—or not usually— concerned with the realistic depiction of particulars but with evoking a mood, commending certain values or conveying general truths—truths which are no less true and important for being simple and obvious. Perhaps, most generally, what he does is to write poetry which corresponds to Peter Marinelli's definition of the essential quality of pastoral, that it is 'a projection of our desires for simplicity.'[23] Sometimes his poems do deal with the concrete particulars of contemporary rural life; 'Packie's Return', for instance, describes the various signs of the return of spring in the natural and human worlds:

> Auld Tummas to the gavle-wa'
> Nails up a cherry-twig;
> An' Mar'an watters, raw by raw,
> Her bleachin' wi' a pig;
> An' yonder—he's been lang awa'—
> Comes packie owre the brig;
> And country lads may noo gang braw,
> An' country lasses trig.

There are finely observed particulars too in the opening stanza of 'The Tinklers':

> The mist lies like a plaid on plain,
> The dyke-tops a' are black wi' rain,
> A soakit head the clover hings,
> On ilka puddle rise the rings.

'The Tinklers' is unusual among Logie Robertson's poems in its depiction of the grim side of traditional life. The reader is likely to be reminded of Hardy in the sharpness of detail and the sardonic humour of its description of the tinker couple travelling along a country road in the pouring rain, 'He foremost wi' a nose o' flint/She, sour and sulky, yairds ahint.' In the case of the man, the poem evokes how he moves rather than what he looks like:

> His haunds are in his pooches deep,
> He snooves alang like ane in sleep,
> His only movement's o' his legs,
> He carries a' aboon like eggs.

The dialect word 'snooves' brilliantly conveys the idea of rapid, smooth and stealthy locomotion, while the last simile reminds us of the usefulness for travelling people of being able to move quickly bearing the spoils from a local farm or croft. But for all its vividness the poem is more than just a vivid depiction of a particular occasion; the scene takes on a kind of representative quality and the picture of the two bedraggled wayfarers dourly facing the unrelenting rain becomes a powerful image of the essential harshness of the travelling life itself.

There is one poem in *Ochil Idylls* which looks forward to MacDiarmid's later attempts to bring the discoveries of modern science into Scottish poetry. In 'The White Winter', the speaker describes an unusually harsh and prolonged spell of cold and speculates about whether it might not represent the beginning of a new ice age. The idea of ice ages separated by interglacial periods was a relatively new one in scientific circles when the poem was written and much of the work which linked present landscape features with the Pleistocene glaciation was done in Edinburgh by the brothers Archibald and James Geikie, who succeeded one another in the Murchison Chair of Geology at Edinburgh University; the latter published his *The Great Ice Age and its Relation to the Antiquity of Man* in 1874. Unlike most of Logie Robertson's other work, 'The White Winter' reflects a distinctly modern sensibility; the poem depends on the perception that things which may appear exceptional—and therefore portentous—in the short-term human perspective, in fact spring from natural rather than supernatural causes. However extraordinary they may seem, events in nature are essentially regular and law-governed in their operation and no human action can influence their impersonal unfolding. Modern science has allowed us to understand this by enormously extending our sense of time and our knowledge of what happened in the remote past; we can now see the short-term rhythms of the seasons (so intimately linked with human life in the literary tradition) as embedded in the enormously longer periodicities of geological and cosmological time. While Logie Robertson's Horation original (the second ode of the first book) begins with the poet praying to the gods to end the violent weather, which has been sent as a punishment, the speaker of the Scots poem sees the unusually severe conditions not as exceptional, but as perhaps being the beginning of a new glacial phase. We know from the geologists that there was an ice age in the past and 'What aince has been may happen twice.' The idea sets the speaker's imagination working and he conjures up a memorable picture of that past (and future?) age which is at once splendid and grotesque; in it, the frozen earth is seen from an extra-terrestrial viewpoint which recalls MacDiarmid's use of a cosmic perspective in his early Scots work:

> This planet's fortune was to fare,
> In ages auld,
> Thro' regions o' the frigid air,
> Past kennin' cauld.

> Nae doot but this was centuries gane,
> When human cretur' there was nane,
> An' this auld warld, her liefu' lane,
> Bowl'd thro' the nicht,
> Wi' tangles hingin' fra a mune
> That was her licht.

The linking up of the human and the cosmic in the stanza that follows is also reminiscent of MacDiarmid's later use of the traditional Scots habit of linking the exalted and the homely:

An eldritch scene that licht display'd!
There lay the continents array'd,
Like corpses o' the lately dead,
In a cauld sheet,
Wi' icebergs sittin' at their head
An' at their feet!

But Logie Robertson is less important as a poetic precursor of MacDiarmid than for the part he played in recovering elements of the Scottish literary and cultural tradition which had been long neglected or ignored; he is an important figure in the genereal reinvigoration of Scottish intellectual life in the late nineteenth and early twentieth centuries which helped to create the conditions in which MacDiarmid's extraordinary achievement was possible. He produced popular editions of Ramsay, of Burns's poems and letters, of James Thomson—and even an edition of Dunbar, though the Makar's work was 'translated' for modern readers into a rather feeble 'literary' Scots and, of course, censored. There is a tribute 'To William Dunbar' in *Ochil Idylls* which, ironically, is couched in the kind of vapid 'poetic' English which Logie Robertson clearly considered the proper idiom for such dignified and serious utterances. But his championship of Dunbar in the *Scots Observer* and elsewhere did help to change the widely held view that Burns was the only really great poet that Scotland had produced—and if, in deference to the current idolatry of Burns he is fairly guarded in what he says about the relative merits of Dunbar and his eighteenth-century successor in 'Our Earlier Burns'[24] the reader forms the distinct impression that he regards the Medieval Makar as the greater of the two.

Much of Logie Robertson's literary output appeared in the pages of the *Scots Observer*, the short-lived weekly which W E Henley edited in Edinburgh between 1888 and 1890 (when the magazine, still under Henley's editorship, moved to London and was renamed the *National Observer*). The often grudging J H Millar writes enthusiastically about the Edinburgh-based *Observer*, referring approvingly to its liveliness and iconoclasm and to the fact that it had a cultural influence out of all proportion to its modest circulation. Henley, friend of Robert Louis Stevenson and himself a poet, was a Tory and an imperialist in politics and the *Observer* had an uncompromising political stance; firmly unionist it consistently ridiculed current demands for Scottish independence yet, at the same time, it had a strongly Scottish emphasis in both its political and cultural coverage. On the literary side, it regularly carried substantial amounts of writing in the vernacular in the form of poems, sketches, short stories and serialisations of longer works; some of the prose, like the short stories contributed by Barrie early in 1889, is almost entirely in Scots. As well as imaginative work in Scots, the *Observer* regularly carried material dealing with the literary and cultural history of Scotland. In March, 1889 for instance, articles appeared on 'Old French Forms in Scottish Poetry' (which referred to Dunbar, Kennedy and Montgomerie), on 'Matchless Montgomerie', as well as on 'The Metres of Burns'. In April there was an article on 'The Origin of Scottish Drama' which discussed Lindsay's *Ane*

Satyre of the Thrie Estaitis and in September, a piece which contrasted 'Scots and English Popular Poetry' to the advantage of the former (the anonymous contributor summarised the effects of the Scottish reformation in a way which would have appealed to MacDiarmid and his renaissance allies, as a process by which the Scots exchanged 'the Maypole and the dances of the village-green for illegitimacy and whisky').[25] Later issues in 1889 contained lengthy and enthusiastic reviews of Francis Child's *The English and Scottish Popular Ballads* and of Small and Mackay's Scottish Text Society edition of the poems of William Dunbar.

The conjunction of an imperialist and conservative politics with an interest in the history and present state of Scottish culture in all its aspects which is found in the *Scots Observer* may seem an unlikely one, but the combination was common among those involved in the earlier phase of the modern vernacular revival. Two of the key figures in that movement, John Buchan and Charles Murray, played significant if contrasting roles in British imperial activity: Buchan's political career culminated in his appointment as Governor General of Canada, while Murray's advancement came in the professional sphere—trained as a surveyor in Aberdeen, he emigrated to South Africa in 1888 and by 1910 had risen to be Secretary for Public Works for the Union. Buchan did write a small amount of Scots poetry in a volume entitled *Poems, Scots and English* in 1917 (in a note prefaced to it he insists on the authenticity of his dialect and its mother-tongue status, describing the language of the poems as the Scots of 'the hill country of the Lowlands, from the Cheviots to Galloway' which 'I could always speak . . . more easily than I could write').[26] Buchan's main significance, however, was as a publicist for vernacular interests; he was an active campaigner on Scottish cultural issues, using his position as a well-known writer and political figure to try to advance them. He was one of the main, though by no means the only, moving spirit behind the formation of the Vernacular Circle of the London Burns Club which, in the years immediately following the Great War, became the main vehicle for promoting the vernacular. In 1924, he published an excellent anthology of Scottish verse, *The Northern Muse*, which C M Grieve admired for the way in which it illustrated the range, confidence and sophistication of which Scottish poetry was capable.

In the case of individuals like Buchan and Murray, interest in and respect for local customs, patterns of life and forms of speech was not only not inconsistent with support for the British Empire, but intimately related to that support. Both represented a particular tradition of imperialist thinking which was essentially federalist in nature and which conceived of empire as a voluntary union (in the end, if not at the beginning), linking different cultures and countries in a way that would bring the advantages of large-scale co-operation without compromising the essential integrity of the individual components.

The great stimulus to interest in—and active literary use of—forms of local speech was the growing strength of forces which seemed to be threatening cultural diversity and which, if allowed to advance unchecked, would create a uniform, standardised national culture. Looking back in the 1920s, the secretary of the Burns Federation, Thomas Amos, referred to some of the main 'disintegrating agents' which had threatened (and were threatening) dialect and other local cultural features, as 'board-schools, railways, music halls . . .'.[27] At the end of the previous century it was the first of these which had been seen as by far the most serious threat to the vernacular because, through the major education acts of the 1870s, a compulsory, rate-supported, universal system of elementary education was created for the first time. After the reform, centralising tendencies were particularly strong in Scotland where, after the creation of the Scottish Education Department in 1878, there was a single controlling body—in England, control was exercised locally. And almost from the start, the Scottish Education Department was seen not just as a threat to local identity and speech *within* Scotland, but as the agent of something even more sinister: the compulsory anglicisation of Scottish culture. Scottish intellectuals, literary men and journalists (overlapping but not identical categories), themselves beneficiaries of extended formal education tended, understandably, to exaggerate its power for cultural change and widespread fears were—and are still being—expressed about the ability of local dialect to survive what many saw as being, in the words of Alexander Mackie, 'a compulsory English education'. The comment, in his 'Introduction and Appreciation' prefaced to the 1884 edition of *Johnny Gibb* is linked with his observation that Alexander caught the Doric of the North-East just in time 'before the Education Act of 1872 began to take effect.'[28] And, looking back on the work he did on the dialect of his own Border region, James Murray said that the aim of his research was to 'photograph the leading features of one of the least-altered local dialects' before it was 'trampled underfoot by the encroaching language of literature and education.'[29]

It was because it reflected these contemporary anxieties that Charles Murray's poem 'The Whistle' caught the popular imagination just after the turn of the century (it appeared first in *Chambers' Journal* in 1906 and was included in the expanded *Hamewith* of 1909). Murray was easily the best-known vernacular poet of the early part of this century and 'The Whistle' by far the most popular of his works, constantly anthologised, learned by heart and recited; it was even praised by Grieve in his otherwise dismissive account of Murray which appeared first in his series of articles for the *Scottish Educational Journal* between 1925 and 1927. Despite being written in dense North-East dialect the poem's popularity—and that of Murray himself—was not confined to his local area: it aroused a national response because it reflected cultural anxieties which were general in Britain as a whole at the time, but which were unusually strong in Scotland because there the threat of cultural uniformity was a threat not only to regional identity (in England, Hardy feared for the survival of the Dorset culture and speech he loved), but to things which were also felt to be elements of a national identity as well. The 'wee herd' in Murray's poem represents the new generation of Scots, the first to be exposed to a lengthy, compulsory—and anglicising—schooling. The whistle he plays on, a folk instrument, made with native materials (a 'sappy sucker') links him with the folk tradition—and with classical pastoral. Although his talents are musical ones, the wee herd stands for a tradition in which music and song are closely linked; if the poem focuses on the threat to one aspect of the folk tradition, it also has implications for the folk-song and folk-ballad tradition and even for the whole area of popular vernacular poetry and story-telling. Murray emphasises the importance of that tradition, which he sees as the fountain-head of all art, by linking his tale of the North-East Scots herd lad to the great classical legend of Orpheus; like the Greek musician, the herd is able not only to move men, but the animals too:

> He blew them rants sae lively, schottisches, reels an' jigs,
> The foalie flang his muckle legs an' capered ower the rigs,
> The grey-tailed futt'rat bobbit oot to hear his ain strathspey
> The bawd cam' loupin' through the corn to 'Clean Pease Strae'.

The allusion is a humorous one, but it dignifies the lad and his music, linking him with venerable and powerful forces and it prevents us from seeing him, as otherwise we might, as an insignificant, coarse and bucolic figure. His 'art' is not a personal and self-conscious one though, expressing the distinctive personality of the individual artist, but a communal and social art, in which what is transmitted is a communal experience and folk-wisdom which is far greater than the personality of the particular performer. So the wee herd can play 'a spring for wooers' very expressively, though he 'wistna what it meant— its meaning is clear however to someone a little older: '. . . the kitchen-lass was lauchin' and he thocht she maybe kent.' The hitherto continuous process of transmission is cut short when the herd has to return to school at the end of the summer; the dominie confiscates and destroys the whistle. It is significant that the poem ends with that act—'. . . the maister brunt the whistle that the wee herd made'—because it gives the schoolmaster's action a quality of finality which suggests that what is being destroyed is not just a particular folk instrument (the herd can easily make another, after all), but, rather what the whistle represents. The master stands for a new and powerful force which threatens not just to weaken vernacular traditions but to destroy them altogether. The poem owed its popularity not, as Grieve disingenuously claims, to the fact that it is the best of Murray's pieces—because it is not— but to the way in which it chimed with widespread contemporary fears for the survival of folk culture, fears which centered particularly on new educational developments.

In his 1926 survey of 'Scottish Poetry of Today', Robert Bain, a Glasgow journalist and ally of Grieve, recognised, if grudgingly, Murray's pre-eminence among the vernacular poets of the early years of the century, saying that 'When Murray's *Hamewith* appeared it brought a new province into Scottish poetry—Buchan—and the fascination of the comparatively unknown dialect considerably helped the vogue of the poet . . .'[30] Bain's use of 'province' with its inevitable suggestion of 'provincial' and his assertion that a dialect spoken over a large area of his own country was 'comparatively unknown' are amusing illustrations of the prejudices of the intellectual and of the critic who thinks of himself as being at the cultural centre; they help to explain why metropolitan observers like Millar and Henderson failed to detect the beginnings of the vernacular revival. Murrray did more than bring a new area and dialect into Scottish poetry; he was the first poet to demonstrate that a regional dialect could be a vehicle for poetry which was distinguished enough to have more than local appeal. In doing so, he set the direction for many of the vernacular poets who followed him—indeed it was the strength of the regional tradition in Scots verse at the beginning of this century which led C M Grieve to devote so much of his abundant energy to attacking it; he felt that enthusiasm for Scots was flowing in entirely the wrong channel. Murray, Mary Symon and David Rorie, together with younger poets like J M Caie and J C Milne, generally use a poetic language which is very close to the spoken Scots of the North-East; the vernacular of Violet Jacob, John Buchan and Marion Angus is more influenced by literary Scots, although it too, has a distinctly regional character. Violet Jacob's literary development shows the influence of Murray's success with *Hamewith*; she had published a comic poem in Scots, written in collaboration with W D Campbell in 1891, but clearly at that stage did not think of Scots as a suitable medium for serious verse—her first collection, *Verses* (1905) is entirely in English. But in her second and third volumes of poetry, most of the work is in Scots and the regional basis of the medium she used is signalled in their titles: *Songs of Angus* (1915) and *More Songs of Angus* (1918). John Buchan too, in the note which prefaces *Poems, Scots and English* (1917) stresses both the authenticity of his Border speech and the fact that it is still current:

> . . . the Scots pieces in this little collection are written in the vernacular which is spoken in the hill country of the Lowlands, from the Cheviots to Galloway. Scots has never been to me a book-tongue; I could always speak it more easily than I could write it; and I dare to hope that the faults of my verses, great as they are, are not those of an antiquarian exercise.[31]

Most of the large number of poets who wrote poetry in a regional Scots in the early part of this century came from the North-East; Murray, Mary Symon, Violet Jacob, David Rorie, Marion Angus and Helen Cruickshank were all either born in the region or came of North-East stock—and all except the last were born in a single decade, the 1860s. They belonged to the first generation of Scots to be affected by the major educational reforms of the time and so were more conscious of language variety and in particular cases probably experienced conflicting dialect claims which provided part of the stimulus to literary activity. The prominence of the North-East in vernacular writing is probably linked with the relative cultural stability of the area in the vast demographic upheavals of the nineteenth century; though there was migration within the area and some migration into it from the Highlands and even from Ireland, it was insignificant compared to the movement of population in central and south-western Scotland. Contemporaries were aware of the complex cultural and linguistic interactions and amalgamations which these developments brought about and tended to see the process as one of disintegration and corruption, leading to the creation of new, hybrid, 'impure' kinds of language. The kinds of Scots which were developing in urban, industrial areas were associated with the squalor and brutality of urban conditions and tended to be looked down on as crude and brutal idioms, quite unsuited to literary activity. The more stable Scots of the North-East, associated with an area still predominantly centered on traditional activities, had no such associations and could be seen as representing the uncorrupted, pre-industrial stage of Scottish culture.

Murray writes about ordinary people and ordinary life, but not of course about the urban and industrial world which most Scots had come to inhabit even by the time he was born in the 1860s. Murray's country-side, however, is not the static, romanticised one of the 'kailyard' tradition (a tradition which is, anyhow, a version of pastoral and not a failed realism); the society he depicts is not a static one without significant conflict embodying all the fundamental moral virtues. As a poem like 'The Packman' indicates, Murray was aware that rural society itself was changing radically and while, like Hardy, he regrets that certain things are being swept away, he also accepts change as being inevitable and even as something which may make life better. In the career of the packman himself, from near vagabond to banker, shopkeeper and elder, Murray not only traces the rise of an individual who has nothing to begin with except his own shrewdness and energy, but uses the packman's progress as a kind of condensation of the economic and social development of the community to which he belongs.

Murray treats the packman's rise with genial humour, inviting us to agree that he deserves his success while, at the same time, he creates scepticism about the idea of 'success' itself. The packman's children are far better placed economically and socially than he was when young, yet the way in which they are described implies that in human terms their lives are actually less successful than his. Though his three sons are all professionally qualified and his daughter has 'married well' the poem leads us to question whether this is an 'improvement'. The clergyman son is dense; the clever doctor son has a lucrative practice in the 'sooth', but also a drink problem; the lawyer is sharp and manipulative; the daughter has married a dolt to improve her social position. We are made aware through all this, too, of the cultural transformation of the community: in the traditional community, the travelling merchant had been a pivotal figure, linking a scattered community at a time when communication was difficult and acting on his journeys like a kind of human communications centre—and full though his bundle is with all sorts of things to sell, it is nothing like as full as his head:

> The birn that rowed his shou'thers tho' sae panged wi' things to sell
> Held little to the claik he kent, an' wasna laith to tell—
> A waucht o' ale to slock his drooth, a pinch to clear his head,
> An' the news cam' frae the packman like the water doon the lade.

The packman is not just the transmitter of present happenings in the community, but also the custodian of its past and its traditions, who could 'redd you up your kith an' kin atween the Dee an' Don/Your forebears wha were hanged or jiled fae auld Culloden on', or who, as part of his sales pitch would sing some of the 'rare auld ballants' on his broadsides. His transformation into banker, merchant and elder suggests that the vernacular culture in which he used to be a central figure has become something marginal surviving only among his itinerant successors, in those groups still beyond the reach of schools and social reformers. The importance in the vernacular poetry of the period—in the work of Murray himself, in that of Violet Jacob, David Rorie, Marion Angus and others—of the figure of the tramp, the tinker, the vagabond or the vagrant, reflects their recognition that in the increasingly tidy, controlled, formally-educated society of the late nineteenth and early twentieth centuries, it was increasingly those on the periphery of settled society who were the last unselfconscious representatives of folk culture; they were the guardians of a once-robust tradition which was rapidly succumbing to the 'improving' forces of the present.

While the technique of 'The Packman' suggests the popular performance art of the comic recitation, bothy ballad or patter song, Violet Jacob's poem on the same theme, 'Pride' is less direct in its method and more 'literary' in its inspiration. The Scots is convincingly idiomatic, but the poem owes a large debt to the Burns of 'Holy Willie's Prayer'; it is spoken by one of the 'unco guid', and rather as Willie expresses his resentment at Gavin Hamilton's social success, so the speaker in 'Pride' expresses hers at the rise of a local fish cadger, 'Fishie Pete' to riches while she, douce, respectable and godly, has to struggle to make ends meet. Just as Murray emphasises the shrewdness, energy and hard work of the packman by making him start out with very little, so Violet Jacob centres her success story on someone who has risen from thoroughly unpromising beginnings. Readers of *Johnny Gibb* will remember that the most shameful thing that happens to the scheming farmer's wife, Mrs Birse, is the marriage of her son and favourite, Pate, to a fish cadger's daughter; alongside her deeply disgraceful social origins, the fact that the girl is pregnant at the time hardly counts at all. In Violet Jacob's poem, however, the focus of attention is not how Fishie Pete rose from crying 'the haddies in Ferry Street' to being 'Set up wi' his coats an' his grand cigars/In ane o' thae stinkin' motor-cars' or, by extension, on social change in the community, but on the state of mind of the speaker. In her resentful outburst—directed we imagine at a circle of nodding cronies—snobbery and jealousy masquerade as moral disapproval and are assuaged by the comforting thought of downfall and disgrace to come. The portrait is entertainingly done but there is no doubt that it was Burns's poem rather than any direct experience which provided the model for the poem. Less of Murray's work derives from established literary sources in this way—though Kurt Wittig, following Grieve, describes him as less 'modern' than either Violet Jacob or Marion Angus and more dependent on the enfeebled post-Burns tradition. As evidence Wittig cites the fact that Murray's poetry has 'most Burns-stanzas',[32] a true, but thoroughly misleading remark since, out of nearly a hundred poems in the *Complete Poems*, Murray uses the Burns stanza or some variant of it in just five.

Murray tended to use a contemporary and colloquial Scots, closely based on the dialect of the area he grew up in because his main talent was for narrative and dramatic verse; some of his most successful poems are dramatic monologues like 'A Green Yule' or 'Dockens afore his Peers' or closely related forms, like the verse-epistle form of 'Fae France' or 'Hairry Hears fae Hame', which purport to be familiar letters from non-literary correspondents and therefore represent a kind of vernacular 'talking on paper'. Violet Jacob's characteristic idiom is more generalised and 'literary', though still clearly regional; as a result her poetry, like that of Marion Angus, who used the same kind of Scots, is more readily accessible to the reader who is not from the North-East than that of Charles Murray or Mary Symon. No doubt that was one of the reasons why Grieve preferred the work of Violet Jacob and Marion Angus and even referred to the former as 'by far the most considerable of contemporary vernacular poets' despite her regrettable tendency to accept 'the stock-conception, the platitude, the "line of least resistance"'[33] and her general reluctance to take poetic risks. It is a description which points, in an unintended way, to the greater originality of Murray's work; in Bain's phrase he 'brought a new province into Scottish poetry' and there is no equivalent in the work of either of the other poets of that sense of the life and character of a specific region which Murray's work communicates so fully.

Violet Jacob's best-known and most-anthologised poem—and the one described by Grieve as her finest but not most characteristic piece—is 'Tam i' the Kirk'. It is a poem which has its roots in the folk-song tradition and probably owed much of its appeal to the way in which it communicates erotic excitement. The speaker, a young man, is sitting in the kirk, but finds he cannot attend to the service for thinking about Jean, who is sitting in front of him with a red rose on her bible which he has pulled for her that morning. The association between the rose and female sexuality is a very old one in the European literary tradition, of course, and the connection between them is made in the third stanza, where the speaker reflects that 'nane but the reid rose kens what my lassie gied him—/It and us twa'. It was this teasing frankness about sex, so familiar in the folk tradition, together with the fact that the poem celebrates the erotic in opposition to a religious tradition which is made to seem selfish and repressive in comparison, which made it appeal to Grieve:

> O Jean, my Jean, when the bell ca's the congregation
> O'er the valley and hill wi' the ding frae its iron mou',
> When a'body's thochts is set on their ain salvation,
> Min's set on you.

The conflict between a repressive, puritanical religious tradition and the passionate, sensual side of human nature is also presented with considerable power in 'The Jaud'. Like many of Violet Jacob's best poems, it owes its force to its use of folk technique; it is a ballad-like exchange between two voices, without any establishing or interpretative commentary and it has the sparse power of the best ballad work. It begins with a familiar kind of question and answer sequence, in which one voice asks the 'auld wife' why she is gazing at

the 'clour'd' gravestone, in a neglected corner of the kirk-yard. The grave is
that of a 'jaud', who had fascinated men, but disgraced her sex and has been
damned as a result: 'When the Last day braks tae the trumpets' ca'/And the
souls o' the righteous rise.' The questioner is particularly surprised at the
auld wife's interest since she herself is such a thoroughly respectable figure,
married to a decent man and with a large family, all successful and settled.
More acute than the inquirer, who is blinkered by a narrow, self-righteous
view of things, the reader recognises that the source of the wife's interest is
her awareness of unrealised elements in her own nature which link her with
the disgraced girl. The moral division between the respectable and the dis-
reputable woman is not an absolute one and the harsh judgement pronounced
by the first voice is unjustified. But more than this, the lovely description of
the dead girl links her with natural beauty and natural vitality in a way which
suggests that moral judgements are irrelevant:

> Her hair was like the gowd broom,
> Her een like the stars abune,
> Sae prood an' lichtsone an' fine was she
> Wi' her breist like the flowers o' the white rose tree
> When they're lyin' below the mune.

What is emphasised in 'prood an' lichtsome an' fine' is a free and confident
sensuality and a sexual independence which challenges prevailing notions of
female sexuality. It is, ironically, the voice representing conventional moral
attitudes which unintentionally reveals the reason for the auld wife's envy of
the jaud for, in its insistence that there is no reason for her to weep, with her
'three braw dochters' all settled and her 'fower bauld laddies . . . ilk wi' a
fairm at his back', the voice is revealing the limitations of a view of women
which sees their role almost exclusively as an other-centred rather than as a
self-fulfilling one. Despite its traditional appearance, 'The Jaud' reflects that
questioning of traditional conceptions of women's social and sexual place
and exploration of female identity which is a characteristically modern preoccupation.

Marion Angus was born in the eighteen-sixties, like many of the other
poets of the first stage of the vernacular revival, but she did not begin to
publish verse till after the Great War. Her late start, together with the fact
that some of her first published work appeared in Northern Numbers, the
series of anthologies of contemporary Scots poetry which Grieve produced in
the early twenties, has led to her being associated with the Scottish renaissance
movement, but the fact that she began to publish vernacular verse after the
war had more to do with the fact that the North-East was the major centre
of vernacular activity in the years leading up to the war.

When Grieve included the work of Marion Angus in the third (1922)
series of Northern Numbers, he was still at the stage of seeing English, that
'immensely superior medium of expression' as the inevitable language of any
ambitious and genuinely contemporary Scots poetry; the vernacular had
become and would remain no more than 'a backwater of the true river of

Scottish national expression.'[34] In other words, it was the already established vernacular movement which nurtured the early work of Marion Angus and not the later and in many ways antagonistic one associated with Grieve— and MacDiarmid. Her best work, like that of Violet Jacob, is rooted in the folk-song and ballad tradition or at least in that tradition as reflected and refracted in literary sources. But while Violet Jacob is largely interested in familiar human feelings and relationships, Marion Angus is perhaps the only modern Scots poet before MacDiarmid himself whose poetry conveys (in the words of a passage from Lytton Strachey quoted approvingly by Grieve) 'by means of words, mysteries and infinitudes.'[35] While Violet Jacob uses folk superstition in 'The Cross Roads' or 'The Neebour' simply to create a frisson of the kind we get from a good ghost story, Marion Angus uses the supernatural elements of the folk tradition for altogether more serious purposes in poems like 'The Seaward Toon' or 'In the Streets thereof' to create a sense of kinds of experience which are beyond the routine, rational and explicable, moments of contact with the numinous, which can only be conveyed by poetic means. 'The Seaward Toon' is a kind of warning against the temptation which the speaker of MacDiarmid's *A Drunk Man Looks at the Thistle* prays to be protected against—of being 'cut aff and self-sufficient' like a standing pool in a 'pocket o' impervious clay', cut off from the 'heichts o' the lift' and 'deeps o' the sea'. Marion Angus's central image of the 'seaward toon' which 'ye' (that is, most people) have failed to reach has affinities with MacDiarmid's use of the sea as a symbol of the fuller energies which most people shut out most of the time. The conception is a familiar one in modernist, as in romantic, writing and is linked with the sense of a fuller and more vital life beneath conscious level which is confined by both personal barriers and social circumstances. Many of the writers who explore this notion in their work, like Lawrence and MacDiarmid, rejected orthodox Christian belief—but they tend nevertheless to relate kinds of experience which have traditionally been regarded as 'religious' to situations in which contact has been established with the mysterious creative area of the psyche and to use traditional religious symbols and images to convey such experiences. Traditional Christian symbolism is used more seriously by Marion Angus, but she may have been aware of current trends in theology which attempted to link up religious experience with the idea of an unconscious life. The other thing that makes her poetry of religious experience memorable is its localisation of the great patterns and symbols of the religious tradition in a setting which is at once familiarly Scots and also strange:

> Ower the bent, an' ower the bent
> Ayont the blawing sand,
> Yer fit wad hae fint a seaward toon
> Ne'er biggit by mortal hand.

> Wi' a glimmer an' lowe fae shinin' panes,
> An' the stir o' eident feet,
> A'thing hapt in a droosy air
> That's naither cauld nor heat.

Thir's ane that cries sae clear and sweet
Three names baith kin an' kind,
Marget, Maud'lin, Lizabeth,
Far ben a quaiet wynd.

The work of Charles Murray, Violet Jacob and Marion Angus illustrates, in different ways, how much popular speech and the folk tradition have contributed to the renewal of vernacular poetry in this century, but perhaps the most telling evidence of all of the debt that the recent vigour of Scottish literature owes to the ordinary vernacular speaking people of Scotland, these mere 'hinds and chawbacons' with their 'gutter dialects' is the most extraordinary literary metamorphosis of the century—the transformation of C M Grieve, scourge of the vernacularists, into Hugh MacDiarmid, Scotland's greatest vernacular poet. The main agent of that transformation, as Grieve himself recounted in his own description of the event in the *Dunfermline Press* for 30 September 1922, was an apparently dry linguistic monograph, one of the products of that impulse which Grieve had denounced so fiercely as being merely conservative—its subject, one of those impoverished fragments of the once great Scots 'language', a regional dialect, and the dialect of a rural region at that. The book in question was, of course, Sir James Wilson's *Lowland Scotch as Spoken in the Lower Strathearn District of Perthshire.*

NOTES

1   T F Henderson, *Scottish Vernacular Literature: a succinct history* (London, 1898), p 458.
2   J H Millar, *A Literary History of Scotland* (London, 1903), pp 679, 690.
3   C M Grieve, 'John Buchan', *Contemporary Scottish Studies* (Edinburgh, 1976), p 2.
4   Grieve, 'Swatches o Hamespun', *Contemporary Scottish Studies*, p 82.
5   Grieve, letter to *Scottish Educational Journal*, 24 July 1925, in *Contemporary Scottish Studies*, p 12.
6   Grieve, 'Sir Herbert Maxwell, Bt. Sir Ian Hamilton', *Contemporary Scottish Studies*, p 26.
7   Grieve, 'English Ascendancy in British Literature', *At the Sign of the Thistle* (London, 1934), p 25.
8   Grieve, 'Towards a Synthetic Scots', *Contemporary Scottish Studies*, p118.
9   Joseph Knight, review of *Underwoods*, *Atheneum*, 10 September 1887.
10 J M Bulloch, introduction to John Mitchell, *Bydand* (Aberdeen, 1918), vi.
11 William Alexander, preface to *Johnny Gibb o' Gushetneuk* (Aberdeen, 1871).
12 'Hugh Haliburton' (James Logie Robertson), *Ochill Idylls and other Poems* (London, 1891), pp 9–10.
13 K M Elizabeth Murray, *Caught in the Web of Words: James A H Murray and the Oxford English Dictionary* (London, 1978), p 74.

14 Robert Louis Stevenson, *Collected Poems*, Janet Adam Smith (ed) (London, 1971), pp 486, 487.
15 William Craigie, 'The Present State of the Scottish Tongue', *Burns Chronicle*, first series, XXXII (1923), pp 28, 29.
16 Bulloch, introduction to *Bydand*, v.
17 Stevenson, *Collected Poems*, p 487.
18 C M Grieve, 'A Scotsman Looks at his World', *Dunfermline Press*, 25 November 1922, 6, quoted in Duncan Glen, *Hugh MacDiarmid and the Scottish Renaissance* (Edinburgh, 1964), p 73.
19 Stevenson, *Collected Poems*, p 487.
20 Stevenson, *Collected Poems*, p 487.
21 'Hugh Haliburton', *Horace in Homespun*, p 97.
22 Ibid.
23 Peter Marinelli, *Pastoral*, Critical Idiom Series (London), p 3.
24 'Hugh Haliburton', 'Our Earlier Burns', *In Scottish Fields* (London, 1890) pp 200–246.
25 Anon, 'Scots and English Popular Poetry', *Scots Observer*, 21 September 1889, p 488.
26 John Buchan, *Poems in Scots and English* (London, 1953), p 7.
27 Thomas Amos, Secretary's Report to Burns Federation Annual Conference, September 1922, *Burns Chronicle*, first series, XXXI, January 1923, p 181.
28 Alexander Mackie, introduction and appreciation, *Johnny Gibb* (Edinburgh, 1951), xxi.
29 Murray, *Caught in the Webb of Words*, p 83.
30 Robert Bain, 'Scottish Poetry of Today', *Burns Chronicle*, second series, I, 1926, p 49.
31 Buchan, *Poems Scots and English*, p 7.
32 Kurt Wittig, *Scottish Traditions in Literature* (Edinburgh, 1958), p 277.
33 Grieve, 'Violet Jacob', *Contemporary Scottish Studies*, p 8.
34 Grieve, 'John Ferguson', *Contemporary Scottish Studies*, p 42.
35 Grieve, 'The New Movement in Vernacular Poetry, Lewis Spence: Marion Angus', *Contemporary Scottish Studies*, p 62.

Chapter 2

Scottish Traditional Song and the Greig-Duncan Collection: Last Leaves or Last Rites?

IAN A OLSON

In the decade before the Great War an Aberdeenshire schoolmaster by the name of Gavin Greig together with his collaborator the Reverend James Bruce Duncan amassed from the North-East of Scotland one of the finest and largest collections of folk song—some 3,500 texts and 3,300 tunes—ever made. This collection was not only of such a size and quality as to make both men famous in their own lifetime throughout Britain and the Continent but was also literally revolutionary in content as far as Scottish culture was concerned. And yet, until very recently, little of this great collection has seen the light of day, its contents languishing on archive shelves, almost forgotten for over half a century. It therefore has had but little influence on either the development or the study of traditional Scottish song and music—even the enthusiastic Folk Song Revival of the 1960s could not draw upon it to any significant extent—and to this day (as in Greig and Duncan's time) Scottish Song is taken to be a mixture of Burns and the other National Song Book arrangers, together with debased Scottish Music Hall, purveying a couthy, maudlin, swaggering, drunken and pseudo-patriotic ethos which the rest of the world (the Scots included, especially the expatriates) has come to accept. The premature deaths of both men (Greig in 1914 and Duncan in 1917) before their work was completed and ready for publication contributed to this sorry tale, as did the advent of the Great War. More important still, a number of powerful influences ensured that the bulk of the collection was suppressed and neglected. The same influences exist to this day.

It would indeed be pleasant to re-tell the standard story of this rural dominie and minister spending their lives rescuing the remnants of traditional song in the North-East before the First World War swept their idyllic pastoral world away for ever, but this is so far from the truth (and indeed forms part of the powerful myth that virtually neutralised their findings, then and now) as to make necessary a proper understanding both of the men and their times. In 1861, for example, at the age of five Greig had watched the first Buchan train go past his father's house at Parkhill, Dyce, just north of Aberdeen; it heralded the rapid development of an extensive rail network throughout the region. A high degree of social mobility resulted and the centre of gravity began to shift from the crofts to the townships. Out through this network, furthermore, swept the communication explosion of the Victorian press when newspapers were rendered universally affordable by the repeal of the 1819 Stamp Act in 1855 (there were to be some forty North-East newspapers alone in Greig's lifetime); they were avidly read by one of the best-educated populations in Britain, thanks to the *Education* (*Scotland*) *Act* of 1872 which consolidated the local tradition of deep respect for education and learning. As far back as 1836 the magnificent Dick Bequest had begun its work of ensuring that even the remote parochial schools of the North-East were staffed by University graduates of the highest calibre by virtually doubling the salaries of those schoolmasters who could pass the stiff qualifying examination and regular inspections of their schools. Even a small remote school like Greig's at Whitehill, New Deer, had been sought after by graduates from all over Scotland and northern England. Greig, however, had been one of the most able men of his generation. Fourth Bursar at the age of seventeen in the fierce open competiton held by Aberdeen University (having turned down the thirty-third place bursary he had won at sixteen) he gained his post in 1879 against stiff competition and thereafter spent his life serving the same school ('one of the most efficient teachers known to the Dick Bequest inspectors') and local community. The Ministry was even more sought after as a career and Duncan with his Honours MA and record of high scholastic achievement at Aberdeen, Edinburgh and Leipzig Universities was by no means unusual; in the days of one Professor and (perhaps) one (temporary) Assistant per University department, even the highest flyers were farmed out to the manses, schools and professions in the North-East hinterland. Greig and Duncan, it must be understood, were but *primus inter pares*; there were many like them in the region, often engaged in research of high quality as a glance through such as the *Transactions of the Buchan Field Club* shows only too well.

Greig and Duncan were born into an era of headlong change, of unrest, instability and excitement scarcely comprehensible today, and a far cry from the rose-covered spectacle of stable rural existence portrayed by the Kailyard writers for their largely Anglo-American readers (themselves hungry for the assurance of such a Golden Age in the turmoil of industrialisation that had swept the West during the nineteenth century). By the end of this century Greig, like so many men of his time, began to experience a sense of overwhelming change and loss of the old way of life; he began a personal crusade to involve and interest the people around him in their past. He gave lectures and recitals, revived a rural drama firmly based on the old agricultural units, the ferm-touns, and wrote and produced musicals based on heroic figures in the region's history (conveniently ignoring the fact that the influence of such as Bruce, Mary Queen of Scots and Bonnie Prince Charlie on the area had been uniformly disastrous). The Jacobite cause and the moving Lowland Jacobite song cycle were dear to his heart (episcopal Aberdeenshire had held strongly to that forlorn hope) and his song-lectures and famous musical 'Bonnie Prince Charlie' moved his audiences to tears. When the twentieth century arrived he had successfully established the worth and importance of their historical, political and literary past in the minds of the North-East folk (and himself as its guardian).

Greig, however, had been troubled by the apparent paucity of indigenous music and song, especially when compared with the wealth and beauty of Scottish national song, which together with the romantic Jacobite cycle, had made Scotland the envy of the musical world for almost a hundred years. In a lifetime in the area he had come across only a couple of such worthy pieces (and rapidly turned one of them—'Logie o' Buchan'—into a Jacobite novel despite the fact it bore no relationship to that cause whatsoever). In 1903, however, Greig grasped the belated opportunity to examine the field once more, for the New Spalding Club (a local historical publishing club of some considerable importance—Queen Victoria and later King Edward were Patrons), was considering the publication of a volume entitled 'The Older Popular Minstrelsy of the North-East', at the suggestion of one of the King's Surgeons-General. It was to contain both secular and religious music, instrumental and vocal, and also, if any remained worth having, folk song and music. Greig ensured that he got the commission to do a preliminary survey, but within thirteen months to his surprise and chagrin he 'discovered' several hundred songs within a three mile radius of his home. Breaking through the polite facade of his neighbourhood he found that people of all classes, ages and occupations were capable of providing him with an apparently inexhaustable supply of genuine folk song. He began to realise that for over twenty-five years they had listened politely while he had lectured the adults and taught their children that the true song of Scotland was the beautiful reworkings of such as Burns, Ramsay and Lady Nairne and especially the Jacobite song composers, for in fact, the songs the local people actually sang bore no relation whatsoever to these. If this phenomenon extended beyond the three mile radius (throughout the North-East? throughout Scotland?) then these findings were revolutionary. Greig was about to propose to the New Spalding Club that he should undertake a full and thorough survey when Cecil Sharp in England published a selection of findings from a similar survey in Somerset and North Devon in the *Folk Song Society Journal* in the spring of 1905. They were presented to a uniquely high standard with every detail and variant carefully set out, and with annotation by a panel of experts.

Greig rose to the challenge immediately. He applied successfully for the first of five large research grants from the newly-formed Carnegie Trust for the Universities of Scotland in order to fund what was clearly going to be an extensive and expensive investigation, gained his old friend and University teacher, James Duncan, as a collaborator (Duncan now lived on Donside but had come from a family of folk singers whose croft was a few hundred yards from Greig's school), and thereafter successfully persuaded the New Spalding Club to promise him one of its prestigious Volumes as a vehicle for his findings. Duncan, it must be said, was of an entirely different character from the ebullient and optimistic Greig, for not only was he more cautious and even pedestrian in his thoroughness but also he had access to the large store of folk song in the memories of his own family, especially his brother George and sister Margaret. It is all the more significant therefore, that Duncan rapidly came to appreciate not only the extent of Greig's findings, but also their significance, for when the pair began fully to cooperate in searching out the traditional music and song of the North-East in a systematic manner, they came to at least two inescapable conclusions.

Firstly, as Greig had already noted, *traditional Scottish song as sung by the people clearly bore no relation at all to what was universally understood to be 'Scottish Song'*. The song culture of the drawing room and concert hall was not only ignored by the North-East folk but also was clearly the work of a handful of influential composers and arrangers such as Burns. Worse still, it became obvious to Greig that his beloved Lowland Jacobite song cycle consisted of fakes or forgeries written long after the events they portrayed. But would it not be possible for Greig and Duncan 'to reconstruct Scottish Song' from the wonderful heritage they had discovered? Unfortunately, this was very far from being the case as Greig explained in his Retiring Presidential Address to the Buchan Field Club in December 1905:

> . . . we must ever carefully avoid the error of supposing that we can assign to it [Buchan] any definite body of ministrelsy. We do indeed find a number of songs, the words of which are, or appear to be, of local origin; but even the most original of these will likely enough be found to be modelled on older ditties . . . Still more are the older tunes common property . . . As his [the folk song collector] collection grows he more and more discovers . . . endless resemblances, affinities, imitations, echoes, until there is woven around him and his subject a web that threatens to strangle both . . . [folk song] admits indeed of no delimitation either in a geographical or a secular way, reaching forth ultimately to the ends of the earth, and back to primeval times.

In other words their second inescapable conclusion was that *the North-East of Scotland contained a thriving song culture which transcended regional, national or even international boundaries.* The cultural and political implications of these findings were considerable, for if they applied to the rest of Scotland then it was clear that 'official' Scottish song was but a superficial sham. The international pre-eminence that the Scots had enjoyed in song and music would be seriously damaged; the political implications of revealing that Burns, the Scottish bard of the common man and universal brotherhood, was ignored by the Scots outwith the concert-hall were even more unthinkable.

In England, the dynamic Cecil Sharp encountered similar problems but selected out from his findings those songs which would appeal to English national sentiment and presented them to a delighted public as *English* folk song. Greig and Duncan, however, could see no other way than to finish their researches and present the 'great Thesaurus' to the world as a contribution to international folk song scholarship. Cecil Sharp brought out annual selections of his discoveries and made sure that they were incorporated into the Novello series of school song books, but although Greig wondered whether they should bring out a popular selection of their work to establish their findings in people's minds (and also show their many contributors that they were in fact doing *something*), Duncan was adamant that they should publish only when their work and its analysis were complete, in order to make their final conclusions both exhaustive and scientific. This quiet, retiring minister, moreover, maintained that a popular selection would entail censorship or bowdlerisation (his notebooks contained many verses or even whole songs which he had felt obliged to record in shorthand) and that this was totally unacceptable. Duncan was prepared to jeopardise his social position for the good of their cause by collecting from all manner of 'unsuitable' people such as travelling folk, and although a staunch teetotaller, he was prepared to carry a flask of whisky to stimulate the memories of diffident informants; he was not, however, prepared to skew the results of their researches in order to conform to public moral standards.

On the other hand, there was no objection to the publication of the literary aspect of their findings or to the use of illustrated lectures to further their work, and this they proceeded to do with great success throughout the region and in Aberdeen itself. Greig even employed that popular device of the time, the folk song column in the newspapers, and from 1907 until 1911 published a regular weekly column in the *Buchan Observer* which in turn brought in a further flood of contributions from throughout the country and abroad. Most important of all, however, was Greig's action in expanding his December 1905 address to the Buchan Field Club into a 27,000 word book entitled *Folk-Song in Buchan*, and later distributing it to the academic and folk song world. Scottish professors of English used it in their lectures (and even set examination questions on it). The English Folk Song Society were so impressed that they asked Greig to give the first in a proposed series of academic lectures in London on folk song (sadly, this was later withdrawn because of 'considerations of expenses entailed in a journey from Buchan'). Professor Brandl of Berlin asked to meet him and for permission to incorporate the work in his next Ballad publication. All this was hardly surprising for it was the first major analysis of folk song—both words and music—to be made in English by active field workers *who were themselves natives of the region* from a large collection of oral material using modern techniques. A copy was sent to Cecil Sharp who was himself in the process of preparing his own major analysis entitled (not surprisingly) *English Folk-Song: Some Conclusions* (1907).

Both Greig and Duncan had been concerned lest their findings should prove too revolutionary, too unacceptable even to their own people, but as they lectured throughout the North-East they soon began to realise that not only was the literary/academic world delighted with their findings but also that no rabid nationalist objected to their revelations concerning Burns and the Jacobite songs; the local musical world—even the middle-class circle—applauded their discoveries and asked for more. The Carnegie Trust (which dealt almost entirely with academics) gave Greig research grant after research grant (even breaking its own rules to assist him in publishing his *Buchan Observer* articles). As yet, however, no-one had actually *seen* the collection as such. The flood of material never abated and although both men struggled to get it ready for publication (they had, as we now know, enough for *eight* large volumes of results) only a volume of Child Ballads and a volume of 'later ballads and folk-songs of a more lyrical nature' were anywhere near completion by the time that Greig (who had been ailing for many years) died in August 1914 and Duncan in September 1917.

After Greig's death, Duncan had struggled on alone, determined to complete these first two volumes with the help of Mary Ann Crichton who had been an assistant teacher at Greig's school and the 'devoted amaneunsis' who had transcribed his work. In February 1917 he suffered a severe stroke which left him paralysed and speechless. He never recovered, and in the eight months before his death his daughter Katharine sought advice from Mr P J Anderson, the Secretary of the New Spalding Club (and also the University Librarian) as to what she should do with the manuscripts of the two volumes. Anderson recommended that they should be handed to William Walker to see if they could be got ready for publication.

Walker, aged seventy-six, had retired from business a few years before to give the whole of his time to the literary work which he had hitherto prosecuted during his leisure moments. In 1887 his *Bards of Bon-Accord* had become a minor classic. He had been Professor Child's principal North-East correspondent for the famous *English and Scottish Popular Ballads*, and held undisputed sway as the grand old man of Scottish balladry. His life-long interest in ballads and the literature of folk song (he had one of the most remarkable private libraries in existence) had culminated in 1915 with his attempt to vindicate the works of Peter Buchan, the early nineteenth-century Aberdeenshire collector, whose validity had been seriously questioned. He had very definite views on what constituted 'true' folk song and Greig and Duncan had found him a formidable critic ('a doughty warrior, death on careless work'). Walker, however, decided to examine the manuscripts of the *entire* collection made by Greig and Duncan which had been placed in Aberdeen University's safekeeping after Duncan's death. He completed the survey in a year but it was another year before he gave his report to Anderson. He had been appalled by what he had found:

> . . . it became very evident to me, that the Collectors, (in so far as *Texts* were concerned) having defined 'Folk-Song' as 'songs which the people sing' opened the door for an inflow of Music Hall Ditties, popular street songs, and the multitudinous Slip-Songs of the Ballad hawker,—these last, prepared in our large towns, for singing and selling at country fairs and markets throughout Scotland and Northern England.—These have sometimes been called 'Bothy Ballads' and have nothing traditional about them.—in the Indices, I have frequently marked 'Broadside' 'Slip-Song' 'Chapbook' 'Book', or 'Music-Hall', anent certain items, to indicate that though these may have *now* become a kind of traditional, they are not *of* the people, but were originally prepared *for* the people by a press whose trade it was to supply such, for street and market singers.—Many of these in passing from mouth to mouth among the people (who added to, subtracted from or modified the original in many ways) have as said, acquired a *kind* of traditional character—but their roots are in the ballad hawker's print, and I do not consider them 'folk-song' at all. Some of

the tunes, however, that they are sung to, however, have a real 'folk-song' smack about them, but probably belong to something better than the texts they are now attached to.—Apart from these, however, the Collection contains many songs and ballads *of* or *from* the people, genuinely traditional stuff, though frequently having traces of defective memories and careless hearers, during the course of their long descent.

By employing such criteria Walker felt able to dismiss the majority of Greig and Duncan's carefully collected songs; the rest of his extensive report concentrated on the one hundred and eight Child Ballads and their variants which had been prepared for 'Volume I' ('I have not touched on the Song section . . . intended for Vol II'). These he felt *were* of value and perhaps worthy of publication, *but*, he went on to point out, 'they are all well represented in Child's monumental work by versions from the same district' (many of them, of course, supplied by Walker himself). Nevertheless, they represented the 'last leaves' of North-East traditional balladry and had 'a distinct claim for preservation', especially those ballads supplied by Bell Robertson of New Pitsligo, as those she remembered her mother and grandmother singing were from the same era as Peter Buchan's collections and could help 'to refute the charge of his later English critics raised anent the "untrustworthiness" of his texts'.

By Duncan's death seventy-six of these ballads had been got ready for publication with texts, tunes and variants carefully collated and with a critical introduction to each ballad. Duncan had followed Child's editorial method to the minutest detail but, as Walker pointed out, 'Child's work was a truly national one . . . and so demanded minuter critical detailings than would be necessary in dealing with forms and variations of a small district like Aberdeenshire'. He therefore recommended that Duncan's 'overediting' be severely pruned and his Introduction to the Volume 'boiled down'. As for the remaining thirty-two ballads, Walker had added appropriate introductory notes ('certainly less analytical and critical than those which Mr D. had been supplying'). If the New Spalding Club were to decide on publication, Walker also recommended other cuts and changes together with methods of censoring those ballads characterised by their 'looseness'.

Anderson wrote to thank Walker for his 'sound and valuable' suggestions and to explain that the Club had in fact suspended its operations and that he did not know when, if ever, they would be resumed (he was to die two years after, bringing it effectively to its end). He thought it 'obviously desirable that all the materials collected by Mr Greig and Mr Duncan, and now critically estimated by yourself, should be carefully preserved so as to be readily accessible to duly accredited workers in the same field; and probably this end can be best attained by their being deposited in the University Library'. Four days later they were duly deposited.

Three years after, in 1922, Greig's friends from the Buchan (Field) Club became concerned over their apparent neglect. Dr J B Tocher, the enterprising Secretary, came up with the suggestion that the Club should publish that part of the Collection made from Bell Robertson. Walker (who had praised Bell in his report in 1919) was adamant that this request be refused; he could not be a party to 'mutilating that Colln'; he insisted that they printed '*the whole*'. (At this point it is important to understand that the 'Collection' Walker was referring to was that thirteen per cent he considered to be of any value—the Child Ballads.) Bell Roberson's material may well have included one of the biggest and best collections of such ballads ever made (although sadly, she could provide no tunes to them) but the bulk of the material she had given Grieg consisted of the type of unworthy song Walker refused to countenance *as* folk song. Such a Bell Robertson volume would, from his point of view, seriously misrepresent the importance of Aberdeenshire to the ballad-collecting world.

Walker had his way. He ensured that the Buchan Club publication consisted only of the Child ballads from the entire collection, for he was immensely proud of the fact that almost a third of Child's prime texts were Aberdeenshire versions, a fact which would be reinforced by Grieg and Duncan's (selected) findings. In his eighties by this time he felt unable to carry out the practical labour of preparing the volume itself and this task was given to Alexander Keith, a local journalist then in his late twenties. Keith followed Walker's suggestions almost to the letter and severely pruned the material. The texts were reduced by almost three quarters and the musical examples by half. He abridged and altered Duncan's introductions (while expanding Walker's notes) and provided his own General Introduction. This consisted almost entirely of a justification, using Greig and Duncan's findings, of Walker's lifelong attempt to vindicate Peter Buchan.

Walker had insisted on the title as well. It was 'Last Leaves of Traditional Ballads and Ballad Airs collected in Aberdeenshire by the Late Gavin Greig'. The removal of Duncan's name and the playing down of his contribution was a bold but necessary step if the all important elegaic note was to be sustained (aided by the fact that Duncan's daughter Katharine had taken away and locked up the notebooks of songs collected from the Duncan family, especially his mother, four years before—taken aback, no doubt, by those 'unsuitable' shorthand entries), for this also meant that the unorthodox opinions of the collectors in the form of Duncan's notes could also be played down. Against all the evidence, the Introduction stated that Aberdeenshire ballad-singing was 'dying out' and that *Last Leaves* was 'the final collection'.

Men of the old school such as Walker believed passionately that the ballads (whatever their mode of origin) had undergone a 'long descent', with their last remnants to be found on the lips of the remote rural peasantry who had 'not enjoyed the last benefits of a liberal education', who were 'not greatly endowed with poetic genius' and who lived 'in rural corners tucked away safely from the chief intellectual amenities of civilization'. This noble peasantry had all but died out and, by definition, the ballads had died with them. By this definition, however, the Aberdeenshire of Greig and Duncan's time was also the last place in the world to have contained great numbers of ballads and ballad singers for it was one of the best educated, best informed, most literate (including musical literacy), technologically advanced areas in existence. With its highly organised communications networks and great social mobility, it had probably fewer illiterate rustics to the square mile than anywhere in Western Europe. Greig and Duncan's informants, moreover, had come from all walks of life—doctors, ministers, farmers, shopkeepers, tradesmen, to name but a few; Bell Robertson, 'the most voluminous transmitter of ballads in the history of ballad-collecting' was, *as Walker well knew*, a literate local poet with publications to her name. In order to sustain his thesis Walker was not only obliged to discount virtually all of the Greig-Duncan Collection but also to deliberately ignore the evidence that the singing tradition that had supplied it was alive and thriving. His influence on *Last Leaves* and his dismissive Report on the Collection ensured that *Last Leaves* served as the last rites for this great and important work. (Fifty years later funding bodies were still refusing support for publication of the entire work on the grounds that everything of value in it had been published.)

The Collection languished on archive shelves but the folk song tradition continued. Around 1930 James Madison Carpenter from Harvard retraced Greig and Duncan's footsteps with similar success; in the 1950s, Alan Lomax, Hamish Henderson and many others were to tread the same paths with the same results (some of their singers such as Jeannie Robertson of Aberdeen or John Strachan of Fyvie were perhaps even more prolific informants than any Greig or Duncan had found). Yet still the powerful myth of a high and noble tradition dying on the lips of a remote, unlettered rural peasantry held sway. In 1954, a distinguished Scots man of letters was to assert (and re-assert defiantly in a 1968 edition):

> Nowadays in Scotland there are no peasants; and ours is not a singing age. The tradition in which Burns wrought died out in the Lowlands during the latter part of the nineteenth century, lingered out a brief decadence in the form of the Bothy Ballad in the relative seclusion of the North-East, and now is gone for ever.

Does it matter that 'Scotland's biggest and finest manuscript collection of folk-songs; biggest in sheer size and finest on account of the integrity, breadth of vision and high scholastic ability of its own two collectors' should not have started seeing the light of day in its entirety until 1981? The tradition it mirrored can be heard to this day (although it is sad that recent Folk Song Revivals were largely deprived of the Collection's treasures despite the efforts of the many enthusiasts who searched through the manuscripts in Aberdeen University Library), but the influence of Greig and Duncan on Scottish music and letters died with them—and was buried effectively by such as William Walker.

Scotland's popular music is thus still a travesty of its traditional music. The serious study and performance of this traditional music is (with honourable exception) almost non-existent (although a simple-minded observer might well be confused by such terms as 'Scottish' Opera, 'Scottish' Ballet, 'Scottish' Orchestras and 'Scottish' Schools of Music and Music Departments). The study of Scottish life and literature has been seriously damaged by an often perverse and persistent misunderstanding of the significance and value of traditional culture, by the myth that only the 'great ballads' (divorced from their music and performance) were of any literary importance and that traditional performers were but poor custodians of a once high and noble tradition, enabling the bulk of their repertoires to be discounted as valueless and without meaning. The final publication of the monumental and scholarly Greig-Duncan Folk Song Collection, however, may even yet act as an impetus for understanding and change, and Scottish culture as a whole be enriched and transformed. The long-standing influence of what Greig described as 'the prig and poetaster, the fool and the fiddler' may yet have had its day.

ACKNOWLEDGEMENTS

The research for this article and related papers was supported by generous grants from the British Academy and the Carnegie Trust for the Universities of Scotland.

FURTHER READING

SOURCES

Greig, Gavin, *Folk-Song of the North-East. Reprints of Articles contributed to the Buchan Observer from December 1907 to May 1911. With Special Index prepared by William Walker*, (Peterhead, 1914). Reprinted together with Greig's *Folk-Song in Buchan* (Peterhead, 1906) with a Foreword by K S Goldstein and A Argo (Hatboro, Pennsylvania, 1963)

Keith, Alexander (ed), *Last Leaves of Traditional Ballads and Ballad Airs collected in Aberdeenshire by the late Gavin Greig* (Aberdeen, 1925)

Olson, Ian A, 'The Greig-Duncan Folk Song Collection and the New Spalding Club', *Aberdeen University Review*, 50, no. 171 (1984), pp 203–28

—— 'The Greig-Duncan Folk Song Collection and the Carnegie Trust for the Universities of Scotland', *Aberdeen University Review*, 51, no. 173 (1985), pp 37–73

—— 'The Influence of the Folk Song Society on the Folk Song Collection', *Folk Music Journal*, 5, no. 2 (1986), pp 176–201

—— 'Gavin Greig's Lecture to the Scottish National Song Society, November 1909. A failure of nerve?', *Northern Scotland*, 7, no. 2 (1987), pp 150–7

Shuldham-Shaw, Patrick, 'The Greig-Duncan Folk Song Manuscripts', *New Edinburgh Review*, Festival Issue (August 1973), pp 3–5

—— and Lyle, E B, 'Folk-Song in the North-East: J B Duncan's Lecture to the Aberdeen Wagner Society, 1908', *Scottish Studies*, 18 (1974), pp 1–37

Walker, William, His report on the Collection and the related correspondence was recently discovered by Dr Dorothy B Johnston amongst Aberdeen University Library Archives MSS 793 'Original MS of Scottish music composed and gathered byWilliam Christie, dancing master, Cuminestown, Monquhitter, *c*.1818.' MSS 793/2/1–6

GENERAL

Buchan, David, *The Ballad and the Folk*, (London and Boston, 1972). The modern classic on North-East balladry which is (unbelievably) out of print

Donaldson, William, *Popular Literature in Victorian Scotland. Language, fiction and the press*, (Aberdeen, 1986). Authoritatively overturns most of our treasured concepts of this era and a *sine qua non* for a linguistic, literary and socio-historical understanding of the period. *See also* his Introduction to the reprint of Gavin Greig's 1899 *Logie O' Buchan* (Aberdeen, 1985)

Harker, Dave, *Fakesong. The manufacture of British 'folksong' 1700 to the present day*, (Milton Keynes and Philadelphia, 1985). Politically biased, historically controversial and often irritatingly perverse, it presents, nevertheless, an unusual and refreshing perspective on folk song studies

Henderson, Hamish, 'The Ballad, the Folk and the Oral Tradition' in *The People's*

Past, Edward J Cowan (ed) (Edinburgh, 1980). A full-blooded, yet constructive antithesis to Professor Buchan's *The Ballad and the Folk*. *See also* his 'Enemies of Folksong', *Saltire Review*, 2 (1955), pp 19–25

Munro, Ailie, *The Folk Music Revival in Scotland*, (London, 1984). Openly biased in a number of directions (especially feminism) it remains a careful, thoughtful and stimulating account of this phenomenon and its aftermath. It also contains the excellent *The Folk Revival in Gaelic Song* by Morag MacLeod

Shuldham-Shaw, Patrick and Lyle, E B (eds), *The Greig-Duncan Folk Song Collection*: Volume 1. *Nautical, military and historical songs, and songs in which characters adopt the dress of the opposite sex*, (Aberdeen, 1981). Volume 2. *Narrative songs* (1984). Volume 3. *Songs of the countryside and of home and social life* (1987). (In preparation): Volume 4. *Songs of courtship, night visiting songs, and songs about particular people*; Volumes 5, 6 and 7. *Love songs*; Volume 8. *Songs of parting, children's songs, nonsense songs, general notes and commentaries on the collections, and indexes*

Chapter 3

Foundations of the Modern Scottish Novel

BETH DICKSON

While looking for a billet in Bombay, the young Joseph Conrad was entranced by a beautiful sailing ship being towed into harbour. Conrad secured a billet on this ship and was able to use her name in the title of one of his novels, *The Nigger of the 'Narcissus'*. She had been built by Robert Duncan in Port Glasgow and was owned by Colin S Caird of the Greenock family of shipbuilders. The growth of Scottish industry in the nineteenth century, one of the achievements of which had so impressed Conrad, reached its peak in the early years of the twentieth century. With 10.5% of UK population, Scotland produced 12.5% of UK output.[1]

Underlying this international success of Scottish commerce, however, was a harsh social reality for those who worked in the shipyards and in Scotland's other heavy industries. Appalling housing conditions, long working hours, and inadequate diet meant that between 1900 and 1920, the rate of emigration was fifty per cent of the natural increase in population,[2] a loss which was not compensated for by the steady flow of impoverished immigrants who were encouraged to take jobs at subsistence rates and therefore maintain the low wage economy on which much of Scottish industry was based.

In this, one of the most industrialised areas of the world, it was rare to find writers dealing with the realities of the social experience. As many critics have pointed out, the major Scottish writers of the period around the turn of the century—George Douglas Brown, J MacDougall Hay, Neil Munro and J M Barrie—rarely acknowledge that they live in an industrial country at all.

Of those authors who did tackle the subject, few deployed real imaginative perception. Blythswood Fergus, for instance, in *The Barmaid and what became of her!* (1902) and Patrick MacGill (an Irish writer) in *Children of the Dead End* (1914) and *The Rat-pit* (1915) both set out to show the conditions of the Glasgow poor. Fergus describes the 'respectable poor' while MacGill, the more detailed and hard-hitting of the two, describes the indigent. The writers preface their novels by claiming that *The Barmaid* is 'practically a novel of facts' and the *The Rat-pit* is a 'transcript from life'. Their primary function is educational, and their value lies in their social description, not their imaginative dexterity. The other end of Scotland's social spectrum was portrayed by Frederick Niven in *The Justice of the Peace* (1914), which deals with a Glasgow warehouse owner and the problems which ensue when this son wants to leave the business and become an artist. Of the three novelists described here, Niven is the most 'literary' and his choice of theme—the young imaginative boy dissatisfied with an unimaginative but socially respectable career—links him with the best writers of the period and with concerns which both reflect the nature of their society and the limitations of their art.

At the core of the novels of Brown, Hay, Munro and Barrie is a regularly repeated set of themes which are more self-reflexive than reflective, and which had the effect of circumscribing the scope of their work as explicit social commentary, though it provides the backbone of many of the assumptions with which the rest of twentieth-century Scottish Literature has to deal: what they imply in their works is that as writers they were involved in a fight for survival in a country which seemed to them to have no place for the literary imagination.

The success of Scotland as a part of the Empire provided for many Scots a coherent world view within a powerful culture to which Scottishness gave an added piquancy: John Buchan supremely exhibits this untroubled dual identity, writing about Richard Hannay as easily as Dickson McCunn, researching *Montrose* as well as *Cromwell*, being appointed Governor-General of Canada, and thus achieving the summit of his imperialist ambitions while still acknowledging his Scottish background by choosing the title Baron Tweedsmuir when being raised to the peerage.

The prestige of English culture had two important effects on Scottish writers. It presented them with a secure literary tradition, but one which was essentially foreign and which was of limited use in helping them to find their own literary identity. And, from a critical perspective, it encouraged the interpretation of Scottish works from an English point of view which obscured or distorted native Scottish traditions in fiction. The ease of assimilation of the English tradition and the obscurity of the Scottish tradition created particular difficulties for Scottish writers in finding a voice and style which matched their surrounding environment. Instead of reacting against or developing from a Scottish tradition, each had to manufacture a tradition in order to make sense of their society.

The lack of an accepted mode of seeing the Scottish past perhaps explains the inclusiveness of so many modern Scottish novels. In reaction against the stereotyped perception of Scotland's history as essentially a conflict between the glamour of the Jacobites and the dour fanaticism of the Calvinists—or Highlands versus Lowlands—they seek to redraw the totality of the Scottish past and to re-establish the 'real' pattern of lost traditions and lost inheritances. Despite this, the novels do not read like 'thesis novels' because their inclusiveness is not a gesture of completed understanding but expresses a restless attempt to analyse a situation which continually escapes them.

If novelists lacked a perceived tradition, they also lacked critical appreciation. The so-called 'Kailyard' novels, although they exhibited an idealised and false version of Scottish life, were enormously successful. The hard facts of Scottish reality had been transformed into the matter of nostalgia and distictive Scottish speech and custom were shown as quaint, old-fashioned, but most importantly, as something belonging to the past and therefore irrelevant to the modern world. Novels which challenged this version of provincial Scottish life, showing it to be stagnant not nostalgic, corrupt not quaint, were regarded with animosity because they forced people to confront at least a part of a Scottish reality they would rather have ignored.

Caught between the apparent lack of a vital tradition, and the lack of an audience prepared to take Scottish issues seriously, the authors had difficulty in forming a stable sense of their own literary identity from which they could tackle the issues that confronted their society.

That the work of Scottish authors cannot properly be comprehended within the presuppositions of the criticism of English literature was not an idea widely accepted,[3] and early twentieth-century Scottish writers, therefore, had by themselves to realise the limitations of the English tradition for their creative purposes and develop a sense of their own distinctive identity before being able to turn their experience into fictional form. And yet, out of this confusion of critical and creative traditions, and despite the fact that the writers worked for the most part independently of each other, they display a remarkable unity in their analysis of their own situation—if not of the Scottish situation as a whole. George Douglas Brown, J MacDougall Hay, Neil Munro and J M Barrie are at one in describing the social stagnation of Scottish communities. They deal continually with the way in which such a society rejects imaginative vitality and they display the consequences of that rejection in characters whose lives are devoid of imagination or whose imaginations return to childhood as the only arena in which it is acceptable. The novels display in their plots the authors' struggle to maintain an imaginative vitality which they feel to be on the verge of extinction: the imaginative characters are constantly defeated, or survive by retreating into childhood.

The single work which was to have the greatest influence on subsequent Scottish writing, George Douglas Brown's *The House with the Green Shutters* (1901), is written against this problematic background. Brown takes as his starting point not the major Scottish tradition of the novel of the earlier part of the nineteenth century—the tradition of Scott, Galt and Hogg—but the typical elements of sentimental Kailyard fiction. Brown's brief career is focused around a violent rejection of the novels which display Scotland as a place of rural quaintness where conflicts will be trivial or resolve themselves in an undemanding spiritual harmony, and around a violent confrontation with the lack of imagination which those novels reveal to be the underlying Scottish sickness.

As the Kailyard novels describe a small rural community, so too does Brown, but into his description he packs a rigorous and scathing analysis so detailed and intense that it becomes an analysis of Scotland itself. Of the institutions which are usually claimed to enshrine a distinctive Scottish ident-ity—the church, the education system and the legal system—Brown describes the first two, showing how empty is their claim because in practice they are so remote as to be irrelevant to the lives of ordinary people. Although Brown's fictional village of Barbie has, for instance, not one but two ministers (as a result of the Disruption of the Church of Scotland in the 1840s), it is a den of spite, entirely lacking in Christian charity. The Church of Scotland minister is a buffoon, respected only for his social status, while the Free Church minister is an academic, whose interest in botany is incomprehensible to the local gossips who smear him as a 'weanly gowk'. The schoolteacher is another institutional figure whose academic interests have no value in Barbie. Shown reading *The Wealth of Nations*, he is linked by Brown with the rich intellectual inheritance of the Scottish Enlightenment. However, he cannot find any way of unlocking the benefits of this knowledge for his pupils. Having to provide rudimentary education for children who only come to school in order to learn to read, write and count, has made him frustrated, brutal and hostile to those he is supposed to help. Salvation by spirit or intellect is not available to the folk of Barbie.

It is in this context that Brown's central figure, John Gourlay, stands out: a man of no imagination, of little intellectual or spiritual substance, he can yet dominate the town by the sheer force of a will power whose brutality demands admiration because it displays a potential that the rest of the community dreads to envisage.

But because the medium of his power is commerce, Gourlay is a prey to forces he cannot control—as he controls his family—merely by the strength of his personality: around him, the world is changing, and the forces of social change which gave him the opportunity to become the most successful man in the town—owner of the house with the green shutters—are also forces which will undermine his position. In the community Brown describes, transcendental values have been replaced by materialistic ones; and the tragedy that he describes is not just the tragedy of a materialistic man brought low by the forces of materialism, but a materialist whose pride in his possessions rises to a kind of spirituality in comparison with the stunted spiritual values of the community in which he lives. Gourlay is an uncouth individual who finds it hard to express himself and whose frustration with his condition as his prosperity evaporates can only express itself in physical violence, but he is surrounded by men whose weakness makes his stunted life and qualities seem heroic by comparison. In the small ingrown community everyone knows everyone else's business, the main activity of most of the men is to meet at the Cross to gossip; their sense of community is held together by nothing but their spite, most of which is directed at Gourlay because he spurns them. Even when Gourlay's position weakens, these men will not have the strength to be able to confront him directly: they remain an impotent, whispering chorus to the downfall that Gourlay brings upon himself. Brown confronts us with a society where there are no positive values with which we, as readers, would want to identify: the 'hero' represents values with which Brown has no sympathy, and yet he is of tragic stature because of the petty impotence of those by whom he is surrounded: the vision of blackness, of a society without positive alternatives, is complete and horrrifying.

Gourlay's strength is his insensitivity; his weakness that that insensitivity destroys the family on whom he depends if his 'house' is to be maintained. Into Gourlay's son, John, Brown projects the imagination that both Gourlay and the community of Barbie lack, but it is an imagination stunted by its environment, incapable of growth or maturity. When life becomes intolerable he retreats into his imagination, but it is an imagination which thrives on vivid and morbid sense impressions. He does not use his imagination to bring history or personality alive, or to explore his environment, but to enliven a gruesome scene so that he can experience some strong emotion, as, when, after reading about Dick Turpin, he wallows in fear and horror.

John's imagination is a source of danger to him. The schoolteacher says that his fault is 'sensory perceptiveness in gross excess of his intellectuality' (Chapter Fifteen) and yet this immature imagination is the only kind that we see in the society. At university John attends a lecture on 'Philosophy and the Imagination' in which the lecturer argues that the information that the mind receives from the universe is diverse and overwhelming. The place of philosophy is to explain such phenomena to the mind, to assure the mind of its own worth and to enable it to produce something valuable from a chaotic universe. Philosophy, however is beyond John: he does not seek to encompass and shape the chaos of his life, but to stimulate his senses by drink. His one success at university—winning a prize for an essay—is based on his presentation of a nightmare journey into a frozen wilderness, which is the only end for his own 'opulent and vivid mind' (Chapter Eighteen) and a model of what the Scottish situation seemed to hold out to the writers of Brown's generation. When, abetted by drink and provoked by one of the 'bodies', John murders his father in his only act of self-assertion in the novel, the enfeebled imagination takes self-destructive revenge on the life that failed to succour it. But if it cannot live in the shadow of Gourlay's repressive power, it cannot live without it: John's imagination is haunted by the 'red e'en' of the father he has destroyed and only suicide will allow him a final escape from being overwhelmed by a riotous imagination.

In discussing Barbie writers who had won the Raeburn prize before John, the bodies note that 'the breed seems to have decayed' (Chapter Eighteen). This statement is truer than they suppose and indeed sums up a key issue of the novel: that for John with his materialistic community and his inarticulate but domineering father, imagination was the impossible gift. It was impossible because Barbie saw no need for it and dangerous because it was such a powerful gift when not properly trained; it threatened the life of its possessor. Brown's projection into fictional form of the conflict between the Scottish community and the creative artist is the most striking of the period, but it is paralleled in MacDougall Hay's *Gillespie* (1914), in J M Barrie's *Sentimental Tommy* (1896) and *Tommy and Grizel* (1900) and in Neil Munro's *Gilian the Dreamer* (1899).

All four writers present a community which is sick. Hay's equivalent of Barbie, Brieston, has its equivalent of Gourlay in Gillespie Strang, whose search for power and wealth destroys his family. For Hay the conflict has a more elemental quality than for Brown: he presents a human society which seems driven by vast forces, forces of a spiritual universe with which humanity has almost lost touch and which, though they may help Gillespie rise to power, will just as implacably undermine that power. The plot is so close to that of *The House with the Green Shutters* in structure that Hay's reputation has suffered from the implication of plagiarism, but the quality of the writing and the sense of human beings' relationship to the world around them is strikingly different. The characters pulse with a vitality that is quite different from Brown's spiteful 'bodies', but because that vitality comes from forces that are outside of the society, that pass through human life from elsewhere, what remains the same is the sense of the littleness of humanity, its feebleness even in its strengths. Gillespie's wife, like Gourlay's, is destroyed by her husband's brutality: the strength of one enforces the weakness of the other, and yet that weakness will undermine the strong partner until it provokes the destruction of both. The structure is tragic, but the qualities of the 'hero' so far from tragic nobility that the impossibility of tragedy is the ultimate tragedy of their situation: in this environment no one has the potential to rise to a tragic *anagnorisis* because no one has the imagination to come to an understanding of their own condition.

As Brown focused the role of education in the decline of Scottish culture, so Hay, who was a minister, focuses on the role of the church. In common with other churches in western Europe, the Scottish church in the latter part of the nineteenth century had to contend with the rise of Liberal scholarship, and between 1880 and 1902 there were several heresy trials as the church tried to come to terms with the new scholarship and what it meant for the faith. Being a *national* church, which had formed the backbone of Scottish identity over the previous centuries, such conflicts had a more than religious significance: they contributed to undermining one of the major pillars of Scottish identity.

The implications of these issues are seen in the series of distressing doubts which characterise *Gillespie*. Hay is particularly concerned with implications for human morality when the existence of God is doubted. The stars and the sea are no longer the expressions of a loving Creator but symbols of human loneliness in a vast universe, empty of God. Unlike Matthew Arnold who deals with loss of faith from a personal viewpoint, Hay shows a distinctively Scottish grasp of the problem by seeing it as one which affects a whole society because Gillespie himself, one of those luminously and gratuitously evil men who dog the pages of the Scottish novel, affects a whole society; and although transcendent values have been superseded by materialistic ones, Hay's dilemma is that though God may not exist, the devil still seems to and there is no way of halting him. Gillespie's evil is unrestrained and he is often described by images of hell or of the devil. To counter this evil, Eoghan, Gillespie's son, begins the search for an alternative source of positive value which takes as its starting point the rejection of Christian revelation, the message of the church. Eoghan dies before he has completed the search but the novel points in the direction which later Scottish novelists will travel as they seek to relocate their spiritual beliefs outside of the walls of the church. Hay concludes by describing a ploughman 'ministering to the faith that is imperishable in the breast of man' (Book Four, Chapter Nineteen). This is not faith in God, but faith in the ultimate triumph of the innate good in man, and in its insistence that 'nothing was left but the earth' it prefigures the confrontation that would be central to the world of Lewis Grassic Gibbon twenty years later.

And as in Gibbon's *A Scots Quair*, in all of the communities described by these writers gossip plays a central role. Gossip is the decayed remains of a folk culture and the decayed remnant of a vital imagination: healthy human energy turns sour and malignant in a social curse which dehumanises perpetrator and subject alike. In J M Barrie's *Sentimental Tommy* gossip is so rife that it dominates all private activity. Anything people want to do but want no one else to know about has to be done with elaborate precautions. Practically none of the characters in Thrums is transparently honest. People create public images which are totally divorced from private reality in order to retain some control over how they are discussed by other people. In *Tommy and Grizel*, Tommy's mother, who lives in poverty and has been abandoned by her husband in London, writes to Thrums assuring her correspondent of her prosperity in the great city because the knowledge that the woman will be galled at her (non-existent) success is sweeter to her than having to endure an insincere pity which is only a mask for scorn and contempt. Barrie treats these duplicities in a more humorous way than either Hay or Brown, but his pungent satire does not lessen the horror of the moral emptiness he describes.

The moral emptiness of Lowland life in Barrie's novels and stories is matched by the moral degradation of Highland in Neil Munro's. The phenomena which he feels show Highland decline are depopulation, the presence of sheep on the hills and the fact that the army recruits most of the community's young men. Munro is aware of an old Highland community of ceilidhs and wars, the ruins of which exist in the surrounding countryside, but now Inverary is a 'stopped and stagnant world' (*Gilian the Dreamer*, Chapter Three). It is full of old soldiers drugged insensitive by war when fighting in the British army. As a troop of soldiers enters his town Gilian thinks, 'And now they were the foreign invader, dumb because they did not know the native language, pitying this doomed community, but moving in to strike it at the vitals' (Chapter Eleven). When the Duke, the area's effective ruler comes home, he does not get involved with the local community, he merely 'threw a glance among his clan and tenantry' before returning to London (Chapter Twenty-three). All around in Munro's work, there is the awareness of an enormous reduction in the scope of human activity so that, when two characters quarrel, one 'revenges' himself on the other, not by raiding his cattle, but by dropping him from his invitation list. Such triviality, even when used for humorous purposes, points towards the novelist's consciousness of dealing with a society whose scale of values is incommensurate with his own demands.

Munro's attitude to the Highland community is doubly split. On one hand he knows that the old culture was humanly satisfying but violent. Thus he never went as far as Neil Gunn in seeing it as an archetypal Edenic community. On the other hand he feels that it had now become so enfeebled that the army are doing a necessary but unpleasant job in wiping it out, except that, despite everything, he still yearns for the cultural self-sufficiency of the old life. It has to be said that although Munro's analysis of Highland society is faltering, he seems to be moving to an interpretation of Highland history which became well known in later novels such as Gunn's *Butcher's Broom* and Crichton Smith's *Consider the Lilies*. In later years Munro was bitterly angry with critics who had, he felt, misdirected him by encouraging him to develop the Celtic Twilight aspect of his work rather than other aspects which, on looking back, he considered to be more important.[4] His Celticism was the response of an imagination, which, like that of his characters, was in flight from a world that seemed to offer it nothing, and despite the superficial differences between Munro and writers like Brown and Hay, he was closer to them than later critics have suggested (Hay dedicated *Gillespie* to him) and he was concerned with the same issues.

Munro's central characters are dreamers in a Celtic Twilight who dream themselves into other worlds because they are dissatisfied with their own but their dreaming is only one aspect of the central problem which all these novelists confront. Their own society offers them no human activity which cannot be encompassed by a parish. In such a society, the child who possesses imagination finds little to feed it on. John Gourlay reads adventure stories or his mother's novelettes. Munro shows that Gilian is cut off from oral Gaelic sources and written Scottish sources. Without sustenance, their imaginations become wild, or wither into morbidity. Eoghan Strang dreams of organising a soldier's solemn funeral. Gilian imagines the feelings of a soldier about to be trampled to death by a horse. Tommy imagines his own death so that he can enjoy beforehand his guardian's distress. Because these boys use their imaginations to escape from or ignore uncongenial reality, their imaginations and actions are often unreliable. Because it is so easy to imagine a different world and because they can conceive of that world so intensely, they can live more comfortably in an imagined world than in this one. When Gilian takes a friend to see a nest which he claims belongs to a heron, his friend, seeing only a nest, asks Gilian how he knows it is a heron's. Gilian does not know. He would rather base reality on imagination and believe that heron live there than base imagination on reality and shin up the tree to establish the facts.

The facility of imagination is seen in the boys' adoption of roles. People looking on have difficulty in characterising them because of the way they can drop in and out of other people's characters with seeming ease. Often the boys are mistaken for the role they adopt, but this is merely a feature of their imagination and signifies nothing about their own personalities. His guardian thinks Gilian would like to be a soldier when he sees him pretending to be one but Gilian is simply enjoying his imagination. Dangers arise, however, when the boys find their own lives uncogenial and try to hide by adopting a role, as has been seen in John Gourlay's case. Gilian pretends that he is a poet whose true love has married somebody else, and though it is clear that the girl he loved does not love him he is not willing to recognise the fact. Tommy adopts so many roles that by the end of the novel it is impossible to describe his personality at all; it is all made up of elements of other people's.

The morbidity of much of these characters' imaginings is only a prophecy of their unfittedness for life in their communities: if they try to confront their world—like John Gourlay and Eoghan Strang—their deaths are inevitable, and the only alternative is a retreat into the childhood in which their imaginations enjoyed the scope of their littleness. Thus Barrie's characters continually fail to face up to the demands of adult life and retreat into childhood. In the sequel to *Sentimental Tommy*, *Tommy and Grizel*, Tommy tries to fall in love with his childhood sweetheart Grizel, but he is so self-absorbed he cannot truly love anybody. While he is trying to tell Grizel he loves her, his thoughts are, 'Ah, if only it could have been a world of boys and girls!' (Chapter Thirteen).

The unclouded vision of their childhood is not, in these writers, a touch-stone of artistic integrity, but an escape back to the potentialities of an imagination which may still have the opportunity to develop in conjunction with a literary tradition and a social context which would have helped them develop. It is not until Neil Gunn's *Highland River* (1937) that this return to childhood is taken up in a way which reveals a unity of purpose between the adult imagination and the child's imagination, the possibility that the child can be father to the man rather than escape from adulthood.

To see in characters like John Gourlay the constricted workings of the artistic imagination may seem rather optimistic on the showing these characters make in the novels. Nevertheless it is the case that characters produce some written work in the novels. John Gourlay writes the Raeburn essay; Eoghan and Gilian write poetry; Gilian's poetry is published. Tommy Sandys becomes a professional writer. The writer of the novel projects his own capacities, in enfeebled form, into the novel as though he can hardly believe his own temerity in asserting his imaginative power over the world in which he has to live. And this lack of self-confidence perhaps accounts for the inconsistency that characterises the work of these novelists. Their best and most powerful work is commonly that which arises from the intense struggle of finding their own literary identity. After *Gilian* Munro writes good but less than profound adventure stories. Barrie left novel writing for the stage where his wit ensured success, though it is appropriate that his English reputation rests on *Peter Pan* (1904), the little boy who never grew up. Brown died prematurely and Munro was convinced that a factor in his death was the pressure put upon him by other Scots to produce a novel of the same standard as *The House with the Green Shutters* as quickly as possible:

> Better were his luck, probably longer his life, and more enduring his influence and memory, had destiny and his fellow-countrymen left him, unobserved and unharassed for a dozen years, to find himself.[5]

Hay died without producing anything to compare with Gillespie. All of them, in their search for a method of conveying their dilemma, mixed styles from a variety of sources: thus there are great swatches of Shakespearean or Authorized Version purple in *Gillespie*, as well as the considerable influence of Dostoyevski; and Brown uses the framework of Greek tragedy in a stringently classical version of Thomas Hardy's attempt to bring tragic structure into the novel. It is perhaps significant that Brown is often more convincing in the places where he mingles Gourlay's 'black glower' with images of the devil taken from the Scots folk-tradition. Unlikely situations occur as plots try to contain themes too momentous for them—of all unlikely ends, the deaths of

Gillespie and Tommy Sandys must rank among the unlikeliest. Finally, because of the impossibility of resolving the issues raised by these novels, all the novels have strained conclusions. Three of the novels end with the horrible death of the young boy and two with the deaths of the other main characters as well. Although *Gilian* does not end with Gilian's death, at the end of the first part, Gilian's criminal negligence almost causes the death of some sailors and certainly hastens the end of Gilian's guardian who, though ill, takes a turn for the worse when he hears of Gilian's behaviour. The second part of the novel could be construed as an attempt on Munro's part to evade the tragic consequences of Gilian's dream nature. These unusual endings make clear the intractable nature of the problems facing the Scottish novelists. Solutions or plans for the future were inconceivable. After they had analysed the problem for as long as they could, they simply had to stop analysing. The plot had to end somehow; more often than not it ended in melodramatic tragedy and violence.

Curiously, perhaps, the same dilemmas do not figure as powerfully in the novels of two women whose work gained the recognition of Henry James but which seems to have had little impact on later Scottish writers. Mary and Jane Findlater are primarily concerned with the problems faced by intellectual and imaginative young women in the nineteenth century. Not all the novels are set, like the recently reissued *Crossriggs* (1908), in Scotland, but their theme is always the same. The most striking characteristic of their novels in the light of the problems of the male novelists, is that they can achieve a positive rather than a tragic resolution of difficult themes. It is hard-won and usually involves suffering and it is not always the outcome the main character wished, but it is a resolution which promises a new and enriched peace for the heroine. This facility for resolution, so foreign to contemporary male writers, reflects the fact that the Findlaters were open to another fictional tradition, that of women's writing. There the difficulties of woman's role in society had been discussed throughout the nineteenth century in English and American novels. Thus unlike their male counterparts who struggled with what seemed to be a failed tradition of Scottish writing, the Findlaters had available to them the whole discourse of the novel as developed by women writers in the nineteenth century. They could quickly define themselves in terms of their position as women, a larger and more inclusive category than nationality, and could devote themselves thereafter to finding strategies to overcome the problems they faced in a society which seemed in so many ways to discriminate against women. While this major structural feature links them to a wider fictional tradition, they present a remarkable example of the broader Scottish tradition which has so often been obscured from critical attention. Indeed, the very analysis of Scottish society as presented by the male novelists of the early part of the century has been so influential in our understanding of the Scottish situation, that its partiality is often ignored. Their view of Scotland as hostile and repressive to the imagination is a view conditioned as much by their own situation as writers on the threshold of the twentieth century as it is by the reality of the Scottish world which most of them escaped before writing their works.

That Scottish novelists did not chart the process of urban social change, that much of the actuality of Scottish life goes undocumented by its novelists, is neither to be deplored nor regretted. Their work operates as an analysis of Scotland's self-perception and psychological condition at a level that does not lend itself to the documenting of the conditions of the industrial urban world. In this, perhaps, they are, despite their search for appropriate traditions, at one with a central strand of the whole Scottish involvement in the novel—i.e. a concern with allegory, myth, parable rather than with the mundanities of documentary realism. Their parishes are real enough, but also sufficiently divorced from the centres of contemporary life to become microcosms of the country as a whole, miniatures of a human condition which is not defined by the contingent actualities of Scotland's 'real' condition.

It was not until the Scottish Literary Renaissance that a new framework for understanding Scotland emerged. J H Miller's *A Literary History of Scotland* (1903) described Scottish writers mainly from a British point of view, but in 1919, G Gregory Smith published his *Scottish Literature* which argues that Scottish literature has distinctive national identity. It is this work which first uses the term 'the Caledonian Anti-zysygy' which was to be taken up by Hugh MacDiarmid and used as a key thought in his ideas about Scotland. He began to think in terms of a separate and distinct Scottish literary tradition, a separate Scottish cultural identity and a style which would reflect these realities. This confident intellectual basis was the catalyst of many Scottish novels which appeared between 1930 and 1950, as later writers began to experiment with new ways of writing about Scotland. Later writers and readers tended to accept at face value MacDiarmid's valid but damning criticisms of both Barrie and Munro and as a result those writers have been neglected ever since. George Douglas Brown was singled out as the man to follow, mainly because of the vehemence of his attack on Scottish society; that attack, however, may have given Brown's work a more 'realistic' edge than his contemporaries, but it did not separate him from their general concerns. It was against the backdrop of those concerns that much of the later work was to be written: however incomplete their analysis or unfulfilled their achievement they provided a 'language' which could be developed and in which the issues of Scottish society could be confronted. They formed, for the writers of the Renaissance, the tradition out of which they could develop until they could recover the wider tradition of Scottish writing from which these writers of the early part of the century felt themselves cut off.

NOTES

1 Christopher Harvie, *No Gods and precious few heroes: Scotland 1914–1980* (London, 1981), p 1

2 T C Smout, *A century of the Scottish People* (London, 1986), p 109–14

3   Belief in a distinct and valuable Scottish identity never died out completely
although it was sometimes quaintly expressed. In a series of essays and poems,
Hugh Haliburton argues that Scottish literature should be taught in universities.
Hugh Haliburton, *For Puir Auld Scotland's Sake* (Edinburgh and London, 1887),
pp 156–62
4   Anne Smith 'In search of the essential Celt' in *The Scotsman*, 11 December 1982
5   Neil Munro, *The Looker-On* (Edinburgh, 1933), p 282.

Chapter 4

Recent Scottish Thought

RONALD TURNBULL and CRAIG BEVERIDGE

'And it's more than economics, in the sense that we are more than economics,' said the Philosopher. 'There is the superstructure of thought, especially, say, of religion. Just as the economic life ebbed, so did the religious. Science, with freethought, was the machine there. When William Bulbreac called me the Serpent he wasn't so far wrong. In my own small way, I was Antichrist. And the awful thing about the Antichrist is that he has nothing to put in the place of that which he destroys. For every personal problem is more than a personal problem: it is a communal one.'

Neil M Gunn, *The Serpent*

PHILOSOPHY AND SCIENCE

The main developments in twentieth-century Scottish thought can perhaps best be approached as critical responses to the intellectual dominance of natural science and the advance of philosophical currents which appear to underwrite those attitudes conveniently referred to as 'the scientific world-view'. To provide a context for more detailed discussion of this Scottish contribution to philosophy it will be useful, at the outset, to compare it in general terms with the philosophical styles which have been ascendent in the English-speaking world as a whole.

Essentially, philosophers in England responded to the increasing intellectual prestige of natural science by attempting to emulate scientific discourse and achieve an approximation of philosophy to science, for instance as the logic of scientific inquiry. Positivism, which might briefly be defined as the equation of scientific knowledge with our knowledge of the world *tout court*, has been an immensely powerful force. It was, in the inter-war years, the dominant philosophical movement in England. As is well known, the positivists banished whole areas of discourse, including ethics, political theory and religion, from the realm of cognitively significant debate to the domain of the unsayable, the unintelligible, or—as some preferred to put it—the 'nonsensical'. To quote one of the texts which has been most influential in twentieth-century English thought: 'The right method of philosophy would be this. To say nothing except what can be said, i.e. the propositions of natural science . . .'[1]

Even after its collapse as a movement positivism lived on as a sort of intellectual reflex, expressed in the overwhelming tendency to link morality and religion with the 'merely' subjective and emotive, and to see in the procedures of natural science the paradigm of objectivity and rationality. Certain important figures have continued, indeed, to identify philosophy with the logic of science.[2]

The subordination of philosophy to science was not restricted to the revival of positivist doctrine. Academic philosophy as a whole has been characterised by a scientific ethos and aspiration to scientificity. These are articulated, for instance, in the deployment of formal technique and specialised vocabulary; in the extreme emphasis on exactness and precision (the deadly sins of modern English philosophy being ambiguity and unclarity); and in the exclusion from philosophical writing of personal discourse.

In Scotland, in so far as the universities have been occupied by English intellectuals and a native intelligentsia committed to Oxbridge mores, the philosophy departments, especially in more recent years, have reflected the trends of English philosophy. However, there has survived another intellectual tradition, in which are inscribed quite different conceptions of the status of science and the nature of philosophy. Here there is resistance to 'the twentieth-century "surrender to science"'. Scottish philosophers have been sceptical of natural science not in the sense of being anti-scientific or irrationalist, but in arguing that scientific knowledge is only one mode of human cognition among others. The distinction between philosophies which accept the restriction of the concept of knowledge to knowledge of the sensible world, and those which interpret knowledge in a much wider sense is one we meet time and again in the works of Scottish thinkers. The Glasgow professor C A Campbell, for instance, in his Gifford lectures of the mid 1950s draws attention to 'a very real divide between those who understand by "experience" merely sensory experience, and those who believe that experience as a source of evidence is far richer than is allowed for by its arbitrary limitation to the sensory'.[3] The Scottish philosophers stress the need to assert and explore our other ways of knowing the world, for instance the various dimensions of moral and religious experience.

Consistent with this aversion to the more extreme claims made on behalf of science is the widespread hostility among Scottish thinkers to the English 'revolution in philosophy': the reduction of philosophy to the logic of science, or to the analysis of linguistic usage—the declension, to quote Professor John Anderson, of philosophy to 'technical exercises', the substitution of *Berufsphilosophie* for critical understanding of self and society.

It is interesting to note that these Scottish positions were still being vigorously defended in the 1960s. We might take as an example an article entitled 'Two Conceptions of Philosophy' by the Hegel scholar T M Knox.[4] Knox was concerned to criticise the approach of 'the dominant group of contemporary English philosophers', and to indicate an alternative view of philosophy. He begins by raising doubts about the revolutionary nature of the linguistic method, which is, he thinks, merely 'English empiricism' in a new guise. He confesses to finding the debates of linguistic philosophers 'intensely uninteresting'. 'The questions they discuss so enthusiastically are questions which, in the main, do not arise for me at all.' On the other hand, the methods they employ seem ill-equipped to deal with genuine philosophical problems, as opposed to 'puzzles': a question such as 'what is the chief end of man?' cannot be settled by an appeal to usage.

The root of the problem with contemporary English philosophy, Knox argues, is acceptance of the dogma that our knowledge of the world is exhausted in natural scientific knowledge. Linguistic philosophers hold that 'science, and science alone, deals with fact'. But this abandonment of all experience beyond the sensory means that almost everything which is of importance is excluded from philosophy. English philosophers neglect the human world, rejecting all those levels of reality—our experience of others, of ourselves, of morality, of beauty, of God—which are not amenable to scientific investigation, and they find their only vocation in the analysis of linguistic usage. (Or rather, he notes—hinting at an element of chauvinism—in the analysis of English usage, 'as if English were the only language'.) 'We are to ask,' according to the linguisticists, 'not what goodness is, or truth, or time, but how these words are used'. Knox rejects this conception of the philosopher's role. A philosopher's answer to the question 'what is justice?', as distinct from a lexicographer's, is not an account of the use of the word 'justice': 'his concern *qua* philosopher is with justice, i.e. with an objective fact which also has its subjective side in experience and so with a fact of a kind outside the purview of physical science'.

The error in the linguistic approach is, precisely, that it excludes subjectivity. Philosophy's task, properly understood, is to explore 'the total experience of subject knowing object'. It is the expression of this personal experience: 'philosophy is always personal'; 'it is not wholly unreasonable to describe philosophy as self-knowledge'. We should not then speak of (impersonal) 'problems of philosophy', but always of a philosopher's problems. Knox goes on to criticise the kind of philosophical scholarship, typical of the analytic tradition, which abstracts a work from its concrete personal and historical setting and treats it 'as if it were not a work of literature but a series of mathematical steps'.

(Students of the recent history of philosophy in Britain will observe that Knox's critique of linguisticism parallels in many ways the arguments made fashionable by New Left critics and the Radical Philosophy movement in the later 1960s and early 1970s.)

A further illustration of this kind of position is provided by H J Paton's Gifford lectures of 1950–1. (Paton was a professor at Glasgow, then Oxford, and a distinguished Kant scholar.) Science, Paton writes, is concerned 'only with certain aspects of reality': 'what remains clear is that it has, and can have, no concern with judgements of value or with judgements of what ought to be: it can treat these only as emotive utterances or psychological events . . . Science seeks to be objective—to concern itself solely with objects and to eliminate all merely personal points of view . . .'[5] For Paton a 'critical philosophy' could not turn away from other forms of human experience, or from the point of view of the person as subject and actor. But the 'arid empiricism' he perceived as the prevailing trend in British philosophy seemed unlikely to develop in such directions.

It was Paton's particular concern that the overblown role now accorded to science and scientific reasoning was threatening the claims of a less narrow conception of reason to demonstrate the possibility of fundamental moral principles: 'it is a serious matter, both for the individual and society, if men are to be told that there can be no objective moral principles because these are not the same as scientific generalisations'.[6] Paton's attempt to elucidate and defend the Kantian ethic of respect for persons was intended, he writes, to counter the undermining of the moral life through the spread of the scientific *Weltanschauung*, 'in these days when the pillars of European society are shaken, and when we are assailed on every side by prophets of unreason for whom moral splendour is so much illusion . . .'[7]

ANDERSON: ANTI-MODERNISM

In *The Crisis of the Democratic Intellect* George Davie puts forward the thesis that the distinctive Scottish contribution to twentieth-century philosophy lies in a critique of modernist optimism which can be read as a secular reassertion of calvinist notions about human fallibility. This is expressed, for instance, in the epistemology of Norman Kemp Smith, who held that knowledge does not develop in a cumulative, evolutionary fashion, but rather, in Davie's words, 'in the course of a critical struggle against illusions which at every turn reassert themselves in new forms after they have been conquered'.[8] But modern Scottish philosophy finds its most eloquent and complex articulation, Davie suggests, in the work of John Anderson, who was for a time a colleague of Kemp Smith's at Edinburgh.

The son of a radical teacher, Anderson studied physics and philosophy at Glasgow. In 1926 he emigrated to Australia to become a professor at Sydney. There he established himself as both a major intellectual force and a somewhat notorious public figure, on account of his unconventional views and a certain relish for polemic. He has enjoyed a remarkable reputation in Australia, where he taught and influenced the likes of Passmore, Armstrong and Kamenka, who has written of Anderson that 'he displayed a combination of unflagging logical incisiveness and acuteness, an outstanding sense of coherence and connection, and an unusually strong and original capacity for creative theoretical imagination'.[9]

Like many other Scottish thinkers, Anderson disagreed with the approach to philosophy fashionable in England, referring to 'the narrow, specialising and instrumentalist attitude that has infected the most influential schools of philosophy at the moment'. Whereas modern English thought, in both its positivist and ordinary language modes, assigns to philosophy the status of a specialism, for Anderson it has 'a central place in any cultural system' (here he echoes the conception inscribed in the traditional curricular arrangements of the Scottish universities, described by Davie in *The Democratic Intellect*). In contrast to the ethos of professional neutrality and the concentration on issues remote from general intellectual concern which are so characteristic of the Anglo–American tradition, Anderson locates the task of philosophy in the criticism of accepted ideas and ways of life (philosophy as 'a basis for social criticism'). The philosopher wages war on complacency, is committed to a life of 'permanent protest, criticism and self-criticism', as Kamenka glosses Anderson's view. This conception, the same writer observes, was rooted in 'a certain Presbyterian intransigence, a Scottish suspicion of things English, of urbanity and self-satisfaction . . .'

In his later philosophy Anderson expressed a deep distrust of all progressive, reformist and meliorist discourse, attacking the vision of a New Jerusalem which, it was widely supposed, the planners and experts would soon be able to create through the judicious application of science and technology. Progressivists, Anderson argued, overlook 'qualitative distinctions and oppositions', ignore the incompatibility of different values and traditions, different moralities and forms of life, and collapse ethics to questions of distribution.

Anderson's early marxism developed, partly under the influence of Sorel, into a political position of great subtlety and insight. He criticised the tendency of leftist thought to concentrate on questions of property rather than control (an issue recently explored by Foucault). He argued that the working class was losing direction through its surrender to consumer values (in this respect he shares something of the position of the Frankfurt School). Welfarism he characterised as a mechanism which functions to undermine genuinely radical projects. He was an early critic of statism, or the reliance on a 'protective' state for the provision of benefits. For, first, states will function above all to benefit those who work directly for them; and second, the desire for provision, for security, is the mark of a servile mentality. The labour movement, he came to believe, had degenerated into a vehicle for this desire; it had thus become the enemy of liberty, responsibility and enterprise.[10]

Anderson's anti-modernist position is crystallised in his philosophy of education. 'Anderson was profoundly conscious', writes George Davie, 'of the incompatibility between the intellectual values embodied in the traditional Scottish curriculum, and the neo-utilitarian reorganisation of education which in the years after World War II was increasingly undertaken by the various governments of the English-speaking world.'[11] His response, for instance in the great essay on 'Classicism', was to re-assert these traditional values against 'the view which prevails among professional educationists who . . . conceive education as the preparation of the pupil for the problems of the real world in which he is to live . . .'[12]

He opposed both the fashionable idea of education as self-discovery, and the orthodoxy he termed 'practicalism', according to which education should be organised on utilitarian lines, with pride of place given to technical and scientific subjects. Such philosophies confuse education with quite different things—in the case of practicalism, with training or the acquisition of useful skills. Anderson, for his part, talks of education in terms of thought, criticism, the awakening of intellectual interests, 'the questioning of received opinions', 'the finding of a way of life'. Essential to the development of critical intelligence, he argued, was cultural comparison, acquaintance with a variety of judgements. This helps us to understand his defence of classics, which was also based on the view that Greek culture was one of the zeniths of the critical, the philosophical spirit, freedom from provincialism and blind adherence to the positive. Attacked for holding an 'elitist' view of education, Anderson replied that 'the only alternative to the development of criticism is the development of submissiveness'; here the progressive view was in the end illiberal, functioning to strengthen existing relations of power.

BAILLIE: KNOWLEDGE AND PERSONS

John Baillie was born in 1886, into a calvinist Highland manse. He studied divinity and philosophy at Edinburgh and later at Jena and Marburg. His academic career took him to Toronto, New York and finally back to Edinburgh in 1934 as Professor of Divinity. Though he can hardly be considered a thinker of the first rank, Baillie's work is of great interest in drawing together themes and concerns which are typical of much recent Scottish thought. Of special importance is the emphasis in Baillie's writing, emerging from a critique of scientism, on the phenomenon of personhood. This tendency is to be found in the work of a number of thinkers, most notably Macmurray, Laing and Macquarrie, who can be seen, with Baillie, as representatives of a Scottish personalist tradition.

What do we know? And of what can we be certain? In answering these basic philosophical questions Baillie takes issue with the epistemological views dominant in the analytic tradition. Above all he wishes to reject the empiricist doctrine that our knowledge is limited to that of the world we experience via the bodily senses. The popularity of this theory has to do with the power of natural science, but it is a dangerous assumption which, if taken seriously, must lead to 'the impoverishment of our total spiritual life'. We should resist the tendency to privilege one way in which we apprehend reality, for the range of human experience is much wider than the empiricists allow. They disqualify and so disesteem our knowledge of ourselves and others, our moral feelings, our sense of beauty and our experience of God. The empiricist maxim that we learn from our experience is acceptable, however, if we interpret 'experience' to mean the totality of human experience: 'I must trust my experience, my sense-experience, my social experience and my moral experience'.

Baillie is also anxious to contest the notion that certainty can only be predicated of natural scientific propositions, arguing that, if we examine our experience, we find that certainty attaches to our knowledge of moral truth. 'There is nothing of which I am more assured than that I must not exploit my fellow man in the interest of my own selfish gain, but must seek his own good no less than my own and, if need be, at the cost of my own. There is nothing of which I am more assured than that Hitler was wrong in attempting to exterminate the Jews'.

But Baillie goes further than claiming that our ideas of experience, knowledge and reality should not be limited in their application to the natural world by urging that it is our knowledge of persons, rather than knowledge of natural fact, which is primary and paradigmatic, and that it is in our dealings with others that we are most assuredly in contact with reality. 'To my mind knowledge of persons is the very type and pattern of what we mean by knowledge. Of no other existents is our knowledge so intimate and direct.' 'Reality is personal', Baillie had written in an earlier work. He supports this way of seeing the world in different ways. Reality can be conceived as that which resists. 'Reality is what I "come up against", what takes me by surprise, the other-than-myself which pulls me up and obliges me to reckon with it and adjust myself to it because it will not consent simply to adjust iself to me . . . The world of natural objects, real as it is on its own level, offers to my will a much less stubborn resistance than that offered by my encounter with my fellow men.'[13] We can also think of reality as that which is present to us. It is then significant that 'we do not normally speak of the presence of a physical object'. Nor do we talk about being 'with' an object. 'It is only persons that I can be with.' Baillie acknowledges his debt here to a number of existentialist and personalist thinkers: Heidegger, Eberhard Grisebach, Gabriel Marcel and, above all, Martin Buber, the German–Jewish philosopher whose teaching that 'others are the real world' has found such resonance among Scottish thinkers. (Buber's works, it is relevant to note, were first translated into English by the Glasgow theologian Ronald Gregor Smith.)

My knowledge of others, then, is deeper and more immediate than my knowledge of things. At the same time, it involves a consciousness of responsibility, it imposes duties upon me.

> When our apprehension is of other selves than our own, we are above all aware of the claim they make upon us, and the response they demand is what we call an attitude of responsibility towards them . . . Where we have to do with personal relations, we do but evade the realities presented to our apprehension if we face them otherwise than responsibly. Nor can we bring the least reason into the discussion of these matters if we approach them disinterestedly, or without the full recognition of the demands they make upon our will and action. Our thinking about them is quite unreal unless it be, in Kierkegaard's phrase, 'existential'.

In a frank personal retrospect appended to his final book, Baillie returns to his objections to 'the school of logical and conceptual analysis which has recently dominated the philosophical thinking of Oxford and Cambridge'. He has learned from and made concessions to the teaching of the analytic movement, but 'when I am asked to swallow it whole, I become angry, and the more of the recent books I read by its representatives, the angrier I become'. The analytic movement is theoretically misguided in restricting the real to the world of sense experience, and knowledge to knowledge of natural fact. But Baillie's disagreement is not merely intellectual. 'Reductive naturalism', by devalorising the world of interpersonal experience, tends to have a disastrous effect on the attitudes of those who come under its influence. 'Nor do I speak here of their morals in any ordinary sense, for we are all miserable sinners, but of a certain painful restriction of outlook, of interest, of understanding and of sympathy which seems to leave them as very incomplete human beings . . . I confess that in my heart of hearts my impatience with them knows no bounds.'[14]

MACQUARRIE: PERSONALIST PHENOMENOLOGY

In conceiving philosophy as concerned with the full spectrum of human experience, as an exploration of the full parameters of subjectivity, the tradition we are considering has more in common with certain Continental schools than with modern Anglo–American philosophy, which is always, we might say, a philosophy of the object. It is not then surprising that in the recent period Scottish thinkers should have been receptive to developments in European thought to a much greater extent than mainstream philosophers in England.

The work of the contemporary philosopher and theologian John Macquarrie (born in 1919) illustrates this affinity for European philosophy. A product of Campbell's philosophy department at Glasgow, Macquarrie is the author of a sympathetic study of existentialism, and co-translator of Heidegger's *Sein und Zeit*, in this latter capacity continuing the Scottish tradition in philosophical scholarship represented by figures such as Paton and Kemp Smith.

In *Existentialism* Macquarrie argues for a mode of philosophical inquiry which avoids irrationalism on the one hand, and the narrowing of reality to mathematics and science on the other.

> What is healthy and valid in the existentialist collision with rationalism is not the attack on logic or the exaltation of the absurd—these are in fact dangerous and negative characteristics that must be resisted in the name of reason. Rather what is valid is the insistence that there are many rich strands in human existence that ought not to be ignored or downgraded just because they cannot be fitted into the logic of mathematics or of the empirical sciences. This is not to condemn logic or to embark on intellectual anarchy. At its best, it is an attempt to develop a logic of persons in addition to our logic of things.[15]

In Search of Humanity illustrates what Macquarrie intends by such a 'logic of persons'. It explores a range of phenomena—freedom, becoming, transcendence, commitment, hope, and so on—which define the nature of personhood. Macquarrie suggests, in his development of what he calls a 'personalist phenomenology', that a key feature of 'the lifelong task of becoming a person' is directedness, the pursuance of some policy of action. Conscience, not as an agency of censure and rebuke, but as an inner voice which discloses what we ought to be or become, figures as an essential moment in directedness: it is the call—Macquarrie here adopts Heidegger's idiom

—of the authentic to the empirical self, the summons of a true nature, but a call all too easily drowned in the *Geschwätz* [chatter] which surrounds us.

The nature of cognition is a major theme in Macquarrie's thought. He has two objections to the traditional concept of knowledge. He questions the possibility of a pure thinking subject possessed of pure and certain knowledge, here drawing on philosophers like Habermas and Heidegger's pupil Gadamer, who stresses the historicity of all knowledge and its inevitable complicity with prejudice and interest. 'The overcoming of all prejudice, that global demand of the Enlightenment', he quotes Gadamer, 'will prove to be itself a prejudice, the removal of which opens the way to an understanding of our finitude.' But if the traditional conception goes too far here, in another sense it does not go far enough. *In Search of Humanity* can be seen, Macquarrie writes, as 'a plea for a wider concept of knowing'. He urges us to recognise forms of knowledge which cannot be reduced to clear and distinct ideas; to ask whether detachment, instead of being, as commonly supposed, a condition of knowledge, might in fact be a hindrance to it; and to pay more heed to our knowledge of ourselves and others. Interpersonal experience is indispensable in the acquisition of knowledge. 'How much knowledge, both explicit and tacit, flows from knowing another person, is incalculable. It is through knowing another that I come to know myself, through knowing myself that I come to know others, through knowing others that I come to know a world.' Other, pre-Cartesian cultures recognised that knowing people, not knowing facts, was primary. Macquarrie comments on the concept of knowledge implied in the text 'Now Adam knew his wife Eve . . .':

> It is an indication of the extent to which we have fallen away from that understanding of knowing by union and participation that modern translations of the Bible substitute quite different ideas, and fail entirely either to comprehend or express what was meant by 'knowing'.

Macquarrie's aim is to establish 'a more human concept of knowledge'. This does not mean 'more subjective', 'but rather the opposite, for the broader concept of knowledge being advocated rests on a correspondingly broader apprehension of the reality with which we are confronted'.

MACMURRAY: DECONSTRUCTING SCIENCE

Both Baillie and Macquarrie acknowledge the influence of a thinker who should perhaps be seen as the *chef d'école* of Scottish personalism: John Macmurray. Born in 1891, Macmurray studied classics at Glasgow, then went to Oxford. His experiences in the First World War crucially shaped his thinking. Philosophy, he was convinced, must address itself to the realities of the age, it must relate to the problems which concern society at large. Macmurray held a number of teaching posts outwith Scotland before returning to Edinburgh in 1944 as professor of philosophy, a position he held until his retirement in 1958. He developed his thinking in over a dozen books, published between 1932 and 1965.

The important philosophical issues, Macmurray believed, are not dictated by academic tradition: they are pressed upon the philosopher by the circumstances of the times. So his own philosophy is a response to what he sees as the central issue of his age, a cultural predicament he terms 'the crisis of the personal'. Critical of the analytic movement, which he saw as a failure to engage with the vital questions, he had some sympathy with the existentialists: 'their sensitiveness to the darkness of human despair leads them to discover the emergent problem of our time', he writes in *The Self as Agent*.

The weakening of religious forms of life is one symptom of 'the crisis of the personal'. The decline of religious practice denotes a severe impoverishment of personal life, an increasing 'loss of the human subject', to borrow a phrase from Ronald Gregor Smith. In emphasising the importance of religious traditions for the maintenance of ways of living which attempt to do justice to our nature as persons, Macmurray is eloquently at variance with the facile secularism of most contemporary thought.

> The decline of religious influence and of religious practice . . . betrays, and in turn intensifies, a growing insensitiveness to the personal aspects of life, and a growing indifference to personal values. Christianity, in particular, is the exponent and the guardian of the personal, and the function of organised Christianity in our history has been to foster and maintain the personal life and to bear continuous witness, in symbol and doctrine, to the ultimacy of personal values. If this influence is removed or ceases to be effective, the awareness of personal issues will tend to be lost, in the pressure of functional preoccupations, by all except those who are by nature specially sensitive to them. *The sense of personal dignity as well as of personal unworthiness will atrophy, with the decline in habits of self-examination.* Success will tend to become the criterion of rightness, and there will spread through society a temper which is extraverted, pragmatic and merely objective, for which all problems are soluble by better organisation.[17]

Macmurray's project can be conceived as a foregrounding of the phenomenon of personal being in face of 'the crisis of the personal'. This crisis has a theoretical dimension. We have been led astray, Macmurray believes, by a set of beliefs concerning reason, knowledge, the intellect and the emotions. In what amounts to a quite remarkable contribution to theory, he proceeds to offer what we should nowadays perhaps call a deconstruction of the whole way of approaching the world and our experience of it which the triumphs of natural science have rendered dominant. (If today such critiques of scientism are no longer new, we should bear in mind that Macmurray was developing and publishing these ideas from the 1930s.)

Again, there is no question of irrationalism. 'Our real nature as persons is to be reasonable and to extend our capacity for reason.' But Macmurray rejects the customary identification of reason with thought or intellect. The equation of reason with 'passionless reflection', and the divorce of reason and emotion are, he argues, 'quite arbitrary and groundless'. Detached, unfeeling reflection is rational, 'but it has no unique claim to rationality, and it is indeed not the primary expression of reason'. He suggests that reason be understood in terms of objectivity rather than intellection: 'reason is the capacity to behave in terms of the nature of the object'. And emotions, like thoughts, can be objective—appropriate to the reality to which they refer.

Emotional rationality can be seen in the sensitive, open, disinterested way in which an artist seeks to apprehend the world. Artists try to get outside themselves, to become fully aware of and absorbed in something, to feel it, as we might say. Reversing the conventional notion that art is somehow less objective than science, less concerned with things as they really are, Macmurray argues that science, which is concerned with general properties rather than individual things, yields a more superficial form of knowledge. Intellectual knowledge is knowledge *about* things, not knowledge *of* them. If we have to choose, we must say that it is the person with the artist's sensibility rather than the scientist's who really knows the world. The success of scientific reasoning, however, has meant the neglect of our emotional rationality, which involves our ability to respond to meaning and value in the world. As a result, we have become blind to value, unresponsive to the full range of being, and the kind of life we now lead is a 'fantastic travesty' of the reality of human life.

Macmurray's thought is an attempt to combat the imperialism of instrumental reason and the disqualification of emotional life, art, our sense of value, personal life and relations as non- or ir-rational fields. For him, it was in the realm of 'persons in relation' that rationality is most fully expressed: 'the capacity to love objectively . . . is the core of rationality'.[18]

LAING: THE DE-REALISATION OF REALITY

In 1960 a young Scottish psychiatrist published a critique of conventional psychiatry which helped initiate an important debate about psychiatry's conceptual apparatus, its practices and socio-political functions. On the basis of this and later contributions R D Laing is perhaps today the best-known of modern Scottish thinkers. Yet the relation of Laing's work to his cultural background is poorly appreciated (though Davie has recently drawn attention to Laing's indebtedness to the Hegelian–phenomenological orientation of the Glasgow philosophy department before the establishment there in the 1950s of the analytic school). In fact, the parameters of Laing's thought—the role of science, the phenomenon of personhood—are those of much recent Scottish philosophy, and the work for which he is most famous may be seen as a practical application of a wider intellectual tradition.

Laing's essential criticism of established psychiatric practices is that they involve the 'depersonalisation' of the patient. Underlying such practices is 'the illusion that one somehow increases one's understanding of a person if one can translate a personal understanding of him into the impersonal terms of a sequence or system of it-processes'.[19] This is based in turn on a failure to recognise that persons are *sui generis*, and cannot be fully understood through models imported from the study of the non-human world. Macmurray, who continually emphasised that 'the Self is neither a substance nor an organism, but a person', seems to have been an important influence here; he is at any rate acknowledged in the opening chapter of *The Divided Self*.

The impossibility of understanding persons in terms of impersonal forces (biological, psychological, social, etc.), is also a discernible theme in *Reason and Violence*, Laing's explication (co-written with D G Cooper) of Sartre's *Critique de la Raison Dialectique*. A crucial virtue of Sartre's thought, as it is presented here, is that it 'traces the life of the person to its own ultimate issues, which are to be found only within personal life itself'.

> This ultimate 'original project' or original choice of self provides the intelligible basis of all the acts and experiences of the person . . . It is only through the discovery of a freedom, a choice of self functioning in the face of all determinations, conditioning, fatedness, that we can attain the comprehension of a person in his full reality.[22]

In these early writings Laing is upholding the specificity of personhood against reductive explanations (explaining everything, but nobody) which rest on the illegitimate extension of natural-scientific paradigms. In more recent work, however, Laing displays a much deeper concern about and hostility towards the dominance of the scientific worldview. Here he echoes the sort of ideas found in the work of Paton, Baillie, Macmurray and others in arguing that the triumph of science has led to a catastrophic neglect and disestimation of such areas of our experience as our sense of value and consciousness of ethical obligation.

Science excludes from its domain much of our ordinary reality:

> We know that meaning, value, quality, love and hate, good and evil, beauty and ugliness, exist in some sort of way, which is not a number or quantity, or a thing. We know, therefore, that we, our existing selves, are immeasurable. Job's balances are not to be found in a physicist's laboratory.
>
> The natural scientist explicitly excludes that subjective morass, he leaves all that behind, he sheds all he can of it, before even embarking on his voyage of scientific discovery.[21]

But this scientific perspective is not a primary or pure or neutral apprehension of reality. As Laing writes in *The Divided Self*, it is not neutral 'to see a smile as contractions of the circumoral muscles'. Science in fact transforms primary experience. It involves a 'de-realisation of ordinary reality' through an ablation of ordinary experience, an exclusion of whole areas perceived, except from the scientific perspective, as real. Reality and objectivity are denied to all those phenomena not amenable to quantification and experimental control.

> All sensibility, all values, all quality, all feelings, all motives, all intentions,

spirit, soul, consciousness, subjectivity: almost everything, in fact, which we ordinarily take to be real is de-realised, is stripped of its pretensions to reality.[22]

The victory of this way of seeing signifies 'a profound transformation of our whole being in the world'. Where ethics is divorced from fact and value from knowledge, where it is believed that 'all our subjective values are objectively valueless', we witness the undermining of human responsibility towards being.

CONCLUSION

The historical commitment in Scotland to general theory has been continued in the recent period by a number of thinkers who have addressed issues of wide intellectual interest. Criticism of 'the scientific outlook', and engagement with 'the crisis of the personal', we have been arguing, lend these contributions a certain coherence. Such concerns can be related to a significant feature of the wider cultural background. Most of the thinkers discussed above enjoyed what would now be called a 'strict' religious upbringing. This helps explain their inclination to question the claims of science, their concern with the threat posed to ethics by the spread of scientistic modes of thought, and their refusal to ignore or disesteem the dimensions of experience, knowledge and reality which are beyond the scope of scientific reasoning. In this way the 'presbyterian inheritance' has helped shape recent Scottish intellectual culture, informing a tradition which, as we hope we have shown, is by no means lacking in vitality, urgency or engagement with the central human issues of the age.

NOTES

1 Ludwig Wittgenstein, *Tractatus Logico-Philosophicus* (London, 1922), 6.53.
2 *See* for example the discussion with A J Ayer in Bryan Magee, *Modern British Philosophy* (London, 1971).
3 C A Campbell, *On Selfhood and Godhood* (London, 1957), pp 36–7.
4 T M Knox, 'Two Conceptions of Philosophy,' in *Philosophy*, Vol XXXVI, No. 138, October 1961, pp 289–308.
5 H J Paton, *The Modern Predicament* (London, 1955), p. 377.
6 Ibid. p. 386.
7 H J Paton, *The Categorical Imperative*, 3rd edn, (London, 1958), p 17. Paton belongs to a tradition of Scottish interest in Kant which has made Scotland, in the words of Lewis White Beck, a 'world-centre' of Kant studies in the twentieth century.
8 George Davie, *The Crisis of the Democratic Intellect*, (Edinburgh, 1986), p 50.
9 Eugene Kamenka, 'Anderson on Education and Academic Freedom,' in John Anderson, *Education and Inquiry*, D Z Phillips (ed) (Oxford, 1980), p 20.

10 *See* for example '*The Servile State*', repr. in *Studies in Empirical Philosophy* (Sydney, 1962).
11 Davie, op. cit., p 61.
12 Anderson, *Education and Inquiry*, p 43.
13 John Baillie, *The Sense of the Presence of God*, (London, 1962), pp 33 and 35.
14 Ibid., p 253.
15 John Macquarrie, *Existentialism*, 2nd edn (Harmondsworth, 1973), p 221.
16 John Macquarrie, *In Search of Humanity* (London, 1982), p 69.
17 John Macmurray, *The Self as Agent*, 1969 edn, (London, 1969), pp 30–31.
18 John Macmurray, *Reason and Emotion*, 1962 edn (London, 1962), p 32.
19 R D Laing, *The Divided Self*, 1965 edn (Harmondsworth, 1965), p 22.
20 R D Laing and D G Cooper, *Reason and Violence*, 2nd edn (London, 1971), pp 24–5.
21 R D Laing, 'What is the matter with mind?,' in *The Schumacher Lectures*, Satish Kumar (ed) (London, 1980), pp 6–7.
22 Ibid., pp 10–11.

Chapter 5

Macdiarmid's Early Poetry

CATHERINE KERRIGAN

When Christopher Murray Grieve was demobbed from the RAMC in 1919 he returned to Scotland a man with a mission. He had spent the last years of the war compiling files on Scottish subjects, writing essays and poems and working on his first prose work, the semi-autobiographical *Annals of the Five Senses*. With an almost military precision he began putting his plan to transform the Scottish cultural scene into action and within a few years Quarter-Master-Sergeant Grieve had metamorphosed into Hugh MacDiarmid, the modern Scottish vernacular poet and leader of what he was optimistically to call the 'Scottish Renaissance'.

MacDiarmid's first literary venture was *Northern Numbers*, an anthology of verse modelled on Edward Marsh's *Georgian Poetry*. Published in 1920, the *First Series* contained poems in Scots and English by a representative group of contemporary Scottish writers, among whom were John Buchan, Neil Munro and the Border poet, Will H Ogilvie. While these well-known names gave the volume a decidedly conservative colouring, the inclusion of John Ferguson's sonnets and the war poems of Joseph Lee and Roderick Watson Kerr (dubbed the Scottish Sassoon) introduced a more radical note. MacDiarmid's own contributions were far from exciting. The poems were those written during his army service, and although some have striking images, they are mainly imitations of the Georgian style and consequently aureate, vapid and backward-looking. They are all in English.

Writing to his former schoolmaster and early mentor, George Ogilvie, MacDiarmid predicted that the *Second Series* (1921) would 'technically and otherwise make a great advance'.[1] In this and the subsequent and final volume, the more traditional poets were dropped and there was a greater representation of work in Scots. There was also a greater number of women poets—Violet Jacob, Marion Angus, Muriel Stuart, Christine Orr, Mary Symon—several of them feminists. The end result of the new format was not only poetry of a much greater vitality but evidence of a new self-assertiveness among Scottish poets. The work in Scots in particular shows that these poets had begun using the vernacular less for its nostalgic colouring than as a direct and viable means of expression in the present. The obsession with a simple but idealised past which had been part of the less positive legacy of Burns was being discarded and modern voices dealing with modern dilemmas were beginning to be heard.

Again, all of MacDiarmid's contributions were in English, but some show a marked development from the earlier pieces. Interested in the work of the *vers libristes*, poems like 'Edinburgh' show a new economy of vocabulary which adumbrates the concision and compactness of his early Scots lyrics. By the time the *Third Series* of *Northern Numbers* was issued in 1922, MacDiarmid was already planning *The Scottish Chapbook*, the journal in which he would publish the cultural manifesto designed 'to bring Scottish Literature into closer touch with current European tendencies in technique and ideation'—as well as the earliest of his poems in the vernacular.[2]

In those years MacDiarmid earned his living as a journalist on *The Montrose Review* and was well aware of the part good journalism could play in cultural change. Many of his own tastes and ideas had been formed by contact with A R Orage's innovative and cosmopolitan *The New Age* and he hoped to have the same success with his own literary journalism in Scotland. MacDiarmid was determined to reclaim Scottish traditions. He recognised that the culture had lost confidence in itself and that what passed for tradition was all too often simply a debased and vulgarised form of a once energetic and homogeneous communal life. In a very important series of articles, *Contemporary Scottish Studies*, published in the journal of the Educational Institute of Scotland, MacDiarmid began to challenge—and to educate—the educators. He produced lengthy articles on Scottish writers past and present and brought a new intellectual weight to his critical assessments. Steeped in the ideas of literary modernism, particularly in the techniques of contemporary Russian poets, he was determined to inject into the Scottish tradition the same kind of concerns which writers everywhere were having to confront in the post-war period. MacDiarmid understood that like the old social orders which had crumbled in the face of world events, so too the old forms of literary expression would no longer hold. The task as he saw it was to find a way of preserving what had been authentic in the past in a new, more vital, context.

But MacDiarmid did not confine his work to the pages of periodicals read solely by intellectuals. He publicised and circulated his ideas in a quite amazing number of newspapers throughout Scotland. His articles were designed to instigate debate and his letters to the editor were a regular feature, particularly of the two leading newspapers, the *Scotsman* and the *Glasgow Herald*. In challenging ingrained cultural concepts MacDiarmid went straight for the jugular and attacked the bardolatry which surrounded Burns. Burns, the people's poet, a poet of revolution, had been tamed into respectability by Scotland's bourgeoisie. The national bard had become a cultural commodity. At Burns Suppers, instead of celebrating his very genuine achievements, these literary vandals had turned his poetry of protest into an 'Excuse for faitherin' Genius wi' their thochts'.

MacDiarmid's attacks on the Burns cult were violent and sustained and made him a very visible figure, which is perhaps the reason why when he began to publish his own Scots lyrics he used his now famous pseudonym. After all, if you have been denouncing one of the country's greatest vernacular poets and you begin to write in that medium yourself, it is as well to be sure that you can surpass his achievement. If you have doubts, then it is only prudent to disguise your identity. It should not go without comment that in MacDiarmid's criticisms of Burns there is more than a hint of an anxiety of influence.

It must have been a considerable comfort (and relief) to MacDiarmid when his lyrics were so well-received. In 1922, the year that saw the publication of Joyce's *Ulysses* and Eliot's *The Waste Land*, MacDiarmid found his own distinctive voice. Lyrics like 'The Eemis Stane' combined the familiarity of the spoken word with a spare, lean language and new and disturbing perspectives:

I' the how-dumb-deid o' the cauld hairst nicht   [the dead of harvest night]
The warl' like an eemis stane   [unsteady stone]
Wags i' the lift;   [sky]
An' my eerie memories fa'
Like a yowdendrift.   [blizzard]

Like a yowdendrift so's I couldna read
The words cut oot i' the stane
Had the fug o' fame   [moss]
And history's hazelraw   [lichen]
No' yirdit thaim.   [buried]

(CP.I, 27)

The incantatory rhythms of such lyrical miniatures evoke the sense of a primitive world at once remote and immediate, a place where the human seems the intruder. The earth as a gravestone upon which even the inscription is indecipherable expresses profoundly the lost history and dislocated identity of the post-war world.

Although originally opposed to work in the vernacular, what his Scots lyrics show is a remarkable burgeoning of confidence. Like those other poets who had already begun to adapt Scots to their needs, the early lyrics have an energy and authenticity which had obviously been repressed by the slavish imitation of English models. Freed from this linguistic dominance, Mac-Diarmid discovered a rich and virtually untapped seam of natural imagery and metaphor, and a vocabulary thick with keen, sinewy words.

With his battle-cry of 'Back to Dunbar' MacDiarmid wanted to short-circuit Burns's sentimental tradition. The work of the Scottish mediaevalists was proof of the potential of Scots. Their verse, known by court and commons alike, had not only been highly experimental, it had also been a poetry of the intellect, and it was exactly that combination which MacDiarmid wanted to recreate in modern Scots poetry.

But in the verse of writers like Dunbar there was also a corporeality which had been lost to modern literature. The work of the mediaevalists conveyed an acute sensual awareness of the physical and an interdependence between the human and the material which had long-since vanished or had been deflected and sentimentalised in 'nature' poetry. In wanting to reclaim this concreteness for language, MacDiarmid was beginning to redefine the relationship between the human and the natural in a post-Darwinian world.

From the mediaevalists he learned how to juxtapose opposites and to express the abstract in terms of the everyday. His images are familiar and domestic and often make use of sound effects: 'Time/whuds like a flea'; Eternity is a dripping tap; God is the sound of a 'bobby's feet/Ootby in the lang coffin o' the street'. The setting of his verses is mainly that of a rural landscape, reflecting his own upbringing in Langholm and his childhood perceptions of the Border countryside. But in this landscape God is in retreat from a world now governed by an evolutionary ethos, and is ready to return to the sea, 'Frae which I brocht life yince' ('God Takes a Rest').

The images of the early work are invariably presented as pairs of opposites. The beautiful and the grotesque jostle and modify each other. Like the architecture of mediaeval churches, 'a gargoyle grinning by a saint' expresses a human, earthly reality which exists as challenge and counterpart to a heavenly ideal. This conflict of opposites activates the verse, gives it a sense of motion which is further accentuated in the use MacDiarmid makes of alliteration, repetition, parallelism, the tetrameter beat and the four-line stanza, that is, the traditional techniques of the ballad. The primitive world of the ballad, a world governed less by a caring God than the indifferent forces of Fate, is also transported to MacDiarmid's verse, giving it an eerie, surrealistic quality.

In the vocabulary of Scots MacDiarmid found a psychology at odds with the prevailing social order. He drew parallels between the '*disjecta membra*' of Scots and the life of the unconscious. The vernacular had retained the sense of the physical world in a way that English had not, 'part of its very essense, is its insistent recognition of the body, of the senses'.[3] In this the vernacular was like the work of those 'moderns', Joyce and Dostoevsky, who had explored the irrational and first given expression to the unconscious. The vernacular was as potentially subversive as 'Joyce's tremendous out-pouring', it was 'instinct with those uncanny spiritual and pathological perceptions alike which constitute the uniqueness of Dostoevski's work'.[3]

MacDiarmid argued that it was this element of irrationalism, found characteristically in the clash of the real and the fantastic in Scottish verse, which was 'the essence of the genius of our race' and working on this basis he built a critical theory which argued for the distinctiveness of the Scottish tradition in literature.[4] Thus, MacDiarmid separated the native tradition from its great rival to the south and used his theory to put forward the view that the renewed interest in Scots was no mere nostalgic revival, but a real spiritual awakening which would have social and political consequences even beyond national boundaries.

MacDiarmid felt passionately that the world had to be restructured in terms of human need. As an early socialist he was committed to changing the political order and working for a more just society. His compassion for the suffering of the world's powerless is reflected in these early lyrics, but not in dogmatic terms. In fact, MacDiarmid's images are often traditional and biblical, as in that short lyric, 'The Innumerable Christ'. There, the image of the crucified Christ becomes a symbol of the countless suffering on countless worlds who still 'maun bleed'. The Christian image of redemption is synthesised with Einstein's view of the universe to create a remarkably reverberative poem in which old and persistent human tragedy is presented in the context of the new physics.

Affected by post-war works like Spengler's *Decline of the West*, he saw the coming cultural and political changes as the kind of antithesis first expressed by Nietzsche in *The Birth of Tragedy* as the opposition of Apollo and Dionysos. The Apollonian represented the rule of order under which the West had grown to cultural maturity; the Dionysian, those more primitive cultures which had been repressed under Apollonian law but which, now that the West was in decay, would come into their own natural cycle of development. The first stirrings of the Dionysian were to be found in literature, again in Dostoevsky and Joyce, two writers who were outside of the English tradition, proving that the emerging Dionysian culture would manifest itself as a challenge to and a displacement of the English tradition. To MacDiarmid's mind, Scotland had already begun to follow the same route, the vernacular was the natural language of the Dionysian.

The publication of MacDiarmid's early verse in *Sangschaw* and *Penny Wheep* showed that he was a poet of promise. But it was *A Drunk Man Looks at the Thistle*, his long, lyric poem with a Dionysian hero, which established his reputation in the Scottish tradition—and in modern poetry.

The narrative line of MacDiarmid's long poem is very simple and immediately recognisable as that of Burns's *Tam o' Shanter*. After a night in the pub with his cronies, a drunk man starts to make his way home to his waiting wife. Unlike Tam, it is not a coven of witches which will terrorise the Drunk Man, his demons have been internalised into the more modern torment of spiritual *angst*. The Drunk Man falls into a ditch where he lies looking at a giant thistle by the light of the moon. This inglorious bed among thistles and weeds will be the starting point of a night of metaphysical adventuring in which this Scottish Ulysses will explore the continents of the mind.

The use of a drunken character as a narrator is a stroke of brilliance, for it gives MacDiarmid the freedom to indulge a whole range of techniques and ideas. By nature a drunk is unpredictable. He is at once rowdy, humorous, argumentative, maudlin, bawdy, philosophical, given to bouts of song (and hiccups) and generally enjoys the kind of psychological and social freedom which sobriety inhibits. A drunk has a certain licence to express outrageous opinions, but rarely sticks to the point and wanders happily from subject to subject. What this means in terms of the narrative is that normal linear progression is disrupted in a way which is quite acceptable. MacDiarmid uses the modernist technique of a disrupted, fragmented narrative, but the character is no undergound man expressing a pathological state of mind. He is an easily identifiable aspect of our common selves. One of MacDiarmid's great strengths was his ability to use the often rarefied ideas of modernism and turn them into the stuff of common experience.

The metaphysical question at the heart of the poem is the relationship between body and mind, what the Drunk Man calls 'The dog-hank o' the flesh and soul'. Now that the old relationships between the human and the divine have been severed, how are these two opposites to be reconciled? Perhaps the answer lies in the sexual love he has for his wife:

> Said my body to my mind,
> 'I've been startled whiles to find,
> When Jean has been in bed wi' me,
> A kind o' Christianity!'
>
> (I, 101)

Or perhaps there are any number of possibilities, not the least of them the whisky which has led to all this philosophising in the first place, an answer suggested by his parody of a famous line of Yeats's—he has difficulty distinguishing 'the drinker from the drink'.

This battle between mind and body is encapsulated in the giant thistle which is the controlling symbol of the work. With its roots stubbornly planted in the earth and its outstretched branches and crowning tops reaching heavenwards, the thistle is like a giant tree of life which unites the human and the divine:

> Nerves in stounds o' delight,   [throbs]
> Muscles in pride o' power,
> Bluid as wi' roses dight,
> Life's toppin' pinnacles owre,
> The thistle yet'll unite
> Man and the Infinite!
>
> (I, 98)

But the image of the thistle is not fixed. As the wind moves and clouds pass over the moon, the shape of the thistle changes, presenting the Drunk Man with a whole spectrum of images. At the same time, in his drunken fantasy the other predominant symbols of the work—water, whisky, sea-serpents, moon and woman—constantly collide and merge.

Writing at the tail-end of the Symbolist movement, MacDiarmid introduces a protean technique which, while it uses individual words and objects as a focus of meaning in the symbolist manner, does not fix on any of them in isolation, but instead establishes interrelationships between them all. Avoiding both the pitfalls of a private, impenetrable symbolism and the mechanical application of collective unconscious symbolism, MacDiarmid's fluid technique shows that he had already begun to see language as a system of semiotics.

The contrasting images collide and separate in the kind of clash of opposites which had appeared first in the early lyrics. But this contrariness is indicative of the Drunk Man's character, his need to be 'whaur extremes meet'. His declaration that he will at all costs avoid the 'curst conceit o' bein' richt/Which damns the vast majority o' men', means that he will always take up his position at a point of conflict. Just as his symbols do not fix on any one meaning, so too his explorations of consciousness and the philosophical questions which arise from them are pursued dialectically. MacDiarmid is master of the internal debate, his Drunk Man takes a position, rapidly pushes it to its limits, then turns it on its head to go on and explore the opposite argument. His method of portraying this is to hop backwards-and-forwards from subject to subject while introducing seeming irrelevancies and intrusions in a way that captures the movement of the mind acutely. Like the symbolism of this poem, the Drunk Man's mind is a whirl of perpetual motion.

So too the prosody. The work uses a vast metrical range in a wide variety of forms from the lyric to the bawdy ballad, all of which are orchestrated into the whole through processes of contrast and comparison. Included in the work are a number of adaptations of poems by Russian and European writers which again makes for metrical diversity. Similarly, like Joyce's *Ulysses*, this poem has a parody of the English tradition running through it and this, together with any number of lifted quotations from a considerable range of writers, creates a quite remarkable cacophony of voices.

But the controlling voice is the dramatic monologue of the Drunk Man as he moves through his stages of inebriated fantasy to sobriety. His epic journey has taken him through hell, to a vision of heaven, and then back to earth again. The poem closes (ironically) with a hymn to silence and the Drunk Man ready to return to the routine of domesticity. What he has left behind him in this 'gallimaufry' of a poem is a testament to the poetic possibilities of the vernacular.

MacDiarmid's poem is by any standards an extraordinary achievement. That it was written in Scots makes it even more of a triumph. Writing a major work in the vernacular was an act of faith in the future potential of the nation, it asserted that Scotland had its own thriving cultural life and that the country could take control of its own affairs. MacDiarmid's poetry and journalism had helped create a climate of self-awareness which was to manifest itself as a new drive for political independence. In 1928 the National Party of Scotland was formed. MacDiarmid was one of the founding members.

MacDiarmid's commitment to nationalism brought him into closer contact with another minority language—Gaelic. He was befriended by the leaders of the Gaelic movement in Scotland and began learning more about Celtic culture and traditions. Scottish Gaelic was a dying language, but MacDiarmid had (among others) the Irish example of how a native language could be restored. In his first major poem after *A Drunk Man* he began incorporating snatches of Gaelic language and the heroes of Gaelic mythology into his work.

The central symbol of *To Circumjack Cencrastus* is one which had appeared in the early lyrics and *A Drunk Man* as a sea-serpent, but which now took on a Celtic colouring. From the intertwining figurations of Celtic art he took the symbol of a curling snake whose movements unite the universe. As MacDiarmid explained it 'Cencrastus is the fundamental serpent, the underlying unifying principle of the cosmos. To circumjack is to encircle. *To Circumjack Cencrastus*—to square the circle, to box the compass, etc'.[5]

Whereas the symbol of the rooted, stubbornly material thistle suggested a unity achieved through the conflict of real and ideal, the Cencrastus serpent leaves the material world altogether to dwell in a high reality. And therein lies its difficulty. MacDiarmid's best poetry arises when the two sides of his character enter into debate. MacDiarmid the materialist wants to know— wants to experience—the thistle as quantifiable matter; MacDiarmid the transcendentalist is always yearning for a moral absolute. In *Cencrastus* he leaves the material world behind to move to cosmic wholeness and, predictably, fails.

While the structure and theme of *Cencrastus* are similar to *A Drunk Man*, in so far as the poem proceeds through linked imagery and its subject is still that of a higher spiritual state, this work does not have the spark and confidence of the earlier poem. The controlling concept of an active unity proves as slippery as the snake it is named after. The symbol appears only randomly and consequently the poem lacks cohesion. Cencrastus rapidly becomes Leviathan and that is because MacDiarmid himself is at heart uncomfortable with the idea of a poem intended to move 'on a plane of pure beauty and pure music'.[6] To represent such an ideal is like setting out 'to prove the ways of God to man', litanies quickly become soporific and you break the boredom by pouring your energy into the defiant spirit of the opposition. Heaven (or the cosmic whole) is no place for an iconoclast like MacDiarmid.

MacDiarmid's sense of frustration with his subject comes across in the quality of the poetry itself. Much of it is poor fare. Earlier transcendental poems like 'A Moment in Eternity' are co-opted into *Cencrastus* to reinforce the mysticism of the whole, which in itself suggests a poverty of inspiration. In many ways the themes carried over from *A Drunk Man*—the post-war state of Scotland, the poet's commitment to his culture, the vision of regeneration—had simply written themselves out and what he needed was a new direction. His own recognition of the dilemma comes across as a sense of personal frustration and anger. Of course, the poem was written at a difficult period in his personal life which accounts for some of its bitterness. But even so, in this work it is clear MacDiarmid is trying to fight his way out of a self-created corner.

MacDiarmid's attempt to tear the veil, to penetrate into the inexpressible, is really a struggle with language itself. The best parts of *Cencrastus* are those which express this problem. His recurrent references to drowning in 'bruit matter' point not only to his inability to leave the physical world behind, but to a certain deficiency of language. His language cannot distance, cannot give him sufficient control over, an external physical reality which constantly barrages his senses and disorients his mind. He acknowledges that consciousness is related—not to some transcendental ideal—but to matter itself and that perhaps the poet's task is to give voice to what is as yet unarticulated in the physical world:

> The consciousness that maitter has entrapped
> In minerals, plants and beasts is strugglin' yet
> In men's minds only, seekin' to win free,

As poet's ideas, in the fecht wi' words,
Forced back upon themsel's and made mair clear,
Owercome a'thwarts whiles, miracles at last . . .

(I, 187)

The poet's struggle with language, 'the fecht wi' words', is the real miracle, it is what extends consciousness. Poetry takes the mind to a higher plane of heightened awareness but that plane is not, and cannot, be realised except in terms of the material. A poet like MacDiarmid, to whom sound—the material dimension of language—had been a formative principle of his verse, should have realised that. Yet, characteristically, he resists that idea because he is frustrated by what he sees as the limitations of language:

> The trouble is that words
> Are a' but useless noo
> To span the gulf atween
> The human and 'highbrow' view
> —Victims at ilka point   [every]
> O' optical illusions,
> Brute Nature's limitations,
> And inherited confusions.

(I, 218)

Here, MacDiarmid is unwilling to acknowledge that language, unlike music, is incapable of expressing pure emotion. The medium of poetry is words and sounds which have their life in the commerce of the everyday and the arbitrary events and circumstances which constitute the familiar. The poet has to operate within this system of signs, shaping it, changing it, stamping it with a form of his own making—something he would do in that remarkable poem, 'On a Raised Beach'. Unable at this point in time to apprehend and articulate his insights about language all that MacDiarmid can do is retreat (as in *A Drunk Man*) into silence. When 'Speech squares aye less wi'fact', the only refuge is to lie fallow.

The sense of creative crisis which permeats *Cencrastus* marks the break between MacDiarmid's early and later work. Henceforth his struggle to understand the nature of language in relation to the poetic act became the centre of his activity. Increasingly self-conscious of language, he had to find a way of admitting to his poetry the dynamics—and motives—of literary creativity.

But that sense of the centrality of language to poetry, of poetry being not merely a medium for 'What oft was thought, but ne'er so well expressed', but the way in which meaning comes into being through the activity of language, is the very keystone of MacDiarmid's work. There is an experiential quality in his use of language. It is as though he is unhappy with the idea of words as simply the counters of an external reality. Instead, he finds in words a sensual dimension which is inseparable from the physical world. In his later work he came increasingly to understand that perception is itself shaped by the material effects of language.

Despite MacDiarmid's intense interest in the structures and effects of language, his verse rarely deteriorates into an arid intellectual exercise. There is a joy in his use of language, a *jeu d'esprit*, expressed as a child-like energy which tumbles over itself in the run of words. MacDiarmid's sensitivity to the way in which language works, coupled with his ability to convey the experience with humour and a self-deprecating wit, offers poetry which begins as challenge and ends in delight.

NOTES

1   Letter to George Ogilvie, 8 Feb 1921, National Library of Scotland, Acc. 4540.
2   *The Scottish Chapbook*, August, 1922.
3   *The Scottish Chapbook*, Feb 1923, pp 183, 184, 210.
4   MacDiarmid's theory rests very largely on G Gregory Smith's work, *Scottish Literature: Character and Influence* (1919) in which the idea of antithesis as a principle of Scottish tradition and character was first aired.
5   Letter to George Ogilvie, 9 Dec 1926.
6   Letter to George Ogilvie, 9 Dec 1926.

FURTHER READING LISTS

PRIMARY SOURCES

Grieve, C M (ed), *Northern Numbers. Being Representative Selections from Certain Living Scottish Poets*, First and Second Series (Edinburgh, 1920 and 1921), Third Series (Montrose, 1922)

—— *The Scottish Chapbook* (Montrose, Aug 1922—Nov/Dec 1923)

MacDiarmid, Hugh *Annals of the Five Senses* (Montrose, 1923)

—— *The Complete Poems: 1920–1976*, Michael Grieve and W R Aitken (eds), 2 Vols (London, 1978)

—— *Contemporary Scottish Studies; First Series* (London, 1926)

SECONDARY SOURCES

Bold, A, *MacDiarmid: The Terrible Crystal* (London, 1983)

Boutelle, A E, *Thistle and Rose: A Study of Hugh MacDiarmid's Poetry* (Loanhead, 1980)

Buthlay, K, *Hugh MacDiarmid* (*Christopher Murray Grieve*). Writers and Critics Series (Edinburgh, 1964)

Gish, N, *Hugh MacDiarmid: The Man and his Work* (London, 1984)

Kerrigan, C, *Whaur Extremes Meet: The Poetry of Hugh MacDiarmid, 1920–1934* (Edinburgh, 1983)

Oxenhorn, H, *Elemental Things: The Poetry of Hugh MacDiarmid* (Edinburgh, 1984)

Chapter 6

Neil Gunn's Drama of the Light

FRANCIS R HART

For many years, I read Neil Gunn's novels with the man at my shoulder. The man Neil is gone now; a new discovery of the author Gunn in his work calls for a new kind of reading. This essay is neither biographical nor critical. It attempts a history of Gunn's story-making imagination throughout his fiction. To reconstruct this imaginative history, I must remember that every human act is carried on in certain socio-historical circumstances; literature has its outer logic as an historical fact and a social institution. But the growth of an imagination has its inner logic as well. Each of Gunn's creations was a step out of what had been created before and a preparation for what was to follow. I will try to trace both logics and suggest their interplay.

My method follows modestly the belief that no act of imagination can be whole or complete, that the finest fiction must grow through its own internal contradictions and tensions. If I emphasise less what is achieved than what is attempted, the emphasis is not intended as criticism. If I emphasise later books, this is because they need and deserve more attention. For a time it was obligatory to argue for Gunn's achievement, but thankfully that time is past, and I assume his place among great Scottish novelists. And since there is no space here for summary, I must also assume a familiarity with his books.

Gunn's imaginative life is summed up well by the artist Joe in *The Lost Chart*: 'The darkness creates drama ready-made for man; but man has to create his own drama of the light. It's not so easy' (178).[1] The struggle for light, for affirmation and wholeness, was never easy, and its victories were often imperfect. What is moving and impressive is the history of the imagination's struggle.

It began when the man Neil was thirty. His Caithness youth, his adolescence in Galloway and London, and his care-free bachelor years were over. The Excise Officer, newly married, was sent briefly to strike-torn Wigan, then reassigned in 1922 to the Caithness coast.[2] Severe post-war depression was making the impoverished Highlands more desolate. Home again with idyllic memories, Neil cycled the coast, inspecting poor crofts and their hopeless elderly. The young were off and away; boats were rotting; deer forests were balmoralised; even the sheepfarming that had emptied the glens was dying. Neil was overwhelmed with a vision of bleak greyness, with an aversion (like Ewan's in *Lost Glen*) 'to touch the realities of life in his native place' (272), with a feeling (like Maggie's in *Grey Coast*) that 'there was nothing to come back for' (63).

The short stories he began to write are populated by lonely, tragic old age and fugitive youth. The imagination's search for life moves through 'hidden doors' into secret visionary intensities.[3] It pictures stolid surfaces with a grim realism, and then—in a style sometimes extravagant and derivative, sometimes subtle and powerful—it transforms those surfaces into symbol and legend. How else, in such a world, could the imagination find life and value?

His first novel, *The Grey Coast* (written 1925), faces the same question with the same imaginative strategy. A stylistic cleft between the 'stolidly obvious' and the 'hidden ways of dream and thought' is likened to the flaw in the great sea-cliffs. The imagination tries to bridge the cleft between quotidian matter-of-fact and secret intensity: 'A certain almost deliberate numbness . . . succeeded to her momentary visioning' (83). Surface rituals of numb dialogue and minimal gesture cover life and death struggles of spirit. On this grey coast, the only compensatory powers are 'visioning' and the elaborate language that half-conceals it.

The author is ambivalent about this visioning. The schoolmaster's visioning is treated with unsettled irony. The schoolmaster is too eager to transform young Ivor's bleak reality into tragic myth: 'But no, that was overdoing it! And for the same reason he could not let it go at that' (41). Gunn's imagination is born in this conflict. He will 'vision' the local fact into imaginative value, but he will hold true to that grey fact. He will and will not be the novelist of a place and its people. Realist and mythmaker are in tension. The figure of his imagination whom Neil later called Mr Balance is uneasy on his tight-rope.

The imagination's risks are subtly identified as we move from the kindly schoolmaster to the evil farmer Tullach. In imagination, the schoolmaster wants to 'fix' Ivor, to possess his secret life. In gross flesh, Tullach wants to possess Maggie and unearth the hidden treasure of her sly old uncle Jeems. The novel's suspenseful plotting is the battle of wits between Jeems and Tullach; the secret, hopeless lovers look on, pawns in the game, The game portends many later versions—Old Hector with the Green Isle managers, Sandy with the blood-hunting policeman. The real power struggle is of the imagination. The aim is always to hide the secret treasure, repossess the lost value. The strategy is always an act of secret defiance, a poaching of the spirit, darkness against darkness to make a drama of light. In a 'great joke', Jeems's revived imagination makes a triumphant end to this story, and Tullach is utterly deflated.

The plotting is absorbing, but Neil was working under Modernist influences, and textures of mood and consciousness mattered more than story. In *The Lost Glen* (written 1926), such influences generated mixed experiments in stream of consciousness, naturalism, surrealism, and tragic myth. The man Neil was now staking his claim to pioneering pre-eminence as novelist of the Renaissance, trying to meet high, unclear expectations. The pressures were strong, and everything about *Lost Glen* shows the strain. It moves on four levels: a densely textured material level; a level of turbulent mood; an explicatory thematic level; a level of myth. This, together with the narrative immersion in several troubled consciousnesses, suggests an imagination trapped claustrophobically in its own creation. But its ambitious struggle is fascinating.

The focus is fitting. The cultured gillie Ewan, betrayed and self-destructive, epitomised what was then Gunn's image of the modern Highlands, exploited by supercilious aliens as a sporting preserve. The problem in tone and perspective is where to distinguish between Ewan and his author.

> Ewan was drunk enough to believe that there was a profound reality in this antithesis, that the Colonel and himself were chance figures in a drama that affected the very earth under his feet. Being chance figures, they did not matter; were indeed figures of melodrama. But none the less did the earth await the outcome of their secret strife, as if they stood for an ultimate conquest or defeat [109–10].

The problem in mode is how to save tragedy from melodrama. While a conciliating, life-giving female consciousness (Claire) looks on, two tragic male stories meet in a single bloodhunt. The pattern runs through the history of Gunn's imagination. But here, the absurd and revolting colonel cannot be a fitting antagonist. The gillie's several roles can't quite coalesce into a single character; his inner conflicts overwhelm the outer struggle. The final catastrophe is accidental. As Ewan feels, 'the burden of [the] story had become too great to carry.' (58).

But with so much invested, it is no wonder Neil was angered by the many publishers' rejections and the hostile critical response. Even Nationalist colleagues wrote him off. A sounder response came from a Faber partner who was an expatriate American Southerner; Morley was astute enough to see this 'damnably fascinating and disturbing book' as Neil's *Hamlet*, wherein 'secret perturbations' worked themselves out.[4] Of more relevance to us is this: blasting pessimism half-hidden by self-mockery was not a state in which Gunn's imagination could live. Creation and delight must move together.

Fittingly, the periodical novel that followed, *The Poaching at Grianan* (written 1928–9), moves toward a new mood with the same materials; the poachers are jovial; the greyness seems friendlier; pathetic violence mixes with comic adventure. But, for whatever reason, Neil uncharacteristically gave up on this novel.[5] His imagination had not found its way, and his new public role in politics offered welcome distraction.

1930–1933: TRIUMPHS OF ARTIFICE

Art grows through the power of artifice, and artifice served as a way beyond tragic realism. The sudden Nationalist upsurge of these years called for 'shouting back' at despair, and Neil wrote three shouting novels, spokesman novels that arise from the unique time when he felt with uneasy exhilaration a part of a communal movement. The public situation cried out for a 'Morning Tide', and a Scottish press would publish it. The acclaim greeting *Morning Tide* (written 1930) says much about public mood. A later reader may think that the artifice cannot quite overcome the dark images. 'All great joy', says the book, 'is a little incredible' (221), and Hugh's joys seem so precarious that he runs from them. The book is of greater imaginative interest than its lovely surface suggests.

Hugh is less a boy character than a figure of imagination. This imagination is revealingly figured in the opening. A boy, alone on a dark beach, is digging for bait, for limpets hidden in tangle. He opens and chews them until flavour fills his mouth, flavour out of dark and windswept desolation. The book has many such images: tiny humans in a dark landscape, tiny human circle at night, tiny returning boats against the storm, a surreal sensory intimacy against vast distances. Sheer style defies the darkness. Here is the style in epitome: 'An occult ecstasy rimmed the dark hollow of his fear with white fire'; 'a new mood . . . thrust out here and there crushed tongues of delight, a secret exultation spurting out of fear' (172). The imagination lacks confidence as yet to break through such language.

Meanwhile, boy and imagination are secretive and withdrawn. 'The brave, fine minds are secretive and strong and kind' (115). The boy's mind 'might have been the anemone on the rock the way it drew in' (20). The boy is a watcher, and the author watches him from a delicate distance. 'Leave the boy alone,' cries the father, for mother and sisters are invasive in kindness. Most threatening because most kind is the older sister. Kirsty is the opposing voice in Gunn's imagination, the voice of *Lost Glen*. She has the legend-maker's tragic vision: she is sure the brother must drown, the mother must die—they do not; she is helpless in a fatal passion. Her images are what Hugh must resist. He 'took a little run to himself to stave off the threatening image' (204). 'No one would guess from a little distance the natural dodgings he resorted to in order to command the world around him' (217). The dodgings of imagination are little rituals of defiance.

Ritualistic, too, is the book's symmetrical design. Croft-life rhythms are ritualised; characters are ritualised into archetypal pairings. The rhythm of the three boats' return expands into the three-part rhythm of the book, each part with its move through fearful darkness to triumphant but fugitive rebirth in the 'red ecstasy of the dawn' (111). The design is a repeated triumph of imaginative artifice.

Sun Circle (written 1932) goes further. 'Imagination has its own rape,' it tells us (386), and the novel is a rape of the imagination; protagonist and reader alike are almost lost in ritualistic frenzy. Neil risked more here than in any other book, more imaginative license, more unbridled participation. No wonder he chose later to forget the book, for it risked his new career. Bewildered readers did not notice how close an imaginative sequel it was to *Morning Tide*.

Its declaration of peace and reconciliation belongs to a moment in Neil's Nationalist activism, but its assertion of anarchic freedom is a radically private act. The imagination takes flight from realism into a legendary past of philosophical combat and erotic violence. Vision and history are one. Plot moves by arbitrary creative fancy. Like the Druid Master, the author is an unbridled impersonative power, and yet a hidden onlooker. Appropriately, he focuses on the vocation of the artist, Aniel, whose very name is suggestive.

Aniel represents an extraordinary effort to transform the tragic figure of *Lost Glen* into the triumphant figure of *Morning Tide*. He is a Celtic Hamlet, flawed with 'weakness of will', too pacific and anarchic to lead, divided in creed and loyalty—an intriguing glimpse into Neil's consciousness in 1932. Aniel finds power only in imagination, in the 'elation' of the solitary. He learns to draw a sun circle around himself, a ritual dodge to keep the demons at bay. He will be a survivor and a maker in a world burned and desolated. But first he must choose his own story, and his choice is between a brilliance that is really darkness (Haakon and Nessa) and a darkness that is really light (himself and Breeta). He is drawn to both. In Aniel is fought out the same imaginative conflict we have seen between Kirstie and Hugh. And when he chooses the drama of the light, Gunn's imagination is choosing an attitude with which to face his next, his darkest, subject.

The history of the Sutherland Clearances held Gunn's imagination throughout life. A strongly possessive feeling for it was tied to a 'revulsion of shame and bitterness.'[6] *Butcher's Broom* (written 1933), Neil said later, was not something he wanted to, but something he had to write. The ambivalence made for a powerful but disturbing book. Gifford rightly observes that he designed it so as to distance a deep bitterness,[7] but the compensatory charity is more rhetorical than real. The book is his most rhetorical in design and voice.

In *Butcher's Broom*, the imagination works under heavy constraints. It was written at the peak of Neil's political leadership. Opposing and opposed by divisive extremisms, he worked as a practical policy-maker for realism and reconciliation. Yet, in the novel he was reopening the most divisive of themes, old wounds, old divisions. The constructive political realist perforce conflicts with the author who feels (in Davie's words) that 'There was shame in it however he looked at it' (316). The enemy was everywhere; 'there was no enemy' (370). Only much later in *The Lost Chart* will we find again such a sense of multiple betrayal.

The constraints were aesthetic as well. Burdensome obligation to an epic subject left little space for imaginative play. Historic authority must be scrupulously observed. So weighty a subject demanded epic scale, sweeping rhythms, grandiloquent voices. Communal grouping must prevail over individual character, and does so to the midpoint, after which the narrative focuses on more individual figures. (By contrast, the comparable *Silver Darlings* will focus on individuals from the start.) Characters are personae in a grand rhetorical drama. Narrative voices have the style of epic oration. The most brilliant of these is Tomas the Drover's, and it is revealing that, when Neil reread the novel years later, he reported getting a 'big kick' out of Tomas's great final curse. But the author in the book cannot allow himself so much ironic indulgence. Indeed, Neil discovered the book's title with its caustic irony as a shocking afterthought. The working title, *Dark Mairi*, suggests a very different design.

The awesome conception of Mairi is key to the imaginative problem. The book's rhythms turn on her moving presence, but she is a choral figure. The epic conception cannot be contained in the implications of Mairi; it opposes them. The novel was to be about women, the 'little black knots' hidden from history, but the male pride of Highland tragedy demands its place. The book seeks to embody what Mairi stood for, but a celebration of what endures mixes strangely with the curse of a shameful end. The end is tellingly dual. Tomas's curse is followed quickly by Mairi's death, and curse and death declare what is ended. But the ritual return of Mairi's body to the shore completes a circle where new life is growing. The imagination is ambivalent about what continuity there can be, cannot settle on an ending, cannot finish the final curse. The irresolution and constraint of the imagination give the book its power. Coherence would have been the final betrayal.

1936–1943 WAR-TIME WITHDRAWAL AND RETROSPECT

When the long lapse between *Butcher's Broom* and *Highland River* (written 1936) ended, Gunn's imagination had changed. As Kenn moves away from community, so does his author; Neil the man was preparing for the most decisive break of his life. He felt in 'danger of losing my identity',[8] and his new authorial identity is radically personal, 'whole and secret and hostile' (31). Thrashings had freed Kenn of obligations to school and master; thrashings in Nationalist politics had freed Neil to explore a newly anarchic attitude. The source of his Highland River is where *individuality* is born, and Kenn's hunt is for a 'solitary, lonely integrity' that is deliberately 'elusive' (238). The boyish impulse of flight becomes the argument of a philosophical adult. Kenn's argument with Radzyn is Neil's argument with his world.

A new style appears. The exuberant voice deriding history's 'greats' is far from the modulated rhetoric of *Butcher's Broom*. Voice and mood are playful. The symbolic mood of poaching has shifted from the fearful intensity of *Morning Tide* to a game-like exhilaration. The prefatory letter to brother John describes the book as a 'poaching expedition' and introduces the ployful dodger of later Gunn. It warns of 'odd behavior' and 'covering tracks'. The narrative voice—there is nothing like it elsewhere in Gunn—is third-person Kenn-and-not-Kenn, a meditative interiority spoken by an Other. I can be myself in my creation, says the book, but you won't catch *me* at it! The *TLS* reviewer caught the paradox well: 'intense immediacy and a sort of enclosed detachment.'

These ploys of perspective join with a new focus on 'moments' of intensely personal experience.[9] The book's subject is the process of recreating these moments. Its form is an intricate 'systolic-diastolic' rhythm that plays against the linear river. The artist-side of Kenn collapses personal memory into mythic paradigm; the scientist-Kenn holds scrupulously to real river and experience. The novel must have been, as Neil predicted, 'appallingly difficult' to compose. Nationalist spokesman no longer, he was making a new claim as an artist with 'something to say', with a will to engage the modern world, with a subtle form of his own. The book was and was not what his anxious publishers (now in London) sought: a river pastoral; a return to *Morning Tide*.

Neil had started his poaching game with his publishers, and it worked so well, won such recognition from the literary gamekeepers, that he seemed 'on the way'. But the way would not prove direct. *Highland River's* argumentative 'saying', elusive 'moments', and narrative slightness posed tough challenges to imaginative integration.

Neil's big move of 1937 is biography, but the adventure and the move opened up new imaginative resources and invited an expansion of world. First came a false start when the new free-lance could least afford it, a reworking of old motifs (gillie and sadist from *Lost Glen*), a confusion of media, as with *The Poaching at Grianan*. He tried a play, 'Second Sight' (written 1938). A friendly critique from Bridie saved him another debacle. Anxious not to waste the work, he turned it to a novel. And between weak play and weak novel, he struck out in another direction.

In *Wild Geese Overhead* (written 1938), the argument of *Highland River* intensifies. The book dramatises a defensive moment in Neil's life. The hero Will is a writer defending his new vision, a critic against critics, an escapist battling city sceptics, a painfully private lover, and a disillusioned socialist defending his apostasy. Will's real struggles are internal—his bouts of shame, his dark nights of the soul—and when, at the end, he almost dies, understandably no one knows the cause. Neil's biography may suggest 'causes'. Margaret MacEwen's London situation may have stirred up the old imaginative linkage of political and sexual danger. Neil's visit to Glasgow slums and his sense of imminent war compounded doubts about retreating to Brae Farm. Anxieties of new free-lance life aggravated uncertainties about form. He must reach for a wider, more 'urbane' readership. There was no going back.

For the first time, he made his mature imaginative ploy. He would test a personal image of wholeness and delight against the world's dark negations and try for a drama of the light. Like Will, he would make himself look at painful things (no more of Hugh's dodges) in a new depth (the stereopticon figure) and see if his new distance could be imaginatively validated.

We move rhythmically in Will's consciousness between city and country. The more he belongs to country life, the more he is drawn into the city's threats and sorrows. The more detached, the more he sees. Within this dialectic of vision, Gunn weaves a dialectic of concept: negative and positive evil, negative and positive escapism, theory and praxis, personality and impersonality. Joe and Felicity (one in politics, one in love) are revolutionaries who have lost touch with the personal. But Will's new personal awareness requires impersonality; Jenny will accept his garden help only if 'impersonal', since she too is running from 'personal entanglements'. *Wild Geese* is the most intellectually complex novel Neil ever wrote. Some critics appreciated its elusive sophistication, but had understandable difficulty finding an integration of concept, private ecstasy, and story. The book is an extraordinary experiment, like *Highland River*, but Gunn had not yet created his narrative form.

Meanwhile, the lapse of the novel *Second Sight* gave greater urgency to what would follow, and what followed triumphantly proved Will's argument.

The new distance permitted a new and in-depth address to the past. *The Silver Darlings* (written 1939–40) is the pivotal work in Gunn's imaginative life. Hereafter, Neil would be institutionalised as the writer of *Silver Darlings*. The triumph was also a trap, for the book could be written only once.

It closes his earlier fiction and opens what will come, and its marvellous design traces a tension between past and future. The archetypal parents of *Morning Tide* and *Highland River* become imaginatively real. The dedication to his father's memory belies how complex that figure becomes. Finn's real father is lost at the start—and how suggestive is the long suspense of his 'return'! His adoptive father is a heroic but inadequate model. Finn's relationship to his mother is a similar dynamic of intimacy and distance, reunion and separation. Both must work out their own new lives. These interpersonal relations are integrated cautiously with communal history. The integration can be seen in Chapter Six, the novel in miniature: the counterpointing of Kirstie and Hendry, of Old and New, land and sea, stasis and motion, tradition and experience, danger and delight, communal and individual. Here is Gunn's Mr Balance in total command, perhaps for the last time, for 'balance' will not hereafter serve Gunn's aesthetic or his world view. The novel is more personal than *Butcher's Broom* and more impersonal than *Highland River* and *Wild Geese*. In design, it perfects the systolic-diastolic *River* rhythm, the ever-widening outward circle, the returns to circle of home and self. In imaginative topography, it moves away from earlier locales even as it recovers them.

Final closure (Chapters 19–26) comes slowly. Finn's personal problems are mysteriously recalcitrant and have little to do with 'epic'.[10] Resolution must be personal, but it can come only through the interweaving of communal ritual, song and story, with private retreats to the House of Peace, and finally (for Finn as for Gunn) in the role of storyteller. At last Finn is able to identify with his lost father. But then he knows he must be his own father, must take the lost past into himself and master his own story. No book better enacts the psychoanalytic achievement: 'The problem of recognising oneself is the problem of recovering the ability to recount one's own history.'[11] The achievement brought imaginative liberation.

And liberation invited an author's holiday. Neil's most delightful, most impersonal book followed, and with it he established a holiday rhythm for writing. He would work at the obligatory, then follow a personal impulse. A holiday was a poaching foray outside of authority—including the authority of literary institutions. With *Young Art and Old Hector* (written 1941), the wise and whimsical old ally of youth replaces the solemn figure of the mother; and part of Hector's role is to guide Art beyond authority. In Art, the solitary, rapturous youths of earlier books are replaced by the close and amused perceptions of a real uncle Neil. Distance and intimacy grow together. The book belongs to the worst war years (along with Highland Pack essays) as a restorative pastoral, a pastoral comprising the cycles and playful paradoxes of folk wisdom. It marks a liberation from social and aesthetic 'importance', from the ambitious architectonics of previous novels. Hector and Gunn prize smallness, and the book moves in brief episodes with a gnomic economy of style, a simplicity Gunn will retain for some complex novels to come. Most lasting in impact, the book focuses on story and story-telling (the fruit of Finn's vocation). Proverbs led him to visualise these stories, Neil reported, and the stories include stories, treat the role of story in human culture.

The holiday would even produce Neil's only sequel, something he normally resisted, for his imagination resisted the linear. It worked by circlings back. Only the circular wisdom of a Hector knows how to go back and find what has been lost—a child, a key, crock, chart, well. Only a Second Childhood knows how to complete the circle, for the circle must be secret and devious to elude repressive authority and linear logic. Henceforth, the desire for wholeness would be the same for Gunn's aesthetics as for his politics. His imagination, delightedly at home with Hector and Art, seized on the figure of the wise serpent with his tail in his mouth, the arabesque of Celtic design.

But first, the holiday temporarily over, he turned from Hector to the similar figure of old Tom, the serene philosopher on his height. In Tom, the imagination would (in Freud's terms) 'return, repeat, work through'[12] abiding images against renewed challenges. *The Serpent* (written 1941) is a philosophical *bildungsroman* and a secretive love story. Biographers may find its integration on an unrevealed personal level. Historians may find another occasion. Neil's need for an anti-collectivist manifesto grew not only from reports of Soviet purges, but from closer to home. Johnston's wartime Scottish ministry with its planning commissions began as the book was being composed, and Neil's responses (as supporter and participant) were divided. A divided imagination cannot integrate its art, but the book offers an intriguing study of what it tried to do. It tried to integrate a statement of philosophical individualism, a timeless tragic story of the betrayed woman, a new preoccupation with patriarchal despotism, and the animistic tranquillity of Brae. The dark images—erotic secrecy, tragic betrayal, spiritual tyranny—are circled by the reminiscent old man's hard-won light. Love story and philosophical memoir are held in balance, but balance is not integration, and the novel remains a statement of wholeness, an image of distance. The effect is of discontinuity. Tom has already outlived the end of his story, and Gunn's imagination has outgrown its retrospective materials.

1943–1948 POSTWAR DIALOGUE AND TRAUMA

Neil was now well established in reputation, a man of public affairs often in Glasgow and Edinburgh, enjoying literary friendships among his own generation—Muir, Mitchison, Bridie. But his status brought younger writers and artists to his door, and as the war moved to an end, the future was reborn. He was far from the serene old age of Hector and Tom, and the future troubled him. Planning for the post-war Highlands was underway. Reports of war atrocities and concentration camps were coming home even to remote Strathpeffer. Out of such concerns grew the five novels of these years, and they came fast. They include two or three of his finest, and yet, at the end of this time his publishers were troubled, sales were dropping, and critics had begun to write him off. What happened?

The imaginative impulse of *The Serpent* had been to test a vision of wholeness and light against the darkest forces his imagination could conceive. He now saw those forces as despotic collective power and disintegrative psychological analysis joined in an image of the concentration camp as a 'research center'. He saw the relationship of Hector and Art as the opposing image. Could such an image survive the psychopolitical menace?

Much has been written about the biographical genesis and ideology of *The Green Isle of the Great Deep* (written 1943). The mystery of a seminal aesthetic decision is not so easily plumbed. The bond of Art and Hector had persisted in Gunn's imagination as a power of comic exhilaration, and it now moved him logically into satiric fable. Utopian fable is satire, and the mode demands the mood: fun, the 'sly wink' of Hector, the ingenious turns on paradisal myth. Fun is the norm, moral and aesthetic, and a whimsically simple style embodies it. The Utopian Managers are ultimately made fools of, for the opposite of wisdom is folly, and satire cures by ridicule. True laughter—not the 'bright and shallow' laughter of the Islers, not Robert's bitter laughter— is the best defiance. The book is a dialectic of laughters, and the reader who loses touch with the fun suffers from poor Hector's temporary weakness. True Highlander, he gives in to solemnity and sadness. Art never does. What finally gives Hector the heart to face God is Art's merriment.

In the novel, the two are separated, and their separation is a key to a brilliant plot. What is to be tested by the Managers—'understood', dis-integrated—is their relationship. This Strange Place has seen nothing like these visitors. How will it 'interpret' them? What might they do to it if they were reunited? They are tested in separation, and the plotting perfectly fits the problem. Separation exposes Hector to the old threat of the Clearances: betrayal. Fugitive Art becomes a test of loyalty: who will hide him? The suspense is whether and how they will be reintegrated. Will Hector find some solitary core of resistance? Will Art remain fugitive long enough to complete his legend? Can wisdom and humour be reunited? The triumph of the dual climax—Art awakens divine power but Hector must face it—is the triumph of story, and hereafter story remains at the centre of Gunn's imagination.

The Green Isle was a fable for the modern world. In *The Key of the Chest* (written 1944), Gunn transformed it into complex novel. He needed a 'popular' genre to exploit, and since he was repeatedly to be charged with mysticism, it might as well be the mystery story. The book's socio-political occasion was a growing concern with the question, 'What does brotherhood really mean?' The novel discovers that true brotherhood is not what it appears, and that true community is a subtle interplay of distance and inter-subjectivity, intimacy and privacy.

Privacy is hard to find, here where everyone wants 'the whole picture', where every component of plot and community 'sees' every other, and eyes are everywhere. The novel is a complex plotting of human space, and the space is virtually created by seeing. Every act of seeing is an interpretation, and the narrative orchestrates many choral views, from ceilidh house to kirk, from shop and sheepclub to intellectual lodge. The uneasy marginal figure who must, like the authorial imagination, integrate all these into a true communal attitude is the doctor.

'Slightly' Highland, unmarried and unchurchly, distanced but sympathetic, the doctor is Gunn's first true imaginative surrogate, the onlooker with the burden of making whole the community and the aesthetic design. In ingenious self-parody, Gunn sets him in dialogue with a writer-philosopher named Gwynn, a kind of counter-preacher who mouths endless arabesques of Gunn's ideas. In the affable but uneasy talk of speculative Gwynn and personal doctor, the key of the story-chest is worked out. Everyone is convinced that he has the 'key', but it is finally the doctor who must assume responsibility for Charlie's story. The narrative integration of later novels is born in this act. The issue henceforth, to its moving climax in *Bloodhunt*, is how to make stories end. The doctor's making must fall short. While much communal healing is achieved, he must stand sadly by as the 'bright ones' Charlie and Flora depart.

Gunn's old 'Charlie' story of the failed 'man who came back' undergoes a brighter transformation in the very different novel to follow. *The Drinking Well* (written 1945) is the huge 'sport' in Gunn's imaginative history. Like *Key of the Chest*, it projects post-war Highland economic development and recalls Nationalist discourse of the 1930s. In idea and programme, it has special documentary interest. But it is Neil's *only* attempt at regional historical fiction, and its lapses reveal how alien this genre was to his imagination. It is, in its own phrase, largely 'historic picture' (321).

The 'picture' dimension of *Drinking Well* reminds us that Neil had been busy scripting the film of *Silver Darlings*. The camera symbolism of *Key* shows this influence. But now he attempted a large novel suited for cinema, and sure enough, a film company did take up an option and 'pay like gentlemen.' Some sections read like scenario; some are genre vignettes of 'local colour', a realism he normally despised. The memorable passages are stirring filmic episodes—the fiddler in the street, Iain's return with the ewes, the father's rescue. Characters are camera-actors and angles; inner qualities foreshorten into stage directions. Theatre had never been Neil's medium.

The 'historic' dimension reminds us that Neil had always been sceptical of history. The novel's historic particularity has little imaginative relevance to its timeless issues of spirit, land, and well. Characters belong to a historic typology; what finally matters about the hero is that he is a 'certain type' of young man. The plot depends on accidents: saving the factor, the office fight, the auto accident. The story problems to be solved are accidents, and the solutions are accidental, reflecting a fundamental disbelief in the logics of history.

A very different approach to history would be taken in the two novels that followed, as if in reaction. Cinematic landscapes and economic discussion give way to personal trauma and reintegration. Two personal styles emerge, equally vivid and direct, remarkably integrated: intimate natural sensitivity and mythic personification. A disintegrated post-war world casts its shadow on the most personal local awareness. Neil had given Faber two successes, and now, in these books, he felt free to do something personal.

In *The Shadow* (written 1946), a private soul writes to a beloved friend (the enemy?) in loving desire to save him as well as herself. The authorial imagination enters into this struggle for light more unequivocally than ever before. It enters through two women who must watch in anguish the blood-hunt of male violence, watch the 'extraordinary power and vitality [of] the destructive mind' (48), and overcome what old Hector fought against: 'the mere quiescence of good . . . to evil' (48). The males move (as Neil wrote to Pick) 'across the female field of vision' as plot.[13] The women carry the imaginative burden of the book's problems and design: to heal the division, to make the story whole. Narrative method is a perfect image of their dual effort. First, Gunn commits his voice and imagination wholly to the young woman. Her struggle demands great spiritual risks, and her love lets her take them. Nan's relapse transfers both narrative centre and imaginative struggle to Aunt Phemie, and this transferral is Gunn's most profound psychoanalytic creation, Aunt Phemie his most revealing imaginative surrogate. Like him, she is 'a soul in an experiment' (127).

With Nan's recovery, the women come together 'like two women sitting at the bottom of the well of the world' (222). Nan chooses her new rhythm of retreat and commitment, and Phemie (like the doctor of *The Key*, like *Bloodhunt*'s Sandy) makes her careful decision about the end of the story. Together, they revisit as exorcists the story's dark images and make their own sun circle. The book's intricate design is like the old birch: 'Oddly enough, he seemed to have no symmetry; an ungainly growth, with branches pulled out like an idiot-giant's arms. But then, as I looked, the marvellous balance, the subtle self-compensating arrangements, were really very wonderful' (58). Neil knew well that such forms might well puzzle publisher and reader alike, but he had his pattern at last: 'like the Celtic pattern that interlaced and went on, exquisite in its subtle line' (*Drinking Well*, 419). In a newly disintegrated world, no easier design would do: 'Man has become more involved, his harmonies have become more involved and his disharmonies' (*Other Landscape*, 110).

Fittingly, Edwin Muir wrote about the next novel, 'this last theme of yours fits your intricate and interweaving Celtic imagination wonderfully . . . so many things brought together by such winding and yet natural ways.'[14] The occasion is still post-war trauma, and yet, *The Silver Bough* (written later 1948) is Gunn's Masque of Innocence. The story of Martin's South Pacific bloodhunt, the most horrible Gunn ever used, is background to his funniest comedy. Nowhere else did he tackle so challenging an integration. The drama of darkness is Martin's world vision of 'dead bones and bloody acts' (169), and the task is to make a different end to the human story. The counter-story is a child's fairytale and talismanic toy, the mood a wise-foolish humour. Farcical pratfalls, absurd scrapes, 'cackles of laughter' are so pervasive that casual readers call the book 'light'. Their reaction is fostered by a haiku-like style of 'antique frolic': 'A catspaw of mirth invaded his face. His eyes chimed'

(84). The humour is true grotesque, and the farcical wonder of skulls and skeletons warrants a title Linklater would use the following year: *A Spell for Old Bones*. At times the laughter is tragic; at times pathetic: 'The heart so moved in her that the first spout of water from the kettle missed the teapot' (126). The book works out a tension between 'final irony' and life-giving frolic, and it does this through the imaginative alliance of irony and innocence.

Two fables, the crock of gold and the silver bough, interweave in playful paradox. The crock survives in being re-lost; the bough serves its archaic function by being recreated. The archaic bones, their tragic story long over, must again be 'lost' in the cairn, while the story of Anna and Sheena is reborn. Foolish Andie and Martin, primitive idiot and savage modern man, are the same and not the same. Paradox leads to insight and liberation. The reader who pursues these arabesques is part of making the end.

In two 1948 novels, then, a post-war moment and a Celtic design occasioned Neil's most affirmative art. But the moment ended with a vengeance, and ironic innocence could not survive the onset of Cold War.

1949–1954 COLD WAR RETREATS AND PROPHECIES

An imagination disintegrated by nightmares of atomic holocaust, fifth columns, Police States longs for peace. Neil was faced by the loss of Brae Farm, financial worries, growing conflict with Faber, a feeling of having 'written enough', a desperate need to write fast. *The Lost Chart* (written 1948) is about reckless haste, moral confusion, imaginative hysteria.[15] The protagonist—ordinary businessman, unwilling police spy—shares the author's obsession with a place to hide, to protect the innocents, when 'civilisation is atom-bombed' (8) and only 'small pockets of humanity' remain (7). But the island of refuge is already betrayed; 'betrayal . . . pervaded all' (299). We can hear Davie's voice echoing from *Butcher's Broom*: 'There was shame in it however he looked at it.' Gunn's imagination could never win out against the shame of betrayal.

Dermot the protector uses the very innocents he would save, taking them on his reckless Buchan adventure in a Le Carré world. Gunn uses spy-thriller conventions alien to his imagination. He uses his World War II radio-play for quasi-legendary background, but this tale of heroic sacrifice can find no valid recurrence, and it produces only a hopeless, brief cry: 'Say it once to your own heart, unashamed, before you grow strong again and ordinary and deny it' (307). Plot moves by activism and coincidence; statement is remote from experience; darkness is everywhere, and 'drama of the light' (the phrase comes from this novel!) is only talk and Gaelic song. But the imaginative struggle, fought out in Dermot's consciousness, is as brave as it is doomed. He knows he is compromised, and his mind falls 'away exhausted' from its 'justification' (299). Author and protagonist are 'running for dear life', not knowing where to go. Would it matter much if nuclear war came, since values were already doomed? Why go on writing?

And yet, Gunn's imagination fought its way home again—albeit a home made in a wilderness camp, remade in the most private of places, an enduring marriage. *The Well at the World's End* (written 1950) returns to the comic-ironic mode of *Silver Bough*, the titular symbol of *Drinking Well*, the source-quest pattern of *Highland River*, the holiday spirit of *Young Art and Old Hector*. We join author and hero in a picaresque game on the boundaries of illusion. Like Dermot of *Lost Chart*, Munro does not know where he is going, but not-knowing is necessary. The true adventurer must lose himself and take what happens by chance. Being lost leads to enchantment and finds the circle back. The arabesques are not elaborative (as in *Highland River*) but essential: 'The eye could even stand away and see that all the arabesques came back on one another like more or less friendly serpents' (138).

The serpents *are* friendly. Quixotic humour is a distancing circle, and the book is explicitly Gunn's *Quixote*. The rapturous quest of *Highland River* is replaced by hilarity: contrast the opening salmon episodes. Munro is pursued by farcical demons—'a wet leg . . . stuck in his trousers', demonic holes in his socks, a threatening drop on an old woman's nose. The hilarity borders on wonder. The love-philtre episode mingles magic and farce. The Spanish adventure is the book in epitome: a sunlit holiday, near-death, mock-heroic rescue, a vision of the timeless, a sunburnt shoulder treated with toothpaste.

But the friends *are* serpents. The fable of the well portends a tragic end. Peril and terror are real. The circle can close only through violence and injury, nights in hell, and rebirth suckling at a ewe's teat in the most grotesque and rich episode Gunn ever imagined. The final rescue by the wife is an ultimate act of ironic self-abasement, and the reader can ponder long the integrity of this dual close, not forgetting the extraordinary biographical revelation of a husband saved by a ewe whose lamb he could not save.[16]

London was bewildered by the typescript, and Faber urged him to put it aside. He was almost past caring. The novel feels like a final inventory and belongs with *The White Hour* (stories, 1950) and *Highland Pack* (essays, 1949) as a summing up. For some of us, *The Well at the World's End* is one of his most memorable books. But the self-parodic control it achieved permitted him to go on and write his most perfectly integrated novel. The epigraph to *The Well* might be, 'In my beginning is my end', and for one wise reader (Nan Shepherd), *Bloodhunt* (written 1951) was Neil's *Four Quartets*.[17]

Its 'soul in an experiment' is old Sandy, and his swithering between deathly serenity and troubled recommitment is its centre. His figure reaches back through Phemie and the doctor, Hector and Mairi, to auld Jeems at the start. All are marginal protectors of life 'beyond the edge of the ordinary world' (149), but the world has changed. In the Cold War world, an old imagination, 'desolation and sadness' at its core, wants only to die in peace. But there is no place to hide.

The oasis of Sandy's croft becomes a physical and moral trap, invaded by fugitive criminal and obsessive policeman alike. Plot moves suspensefully on a level of practical ingenuity—the lock, the food, the money—and larger implications are muted. Styles move quietly among spare matter-of-fact, stream of consciousness, witty dialogue, simple aphorism. The focus is always on story, the simple and absolute choice between two immortal stories: Cain or Christ. Trapped and hopeless, Sandy sees the bloodhunt story of Cain as inevitable. There is no way to save the fugitive who killed his girl's seducer. But Sandy is trapped again, this time by life. The ludicrous, natural accident with his cow leaves him helpless, and the kindly, bossy women take over. In their train comes the pregnant girl, and Sandy is jolted into life. He sees that the story can end differently, and here he is one with the authorial imagination, and the reader too is implicated in choosing. The aesthetic and moral choices are the same: drift with the easy drama of darkness, the old law, the old design, or make a drama of light, new life.

The widow Macleay, being a woman, makes her choice easily: 'She had arranged her own kind of battle in the wide sweep of personal and public affairs' (176). This statement perfectly suggests the novel's masterful, quiet integration of small human drama and cosmic implication. The same quiet joining of local simplicity with mythic resonance is seen when, at last, Sandy must suddenly help deliver the child like a lamb in his barn. From this, his final wisdom follows easily. It is the wisdom of the 'old man of the tribe', and when we realise its similarity to the compromises of *The Lost Chart*, we sense that the imaginative confusion of that earlier Cold War parable has been resolved.

Of fiction, there remains only the haunting postscript of *The Other Landscape* (written 1953), a novel that tries to do what it knows can no longer be done, to say what it says cannot be said. As an expression of Neil's later thought and meditation, it is fascinating. As a novel, it shows the two strongest of his imaginative aspirations meeting their nemesis: to lift the personal into the impersonal; to make all stories 'meet in one story' (294). Its plot quest is to know a mysterious author who cannot be known. Nowhere else is Gunn so painfully involved and so carefully hidden—behind his only dramatised 'I' narrator, behind 'verbal thickets' and 'looping arabesques', a 'confounding mixture of tilting planes and noisy association' that drives some to ask (with the Major), 'Are you trying to be infernally funny or are you in a bloody trance?' (197, 203). *This* reader suspects the parodic self-allegory of an author having his final joke at London's expense.

The biographical matter includes marital tragedy, accidental still-birth, blow-ups over other women, the couple's retreat, the artist's struggles and his feelings of guilt which 'dogged him when he had fought for a happy ending' (112). The bitterness spills over into the young narrator's inexplicable revulsions, miraculous exaltations, and visions of man's 'revolting planet . . . composed of the sort of dough that would give indigestion to a moonbeam' (270). And yet, this strange imaginative surrogate strives for impersonality and integration. The dual stories of the defeated titans, the Major and Menzies, are deeply divided, and the narrator uses the first as defence against the second as long as he can. The Major's story is grotesque humour, and it ends in an infernal joke. Menzies' story is tragic mysticism, and it ends in sacrificial death. The narrator wishes to 'hang onto' both, to bring them finally together, all stories meeting in one story, but finds this impossible. 'Heavens,' he asks, 'had life got any sort of pattern?' (187). The author is asking with him.

The Wrecker has won, but he has been bravely confronted. The struggle—for the impersonal, for integration, for light—is the same long struggle of Gunn's imagination. The struggle had produced a remarkable number of fine novels, and now it was over. The novel had outlived its imaginative relevance, and Neil turned to other things. Having tried to trace his imaginative presence through the novels, we may well end with *The Other Landscape*'s narrator, with his resignation, but also with his consolation:

> I had the feeling that I knew him better than any other person on earth and yet I realised that I would never know him. But this did not offend, hardly disappointed even, for I realised, by a lifting further intuition, that what moves the spirit profoundly can never be fathomed. [260)

NOTES

1 Unless otherwise indicated, all page references are to the original British editions of the novels.

2 Biographical information and inference are based throughout on J B Pick and Hart, *Neil M Gunn: A Highland Life* (London: John Murray, 1981). Identified as *HL* herinafter.

3 *See* the title story to the first collection of short stories, *Hidden Doors* (Edinburgh: Porpoise, 1929).

4 *HL*, pp 80–81; review by Frank Morley for George Blake of the Porpoise Press.

5 The novel was serialised in eight instalments in *The Scots Magazine*, beginning September, 1929. Gunn then reported simply that he would not publish it as a book—probably a wise decision.

6 The quote is actually from *Highland River*, p 131.

7 Gifford's view appears on p 22 of his fine study, *Neil M Gunn and Lewis Grassic Gibbon* (Edinburgh: Oliver and Boyd, 1983).

8 *HL*, p 107; letter to F Marian McNeill in late 1934.

9 *See* J B Caird's excellent essay, 'Neil M Gunn: Novelist of the North', in *Essays on Neil M Gunn*, ed D Morrison (Thurso: Caithness Books, 1971), with its Proust comparisons (especially p 50); *also*, Gifford, p 27, and Gifford's 'The Source of Joy: *Highland River*', in *Neil M Gunn: The Man and the Writer*, ed A Scott and D Gifford (Edinburgh: Blackwood, 1973), the crucial first collection for any student of Gunn.

10 For the epic view of the novel, *see* Alexander Scott, 'Folk Epic: *The Silver Darlings*', in Scott and Gifford.

11 Paul Ricoueur, in the *JAPA*, **25** (1977), 862.

12 Peter Brooks, *Reading for the Plot* (New York: Vintage, 1985), p 111.

13 *HL*, p 206.

14 Quoted from *Selected Letters of Edwin Muir*, ed P Butter, in *HL*, p 214.

15 *See* Gifford, p 41, on the 'thrillers', and Pick in *HL*, pp 215–18.

16 *HL*, pp 126–7, concern the most traumatic event of Gunn's personal life.

17 Letter of Jan 1953, quoted in *HL*, p 239.

Chapter 7

Novelists of the Renaissance

ISOBEL MURRAY

It is convenient to separate Neil Gunn from the other main novelists of the time, as the organisation of this book has it, because Gunn's presence in the group of novelists I shall chiefly be dealing with has been distorting to a general view. The three novelists whose claims to treatment here are to me indisputable have far more in common with each other than they have with Gunn. These three are Naomi Mitchison, Eric Linklater and James Leslie Mitchell, better known as Lewis Grassic Gibbon, the pen-name under which he wrote his masterpiece, the trilogy known as *A Scots Quair.* Apart from anything else, all three wrote fiction which was sometimes deliberately and self-consciously Scottish, and sometimes something very different.

Mitchison, Linklater and Gibbon were born within four years of each other, and all three responded very directly to the cataclysm of the First World War. Linklater, born in 1899, forged an earlier date of birth on his documents so that he could be sent to France late in 1917. He was very nearly killed in 1918 by a bullet that went right through his tin hat. He treasured the tin hat thereafter, and in one of his three autobiographical volumes, *Fanfare for a Tin Hat* (1970), he recalled that nothing in his later life had equalled the intensity of three weeks as a sniper. I shall quote this volume frequently. His description recalls Yeats's poems about the intensity of life and death symbolised for him by Major Robert Gregory, or some of the characters in Hemingway's *Fiesta* who remember the war, for all its horrors, as the most exciting time of their lives. Linklater writes of an intensity:

> which I have never known since. I have, on the whole, had a happy life, and I have known much pleasure. But in my nineteenth year I lived at a high pitch of purpose, a continuous physical and mental alertness, that has never again suffused my brain and body.

So Linklater knew and repeatedly illustrated the paradox of the horrors of war on the one hand and on the other hand its intensity, and his unfailing admiration and love for the soldiers who carry on the war. He wrote a great deal about war, in histories, plays and pamphlets as well as in fiction, but his best war novel is *Private Angelo* (1945). And the unforgotten intensity of that nineteen-year-old left the mature writer liable to search for novelty, change and action that moulded much of his fiction, and ensured that travel would be a central feature of his most effective novels.

Naomi Mitchison was seventeen when the war broke out, and lived in

Oxford, knowing a large number of young men through her beloved elder brother, Jack Haldane. Her memoir, *All Change Here*, recounts the devastation, as a whole generation seemed to be destroyed. Her marriage to Dick Mitchison was accelerated because of the war, as were so many others, and when Dick was seriously wounded in 1916 she travelled to France and was allowed, because of her VAD training, to nurse him through the worst. For Mitchison as for Linklater, the war was not only appalling but a crucial formative experience that destroyed many old ways and left a future for which it seemed every foundation had to be newly prepared. Francis Russell Hart has drawn attention to 'a brief flourish of archaic recreation in the novel'[1], when Gibbon, Gunn, Mitchison and others almost simultaneously turned to historical fiction. When I asked Mitchison about this, whether there was some common need felt and understood here, she answered simply: 'Well, I think in a sense we were making something to stand on.'[2] Mitchison of course stuck to history more determinedly than the others. Her historical fictions could on the one hand explore the nature of civilisation, government, slavery and war, serving as such a basis for reconstruction, and on the other hand they could often have a discernible contemporary relevance. In this way her first novel *The Conquered* (1923) was a tale of Gaul gradually united under Vercingetorix to oppose Julius Caesar, and at the same time a clear indictment of Britain's contemporary treatment of Ireland.

She was to search deeper still in her first really large scale fiction, *The Corn King and the Spring Queen* (1931), where she sought a mythic basis for Western civilisation in Sir James Frazer's *The Golden Bough*, which she had read voraciously for the stories, even before she was old enough to follow all the arguments. So in effect, Mitchison shared many concerns with T S Eliot and *The Waste Land*, and her novel probed the very distant past where myth grew into history and man grew into full self-consciousness. But Mitchison believed in action as well as literature, and during the 1920s and 1930s, while bringing up her family and supporting her husband's political career as a Labour MP, and writing an astonishing number of books, she worked tirelessly for the causes she wholeheartedly espoused, including Socialism, Feminism and the making available of birth control information.

Lewis Grassic Gibbon, the youngest of the three, was only seventeen when the War ended, so naturally did not take part. But his work shows all too vividly his awareness of its impact, on individuals and communities alike: he presented it as one of the last throes of a civilisation which is dying. In *Sunset Song* even a brief acquaintance with army life brutalises the previously kindly Highlander Ewan Tavendale, and the tiny hamlet of Kinraddie is deprived of its most outstanding men of military age, while the Prelude and Epilude most deliberately draw attention to themes of change and destruction, of the end of old ways and the peasant tradition. His inevitable non-participation in the War did not delay the formation of Gibbon's political and social views about the world: by age seventeen he had become a Communist, and had begun speaking from public platforms in Aberdeen. Ironically, he went on, in a time of bad unemployment, to serve time in both the Army and the Air Force: 'His stomach had conscripted him', he says of one of his characters.

All three of these writers, then, experienced the War as an earth-shaking preliminary to adult life, and like others of their generation across Europe and America they reacted strongly to it. They all found it natural to be at least to some extent political animals, and this can be seen throughout their fictions, although none of them allowed his or her best work to be vitiated by mere propaganda messages. All three in due course paid careful attention to the case for Scottish independence, and Linklater was sufficiently convinced of it, for a while, to stand at a by-election for the National Party of Scotland in 1933, while Mitchison was Labour candidate for the Scottish universities in 1935: both were unsuccessful, but Mitchison saved her deposit!

Gibbon became less politically active as time went on: his spells in HM Forces may partly explain that, and most of his phenomenal energies were more and more directed toward his writing. As well as being for the most part a fairly individual, non-aligned Socialist, he had a great interest in Diffusionism, which is most clearly illustrated in the books published under his own name, James Leslie Mitchell, and in his Grassic Gibbon essay, 'The Antique Scene'. This is the idea that civilisation itself is the cause of all our discontents and miseries, that until man the nomadic hunter settled down to tilling the soil and agricultural life, he lived in a Golden Age. It was agriculture that brought all the institutions and evils of civilisation, and distorted and crippled man's better nature. Critics are much divided over the extent to which his masterpiece, *A Scots Quair*, is governed by Diffusionist or Socialist ideas: Bob Tait and I have argued in *Ten Modern Scottish Novels* that the importance of Diffusionism to the *Quair* has been over-stressed. Indeed, I would suggest that the trilogy preaches neither creed, but leaves the reader at the end with a kind of choice: to follow either the bleak and passive realism of Chris Guthrie or the political activism of her son Ewan: Chris sees the final futility of all efforts to redirect the destined, changing chaos that life offers, while Ewan sees some advantage in fighting for some improvements in people's lives, however transitory.

Gibbon, then, responded to the political climate of the twenties and thirties by embracing Communism (with some individuality) and condemning Fascism—and of course he was a self-conscious Nationalist too, as is evidenced by his co-operation with Hugh MacDiarmid in *Scottish Scene* (1934), a curious compilation of Scottish essays and stories. His contributions to that volume can be found in *A Scots Hairst*. Even more remarkable in a way, was his organisation of a series of volumes called *Voice of Scotland*. He did not survive to complete his own contribution—in MacDiarmid's phrase, on 'the Burns business', but he succeeded otherwise in building an astonishing list of contributors, including MacDiarmid, Gunn, Linklater, Edwin Muir, Willa Muir, A S Neill and Compton Mackenzie. Like MacDiarmid, then, in his own way, Gibbon was partly responsible for orchestrating the 'Scottish Renaissance', but his early death in 1935 meant that he had hardly time to start issuing warnings about the Second World War.

Mitchison and Linklater both did just that, however. Mitchison published her first non-historical novel in 1935, a thinly disguised account of her own family situation and hopes and fears for civilisation, which ended with a fearful warning vision of a counter revolution and a Fascist dictatorship in Britain. *We Have Been Warned* is not one of her best novels: it is too crowded, and partisan, and involved, but its very title sounds the alarm. In this novel and in her memoirs, too, she relates how she went to meet and refresh the very Hunger March from Scotland that Ewan Tavendale set out to lead the previous year, at the end of *Grey Granite*. She went to Vienna to report on the counter revolution of Dolfuss in 'Red Vienna', and published her *Vienna Diary* in the same year, 1934: she wrote a book on moral and political philosopy, *The Moral Basis of Politics* (1938): and her next novel, *The Blood of the Martyrs* (1939), set in Rome at the time of the persecution of early Christians, deals again with the issues she saw as most urgently confronting the citizens of a free democracy in the face of Hitler's Germany.

And when the war was responsible for the longest publishing hiatus in her adult life, she worked unceasingly at Carradale, Kintyre, caring for her children, helping in local politics, dealing with refugees, and Free French soldiers, and political bigwigs, and producing two very different books about the war. The first was in the form of a diary written for Mass Observation, which ran to over a million words. An absorbing selection edited by Dorothy Sheridan was published in 1985 as *Among You Taking Notes...* The composition of the second is partly documented in the first, where we learn of the seven years of planning and research that went into the composition of her Scottish masterpiece, *The Bull Calves* (1947).

We will come back to *The Bull Calves*, but it must be saluted here as perhaps the best example of the remarkable economy whereby she could do several things at once, first demonstrated in *The Conquered*. *The Bull Calves* is a Scottish historical novel, set in 1746, the year after the second and last important Jacobite Rising which divided the people of Scotland. Francis Russell Hart has said that it 'comes closer to the historical romance of Scott than any other later Scottish fiction I have read' (190). But it is not concerned to take sides. Mitchison told us: 'No, it very much doesn't take sides, . . . and there's no nonsense about the Prince.' At the same time it is an exploration of Mitchison's own ancestors, the Haldanes of Gleneagles. And it also reflects the European situation two hundred years later, with nations divided and exhausted by a punishing war, and it deals with themes of reconstruction and regeneration.

Linklater was to deal with some similar themes in *Private Angelo*, which he wrote in 1944-5 when an Allied victory seemed certain, but in which he pushed the reconstruction of Italy on by a couple of years, so confident was he in the resilience of the people and the final indestructibility of their art and history. But between the wars, unlike Gibbon and Mitchison, he saw Communism as just as dangerous as Fascism, and because of this he was emotionally disabled by the Spanish Civil War, finding it possible to support neither side wholeheartedly. His fictional response was *The Impregnable Women* (1938), a loose adaptation of the *Lysistrata* of Aristophanes. As he said, it was 'inspired by angry revulsion against the prospect of war's renewal', and it is an uneven novel. But *Judas* (1939), with its themes of loyalty and treachery, was inspired by the way Britain and France in particular deserted the cause of Czechoslovakia in the name of appeasement. It makes an interesting contrast to Mitchison's treatment of the same gospel story in *Behold Your King* (1957).

Private Angelo remains Linklater's best novel concerned with or reflecting on the war. By a series of lucky chances, Linklater was able to spend a year in Italy as the Allied armies fought their way up, covering the campaign, gestating the novel and making the extraordinary discovery of Italian art treasures that he describes in *Fanfare for a Tin Hat*. Linklater's own secret kisses for Bottticelli's flower girls stand behind Angelo's adoration of the della Francesca Virgin, and the author describes his love affair with Italy as 'a state of idealistic adultery', whose fruit was *Private Angelo*: 'The subject of my novel was not only war and its capacity for destruction, but Italy and its genius for survival'.

So we have three exceptionally energetic and wide-ranging novelists, all interested in history and its lessons, all deeply involved in contemporary life, and all impelled, it seemed, to a fury of production that was more than a desire for money or reputation, although it certainly included these too. No time was wasted organising a specific 'Novelists' Renaissance': while Gibbon was coadjutor with MacDiarmid, Linklater was for long detached: his account of Magnus Merriman's gradual and temporary interest in the Scottish ferment seems only a heightened version of his own experience. And Mitchison was not yet really identified in a public way as Scots, although Gibbon specifically included her among other [Scottish] writers in English, whom he refused to acknowledge as Scottish writers in his essay 'Literary Lights'.

Mitchison's specifically Scottish writing began with *We Have Been Warned*, but did not coincide with her best work until *The Bull Calves* and the stories of *Five Men and a Swan*, some of which dated from the early 1940s. All three writers wrote for a wider audience than simply and solely the Scottish one, although the Scottish one was most important, and rave reviews from round the world for *Sunset Song*, including one from Linklater, could not console Gibbon for the narrow and parochial responses the novel provoked in his native land.

They poured out books, all writing other books as well as fiction. If we take as example four years at the beginning of the 1930s—1931 to 1934—the last years of Gibbon's life, we find a quite phenomenal production of books, a flood so astonishing that it is perhaps inevitable that in all three cases the quality was uneven.

For Gibbon, these years saw the separate publication of the three novels that were to form *A Scots Quair*, and his celebrated collaboration with MacDiarmid, *Scottish Scene*. But as James Leslie Mitchell he also published six novels, one volume of short stories and three histories, the last of which for some reason was co-authored by Gibbon and Mitchell. Of these *Spartacus* certainly survives as a good novel, independent of the reputation created by the *Quair*, while *The Thirteenth Disciple*, a lesser novel, has clear biographical interest. Mitchison published *The Corn King and the Spring Queen* in 1931, and six other titles in the four years, not counting *We Have Been Warned*, which was delayed by timorous publishers because of its alleged outspokenness on sexual matters, chiefly the mention of contraceptive rubber goods. And Linklater published *Juan in America* and *The Men of Ness* in the same year, 1931, and seven more books in the period, fiction, stories, histories and a play. And the energy of composition was such that in each case the best work is marked by new developments in the novel, and a variety of experimental techniques. The two survivors of these years, Mitchison and Linklater, continued to innovate and experiment, to an extent that put off the kinds of reviewers and critics who like to pigeonhole writers neatly, and to know, more or less, what to expect.

The differences between the three writers are also great and must be acknowledged, by at least a minimal separate treatment. Their backgrounds could hardly be more diverse. Gibbon was born in 1901 in Auchterless, Aberdeenshire, and raised as the son of a small tenant farmer, who was expected either to 'better himself' with education, or 'take a fee', a farm labourer's job. He was to value the perspective this gave him when he came to write: in his projected autobiography he intended to describe the class war, 'from the viewpoint of one who in origins (peasant) was outside the war.'

His great trilogy is very self-consciously Scottish, and perhaps its single greatest strength is the adaptation of Scots in which he writes it, a Scots based on North-East speech which is kept easy to read, and does not use an incomprehensible vocabulary or indicate dialectal differences orthographically. It does not repel the non-Scot, but captures a ring and an intonation that is compelling and expressive. *A Scots Quair* was composed in three parts—Douglas Gifford has called it 'one great novel with three massive movements'. It is inventive and experimental in its subtle rendering of point of view, and in the apparent starkness of its structure. We can say with truth that *Sunset Song* deals with the heroine's youth and first marriage, and life on a croft and in a small hamlet: *Cloud Howe* deals with her second marriage, to a minister, and life in a small town, and *Grey Granite* covers her move to a grim industrial city with unemployment and labour problems, and a disastrous third marriage. But although the structure is indeed as clear as this, that summary indicates a formulaic strictness that is quite at variance with the experience of reading the trilogy.

The heroine Chris Guthrie is central to that experience, and the reader is privy to her emotional development in adolescence and youth, and her gradual defensive retreat into a stoic self-sufficiency, in an attempt to escape first the loneliness and hurt of the later years with Robert Colquhoun and then the nullity of her third marriage. Critics who agree about little else all, I think, agree on the centrality of Chris. Her internal emotional battles continue into *Grey Granite*, where she weeps with 'a sudden wild woe' that defeats all her rational arguments:

> things would redd up in time, she wasn't hungry or starved, she had friends, she had Ewan . . . SHE HAD NOTHING AT ALL, she had never had anything, nothing in the world she'd believed in but change, unceasing and unstaying as time, light after light went down, hope and fear and hate, love that had lighted hours with a fire, hate freezing through to the blood of one's heart—Nothing

endured, and this hour she stood as alone as she'd been when a quean in those wild, lost moments she climbed the heights of Blawearie brae.

Gibbon is the only one of these writers who has as yet received much serious critical treatment, and the most vexed questions in the lively and ongoing debate seem to be these: how important to the trilogy is the author's Socialism? and his Diffusionism? How important is it to read the whole *Quair* as a unity, as Gibbon intended, or is it a legitimate reading to find a falling off in the second and third volumes, and to concentrate on *Sunset Song*? How should we read the ending? Should we read the *Quair* as Kurt Wittig first I think suggested in *The Scottish Tradition in Literature*? His reading was schematic, and has since been carried further. He wrote: 'The story moves on three distinct levels: personal, social, and mythical.' Bob Tait and I have argued in *Ten Modern Scottish Novels* that there are perils in this last approach, most crudely illustrated when a school edition can provide a key to the novel, in which Chris is equated with 'Scotland herself' or 'the land', her first husband is 'the Gael' and her second 'the Protestant Kirk', while her desperate mother, who commits murder and suicide when assailed by yet another pregnancy, can be cheerfully labelled 'Woman personified' or 'Mother Eve'. It seems to me undeniable that this emphasis is liable to blur the realistic impact of the trilogy, to mutilate the reading experience.

But it is clearly possible to hold a symbolic or allegorical interpretation alongside the others (if possible, rather in the background!), and the evidence allows this, while the emotional force of the narrative is most obviously spent on the personal level. So it is both natural and right to see *A Scots Quair* as a deliberate effort to produce a national epic or myth, with a force on every level that sets it beside, say, *Heart of Midlothian*, with no need for apology.

The inventiveness of *A Scots Quair* crucially contributes to its success. Gibbon invents not only the effective Scots rhythm of the whole, but the very narrative method, in which voices unobtrusively replace each other, and the story is conveyed retrospectively, when Chris retires alone to reflect on her experiences, at irregular intervals in the novels. He invents the framing devices of local historical lore and opinion, in a strong local voice, which introduce Kinraddie and Segget, but which significantly disappear with the anonymous industrial city of *Grey Granite*. He modulates the narrative voices with unique expertise, coming in the last volume to a new and most effective way of rendering industrial (or unemployed) man in a communal experience in which he acquires self or group confidence.[3]

It is a bleak epic in its impact at the very end, where Chris is alone at last, and has retired alone to her birthplace, facing a final recognition that life has no grand meaning, no stability, no reality but the inevitability of change. By the end that inevitability is 'the best deliverance of all, as she saw it now, sitting here quiet.' She had achieved a certain equanimity on her first return to Cairndhu: after a stark recognition that life was only 'that dreich, daft journey that led nowhither', she then realised: 'THAT didn't much matter—daft the journey, but the journeying good'. So while young Ewan sets off with the Hunger Marchers at the end of the novel, straight into contemporary history (and toward Mitchison's welcome in Oxford), the reader remains behind with Chris, motionless and silent.

Eric Linklater was born in Penarth, Glamorganshire, in 1899, son of a master mariner who was himself an Orcadian, and an English mother. He was to describe her as 'a woman of fierce and determined character who had arbitrarily decided that she was Scotch', and he followed her in all of these, creating a legend that lasted for decades, of having been born in an ancestral Orkney. His devotion to the Orkney Islands and the northern counties of Scotland was both genuine and part of a self-made mask. After his narrow escape from death in France he read English at Aberdeen University, and gained experience there in teaching and in journalism in India before the American visit, ostensibly for postgraduate research, that gave him material for perhaps his best known novel, *Juan in America*. After that he was a full-time writer.

Juan in America (1931) has been widely praised. Linklater called it a historical novel, for in it he caught the flavour of 1920s America even as it was vanishing. It is a picaresque novel, a series of adventures linked largely by the personality of the chief character, Juan Motley, a descendant of Byron's Don Juan, whose amorous adventures are for the most part occasions for witty and mordant travelogue. Linklater called it 'a romantic period in which money, bootleg whisky, and blood flowed freely, and a new mythology was created'. Not surprisingly, perhaps, Linklater thought the great American novel of the twenties, *The Great Gatsby*, over-rated, but he and Fitzgerald can be seen to identify and use the very same quality. Linklater much later wrote that 'innocence . . . was what I saw beneath the fabulous wealth of the United States, and it was that which let me write, as I did, *Juan in America*. I wrote it, open-eyed, with delight and a total acceptance of what I saw'.

Linklater's best fiction often uses myth as a central structural device, and his choice here of Byron's Don Juan was inspired. Linklater's Juan has very little character: he likes comfort, sex and freedom, and the reader enjoys these vicariously. The secret of Juan's success is that he lives almost entirely in the present: neither past peccadilloes nor future commitments are allowed to disturb his present spontaneity:

> And never a thought came to his mind of the last time he had sung that song, for such a morning was not meant for memory but present joy—

And after that his greatest gift is perhaps the gift of laughter.

With this genial rogue-cum-innocent as lens and register, the reader discovers Prohibition America, college life and American football, bootlegging and gangsterism, a presidential inauguration, the Deep South and Hollywood. The plot is spiced with coincidence and unlikely reunions, and the text, like Byron's, is littered with great set pieces—of fat people undressing on express trains, of a shoot-out at a gangster's funeral, of a dismal old man patiently and systematically smashing bottles of illegal whisky.

Linklater's output was deliberately varied, and after *Juan in America* he published his own version of a viking saga, *The Men of Ness*, following the saga tradition of economy and understatement, as different from its predecessor as can be imagined. Much of the material is ingeniously derived from genuine sagas, but Linklater prided himself that the long sea voyage was original, and authentic. And Marjorie Linklater suggested in a recent introduction to a new edition that the truly original character in the book is Gauk, the anti-hero, the small man, the hen-pecked, artful survivor who returns home when all the heroes are dead. The next novel was *Magnus Merriman*, clearly based to some extent on Linklater's own discovery of the Scottish Renaissance and the National Party of Scotland. It has splendid set pieces, as in *Juan in America*, and abundant comic vitality, but it lacks either a myth or a narrative logic that would provide a satisfactory structure: it remains a comic textbook of the Renaissance and a novel that falls short of Linklater's best.

I shall point to two of these best novels. *Private Angelo* was one of the first novels to take account of the war, and I would argue it inspired or directed the course of others. The character of Sergeant Vespucci, the 'Free Distributor' who has seen and exploited commercial opportunities, whom Angelo considers to be 'doing well in life, not only for himself but for his country', seems to stand behind the creation of Milo Mindbinder in Heller's *Catch 22*: and the pleasant young Englishman who has an affair with Angelo's fiancée and leaves her pregnant, Corporal Trivet, has surely some small part in the inspiration of Waugh's unpleasant anti-hero Trimmer in *Unconditional Surrender*, who leaves Guy Crouchback's divorced wife Virginia in similar condition.

Angelo has led a rout of Italians fleeing from battle, and is dismissed by his natural father the Count in the first sentence as lacking the gift of courage. But the idea of courage will be re-examined, and the importance of understanding will also be stressed. By the end Angelo has served in three armies, Italian, German and British, although his development of discipline to overcome fear in the last is rather unconvincing, and he has become the legal father of five, three of them other men's bastards, one English, one Polish and one Moroccan. The tenor of the book is against nationalism, and Angelo's happy settling into a family scene, even with a living-in mistress, is uncharacteristic Linklater. Elsewhere his central characters tend to be presented parentless and childless, and to be seen in contexts other than family ones.

The book exposes many of the absurdities and horrors of war: even the innocent Angelo learns to say: 'I hope you will not liberate us out of existence.' As armies bomb their own troops, and Angelo deserts again and again, we see the folly of war. But the wandering refugees, and the rapes of both Angelo and his fiancée, remind us of serious horror, and Linklater's conviction that this is a just and necessary war is clear.

An older man who seems to have come to satisfactory terms with life is the central figure of *A Man Over Forty* (1963), one of the most accomplished novels. Edward Balintore is a TV personality who unconcernedly submits to a grilling interview on air, only to collapse suddenly and dramatically after confessing he is afraid 'of being found out'. The book charts Balintore's comic journey in search of peace, and his gradual self-discovery, and the exorcising of his guilt. He escapes to Jamaica, Ireland, Greece, repeatedly meeting characters who accuse him of past misdeeds, so that each refuge becomes a new situation from which to escape. The basic myth is that of Orestes, as the reader slowly becomes aware; and Balintore's buried memory of matricide and his pursuit by twentieth-century Furies form the sober centre of a comic novel which combines all the ingredients Linklater is best at.

The success of his best books often depends on this use of myth. The Don Juan myth is a perfect cover for the satirical travelogue of *Juan in America*, and Juan owes something also to Candide. Dissimilar though they are, both Gauk and Angelo owe something to *The Good Soldier Schweik*, and it is no coincidence that Linklater was adapting *Don Quixote* for radio before he embarked on *Private Angelo*. In *A Man Over Forty* the central myth of Orestes not only supports a clear structure, which gradually emerges from apparent picaresque chaos, but also allows an investigation in modern terms of perennial questions of evil and guilt.

Mitchison was brought up in Oxford, daughter of a distinguished scientist and academic, and co-heir to the status and responsibilities she was aware of from early on: she knew she was one of 'the intelligentsia, and . . . the people who should be giving a lead'. Like Linklater, she has published splendid volumes of memoirs. And she has written dozens of other books, many of the more recent ones for children and young people.

The Corn King and the Spring Queen (1931) is a giant book that can in a sense be summarised: Mitchison acknowledges this by the clear and simple summaries she provides at the end of each of its nine parts; 'because it is a long and crowded book and it is rather difficult to remember just what happened from time to time.' Summary is legitimate, then, but it does not begin to substitute for the long and absorbing experience of reading it. And a summary as short as the following can say very little.

In the novel, Mitchison balances two stages of civilisation, treating them alternately. There is the ancient Scythian kingdom of Marob, ruled by Tarrik, the Corn King, and Erif Der, a witch, who becomes his Spring Queen at her father's urging, to destroy and supplant Tarrik, but who in the end loves and saves him. Tarrik and Erif are barbarians, susceptible to magic, in tune with the seasons and their rituals, and necessary to the prosperity and fertility of Marob.

Consciously rational Greeks on the whole despise the barbarians of Marob, and Erif's magic does not work on the clear, rational mind of Sphaeros, the Stoic philosopher, for example. The narrative moves repeatedly from Marob to Sparta, and many of the characters journey there also. Here a long period of decadence has destroyed ancient ways, creating an oligarchy, a dictatorship of the wealthy, the enslavement of the poor. Agis and Kleomenes, successive Spartan kings, seek to lead a revolution which will restore the ancient ideals of equality and fellowship, but although like Tarrik (and later Jesus) they are kings willing to die for their people, the sacrifice of their deaths does not bring about the desired result. The ideal of Sparta is lost, but by the slow end of the epic—it is deliberately slow, and enormously readable,—Tarrik and Erif Der are cleansed of their troubles and restored to Marob, Corn King and Spring Queen again, but with a flow of Hellenic enlightenment that transforms them as individuals, but is not fully passed on to their successors, who are less troubled, and more fortunate.

Although Marob is an imaginary kingdom, necessarily, as written records would never be made of that kind of civilisation, Sparta is carefully documented here. Mitchison's fictions of the Hellenic world return repeatedly to the antithetical claims to allegiance of Athens and Sparta, a kind of democracy in however exhausted a phase, and a place of iron discipline and austerity, and a certain totalitarian quality. In the twenties and thirties Mitchison recognised this totalitarian quality in Germany and Italy, with the rise of the Fascist dictatorships, and to some extent in Russia too: on her 1932 visit to the USSR she notes at one point in her diary, with sad disapproval: 'A lot of Sparta about this.'

Any attempt to 'cover' Mitchison, even on this scale, would be ludicrous, for she has published more than seventy books. I shall only gesture at *The Bull Calves*, and at my own edition of *Beyond This Limit: Selected Shorter Fiction*, in the Introduction to which I have attempted a slightly fuller sketch map of her adult fiction. Like *The Corn King and the Spring Queen*, *The Bull Calves* was composed over many years, and involved painstaking research, research doubly interesting to the author because the Haldanes of the story were her ancestors: 'of course, what was great fun was doing the characters who were actually my ancestors: one's sort of interested in the genes . . . And Patrick in a sense is partly based on my brother, so that it was all very close to the heart.' Like *We Have Been Warned* among others, it particularly addresses 'the intelligentsia, and . . . the people who should be giving a lead.'

The novel has a very ingenious structure. It covers only three days of a family get-together at Gleneagles in 1746, but by a series of conversations in which characters come to confide in other members of the family, it goes way back into the earlier lives and sufferings and errors of a mature, fairly recently married pair, from opposing backgrounds, while in the foreground a simple and not-too-urgent plot relates to the aftermath of the Forty-Five. It is a sizeable book, with a great apparatus of notes appended, 'an essential critical text of the novel in Scotland,' says Francis Russell Hart (184).

These novels are particularly large in scale, and even Mitchison's shorter fictions tend toward novella-length at times. But a selection of these seemed to me the most practical way of conveying the range and variety of Mitchison's work, and the presentation of many themes, to an audience brought up in ignorance of her existence. *Beyond This Limit*, the title story, is set in contemporary Paris, London and Oxford, with a through-the-looking-glass quality of fantasy that renders it unique. Here Phoebe is trying to out-run heartbreak in the Paris metro:

> Phoebe ran and ran and the station must have been a long way back, with the lighted trains coming noisily in under their wide arches. She had certainly been pierced to the heart, but that was some time ago. Since then the wood-wind Creature, the piercing oboe, the cloudiness that was no doubt the beginning of

the cello's answer, had gone right through her, come out ahead of her and flapped away into a dazzle. Phoebe Bathurst was chasing it; she had to try and get it behind her again, for unless she did that why was she in Paris at all, why not at home?

Thereafter the stories range from primitive man and the cave-painters of Lascaux, through an ancient Greek tale of citizens enslaved, to Scottish and African tales of a more recent vintage. There are repeated treatments of physical and psychological slavery, and the exercise of unjust or irrational power in human relationships is often illustrated by cases of rape: particularly interesting are the pragmatic solutions variously arrived at, often by the women involved, to cope with the reality and the aftermath of such incidents. The African stories underline different cultural attitudes to sexuality, and to polygamy, and something of the nature of western imperialism.

The selection ends with 'Remember Me', an account by a survivor of a 'minor' nuclear holocaust in Scotland: it is remarkable for the authenticity and quiet desperation of the narrative voice, and the finely judged use of significant detail. This subject is typical of much of her more recent work, which tackles huge issues of conservation, ecology and famine, sometimes in a kind of science fiction. The selection juxtaposes Mitchison's abiding preoccupations, as in her most recent longer fiction. *Not By Bread Alone* (1983) investigates possibilities of great advances in world food production, with terrible consequences when new foodcrops become susceptible to new diseases; and her most recent work, *Early in Orcadia*, attempts to recreate the lives and outlooks of early settlers in Stone Age Orkney—primitive man, but always centrally, discernibly human.

Among other novelists of the period I shall point to two who deserve more critical attention than they have received hitherto. Fionn MacColla was a maverick novelist, and he has often been brought in to critical comparison to illustrate the virtues of others by contrast. He was an awkward and intemperate personality, espousing extreme forms of causes in ways that were often aggressive. Like MacDiarmid and Gibbon, he adopted a name: Tom Macdonald of Montrose chose to become Fionn MacColla of the Gaidhealtachd. He learned to speak Gaelic, and became a Nationalist of the extreme variety that can embarrass other Nationalists, claiming that England had waged unceasing war for centuries to destroy the Gaels and their language. He opposed Scottish Calvinism, blaming it for every Scottish ill, and became himself a convert to Roman Catholicism. His opinions are openly urged in his autobiography *Too Long in This Condition* (1975) and his extraordinary book of polemic *At the sign of the clenched fist* (1967), and they are made clear in his fiction also, but Bob Tait and I argued in a chapter of *Ten Modern Scottish Novels* that his novel of the Clearances, *And the Cock Crew* (1945), is not unduly marred by the violence of his opinions, because of his inspired choice of perspective.

If the same cannot quite be argued for his first novel, *The Albannach* (1932), it is a vehement and highly coloured novel that deserves consideration. This is the in part tragic story of a young Gael, Murdo Anderson, who finds himself at odds with his parents, and their perception of life, and in particular their religious attitudes. He watches his mother at prayers:

> Just now the black brows were bent on the Book, and her reading spectacles balanced far down on a reverent nose. He used to keep a watchful eye on the black fringe on her upper lip whenever there would be anything in the chapter about the Philistines or any of those clans the Lord was always smiting, because whenever He did the hairs used to bristle and she gave a toss of her head and a flap at the loose skin between the chin and the scraggy neck of her as if to say, 'Sin a bhalaich! Well done, God! That'll learn them!'

If MacColla has had cursory attention, the novels of Willa Muir have received virtually none at all. Willa Muir is known to posterity as wife of the more famous poet, of course, and co-translator of Kafka and the rest. She was also author of a delightful book in Grassic Gibbon's *Voice of Scotland* series, called *Mrs Grundy in Scotland*, and a book on ballads. But she wrote two novels of considerable interest and sophistication which have been unjustly neglected. Edwin Muir's novels are interesting to any student of his poetry or his work generally, but tend to be somewhat flat and lifeless: Willa's novels are full of energy. *Imagined Corners* (1931) is set in her native Montrose, thinly disguised as the east coast town of Calderwick. Without stridency, the author demonstrates the suffocating quality of life for respectable young women there, as a member of the family who escaped to more interesting unrespectability years before returns and observes the similar struggles of a younger woman in 1912. Muir makes the same kind of point that Catherine Carswell made in *Open The Door!* (1920), but with an assurance and skill that are unusual.

Her second novel, *Mrs Ritchie* (1933), can briefly be described as a descendant of *The House with the Green Shutters*, *Gillespie* and *Hatter's Castle*, a tale with all the bleakness of the anti-Kailyard. Here is another oppressive family unit where children are terrified of parents, and fears, of God, church and public disgrace, are the dominant weapons against rebellious, even in the last resort murderous, youth. The fascinating difference is that this time it is the woman who is the central monster, with a 'terrifying intensity of self-assertion' which is unrelentingly destructive of her family.

NOTES

1 Francis Russell Hart, *The Scottish Novel: A Critical Survey* (London, 1978), p 250. Other page references bracketed in the text.
2 In a recorded interview with Isobel Murray and Bob Tait, September 1984. Other unattributed quotations also from this source.
3 For a fuller discussion, see my 'Action and Narrative Stance in *A Scots Quair*' in David Hewitt and Michael Spiller (eds), *Literature of the North* (Aberdeen, 1983), p 109–20.

FURTHER READING

Information on primary publications and criticism of the writers can be found in:
Aitken W R (ed), *Scottish Literature in English and Scots: A Guide to Information Sources* (Detroit, Michigan, 1982)

The only extensive critical treatment is in:
Hart, Francis Russell, *The Scottish Novel: A Critical Survey* (London, 1978)

See also
Bold, Alan, *Modern Scottish Literature* (London, 1983)
Craig, Cairns, 'The Body in the Kit Bag: History and the Scottish Novel' in *Cencrastus* 1 (Autumn 1979), pp 18–22
Craig, Cairns, 'Fearful Selves: Character, Community and the Scottish Imagination' in *Cencrastus* 4 (Winter 1980–81), pp 29–32

Selected criticism on Gibbon since Aitken:
Calder, Angus, 'A Mania for Self-Reliance: Grassic Gibbon's *Scots Quair*', in Douglas Jefferson and Graham Martin (eds), *The Uses of Fiction: Essays on the Modern Novel in Honour of Arnold Kettle* (London, 1982)
Campbell, Ian, *Lewis Grassic Gibbon*, Scottish Writers Series (Edinburgh, 1985)
Gifford, Douglas, *Neil M Gunn and Lewis Grassic Gibbon* (London, 1983)
Malcolm, William, *A Blasphemer and Reformer: a study of James Leslie Mitchell/Lewis Grassic Gibbon* (Aberdeen, 1984)
Murray, Isobel and Tait, Bob, *Ten Modern Scottish Novels* (Aberdeen, 1984), pp 10–31
Murray, Isobel, 'Action and Narrative Stance in *A Scots Quair*', in David Hewitt and Michael Spiller (eds), *Literature of the North* (Aberdeen, 1983), pp 109–20

On Linklater since Aitken:
Parnell, Michael, *Eric Linklater: A Critical Biography* (London, 1984)
Rutherford, Andrew, 'Eric Linklater as Comic Novelist' in David Hewitt and Michael Spiller (eds), *Literature of the North* (Aberdeen, 1983), pp 149–61

On Mitchison since Aitken:
Murray, Isobel, 'Introduction' in *Beyond This Limit: Selected Shorter Fiction of Naomi Mitchison* (Edinburgh, 1986)
Scott, Alexander, 'Naomi Mitchison: Great Grandmother' in *The Scottish Review: Arts and Environment* No 25, (February, 1982), pp 15–19

On MacColla since Aitken:

Murray, Isobel, 'Fionn MacColla: Pilgrim of Independence', in *Leopard Magazine* 59 (February, 1980), North East Review, pp i–iii
Murray, Isobel and Tait, Bob, *Ten Modern Scottish Novels* (Aberdeen, 1984), pp 55–77

Chapter 8

Inter-War Criticism

MARGERY McCULLOCH

Scottish criticism in the inter-war period is dominated by three of the principal creative writers of the time: C M Grieve (Hugh MacDiarmid), Edwin Muir and Neil M Gunn. The immediate post-war years and the 1920s see the beginning and development of the movement which has come to be known as the Scottish Literary Renaissance, initiated by Grieve and greatly assisted by the poetic achievement of his *alter ego* MacDiarmid. The question of language predominates, initially through Grieve's hostility towards attempts by the newly-formed Vernacular Circle of the London Burns Club to promote a revival of the use of the Scots language, 'the Doric', for literary purposes; and subsequently, after his own conversion to the use of Scots as a literary medium as a result of the success of Hugh MacDiarmid's Scots lyrics, through Grieve's vigorous campaign in journal, newspaper and public platform on behalf of the Scots language, and later on behalf of Gaelic also. The development of criticism in this 1920s period therefore closely follows the pattern of Grieve/MacDiarmid's career, much as in the contemporary English scene, the re-orientation of the traditional canons of English literature attempted by T S Eliot in his critical articles was directed towards creating an audience for his own innovatory poetry.

Language appears to be dominant during the 1930s also, primarily as a consequence of Edwin Muir's advocacy of the adoption of the English language and literary tradition in his critical study *Scott and Scotland*, and the hostile reaction which this provoked on the part of Grieve/MacDiarmid. However, a closer examination of the critical writings of the period demonstrates that the cultural and political decline of Scotland which lay behind the language and literary identity arguments of the 1920s has now moved closer to the centre of the stage. While Muir's *literary* conclusions in *Scott and Scotland* have received much prominence, they grew out of his surveys of the cultural and economic situation of Scotland in the 1930s in *Scottish Journey* and in his periodical articles of the time. The content of the many books on the condition of Scotland which he reviewed for the *Spectator* demonstrates that social and economic decline was a dominant preoccupation of these years of Depression, in Scotland as elsewhere. Additionally, however, Scotland had the continuing problem of cultural decline and loss of national identity to contend with, and it is in this context that we find questions of language and literature debated.

The wider cultural context is explored also in the critical writings of the

119

Highland novelist Neil M Gunn, a writer whose non-fiction articles of the 1930s and early 1940s are of much significance in any examination of Scotland's cultural crisis and whose work in this area has too often been neglected in favour of the more stylistically attractive and literature-oriented criticism of Edwin Muir.

One of the complaints made by C M Grieve when he began his post-war literary work was that there was no Scottish literary criticism worth speaking of: 'Scottish literary criticism . . . as distinct from British (which really means English)—scarcely exists at all,' he wrote in the *Scottish Chapbook* of April 1923. (241) There was also in his view no Scottish literary periodical which could accommodate the criticism of a writer such as Edwin Muir whose articles were appearing regularly in the English *New Age* and American *Freeman*. Grieve proposed to remedy this situation through the periodicals he edited such as the *Scottish Chapbook* and *Scottish Nation*.

This absence of literary criticism and literary periodicals is not surprising in view of the steady decline in Scottish language and literature since the two Unions of 1603 and 1707. By the early twentieth century we find a recurrent questioning as to whether there is in fact a distinctive Scottish literature. 'There is a sense in which we have no Scottish literature in the same way as there is French and Welsh literature, because we have not a language of our own', was T B Peattie's pessimistic comment as he proposed the toast of Scottish literature at the Burns Federation Conference in 1922. Critics such as W MacNeile Dixon, editor of the *Edinburgh Book of Verse* (1910) and G Gregory Smith in his book *Scottish Literature: Character and Influence* (1919) emphasised the English dialect origins of Scottish language and literature at the expense of indigenous development, and in consequence found Scottish literature inevitably provincial and idiosyncratic in character.

Gregory Smith's book and his analysis of what he saw as the characteristic trait of Scottish literature, that 'antithesis of the real and the fantastic' which he described as the ' "polar twins" of the Scottish Muse' (20) are now of interest principally in relation to Grieve/MacDiarmid's transforming of this 'Caledonian Antisyzygy' (4) concept with its somewhat negative (from Smith's point of view) attributes into the positive characteristics of his own literary revolution. Despite Grieve's admiration for his book, Gregory Smith was representative of a critical attitude towards Scottish literature which was the 'polar twin' of his own forward-looking vision and one which had to be overcome if his literary revival was to succeed.

This question of a distinctive Scottish identity in literature was in the foreground of Grieve's critical and editing work when he returned to civilian life after the First World War. The progress of his campaign for the revitalisation of Scottish literature can be charted in the three series of the poetry anthology *Northern Numbers*, in the periodicals he edited such as *Scottish Chapbook*, *Scottish Nation* and *Northern Review* and in the many articles he wrote for Scottish newspapers and journals in the 1920s.

At first, however, the Scots language did not seem to feature prominently in Grieve's plans for a literary revival. Ironically, Gregory Smith's rejection of 'compulsory Scots' for Scotland's poets and his vision of the vernacular surviving at best as 'the delicate colouring of standard English with northern tints' (149, 148), is not far removed from Grieve's pre-'Watergaw' rejection of 'the Doric' and his insistence on the use of what J C Bulloch of the London Burns Club called 'Albyn-Place English'[1] as the superior literary medium: 'It is safe to predict that the majority will write in English—for the simple reasons (1) that they will reach a larger public (2) that the English language is an immensely superior medium of expression.'[2]

In this immediate post-war period Grieve's eyes were turned towards Europe and, despite his later reputation for Anglophobia, towards England. The *Scottish Chapbook*, which first appeared in August 1922, had among its aims the attempt 'to bring Scottish literature into closer touch with European tendencies in technique and ideation,' while the *New Age*, edited by A R Orage, provided an intellectual life-line for Grieve and Edwin Muir. Both were contributors and it provided also a working model for the periodicals which Grieve himself edited and published, as the English Georgian Poetry anthologies had provided a model for *Northern Numbers*. The reading material mentioned in Grieve's war-time letters to George Ogilvie is predominantly English and European. Scottish literature is significantly absent.

On the other hand, despite his initial emphasis on the English language as literary medium, Grieve did not see a Scottish literary revival as being based in the English literary tradition, as Edwin Muir was to suggest in the 1930s. Grieve was always quick to emphasise that while he envisaged Scottish writers of quality and ambition using English, what they wrote would not be 'English on that account. . . . It is not English in content—although in form it may owe a great deal to contemporary English tendencies.'[3] For him the difference—as he was to say also of an indigenous Scottish drama—'will be equivalent to the stupendous and tremendously underrated difference between Scottish and English psychology.'[4]

Grieve's critical criterion was at this point primarily literary merit and this fact lay behind his initial hostility to the London Burns Club's attempt to revive the Scots vernacular. Like the nationalist movement and other public organs of the time, the Burns Federation and its journal the *Burns Chronicle* were concerned at the loss of cultural identity in Scotland, at the loss of customs and traditional ways of life, of knowledge of Scotland's history and literature and, especially, at the loss of language. Although Grieve supported the connection between literature and nationalism: 'I believe in the future of Scottish literature just as I believe in the continuance of Scottish nationality',[5] for him literary merit must come before insistence on the use of an outworn national language. And at this point the Doric did seem to him just such an outworn language: 'a modern consciousness cannot fully express itself in the Doric as it exists.'[6] Despite his encouragement in *Northern Numbers* of more adventurous Scots-language poets, he clearly did not see the future of the literary revival as lying with them: 'The whole trouble with the Doric as a literary language today is that the vast majority of its exponents are hopelessly limited culturally—and that the others . . . only use it for limited purposes,' he wrote in the *Chapbook* of October 1922. (63) In his view, the attempt by the 'perfervids attached to the London Vernacular Circle' to promote a

'Doric "boom"'' at this point in time 'would be a gross disservice to Scottish life and letters.'[7]

Grieve's personal literary ambitions as English-language poet and the success of the new direction in Scottish literature which *Northern Numbers* heralded depended upon maintaining the flight from the Kailyard into the more invigorating atmosphere of contemporary European letters. In this context, the conservation activities of the London Vernacular Circle must have seemed an attempt to close the Kailyard gate before the new literary horses had had an opportunity to bolt!

Grieve's conversion to the vernacular is documented principally in the *Scottish Chapbook*. The third issue of October 1922, which also contained 'The Watergaw' by the new poet 'Hugh M'Diarmid', marked a shift in his previously negative attitude: 'One of the objects of "The Scottish Chapbook" is to supplement the campaign of the Vernacular Circle of the London Burns Club for the revival of the Doric.' This was quickly qualified, however: 'I do not support the campaign for the revival of the Doric where the essential diversity-in-unity is forgotten, nor where the tendencies involved are anti-cultural.' (62) By February 1923 the editor's Causerie was attempting 'A Theory of Scots Letters' and a more organised investigation of the potential within the Scots language. The criteria insisted on, however, were still literary effectiveness and modern thought: 'Whatever the potentialities of the Doric may be, however, there cannot be a revival in the real sense of the word . . . unless these potentialities are in accord with the newest and truest tendencies of human thought. . . . If all that the Movement is to achieve is to preserve specimens of Braid Scots, archaic, imitative, belonging to a type of life that has passed and cannot return, in a sort of museum department of our consciousness—set apart from our vital preoccupations—it is a movement which not only cannot claim our support but compels our opposition.' (182)

Although his *Chapbook* Causeries are often unfocused, Grieve is especially interesting in this February Causerie when he defines the creative qualities which, in his persona of MacDiarmid, he was increasingly finding in the vernacular: 'We have been enormously struck by the resemblance—the moral resemblance—between Jamieson's Etymological Dictionary of the Scottish language and James Joyce's *Ulysses*. A *vis comica* that has not yet been liberated lies bound by desuetude and misappreciation in the recesses of the Doric: and its potential uprising would be no less prodigious, uncontrollable, and utterly at variance with conventional morality than was Joyce's tremendous outpouring.' (183) In addition to this link with the modernist Joyce, he finds that 'one of the most distinctive characteristics of the Vernacular, part of its very essence, is its insistent recognition of the body, the senses' (184): a comment given substantiation in the MacDiarmid poem 'Wheesht, Wheesht' to be found on a following page. The Blakean nature of the vernacular, 'the reconciliation it effects between the base and the beautiful, recognising that they are complementary and indispensable to each other' (184) was a quality he was to promote most powerfully in *A Drunk Man Looks at the Thistle*.

By Part II of 'A Theory of Scots Letters', Grieve's conversion to the use of Scots would seem to have been completed: 'The Scots Vernacular is a vast storehouse of just the very peculiar and subtle effects which modern European literature in general is assiduously seeking.' And in the Scottish dimension it is 'a vast unutilised mass of lapsed observation made by minds whose attitudes to experience and whose speculative and imaginative tendencies were quite different from any possible to Englishmen and Anglicised Scots to-day.' (210) By the end of this March Causerie, Scots has replaced English as the medium of the Scottish literary revival: 'Another feature of the Doric . . . is the fashion in which diverse attitudes of mind or shades of temper are telescoped into single words or phrases, investing the whole speech with subtle flavours of irony, commiseration, realism and humour which cannot be reproduced in English. In onomatopoeic effect, too, the Doric has a wider range and infinitely richer resources than English.' (211)

Grieve's mastery of Scots for poetic purposes had been establishing itself throughout this period of the *Scottish Chapbook*'s debate. His account of what he finds of value in the vernacular is an illuminating commentary on his Scots lyrics and on *A Drunk Man Looks at the Thistle* which was yet to come. Most importantly, the qualities he found in the vernacular seemed at one with the qualities to be found in European modernist art—in literature, painting and music. Clearly, for Grieve at this stage, the Scots language was now able to satisfy both the European orientation of the literary renaissance and the need to explore Scottish identity, both literary and cultural.

Having accepted the efficacy of Scots as poetic medium, Grieve seemed to lose interest in the language debate, at least so far as the *Scottish Chapbook* was concerned. First 'A Theory of Scots Letters', then the Causerie itself ended. The periodical ceased publication in December 1923.

Grieve's subsequent critical writing of the 1920s is to be found principally in the *Scottish Nation*, the *Northern Review* and *Contemporary Scottish Studies* (1926). As opposed to the emphasis on poetry in *Scottish Chapbook*, the *Scottish Nation* followed the *New Age*'s pattern of a more widespread coverage of the arts, with Grieve himself writing many of the European literature articles and contributing music criticism and additional international criticism under the pseudonym of Isobel Guthrie. Edwin Muir also contributed to the *Scottish Nation* and in the article 'The Assault on Humanism', an attack on D H Lawrence which provoked a dissenting reply from Grieve, we have a foretaste of the literary and philosophical divergence between the two men which was to colour the language and literature debate of the 1930s.

Like the *Scottish Chapbook*, neither the *Scottish Nation* nor the *Northern Review* was long-lived and by late 1924 Scottish literature was once again without a literary periodical capable of accommodating the new tendencies in poetry and criticism. With hindsight, it is clear that in his attempt to revolutionise Scottish letters, Grieve had taken on an almost impossible task with insufficient resources. Although there were several good supporting players in the Scottish Renaissance cast, the drama needed more principal actors, especially in analytical and literary history roles. Grieve was a splendid propagandist and a master of the provocative phrase, his 'war-like' criticism akin to the Russian kind he advocated in the *Chapbook*'s Causeries. His approach was not analytical, however, but diffuse and generalised—except where the effects he described related to his own use of Scots in his poetry. In his determination to take Scottish literature into the modern world, his writing was often adversarial and insensitively destructive. The negative nature of many of the articles in *Contemporary Scottish Studies*, destructive even when it seemed he had set out to praise, must have alienated many readers and potential financial backers of his various literary enterprises. Yet at the end of an essay one seldom is clear about the *specific* literary criteria by which a writer is condemned or (with qualification) applauded. Too often an argument is lost in a swamp of quotation. We do not find in Grieve the carefully constructed arguments of T S Eliot's early criticism when he similarly sought to change literary sensibilities to accord with his own poetic practice. Nor do we find the kind of historical account of the rise and fall of Scottish literature which Professor W A Craigie provided in his lecture to the London Vernacular Circle, 'The Present State of the Scottish Tongue'[8]: an educational dimension the Renaissance movement badly needed. It is difficult to escape the conclusion that in the early and mid 1920s at least, Grieve's knowledge of Scotland's past literature was scanty. Apart from Burns, his references are principally to contemporary or late nineteenth-century figures. Fiona Macleod (William Sharp) surprisingly receives several flattering mentions, while John Galt finds himself condemned to the Kailyard. Robert Ferguson does not receive even the qualified appreciation extended to Burns. The famous slogan: 'Not Burns—Dunbar' does not itself appear until *Albyn* (1927).

The ending of *A Drunk Man Looks at the Thistle* and the Drunk Man's refusal to take up his Scottish place on the Great Wheel of Life hint at a growing pessimism on Grieve's part with regard to the progress of the Scottish literary revival. Edwin Muir, one of the earliest critics to write perceptively about MacDiarmid's poetry, was to say in *Scott and Scotland* that the poet had received no criticism in Scotland which could help him to assess what he had achieved in such an ambitious work. *To Circumjack Cencrastus* (1930) is the poem in which Grieve/MacDiarmid's struggle with his unresponsive Scottish environment is most fully given expression. In this poem, as in the prose-book *Albyn* and in essays such as 'The Caledonian Antisyzygy and the Gaelic Idea' (1931–2) and 'English Ascendancy in British Literature' (1931), he turned increasingly to the idea of Gaelic and the Catholic Celtic culture of the Scottish Highlands and Irish immigrants in the attempt to heal Scotland's fragmented identity. Yet despite the increase in Gaelic studies and writing in the early twentieth century and despite Grieve's wish to bring Gaelic into the literary revival, the Highland Celtic culture was not easily accessible to a Lowland writer and critic. By 1930 we find the *Cencrastus* poet lamenting that he is 'a pool cut aff frae the sea,/A tree withoot roots that stands/On the ground unsteadily.'[9] By 1930 also Grieve was in London with Compton Mackenzie's *Vox* project and writing to George Ogilvie that 'I ought to have been here years ago.'[10] The Scottish Renaissance movement seemed, temporarily at least, to be marking time.

With Grieve in virtual exile on the small Shetland island of Whalsay after his return to Scotland in 1932, his place in the foreground of Scottish literary and cultural criticism was taken by Edwin Muir and Neil M Gunn. Edwin Muir returned to live in Scotland in 1935, having spent much of the 1920s and early 1930s either in Europe or England. As Orkneyman, he had an ambivalent relationship with what he called his 'second country' and this was a source both of strength and weakness in his writing about Scotland and its problems. Muir's sense of detachment and his European experience brought fresh perspectives to bear on the contemporary Scottish scene, yet he was also sufficiently a Scotsman to understand the nuances of the cultural situation as no total outsider could have understood them. This perceptive detachment is one of the strengths of *Scottish Journey*. On the other hand, his Orkney origins and his consequent sense of linguistic dislocation both from the rich spoken Scots of the Borders in which Hugh MacDiarmid's Scots poetry was based and, to a certain extent, from English also, may have led him to overestimate the significance of language in his prognostications for a Scottish literary revival.

The chief part of Muir's literary and social criticism which relates specifically to Scotland is to be found in the reviews he wrote in the 1930s for Scottish periodicals such as the *Modern Scot* and its successor *Outlook*, the London *Bookman* and *Spectator* and in the two books *Scottish Journey* (1935) and *Scott and Scotland* (1936). Muir's criticism took place in a context of increased interest in Scottish matters within and without Scotland, much of it the result of Grieve/MacDiarmid's literary work in the 1920s. In December 1932 the *Spectator* announced an editorial policy of regular coverage of Scottish affairs, and it is frequently in the *Spectator* that one first finds Muir exploring the social and cultural themes which were to form the arguments of his Scottish books.

Scottish Journey incorporated one series of Muir's investigations of the contemporary and historical situation of Scotland. As in many other ostensible travel books of the period, Muir's journey is an interior journey where description of landscape and incident becomes a metaphor for a deeper psychological and philosophical search, what Grieve/MacDiarmid in the *Islands of Scotland* (1939) was to call the attempt 'to expose through the physical form the spiritual meaning of Scotland today.' (xix)

In *Scottish Journey*, as in the review articles 'The Problem of Scotland' and 'Scotland: That Distressed Area',[11] Muir's concern is with Scotland's decline as a consequence of the loss of national responsibility and cultural identity, a process which he saw as having begun with the Reformation and the Union of the Crowns, and one which was being accelerated in the twentieth century by the increasing centralisation of economic and political decision-making in London. His argument is that the aimlessness and emptiness which he finds in Scottish contemporary life have a deeper source than the growing anonymity which threatens all societies in the modern world. A country such as Scotland is particularly vulnerable in that being no longer a nation, with the tangible political and social institutions related to nationhood, all Scotland has left is 'a distinctly marked style of life; and that is now falling to pieces, for there is no visible and effective power to hold it together.' (25)

In *Scott and Scotland* the loss of the Scots language was to become for Muir the critical aspect of Scotland's struggle to retain what was left of her cultural autonomy, but in *Scottish Journey* he accepts that the adoption of the *English* language need not mean the surrender of one's Scottishness: 'The ability to speak English . . . does not involve any wish or any intention of becoming English or denying the Scottish tradition. And besides, English as it is spoken in Scotland is very different from English, and certainly very full of Scottish character.' (27)

Muir explores Scotland's cultural crisis through manifestations such as the Burns Cult and Kailyard literature, through the vitality of the Borders and their Ballads to a present where 'almost the only thing that remains now is a sentimental legend.' (47) Economic decline is investigated through the slums of Glasgow and its industrial environs and the contrasting but related problem of the unproductive and depopulated Highlands. 'The only desirable form of life' he found on his journey was in that 'erratic fruition', Orkney. (241)

Muir's double conclusion is that 'the real obstacle to the making of a nation out of Scotland lies now in the character of the people, which is a result of their history' (232) and that regeneration must come not through nationalism but socialism: a paradoxical conclusion which seems to war with the need for the resolution of the Scottish identity question which his investigation of Scotland's cultural malaise in the book has demonstrated.

Scott and Scotland followed *Scottish Journey* one year later and transferred its cultural and social/economic investigations into a predominantly literary context. In *Literature and Oatmeal* (1935), a companion volume in the *Voice of Scotland* series, William Power had titled his first chapter: 'Does Literature Mean Anything to Scotland?' Here we find Muir asking, as critics in the early part of the century had done, 'whether Scotland could be said to have a literature.' (1)

The arguments of *Scott and Scotland* are anticipated by Muir's *Spectator* review of R L Mackie's *A Book of Scottish Verse* (20 Apr 1934) and his article 'Literature in Scotland' (25 May 1934), as they are also to some extent by George Blake's *The Heart of Scotland* (1934). In 'Literature in Scotland' Muir discusses the related problems of 'a renaissance without a centre' and the viability of the Scots language: 'that Scots will ever be used again as an independent language capable of fulfilling all the purposes of poetry and prose is, I should think, very doubtful.' (823)

Scott and Scotland is a provocative book, but it is in many ways unsatisfactory as a critique of Scottish literature. Muir's central thesis is that, as a consequence of the decline of the Scots language in the wake of the Calvinist-dominated Reformation and the Unions of Crowns and Parliaments, 'Scotsmen feel in one language and think in another . . . their emotions turn to the Scottish tongue with all its associations of local sentiment, and their minds to a standard English which for them is almost bare of associations other than those of the classroom.' The literary consequences of this dissociation have been severe: 'For the major forms of poetry rise from a collision between emotion and intellect on a plane where both meet on equal terms; and it can never come into existence where the poet feels in one language and thinks in another.' (21)

This theory is strikingly similar to T S Eliot's concept of the dissociation of sensibility in 'the mind of England between the time of Donne or Lord Herbert of Cherbury and the time of Tennyson and Browning.'[12] Muir admired Eliot's criticism and one can see the influence of Eliot's impersonality in art theory in Muir's 1924 *Latitudes* essay 'A Plea for Psychology in Literary Criticism'. It may be that he was unconsciously influenced by Eliot also when he came to examine Scottish literary development, and that the dissociation theory answered his own sense of linguistic dislocation, just as the impersonality of art concept had appealed to his earlier need to distance himself as poet from the problems of his personal life.

Muir over-emphasises the linguistic disparity between Scots and English in the development of his argument and ignores a linguistic *similarity* which made the adoption of the English 'sudroun' only too easy when it became socially and economically politic to do so; a similarity which, if acknowledged, would have rendered his extreme view of the Scottish dissociation of sensibility unviable.

There is a similar simplistic quality in Muir's assertion that Coleridge's criticism of Shakespeare was a product of 'the most close communion between the critic's mind and the poet's through the medium of a single language' (34), while a 'Scottish writer dealing with the poetry of Burns in English . . . cannot use Burns's language' and 'has no working standard, therefore, for measuring the excellence which Burns attained in it.' (32) Such a view takes no account of the changes in the *English* language and sensibility from the experimental and unsystematised language-use of the Elizabethans through the neo-classicism of the late seventeenth and eighteenth centuries to the 'rediscovery' of imagination and feeling in the Romantic period. Coleridge, writing in the early nineteenth century, was at least as distanced from Shakespeare as the twentieth century Scottish critic, writing in Scottish-English, is from Burns. Had Muir used the fifteenth century Makars as example, his charge of academic criticism in the Scottish context might have had more substance. However, like MacDiarmid's poetry in the twentieth century, much of Burns's most successful verse was written in what David Daiches has described as 'an English tipped with Scots.'[13] Apart from the need to use a glossary more frequently, the twentieth century reader should not be far behind his eighteenth century counterpart in the understanding of Burns.

Muir's charges against Calvinism are also difficult to sustain—in the literary sphere at least. While the ideological narrowness of the Scottish Kirk and the break with Scotland's cultural past which the Reformation effected have certainly had an adverse effect on the country's cultural life, one can hardly ascribe Scotland's partial poetry tradition to the Kirk's suppression of poetic drama, as Muir does here. And with Wyatt, Surrey, Sidney and Spenser as witnesses, it is difficult to accept that before poetic drama in England one finds only 'the simple lyric with all its natural thoughtless grace.' (25) As with

Grieve's limited knowledge of Scotland's past literature in his criticism of the early 1920s, Muir is here historically weak.

Muir is no more persuasive when he leaves the past for the present. He ignores the changed context produced by the Scottish Literary Renaissance movement and Grieve/MacDiarmid's attempt to restore Scots as the poetic medium as he applies to the contemporary situation the dissociation theory he had previously discussed in relation to Burns and Scott. No distinction is made between those who, like MacDiarmid, developed literary Scots from a natural spoken-Scots base, and those whose natural language was Scottish-English and whose adoption of Scots for literary purposes might be truly described as 'translation'—even if the reverse side of the translation coin referred to by John Galt in the early nineteenth century.[14] Nor does Muir acknowledge the philosophical, intellectual attributes of MacDiarmid's Scots lyrics: a feature which in Muir's view of the language divide should not exist. His conclusion—which, stated as it is at the outset of his investigation, compromises his ability to conduct an objective analysis—is that 'a Scottish writer who wishes to achieve some approximation to completeness has no choice except to absorb the English tradition.' If, however, he 'roots himself deliberately in Scotland, he will find there . . . neither an organic community to round off his conceptions, nor a major literary tradition to support him, nor even a faith among the people themselves that a Scottish literature is possible or desirable, nor any opportunity, finally, of making a livelihood by his work.' (15)

Although Muir's pessimistic literary assessment caused a breach with Grieve/MacDiarmid which was never healed, the latter part of his comment had already been given poetic expression in *A Drunk Man Looks at the Thistle* and *To Circumjack Cencrastus*, as it had also in the progress of Grieve's career as poet and critic. Like Muir, the Drunk Man found when he confronted the Wheel that

> A Scottish poet maun assume
> The burden o' his people's doom,
> And dee to brak' their livin' tomb.
>
> Mony ha'e tried, but a' ha'e failed.
> Their sacrifice has nocht availed.
> Upon the thistle they're impaled.
>
> You maun choose but gin ye'd see
> Anither category ye
> Maun tine your nationality.[15]

The predicament described arises, however, as Muir himself had demonstrated in *Scottish Journey*, principally from the loss of national sovereignty and confident consciousness of identity. Similarly the adoption of the English *language* does not necessarily mean the adoption of the English *tradition*— as Grieve had argued before his conversion to the use of Scots, and as Muir himself had accepted in *Scottish Journey*. However stimulating his views have proved to be to later critics, Muir's assessment was not logical in the face of the language conditions which pertained in Scotland in the 1930s and in relation to the identity crisis which he had uncovered in *Scottish Journey*.

Muir's views were, however, similar to those of the novelist Leslie Mitchell (Lewis Grassic Gibbon). In *Scottish Scene*, the book which he wrote jointly with Grieve/MacDiarmid in 1934, Mitchell was dismissive of the Scottish Literary Renaissance, finding that 'Modern Scotland . . . is a nation almost entirely lacking a Scottish literary output.' (199) As with Muir, language was for Mitchell the critical factor. In his view, a Scottish writer using English '*translated* himself'; Neil Gunn was merely 'a brilliant novelist from Scotshire', while Hugh MacDiarmid and Lewis Spence, both writing in Scots, were 'the two solitary lights in modern Scots Literature.' (196, 200, 203) While describing his own attempts as Lewis Grassic Gibbon to rework the English language for his Scottish purposes, he was cautious about his ultimate success: 'Whether his technique is adequate to compass and express the life of an industrialised Scots town in all its complexity is yet to be demonstrated.' (205) Despite his inclusion as a writer of the Scottish Renaissance on the basis of *A Scots Quair* and his Scottish short stories, Mitchell was never involved in the Renaissance critical debate to any extent and his affiliations were with socialism rather than nationalism.

The Highland novelist Neil M Gunn was quick to criticise Edwin Muir's conclusions in *Scott and Scotland* in his review of the book in the *Scots Magazine* of October 1936. Unlike Muir, Gunn was securely rooted in his Scottish environment and unambiguously supportive of the principal aims of the Scottish Literary Renaissance movement, although he himself used English in his work. Language, for him, did not occupy the central position that it did for Muir, Mitchell and Grieve.

Gunn's criticism is to be found principally in the articles he wrote for the *Scots Magazine* in the 1930s and early 1940s, many of which relate to the social, economic and cultural decline of the Highlands, a topic explored also in his novels of the period. Like Muir, Gunn was acute in isolating the cultural and social implications in a work of art and, conversely, the effect on the artist of the fragmented cultural situation which existed in Scotland. He was, however, unlike Muir and like Grieve, a nationalist who believed that the resolution of the identity crisis could come only through Scotland taking responsibility for its own affairs.

Several of Gunn's *Scots Magazine* articles explore his conception of nationalism as 'a growing and blossoming from our own roots',[16] a definition which relates to his belief in the importance of tradition and a rootedness in one's own culture. This is the theme of 'Highland Games' (1931) where the heroes are not men apart but 'of the people, doing the day's tasks about steading or shore.' (414) In 'The Ferry of the Dead' (1937) the Gaelic Mod is dismissed as standing for 'the remembrance of things past' because it 'does not envisage a future in terms of that past.' (20) Gunn's contribution to the *Scots Magazine* symposium 'Preserving the Scottish Tongue: A Legacy and How to Use It' (1935) concluded that his bequest would go to 'whatever body existed with the object of keeping Scotland the nation alive.' For 'whenever the conception of the nation is reborn, immediately everything that distinguishes that nation is reborn, including in particular its forms of expression.' (110)

The forces which were working against keeping Scotland the nation alive were investigated in fishing articles such as 'One Fisher Went Sailing . . .: The Plight of the West Coast Herring Ports' (1937) and 'The Family Boat: Its Future in Scottish Fishing' (1937) while the problems of the depopulated Highlands were the subject of ' "Gentlemen: The Tourist!"—The New Highland Toast.' (1937) Like Muir in *Scottish Journey*, Gunn in these articles points to the cultural consequences of a loss of nationhood and responsibility for taking one's own decisions, while he lays bare also the economic consequences of increased centralisation and the application of political and economic decisions which go against the traditional ways of life of the people. For Gunn, a nation's traditions are irrevocably linked to its life and health and provide also the means through which nations can meet in true internationalism: 'A nation's traditions are the natural inspirations of its people. . . . And it is only when a man is moved by the traditions and music and poetry of his own land that he is in a position to comprehend those of any other land, for already he has the eyes of sympathy and the ears of understanding.'[17]

Although Gunn's *investigation* of Highland decline therefore had many parallels with Muir's similar investigation of Scottish decline, Gunn's response to his findings was much more positive than was Muir's. While Muir could find little hope for Scotland's future, Gunn set out his belief in Scotland and its traditions and pointed in articles and novels to the significance of these traditions for the way we lead our lives.

In the area of literature also Gunn's approach was a positive one. Articles such as 'Literature: Class or National?' from *Outlook* (1936), 'Tradition and Magic in the Work of Lewis Grassic Gibbon' (1938) and 'The Theatre Society of Scotland' (1938) from the *Scots Magazine* all, like the 1946 article 'The Novel at Home' stress the importance for the writer of working out of his own culture. 'Literature: Class or National?' also takes up the question of nationalism and internationalism in a literary context and dismisses the notion that one can have a vital literature of universal or international significance which disregards national origins. This argument runs counter to Muir's suggestion that the only way forward is to reject what is left of the Scottish tradition and adopt the English. Gunn points to the Irish playwright Sean O'Casey who 'out of conflict in the national spirit . . . created his vivid drama' and to the Scottish Leslie Mitchell/Lewis Grassic Gibbon who 'had to come back to his own country, his own people, before what moved him so deeply received its profoundest expression.' (57, 55)

Despite Mitchell's own hesitancy about his language experiments, Gunn's comments about language are very pertinent to the critical debate of the 1920s and 1930s. In 'Tradition and Magic in the Work of Lewis Grassic Gibbon', he finds that while the magic of *Sunset Song* springs from its 'life's being rooted in the breeding soil of tradition,' the medium for this magical tradition is the English language reworked to achieve 'not a new language but an old rhythm' and a rhythm which is 'utterly un-English' and 'of the soil of which Mitchell writes.' (29, 30)

Gunn's cultural criticism is less literary in its orientation than that of Muir and Grieve. It can nevertheless be seen to be of much significance in the literary revival debates of this inter-war period. His comments on Mitchell's reworking of the English language for his Scottish purposes, together with his own novel-writing in English about essential Highland life and traditions, point to the fact that there can be a middle way in the language controversy between the 'polar twins' of Grieve's insistence on Scots and Muir's viewpoint that if the Scots language is lost, then both English and the English *tradition* must be adopted. Gunn's investigation of the relationship between a nation's traditions and its life demonstrates that a nation's culture consists of more than language, however important language may be. And although as critic Grieve for long continued to insist on the necessity of using Scots as a literary medium, as poet his own practice increasingly involved the use of English, thus giving support to Gunn's views.

Gunn continued throughout the war period to explore Scotland's cultural situation in article and novel. Muir, on the other hand, would seem to have been taken aback by the furore aroused by *Scott and Scotland* and his articles on Scottish matters subsequently became fewer in number. Those he wrote were noticeably less provocative in attitude, distanced in a way that the involved writer of *Scottish Journey* and *Scott and Scotland* was not, to some extent accepting the Scots and their country as 'characters'. Grieve, though still in Shetland in the late 1930s, was active in his rejection of Muir's language views and by 1938 he was once more in business as editor, his *Voice of Scotland* having a short life before it was temporarily halted by the outbreak of war. The outcome of the critical debate had therefore not yet become clear at the end of the 1930s. What is clear fifty years later is that the vitality and variety of creative writing in all three of Scotland's languages in the post-war years are in large measure due to the vigour of the critical, no less than the creative activities of this inter-war period.

NOTES

Numbers in parenthesis after quotations relate to pages of books immediately referred to.

1 See *Aberdeen Free Press* correspondence, *The Letters of Hugh MacDiarmid*, Alan Bold (ed) (London, 1984), pp 749–56.

2 C M Grieve, quoted in Duncan Glen, *Hugh MacDiarmid (Christopher Murray Grieve) and the Scottish Renaissance* (Edinburgh & London, 1964), pp 73, 78.

3 Ibid, p 74.

4 C M Grieve, *Scottish Chapbook* Vol 1 No. 4, November 1922, p 91.

5 C M Grieve, *Scottish Chapbook* Vol 1 No. 2, September 1922, p 43.

6 C M Grieve, *Scottish Chapbook* Vol 1 No. 3, October 1922, p 62.

7 *The Letters of Hugh MacDiarmid*, pp 751, 755.

8 W A Craigie, 'The Present State of the Scottish Tongue', *Burns Chronicle* No. XXXII, January 1923, pp 26–38.

9 Hugh MacDiarmid (C M Grieve), 'To Circumjack Cencrastus', *Hugh MacDiarmid: Complete Poems 1920–1976*, Michael Grieve and W R Aitken (eds) (London, 1978), p 191.
10 *The Letters of Hugh MacDiarmid*, p 101.
11 Edwin Muir, 'The Problem of Scotland', *Spectator* 2 November 1934, p 676; 'Scotland: That Distressed Area', *Criterion* XV no. LIX, January 1936, pp 330–32.
12 T S Eliot, 'The Metaphysical Poets' (1921), *Selected Essays*, 3rd enlarged edn (London, 1954), p 287.
13 David Daiches, *The Paradox of Scottish Culture: The Eighteenth Century Experience* (London, 1964), p 88.
14 *See* John Galt, 'Biographical Sketch of John Wilson', *Scottish Descriptive Poems*, J Leyden (ed) (London, 1803), p 14.
15 Hugh MacDiarmid, *Complete Poems*, p 165.
16 Neil M Gunn, 'Highland Games', *Scots Magazine* XV No. 6, September 1931, p 414.
17 Neil M Gunn, 'Nationalism and Internationalism', *Scots Magazine* XV No. 3, June 1931, p 187.

FURTHER READING

Blake, George, *The Heart of Scotland* (London, 1934)

Buchan, John (ed), *The Northern Muse* (London, 1924)

Craigie, W A, 'The Present State of the Scottish Tongue', *Burns Chronicle* XXXII, January 1923, pp 26–38

Gibbon, Lewis Grassic and Hugh MacDiarmid, *Scottish Scene or The Intelligent Man's Guide to Albyn* (London, 1934)

Glen, Duncan, *Hugh MacDiarmid (Christopher Murray Grieve) and the Scottish Renaissance*, (Edinburgh & London, 1964)

Gunn, Neil M, *Landscape and Light: Essays by Neil M Gunn*, Alastair McCleery (ed) (Aberdeen, 1987)

McCulloch, Margery, 'Edwin Muir's Scottish Journey 1935–1980', *Scottish Review* 17, February 1980, pp 47–52

—— 'Edwin Muir and Scotland', *Akros* Special Edwin Muir Number, 16, No. 47, August 1981, pp 67–81

—— 'Neil M Gunn: Tradition and the Essence of Nationalism', *Cencrastus*, June 1987

MacDiarmid, Hugh (C M Grieve), *Northern Numbers*, Edinburgh, 1920; Second Series, Edinburgh, 1921; Third Series, Montrose, 1922

—— *Scottish Chapbook*, C M Grieve (ed), Aug 1922–Dec 1923

—— *Scottish Nation*, C M Grieve (ed), May 1923–Dec 1923

—— *Northern Review*, C M Grieve (ed), May 1924–Sept 1924

—— *Contemporary Scottish Studies* (London, 1926)

—— *Albyn, or Scotland and the Future* (London, 1927)

—— *At the Sign of the Thistle* (London, 1934)

—— *Voice of Scotland*, C M Grieve (ed), June 1938-Aug 1939

—— *The Islands of Scotland* (London, 1939)

—— *The Uncanny Scot: A Selection of Prose by Hugh MacDiarmid*, Kenneth Buthlay (ed) (London, 1968)

—— *Selected Essays of Hugh MacDiarmid*, Duncan Glen (ed) (London, 1969)

—— *The Letters of Hugh MacDiarmid*, Alan Bold (ed) (London, 1984)

Muir, Edwin, *Scottish Journey* (London, 1935)

——*Scott and Scotland: The Predicament of the Scottish Writer* (London, 1936)

——*Edwin Muir: Uncollected Scottish Criticism*, Andrew Noble (ed) (London, 1982)

Power, William, *Scotland and the Scots* (Edinburgh, 1934)

—— *Literature and Oatmeal* (London, 1935)

Ramsay, M P, *Calvin and Art: Considered in Relation to Scotland* (Edinburgh & London, 1938)

Smith, G Gregory, *Scottish Literature: Character and Influence* (London, 1919)

Thomson, David Cleghorn (ed), *Scotland in Quest of Her Youth* (Edinburgh, 1932)

Chapter 9

Edwin Muir

RITCHIE ROBERTSON

Despite its simple language, Edwin Muir's poetry is often enigmatic. Many readers, therefore, prefer to approach it through his autobiography. Muir's direct, unadorned, meditative style makes this work seem artless and transparent. We encounter a naturally pious man searching undogmatically for the 'fable' underlying the 'story', the biographical contingencies, of his life, and we tend to overlook the artifice with which Muir has shaped his recollections. To link 'story' with 'fable' he adopts the genre of the crisis-autobiography, inaugurated by St Augustine's *Confessions*. Such books derive their structure from a crisis of faith that the author has recently experienced; the author interprets his past as leading up to the crisis, and distinguishes sharply between his new life and his unregenerate previous life. Muir's crisis came in February 1939, when he first had what he called 'something like a sense of the presence of God'.[1] The first version of his autobiography, *The Story and the Fable*, was written in the aftermath of this experience, and narrates his earlier life as a preparation for it.

One of the narrative models Muir uses is the Christian story of fall and redemption. Orkney, where Muir was born in 1887, represents prelapsarian happiness. The fall is his family's move to Glasgow in the winter of 1901–2. They could not adjust to urban squalor and economic competition. Within five years Muir's parents and two of his brothers died. The young Muir, earning his living as a clerk, is depicted in retrospect as compensating for solitude and misery by Nietzschean fantasies of intellectual and moral superiority. The spiritual arrogance of this phase serves as the antithesis to the Christian humility Muir had acquired at the time of writing. Marriage (to Willa Anderson in 1919), psychoanalysis, Continental travel, and the first steps in writing poetry, are portrayed as stages in a journey of self-discovery which culminates in the discovery of faith. *The Story and the Fable* ends with a selection of diary entries, indicating that his religious quest is not securely over; the later version, *An Autobiography*, replaces these with additional reminiscences which recount the deepening of Muir's faith but blur the underlying narrative pattern.

Another narrative model comes from Muir's interpretation of history. Orkney exemplifies pre-industrial society: a small-scale, close-knit community, its past recorded in collective memory, with a popular culture represented by oral poetry. Glasgow embodies industrial mass society, in which relentless competition destroys social bonds and reduces people to helpless monads. In this pattern, Muir's Nietzscheanism illustrates how the denizens of this soulless society compensate for their weakness by embracing pseudo-religions. His subsequent progress via Socialism to Christianity gradually refines his conception of what society might be. In discovering faith, he also comes to understand the mystical bonds that hold all human beings together in an invisible community.

With this perspective, Muir the autobiographer could hardly represent his earlier self faithfully. In Willa Muir's memoirs (*Belonging*, 1968) the young Muir appears, not as a neurotic introvert, but as a lively, witty womaniser, with an engagingly bookish streak. His early writings, under the pen-name 'Edward Moore', are assertively 'modern'. His heroes were Nietzsche, Ibsen, Dostoyevsky. He kept up with contemporary literature and thought by reading *The New Age*, edited by A R Orage, in which he published first the aphorisms headed 'We Moderns' (1916–18), later issued in book form, then the notes on current affairs headed 'Our Generation' (1920–2). The political philosophy advocated by *The New Age* was Guild Socialism, which wanted workers to manage their own industries through guilds developed from the existing trade unions. This provided Muir with a middle way between Marxism, whose collectivism he rejected, and Fabianism, which, he thought, aimed merely to bring industrial society under new management without altering its fabric. Later, like Pound and MacDiarmid, he was to follow *The New Age* in adopting the economic theory of Social Credit.

In the callow but brilliant *We Moderns*, Muir places himself in the tradition of emancipatory polemic represented by Heine, Ibsen, and Nietzsche. Like other eclectic 'advanced thinkers' of the Edwardian period, Muir believes it possible to combine Nietzscheanism with Socialism, Edward Carpenter's sexual liberation with Bergson's 'creative unconscious'. Muir's Socialism appears in his attack on industrial mass society as a gigantic machine holding both the worker and the employer in its grip, and in his demand for economic emancipation. Mostly, however, he conducts cultural rather than social criticism, attacking the complacency and hypocrisy of his society in the name of an individualistic humanism.

Muir criticises the secularised modern age for its artistic and spiritual impoverishment. While the great art of the past created images of human possibility in myth and tragedy, literature has now lost contact with tradition and declined into shallow realism or decorative aestheticism. Religion has become ossified into doctrines of 'Original Sin', which glorify mediocrity, disparage greatness, and try to repress the instincts. Instead, Muir exalts pride, self-discipline, and 'Creative Love'. This seems to be an amalgam of Nietzsche's Dionysiac ecstasy and Bergson's life-force. It proceeds 'from the very well spring, the very central ego of Man, out of the unconscious, the innocent, the real'.[2] Modern man must return to this source for spiritual renewal.

This essentially religious concern also underlies the comments on current events in 'Our Generation'. Muir's targets include unemployment, the cruelties of the legal system, the venality and triviality of the press, and the antisocial destructiveness of capitalism: 'Financial lawlessness and freebootery are the practical expression in our society of animality, of pre-human impulses and pre-human values, just as law and civilisation are the practical expression of humanity.'[3] In placing greed and self-interest above social ties, capitalism denies man's spiritual nature. Organised Christianity has meanwhile declined into 'hocus-pocus'.[4] It no longer tries to provide society with a living spiritual centre. Its role in interpreting life, and its therapeutic function, have passed to art and psychoanalysis. Deploring the banality of contemporary literature, Muir observes caustically: 'A few bad works about the destiny of man would come as a relief.'[5] Psychoanalysis, he argues, can not only increase our understanding of society and culture, but also provide an equivalent for the experience of spiritual rebirth. 'Psychology has rediscovered religion; for religion is just an art of the soul which we have forgotten.'[6]

When he made these claims, Muir was undergoing a Jungian analysis. This began releasing his imaginative powers, first in mythopoeic dreams, later in the poems based on them, published as 'Ballad of Rebirth' and 'Ballad of Eternal Life' in *First Poems*. Two years' residence in Prague, Germany, Austria, and Italy (1922–4) helped to expand his horizons. He learnt German and immersed himself in the meditative lyrics of Hofmannsthal and the visionary hymns of Hölderlin. His own poetry, however, was still stumbling and imitative, and the new themes he was exploring are best revealed in his criticism and his novels.

Muir's critical method is to illuminate individual authors by subsuming them under concepts, often arranged antithetically. Thus the important three-part essay 'The Meaning of Romanticism' contrasts romantic and classical representations of the world; and 'North and South', one of the most interesting essays collected in *Latitudes*, contrasts the distinctive qualities of Germanic and Romance literatures. Perhaps the most impressive result of this method is *The Structure of the Novel*, a typology of ways of representing time and space through narrative structure, which resembles the contemporaneous studies of the novel by Lukács and Bakhtin.[7] Muir may well have been the first British critic to explore how the ideological content of a literary work is implicit in its form.

'The Meaning of Romanticism' reveals a shift in Muir's thinking. It is an attempt to understand the situation of modern writers, including himself, by examining their relation to Romanticism. Visionaries like Wordsworth and Hölderlin responded to the secularisation of society by imagining new destinies for mankind in a transfigured world. Their successors, like Heine, the early Ibsen, and Nietzsche, degraded these visions by trying to imagine such destinies over-literally. In thus criticising his former idols, Muir is repudiating his own earlier vague faith in emancipation. Worse still, the Socialist utopias of Morris and Wells denuded Romantic visions of all their spiritual content. The modernism of Eliot, Joyce, and Lawrence, examined sceptically by Muir in *Transition*, has reacted against Romanticism without breaking new ground. It represents no more than a transition to some new, still unimaginable vision of the world.

Muir himself is seeking a new way of viewing the world *sub specie aeter-*

nitatis. In the 1920s he is fascinated by literature depicting dramatic crises, in which the intensity of the protagonist's passion or terror seems momentarily to fix him in a timeless attitude, excluding reflection or moral judgement, and to evoke a background of eternity. Muir finds such dramatic intensity in Shakespearean tragedy, and also in the Scottish ballads, in which life is seen 'on a greater and more intense level, as a vision of sin, tremendous, fleeting, always the same and always to be the same, set against some unchangeable thing'.[8] Muir's long poem *Chorus of the Newly Dead* tries to evoke such crises. Its seven anonymous, archetypal characters (the Hero, the Harlot, the Mystic, etc.), recall crucial moments which seem to encapsulate the meaning of their recently ended lives. And all three of his novels are built round crises in the lives of their protagonists.

The Marionette illustrates Muir's interest in madness, which he had begun exploring through the Idiot in the *Chorus*. Muir seems to suspect that the heightened and simplified perceptions of the insane may disclose truths unavailable to the sane. His protagonist here is a mentally retarded Austrian boy, Hans, who becomes obsessed with the puppet-play of *Faust*. Hans himself acts the role of Faust with a marionette representing Gretchen. In a fit of rage, Hans smashes the Gretchen marionette. After suffering a nervous collapse, he dreams that the 'dead' Gretchen, imagined as a human being, returns to life and walks with him through a green landscape at sunrise, still dressed in her white grave-clothes. These actions are intended to be analogous to Faust's betrayal of Gretchen and his subsequent forgiveness and reunion with her. The analogy implies that on some level Hans has undergone the experience of sin and redemption. Besides this religious core, the novel abounds with psychologically intriguing images. Role-playing and mirror-reflections help Hans to construct his personality and defend it against schizophrenic divisions and fantasies of persecution. It is Muir's most ambitious attempt to approach religion via psychology.

The Three Brothers, set in Reformation Scotland, centres on the conflict between good and evil. This conflict is located partly in the psyche of the hero David Blackadder, and played out in his symbolic dreams; partly in the antagonism between David and his brother Archie, an amoral, greedy creature without fraternal loyalties or spiritual aspirations. The third brother, Sandy, represents the natural man, sensual but with a confused striving towards the good. These spiritual conflicts take place amid political and religious turmoil. Calvinism is portrayed as a totalitarian ideology too shallow to resolve the problem of evil which obsesses David. At the end he has a vision of the Last Judgement; but his spiritual unrest remains unappeased.

In *Poor Tom*, set realistically in the Glasgow of his youth, Muir borrows some modernist techniques from Hermann Broch's *Die Schlafwandler*, which the Muirs had translated as *The Sleepwalkers*. Like Broch, Muir varies dramatic scenes with essayistic reflections, and preserves an ironic distance from his characters. Since Tom's death is seen approaching from the outset, there is virtually no plot. The title, taken from *King Lear*, announces a portrayal of 'unaccommodated man', and the loosely connected scenes illustrate Muir's view of man as mortal and guilty. Tom's death is indirectly the fault of his brother Mansie, who took Tom's girl-friend from him; Tom's subsequent heavy drinking led to an accident which caused the brain tumour from which he dies. Thus Muir shows guilt arising from the unavoidable conflict among people's material and sexual appetites. At first Mansie's commitment to Socialism, presented ironically as a delusory substitute for religion, conveniently blinds him to his guilt. But a mystical vision by Tom's death-bed humbles him and teaches him that redemption from guilt is only possible within an eternal order of things.

Fiction led Muir from psychological to social themes and enabled him to portray the inadequacy of secular ideologies to supply man's spiritual needs. In the 1930s, caught like other intellectuals between the ideologies of the far left and the far right, he had to define his position. Politically he remained convinced that economic justice and individual liberty could only be reconciled by non-Marxist Socialism. He rejected Scottish Nationalism on the grounds that without a Socialist economic order it was frivolous, while the achievement of Socialism would make it superfluous. 'I am quite clear in my mind,' he writes in 1939, 'that society must change, that Capitalism must be transcended; but if the change comes through the terrible Marxist machine of Materialist Determination, it will be a major calamity, for it denies the soul, and there cannot be a more fundamental denial than that.'[9] But he devoted less energy to political activity than to working out the religious humanism expressed in his essays and poems from the 1930s onwards.

To understand the modern world, Muir went back to its origins in the Renaissance, when the traditional ties holding together medieval society were weakened by individualism and religious dissension. Greater appreciation of the individual produced an enriched Christian humanism, represented for Muir by Rabelais. Rabelais accepts as good the sensual appetites of his natural man, Panurge, and civilises them by admitting Panurge to the humanist circle around Pantagruel. But the political individualism of Machiavelli rejected tradition as a moral sanction and taught rulers to gain their ends by a strictly rational calculation of the means. This amoral rationality also supplied capitalism with its methods and with its conception of 'economic man' as placing self-interest above social loyalties and responsibilities. The poem 'Scotland 1941' summarises this process and portrays it as a descent into hell. The medieval 'rustic day' ended when Calvinism 'fell[ed] the ancient oak of loyalty' and carved out the 'towering pulpit of the Golden Calf' which is modern Scotland, with its 'cities burning in their pit' (97-8).[10]

Besides individualism, the Renaissance also inaugurated totalitarianism. Muir's research for his biography of John Knox made him especially attentive to Calvinism, in which he saw numerous analogies to twentieth-century Communism.[11] Both replace the authority of tradition with that of a central text; both aim at a rationally planned society; both are deterministic; and both operate with a reduced version of humanity. Totalitarianism rejects the humanist view of man as both natural and spiritual. Twentieth-century totalitarian ideologies resemble such writers as Lawrence and Hemingway in glorifying man's animal energies and appetites. While Communism does try to teach the natural man, Fascism exalts his animality, regarding intellect and spirit as useless appendages. Muir sets Christian humanism against totalitarianism in 'The Incarnate One', written some years after he had witnessed the Communist takeover of Czechoslovakia in 1948. The medieval dream of 'Christ, man and creature in their inner day' has been threatened first by 'Calvin's kirk' and now by the spreading 'cold empire' of Communism, both based on 'the fleshless word' and 'the abstract man' (228).

Muir's task, therefore, was to preserve in poetry the humanist image of man. At first he was hampered by clumsy technique. From his favourite English poet, Wordsworth, he acquired a poetic model in which the 'I' utters reflections stimulated by a landscape which serves as their symbolic correlative. In his early poetry, he tries to convey his meaning through visionary landscapes, but often fails through verbosity and over-explicitness. He seems to have learnt how to transpose thought into image from Kafka, whose work he discovered in 1929. He particularly admired the expression of thought through images in Kafka's aphorisms. For example, Kafka condenses the theme of *The Trial* into the aphorism: 'The hunting dogs are still playing in the courtyard, but the hare will not escape them, no matter how fast it may already be flying through the woods.'[12] This reappears in Muir as 'The hunting roads ran on/To round the flying hill/And bring the quarry home' (140). It has become part of a system of symbols with shifting meanings ('road', 'day', 'harvest', 'wood') which requires, but has hardly yet received, the kind of patient exegesis that has been devoted to Kafka or Rilke. Muir's poetry is most successful when precise thought has been translated into symbols set in complex relationships. Since such poetry must be cryptic, however, Muir has unfortunately become best known by more accessible but inferior poems like 'The Combat', with its over-obvious allegorical images, or 'The Horses' and the mawkish 'The Good Town', in which pastoral imagery is awkwardly superimposed upon recent or foreseeable history.

The success of Muir's poetry also depends on the verse-form used. Pentameters generally tempt him into verbal padding and flaccid rhythms. But he excels in trimeters and tetrameters whose metre shifts between iambs and trochees with a flexibility that defies rigid scansion. Their concision permits the translation of thought into image, with occasional unobtrusive word-play ('a little paradise/Held in the world's vice', 159). At times Muir abandons imagery for bare statement such as he had praised in the Scottish ballads: it is no small feat for a poem to end with the words 'Pride and fidelity and love' (220) without being embarrassing.

Except in some early ballads, Muir did not try to write in Scots. He justifies this by arguing, in *Scott and Scotland*, that since Knox's decision to write in English and the acceptance of the English Bible, the use of English for intellectual purposes has given Scots a divided sensibility. They feel in one language and think in another. Their poetry is chiefly ballad and lyric; their prose is either bloodless or baroquely extravagant (Carlyle). He therefore maintains that a Scottish literature expressing a full range of experience can only be written in Gaelic or English, like the literature of the Irish Renaissance. Whatever the truth of this (and Muir does not even mention the work of Grassic Gibbon and MacDiarmid), it describes Muir's own practice. He blamed the Scots' divided sensibility for the fleshless rationality of Calvinism and the sentimentalism of the Kailyard. By contrast, his humanism required that reason should remain linked to feeling. He therefore needed, and found, a literary voice that served for both prose and poetry, expressing emotion and argument with the same simplicity and warmth.

Muir's poetry of the 1930s portrays the world of secular ideologies in which time is unrelated to eternity. Mankind becomes 'the mock of Time,/While lost and empty lies Eternity' (48). In secular history, no spiritual goal can be reached. Hence progress seems illusory, a 'stationary journey' (40, 57). Nietzsche's concept of eternal recurrence provides no escape from time. It merely trivialises dramatic events (shipwreck, crucifixion, murder) into a 'great non-stop heraldic show' (104). Secular ideologies presuppose a deterministic world, 'patrolled by stars and planets' (59). They are vindictive, seeing history as a record of 'wrath' ('The slowly twisting vine/Scribbled with wrath the stone', 140), without mercy for victims: repeatedly 'time's deer is slain' (61). They are destructive: civilisation is being 'eaten out by time' (76) and falling under the bureaucratic tyranny of 'men obsessed and neat' (77). Yet they do not satisfy even their adherents. Despite their utopian promises ('And when Time is grown/Beneath your countless hands/They say this kingdom shall/Be stable and beautiful', 86), people cannot stop blindly battering at the unanswering stronghold of eternity.

History acquires meaning and value only from the Incarnation, the unique entry of eternity into time. 'If Christ live not, nothing is there/For sorrow or for praise' (116). This provides assurance that a transcendent reality does exist, though it cannot be attained in history. The longest and most philosophical of Muir's mature poems, 'The Journey Back', concludes that the beginning and end of history are inaccessible, except insofar as they are always present at each moment, which is history's 'perpetual end and flawless bourne'. History does have purpose, but as a race whose 'prize is elsewhere,/Here only to be run for'. Its transcendent goal is visible as 'the golden harvester' (175), i.e. the harvest moon lit by the rays of the sun which has sunk below the horizon. Eternity can be apprehended only as 'double absence' (239) in time.

It is therefore pointless to seek an earthly utopia at either the beginning or the end of history. The dwellers 'outside Eden' do not try to recolonise Paradise but are content to see 'the radiant hill' (212) in the distance. The pilgrims in 'The City' are amazed to find farmers tranquilly living outside Jerusalem, and press on towards their utopian goal, only to unleash centuries of warfare (107–8).

Many poems depict a pastoral landscape, not as a blueprint for a regression to pre-industrial society, but, as in all literary pastoral, as a metaphor for certain human values. In Muir's pastoral, life is structured by the agricultural year, culminating in harvest which symbolises the consummation available only in eternity. Man and animal share an 'archaic companionship' (247) within 'an order natural and wise' (107). The landscape they inhabit is rough and unfriendly, 'a difficult country' (238) of 'famished field and blackened tree' (227), where a 'thorny waste' surrounds the 'flourishing grove' (213). Its 'corn and tares compactly grown' symbolise the ineradicable mixture of good and evil in 'the fields of charity and sin'. Their 'strange blessings' (227) would have been impossible in the over-simple goodness of Eden, confined 'within the great wall's perfect round' (142). The farmers do not descend into the world to 'browse in sin's great library' (213). Their simplicity keeps them close enough to the original purity of mankind to resemble 'the natural shape we take' (121).

Muir's farmers are linked to the past by memory and tradition. Memory is ambivalent, 'tarnished gold': it records 'the fathers' anger and ache'. Yet we owe it to our ancestors to commemorate their 'past agonies' (139). The farmers' 'long memories' (213) simplify history, summing up the Napoleonic wars in the sentence: 'There was a great war then' (304). Transmitted down the generations, memory interprets 'the hazard and the danger' of history's 'imperial highways' (222). Without it, history would be a record of 'carnage' and 'confusion' in which 'armies like forests fall' (148). Further back, Muir occasionally employs the Jungian fiction of racial memory linking mankind to the remotest past: 'I wear the silver scars/Of blanched and dying stars/Forgotten long,/Whose consternations spread/Terror among the dead/And touched my song' (171). (Note the subtlety with which the German 'Stern', 'star', has replaced the second syllable of 'constellations'.)

If memory links us to our ancestors, the imagination links us to all other human beings, in life and in literature. Muir upholds the Kantian doctrine that imagination supplies schemata with which to structure our experience. Knowledge gathered from 'the day's shrill complexity' is shaped by the imagination's 'speech that from the darkness grew' (240). Similarly, archetypal patterns enable us to understand particular narratives: 'Even a story to be true/Must repeat itself' (135). Common human experiences provide the imagination with content and equip us to understand other people. Hence Muir defines imagination as 'that power by which we apprehend living beings and living creatures in their individuality, as they live and move, and not as ideas or categories.'[13] But understanding implies also the recognition of difference, and the imagination enables us to bridge the gulf of time separating us from Homer's people. Thanks to it, we are 'into thirty centuries born' (249). Muir keeps returning to archetypal individuals from literature and legend—Abraham, Prometheus, Orpheus, Odysseus, Penelope, Oedipus—in order to meditate on the basic human situations which they embody. From them, and from individuals like Boswell's Johnson and Tolstoy's Ivan Ilyich, we learn things about human life which no theory could tell us. This particular knowledge feeds into our knowledge of mankind in general, helps us to 'retrieve the shape of man,/Lost and anonymous' (148), and leads back ultimately to 'the lost original of the soul' (217).

Muir's humanism shows itself in his efforts to enter into unfamiliar states of mind. In 'Sappho' he imagines how someone on the verge of suicide perceives the world as drained of substance, reduced to 'dumb hulks of being' (131). His strangest poem is perhaps 'The Child Dying'. Its imaginings could only be conveyed in naïve yet puzzling phrases, like the opening lines: 'Unfriendly friendly universe,/I pack your stars into my purse'. In the perspective they create, the whole world seems focused on the minute area occupied by the fading consciousness of the child about to enter 'nothing-filled eternity' (178). By negating positive expressions, Muir comes as close as he can to imagining the barely conceivable. Similarly, in 'The Animals', he uses negation to explore the consciousness of beings who are 'not in time and space' and 'were never in any place' but inhabit a perpetual, wordless present, devoid of memories, in which 'all is new and near' (207–8).

Many of Muir's finest poems celebrate personal relationships. He commemorates dead friends (91, 156), appeals to a former friend for reconciliation in a quarrel caused by 'the outward eating rage/And murderous heart of middle age' (98), and warns against the fantasy that one can possess another person entirely (191). Central to his work are the love-poems which made John Holloway call him 'with Graves perhaps, the outstanding British love poet since Yeats'.[14] Even in the 'iron reign' of contemporary history, love in which body cannot be separated from soul summons 'the rare/Spirit to breathe and live' (117). In 'The Commemoration', written after more than twenty years of marriage, Muir contrasts time's destruction of material things with the 'invisible virtue' generated by love and the immaterial harvests 'safely won/In hollow heart and brow' (119). He celebrates fidelity by repeatedly evoking Penelope's twenty-year wait for Odysseus (114, 125, 219, 243, 277), and in the deeply enigmatic 'Orpheus' Dream' he imagines a spiritual reunion with Eurydice so intense that Orpheus can look back with impunity at 'the poor ghost of Eurydice,/Still sitting in her silver chair/Alone in Hades' empty hall' (217).

On the few occasions when Christianity enters explicitly into Muir's poems, it is pervaded by his humanism. 'The Annunciation' is based on a plaque Muir had seen in Rome, in which the enraptured mutual gaze of the angel and the Virgin reminded him of Dante's lovers Paolo and Francesca. The poem accordingly depicts the encounter of heaven and earth, of the timeless with time, as a meeting of lovers who 'stare into their deepening trance/As if their gaze would never break'. Their 'immediacy/Of strangest strangeness' (223–4) hints both at the mystery of the Incarnation and at that of human love.

In Muir's later poetry such moments of personal encounter replace the grandiose visions of universal redemption with which he had ended his novels. Soon after his acceptance of Christianity, however, he did write a visionary poem, 'The Three Mirrors'. It contrasts three visions: a time-bound world ruled by 'incomprehensible wrath'; a more familiar world in which good and evil are 'locked in love and grief' (140–1); and finally what Muir, in a prose gloss, calls 'the supreme vision of human life' which 'reconciles all opposites' and 'in which both good and evil have their place legitimately'.[15] King and rebel coexist securely as (to quote another poem) 'irreconcilables, their treaty signed' (116). This all-embracing vision is not static but animated by 'the quick god everywhere'. Its universality is underlined by the last words of the poem, 'And you and myself there' (141), with which Muir also disclaims any pretence of impersonal prophetic authority, and reminds us that his humanism, even in this mystical elaboration, is based on the knowledge of another individual.

Within its narrow range of expression, Muir's poetry addresses highly ambitious themes. His stature as a writer, however, is still problematic. His poetry is underrated, partly because of the currency of inferior poems, partly because his technique of condensing thought into symbol has not yet been properly understood. To the monoglot reader, its Wordsworthian affinities, its remoteness from the modernism of Eliot and MacDiarmid, make it seem strangely old-fashioned; one needs a European perspective to see that Muir shares the modernism of Kafka and Rilke. His work also needs to be seen as a whole, with his poetry intimately related to his criticism and his fiction. His rejection of nationalism may be thought to place him outside the mainstream of twentieth-century Scottish literature, while some readers are put off by his humanist Socialism and by his Christianity, tentative and undogmatic though it is. There is still a tendency to suppose that one cannot admire both Muir and MacDiarmid. And an unqualified admiration for MacDiarmid would probably presuppose aesthetic and political choices that discouraged an appreciation of Muir. But these choices would also carry the risk of a dogmatism alien to Muir's open-minded humanism. Rather than MacDiarmid, the modern Scottish writer with whom Muir can be most profitably compared is Neil Gunn. Both share a lucid English style, an interest in traditional communities and the pastoral mode, and a concern with psychology and religion. And the best work of both keeps rewarding patient re-readers with new subtleties and profundities.

NOTES

1   *Selected Letters of Edwin Muir*, P H Butter (ed) (London, 1974), p 118.
2   *We Moderns* (London, 1918), p 179.
3   'Our Generation', *New Age*, 6 July 1922, p 116.
4   'Our Generation', *New Age*, 7 Apr 1921, p 270.
5   'Our Generation', *New Age*, 22 Dec 1921, p 88.
6   'New Values', *New Age*, 5 Feb 1920, p 224.
7   Cf. Georg Lukács, *The Theory of the Novel*, trans Anna Bostock (London, 1971); 'Forms of Time and of the Chronotope in the Novel', in M M Bakhtin, *The Dialogic Imagination*, trans Caryl Emerson and Michael Holquist (Austin, Texas, 1981).
8   'A Note on the Scottish Ballads', in Edwin Muir, *Uncollected Scottish Criticism*, Andrew Noble (ed) (London, 1982), pp 155–65 (p 165).
9   *Selected Letters*, pp 107–8.
10 Page numbers alone refer to Edwin Muir, *Collected Poems*, 3rd edn (London, 1984). The pagination corresponds to that in the 2nd edn (London, 1963).
11 See 'Bolshevism and Calvinism', in *Uncollected Scottish Criticism*, pp 123–30. Cf. Michael Walzer, *The Revolution of the Saints* (London, 1966).
12 Franz Kafka, *The Great Wall of China*, trans Willa and Edwin Muir (London, 1933), p 264.
13 *The Estate of Poetry* (London, 1962), p 81.
14 John Holloway, 'The Modernity of Edwin Muir', in *The Colours of Clarity* (London, 1964), pp 95–112 (p 102).
15 'Yesterday's Mirror: Afterthoughts to an Autobiography', *Scots Magazine*, 33 (1940), pp 404–10 (p 406).

FURTHER READING

Place of publication is London unless otherwise stated.

POETRY

First Poems (1925)
Chorus of the Newly Dead (1926)
Six Poems (Warlingham, 1932)
Variations on a Time Theme (1934)
Journeys and Places (1937)
The Narrow Place (1943)
The Voyage (1946)
The Labyrinth (1949)
One Foot in Eden (1956)
Collected Poems, third edition (1984)

NOVELS

The Marionette (1927)
The Three Brothers (1931)
Poor Tom (1932)

AUTOBIOGRAPHY

The Story and the Fable (1940)
An Autobiography (1954)

CRITICISM

We Moderns (under pseudonym 'Edward Moore') (1918)
Latitudes (1924)
Transition (1926)
The Structure of the Novel (1928)
Scott and Scotland (1936)
The Present Age (1939)
Essays on Literature and Society, second edition (1965)
The Estate of Poetry (1962)

BIOGRAPHY

John Knox (1929)

TRAVEL

Scottish Journey (1935)

POLITICS

Social Credit and the Labour Party (1935)

CRITICISM

Butter, P H, *Edwin Muir, Man and Poet* (Edinburgh, 1966)
Huberman, Elizabeth, *The Poetry of Edwin Muir* (New York, 1971)
Marshall, George, *In a Distant Isle: The Orkney Background of Edwin Muir* (Edinburgh, 1987)
Wiseman, Christopher, *Beyond the Labyrinth* (Victoria, British Columbia, 1978)

Chapter 10

Somhairle MacGill-eain

TERENCE McCAUGHEY

In what is probably a quite unrepeatable way, Sorley Maclean writes from within the Scottish Gaelic tradition, yet acts upon it. Contextualising it within the framework of wider concerns and pre-occupations of twentieth-century consciousness, he has been able to avoid the pitfalls which so often endanger the work of those who write in the 'less-used' languages of Europe. It has been observed that the Scottish Gaelic poet must steer between the twin dangers of *parochialism* on the one hand, and *esotericism* on the other. A peculiar confluence of influences has made it possible for Sorley Maclean to do just that.

He was born in 1911 in Osgaig on the east side of the Isle of Raasay, an island some ten miles long between the east coast of Skye and the mainland of Wester Ross. Childhood in Raasay brought him into sharp contact with three things which (to a greater or lesser extent) helped to form most people growing up in Scottish Gàidhealtachd of his time i.e. the Gaelic tradition in song and story, the physical evidence and the social and psychological results of land clearance and (in the Protestant Highlands) Calvinist orthodoxy, as promoted and sustained in the Free Presbyterian Church to which the majority in Raasay adhered.

Although the third of these attempted (in line with the example set by the later Evangelicals) to suppress the first, a *modus vivendi* was arrived at—even in an island like Raasay—whereby only that minority who became communicant members of the church had an obligation to turn their backs entirely on 'worldly' things, including songs and the music of the fiddle and the pipes.

The house in which the poet grew up was full of music: his father who ran a tailoring business in the island was a good singer, and his father's sister Peggy who visited Raasay for about a month each summer, had a wide repertoire from which Sorley Maclean still often quotes to this day. His mother's people, the Nicolsons, were pipers and singers of distinction and one was a bard. It was through his mother's brother Calum that the youthful Sorley first came to know the songs of Màiri Mhór nan Òran (Mary Macpherson, 1821–98). It is not surprising that the songs of this remarkable woman who only began to compose when she was fifty years of age under pressure of poverty and injustice, who herself was reputed to have a repertoire of earlier Gaelic song of some thousands of lines, and who became an unofficial bard to the land agitation of the 1870s and 1880s, should attract the young Maclean. On his own account, he had relinquished Calvinism for Socialism at the age of 12 and at that stage cherished the idea of entering politics 'helping to change the world'. Màiri Mhór nan Òran was in herself a link between the Gaelic tradition and that radical movement of tenants and crofters in defiance of Lord Macdonald the landlord which came to a head in the so-called 'Battle of Braes' in 1882 (*See* J Hunter, *The Making of the crofting community*, I F Grigor, *Mightier than a lord*, Stornoway 1979, 42–9). Braes is that part of Skye coast-line immediately opposite Raasay, from which the Nicolsons came, and to which Sorley Maclean and his wife went to live after his retirement from the headmastership of Plockton School in 1972. Memories of that struggle were lively, as was the bitter recollection of George Rainy the pious Edinburgh merchant who purchased the island from the last resident Macleod of Raasay in 1846 and proceeded to clear 94 families from 12 townships off the island. These terrible events run like a *leitmotiv* through the verse—notably in *'Hallaig'* (RC. 143–5), where the very townships which Rainy cleared are the poignant starting-point for a poem on the transcendence of Time and the capacity of loving imagination to redeem (if only for a time) the betrayals and irretrievable wrongs of history. The ship which carried what the landlords of Skye had come to think of as surplus population off to North America is directly spoken of in *'The Chuilithionn'*, 'The Cuillin', Pt. vi (4 PS. 124–5) in the person of a girl carried off on it against her will while gathering shellfish on the shore at Geusdo in Skye. It becomes a prototype of the universal suffering of the masses in the following:

> Dé gach cuach de d' chual òr-bhuidh
> ris gach bochdainn, àmhghar's dòrainn
> a thig 's a thàinig air sluagh na hEorpa
> bho Long nan Daoine gu daors' a' mhór-shluaigh?

> (What every lock of your gold-yellow head/to all the poverty anguish and grief/that will come and have come on Europe/from the Slave Ship to the slavery of the whole people?)
>
> (RC. 13)

The townships which Rainy cleared of people were not entirely cleared of beauty, but now Rainy too is gone and the Sound is filled with the harbingers of nuclear threat which will leave behind nothing:

> Thogadh ròn a cheann
> agus cearban a sheòl,
> ach an diugh anns an linnidh
> togaidh long-fo-thuinn a turraid
> agus a druim dhubh shlìom
> a' maoidheadh an nì a dhéanadh
> smùr de choille, de lianagan 's de chreagan,
> a dh'fhàgadh Screapadal gun bhòidhche
> mar a dh'fhàgadh e gun daoine.

The presence in Raasay, during Sorley Maclean's formative years, of a few

men who had known John Maclean the union leader of Clydeside, who had
protested against workers' involvement in what he took to be a capitalists'
war (1914–18) and been jailed for his pains, gave the young Sorley Maclean
a perspective on the labour movement in Glasgow, which was later to be
given an international dimension in the perceived parallels between John
Maclean in Scotland and the protests of James Connolly in Ireland and
Liebknecht in Germany.[1]

Recent work on the poetry of Sorley Maclean has emphasised the abiding
influence upon the poet of the Calvinism in which he was brought up and by
which he has been surrounded for the greater part of his life. He himself has
borne witness to the significance of the lengthy Gaelic sermons and extempore
prayers. Writing of the almost wholly extempore and unrecorded sermons
and prayers of the nineteenth century, he goes on to say:

> Even to this day there may be heard Gaelic sermons in which the thought is
> essentially that of St Augustine, Calvin or even Pascal, and the prose one of
> great tension and variety.[2]

He ends by acknowledging the debt which modern Gaelic poets owe to 'the
almost lost prose' of these sermons of the period after the Clearances when
the survivors, bewildered by the treacherous greed of their 'natural' leaders,
as John MacInnes puts it 'eagerly accepted the demands of a passionate and
uncompromising faith. Here was a new dialectic, powerful enough to replace
the deep loyalties of the traditional order. It was a theology that now supplied
an identity and a world view of history, partly in millenarian terms'.[3]

Sorley Maclean himself has condemned the Evangelical Movement for
encouraging an individualism which, at the political level, led to supineness
and quietism. Certainly this can be documented from the evangelical literature, but it is not the whole story. In the case of poets whom he himself
admires—Mary Macpherson, already mentioned, or Iain Mac a' Ghobhainn
of Iarsiadar (1848–81) there emerges both from the rhetoric and from the
substance of evangelical Calvinism, an indignant protest against landlordism
which (though it may have suffered a sea-change) informs Sorley Maclean's
own verse.

So it can be said that even before Sorley Maclean left Raasay to go to
Portree High School in 1924, and certainly by the time he left Portree to go
to Edinburgh University in 1929, certain centrally important influences had
already made an indelible mark upon him.

On arrival at Edinburgh University he decided, after considering the possibility of Celtic or History, to opt for English during the professorship of
Herbert Grierson who, with T S Eliot, was at that time restoring the prestige of
John Donne and the English Metaphysicals. Some trace of the metaphysicals'
technique can be discerned in Sorley Maclean's own verse, for instance in 'An
Sgian', 'The Knife' in which a single conceit which is announced in
the first quatrain, is followed through and exploited right through to the
last:

> Rinn sgian m'eanchainn gearradh
> air cloich mo ghaoil, a luaidh,
> is sgrùd a faobhar gach aon bhearradh
> is ghabh mo shùil a thuar.

(The knife of my brain made incision/my dear, on the stone of my love,/and the blade examined every segment/and my eye took its colour.)

(RC. 45–7)

During his time in Edinburgh University he dropped the habit of writing in English on the ground that his verse in English was 'imitative of Eliot and Pound . . . over-sophisticated, over-selfconscious and that what I had written in Gaelic was better in the sense that it was more myself.'[4] By 1922, i.e. before he had met Hugh MacDiarmid who is sometimes credited with promoting Maclean's commitment to writing in Gaelic, he tells us that he had consciously preserved *'A' Chorra-ghritheach'*, 'The Heron' (RC. 3–5), 'and some other Gaelic poems which I thought much more true to myself than anything I had done in English'. Of course, Hugh MacDiarmid was to have an influence on Sorley Maclean from their first meeting in 1934 while Maclean was doing his teacher training in Moray House Teacher Training College, Edinburgh, as he did on almost every creative artist working in Scotland from the 1920s onwards for four or five decades. The friendship between the two men lasted till MacDiarmid's death in 1978. But Sorley Maclean was actually introduced to MacDiarmid's early lyrics by two men whom he met in his own final year at Edinburgh (1933)—James B Caird and George E Davie, author later of *The Democratic Intellect*—committed Scots with a catholic enthusiasm for ideas. Together with Hugh MacDiarmid these two men no doubt helped the Gaelic poet and student of English to re-appropriate the whole Scottish tradition without any strident cultural chauvinism. Certainly MacDiarmid, with whose particular brand of Socialism Sorley Maclean was to find himself in disagreement from time to time, together with the rise of Fascism in those years, served to internationalise his understanding of the struggle and his socialist analysis enabled him to contextualise the peculiar tragedies of the Highlands. A fierce and compassionate indignation is to be found in *'Ban-Ghàidheal'*, 'Highland Woman' (RC. 77–9), which he wrote in Mull during the year he spent there (1938) after leaving Portree High School staff, where he had taught from 1934 to 1937.

The outbreak of the Spanish Civil War in 1936 was a focus of commitment for most politically sensitive young people and Maclean shared this experience. Many of the poems written at this time juxtapose the intense personal love which he was experiencing and the struggle of the Government and people of Spain against insurgent fascism of the Spanish army.

Two poems in particular, *'Gaoir na hEorpa'*, 'The Cry of Europe' (RC. 13), and *'An Roghainn'*, 'The Choice' (RC. 25–7), indicate what was involved. The first of these opens with a burst of the rhetoric we associate with *amhran*—metre love-songs of the eighteenth century, alliterative, flowery, discursive:

> A nighean a' chùil bhuidhe, throm-bhuidh òr-bhuidh,
> fonn do bheòil-sa 's gaoir na hEorpa,

a nighean gheal chasurlach aighearach bhòidheach
cha bhiodh masladh ar lathe-na searbh 'nad phòig-sa.

(Girl of the yellow, heavy-yellow, gold-yellow hair,/the song of your mouth and Europe's shivering cry,/fair, heavy-haired spirited, beautiful girl,/the disgrace of our day would not be bitter in your kiss.)

There follow five quatrains, each one an urgent rhetorical question:

An tugadh t'fhonn no t'àilleachd ghlòrmhor
bhuam-sa gràinealachd mharbh nan dòigh seo,
a' bhrùid 's am meirleach air ceann na hEorpa
's do bhial-sa uaill-dhearg 'san tseann-òran?

(Would your song and splendid beauty take/from me the dead loathsomeness of these ways,/the brute and the brigand at the head of Europe/and your mouth red and proud with the old song?)

His love's beauty is set in a sort of see-saw opposition to the treachery and spite of a bourgeois and enfeebled Scotland. The question is asked, could her beauty put from him 'the frailty of this lasting cause' (breòiteachd an aobhair bhuain seo), 'the Spanish miner leaping in the face of horror and his great spirit going down untroubled' (am méinear Spàinnteach a' leum ri cruadal/is anam mórail dol sìos gun bhruaillean). The poem ends unresolved with a great and essentially pessimistic question which looks, not alone at present suffering, but at further suffering and possible defeat to come.

Already in 'Gaoir na hEorpa' there is a hint that more is involved than the love of one woman. Behind that love stands the demands of his art and the development of individual consciousness. News of the death of the young poets Cornford, Julian Bell and Lorca in the Spanish conflict strips away any effort at rationalising:

ach 'sann duinne tha am bròn
ann am breòiteachd a' chinne:
Lorca, Julian Bell is Cornford,
nach d'fhan ri glòir nam filidh.

O mhachraichean na Spàinne,
a chunnaic àmhghar thruaghan
cha d' ghabh mise bhur cràdhlot
is sàthghal bhur buairidh;
an fheadhainn 'an tugadh bàs leibh
fhuair iad sgàil na huaghach;
dh'fhàg cuid dhiubh sonas saoghail
is cuid dhuibh gaoir na truaighe
. . . bu sheachd feàrr leams' bhur n-eug
seach éiginn mo thorchairt!

(But the grief is ours/in the sore frailty of mankind, Lorca, Julian Bell and Cornford, who did not wait for the fame of poets/O fields of Spain/that saw the distress of miserable ones/I did not take your agony/and the full grief of your passion:/those to whom you gave death/found the shade of the grave/some of them left a happy world/and some the shriek of misery . . . to me seven times better your death than the necessity of my case.)

(RC. 81–83)

But in '*An Roghainn*', 'The Choice' (RC. 25–7), he probes the psychological basis of what he laments in *Cornford*:

> Choisich mi cuide ri mo thuigse
> a muigh ri taobh a' chuain . . .

(I walked with my reason/out beside the sea . . .

In that liminal setting of the shore-line, which assumes the more dramatic and ultimate aspect of a headland by the end of the poem, the poet is addressed by his reason/understanding (*tuigse*) and is forced to admit that he has just come to hear of the forthcoming marriage next Monday of his 'beautiful white love'. This wrings from the poet three agonised rhetorical questions which, in a way, parallel those of the other poem, each one beginning 'Ciamar . . .?'/'How . . . .?' How could he imagine it would be possible to grab at 'the radiant golden star' and pop it prudently in his pocket. And then with a devastating use of the imagery of impotence, he asks:

> Cha do lean mi ach an t-slighe chrìon
> bheag ìosal thioram thlàth,
> is ciamar sin a choinnichinn
> ri beithir-theine ghràidh?

(I followed only a way/that was small, mean, low, dry, lukewarm/and how then should I meet/the thunderbolt of love?)

But this poem does arrive at a resolution of conflict:

> Ach nan robh 'n roghainn rithist dhomh
> 's mi 'm sheasamh air an àird,
> leumainn á neamh no iutharna
> le spiorad 's cridhe slàn

(But if I had the choice again/and stood on that headland,/I would leap from heaven or hell/with a whole spirit and heart.)

In the light of that resolution, it is no surprise to find that Sorley Maclean was in the Signals Corps by September 1940. In this enthusiastic decision he was out of agreement with Hugh MacDiarmid who, perhaps still thinking in terms of the arguments of Maclean and Connolly, saw no point in fighting Fascism in the army of Britain or France. Maclean spent much of 1941 awaiting embarkation orders and from December of that year until March 1943, served with the Royal Horse Artillery in Egypt and North Africa. During that time in spite of the difficulties and shortages of war, friends with whom he had left his poems, arranged for the publication of *Dàin do Eimhir* which came out in 1943. Douglas Young, lecturer in Greek (later professor) in St Andrews wrote a short introduction, and the illustrations were by a young Scottish artist, William Crosbie. There were two sections—one of 48 love poems—the 'Dàin do Eimhir', and another of poems on various themes, 'Dàin Eile'. Selected poems were provided with translations into English.

The poet was wounded in the fighting which followed El Alamein and was sent home. He took up his duties again in Boroughmuir School in Edinburgh in 1943 and remained there (latterly Principal Teacher of English) until 1956, when he resigned to take up the principalship of Plockton Secondary School on the mainland of Ross-shire immediately opposite Skye and his native Raasay. He remained there until his retirement in 1972.

The war experience was responsible for a number of poems. In one of them, *'Glac a' Bhàis'*, 'Death Valley' (RC. 121–3), he comments with heavy irony on the statement of some Nazi that the Führer had restored to the youth of Germany the 'right and joy of dying in battle'. Gazing at a young German soldier dead on the North African sand 'his forelock about his cheek and his face slate grey'/ . . . 'gille òg 's a logan sìos m'a ghruaidh/'s a thuar grìsionn' he is not betrayed into any kind of sentimentality. The boy may have been among those who abused Communists and Jews or simply was conscripted for battle without conviction for the sake of rulers, like thousands through human history. Betrayed by the Führer's lies, his corpse gives the lie to the Führer:

> Ge b'e a dheòin-san no a chàs,
> a neoichiontas no mhìorun
> cha do nochd e toileachadh 'na bhàs
> fo Dhruim Ruidhìseit.

(Whatever his desire or mishap,/his innocence or malignity,/he showed no pleasure in his death/below Ruidhìseit Ridge.)

There is compassion for the boy all right, but it is held in tension with a greater tragedy of which that boy's corpse is part.

Another poem from this period, *'Latha Foghair'*, 'An Autumn Day' (RC. 123–5), is concerned with the arbitrariness of human fate, a theme he speaks of by means of the term 'Election' a theological doctrine he had long rejected, but which in the hands of the ministers of this youth had come to be a terrifying doctrine of the arbitrary power of the Deity. He deploys it, as in the poem *'Annsa' Phàirce Mhóir'*, 'In the Big Park' (RC. 153), to indicate an inate and inescapable destiny.

Side by side with the somewhat fatalistic world-view of *'Anns a' Phàirce Mhóir'* there is to be discerned something brighter—a vision of what Hugh MacDiarmid called 'the great end in view'. In *'A' Bheinn air chall'*, 'The Lost Mountain' (RC. 165–7), he hails (though he does not characterise) that end:

> Tha bheinn aig éirigh os cionn na coille,
> air chall anns a' choille th'air chall . . .

(The mountain rises above the wood,/lost in the wood that is lost . . .)

And the wood here, as in the great symbolist poem *'Coilltean Ratharsair'*, 'The Woods of Raasay' (RC. 89–105), symbolises our symbol-system—the trees we plant and those we inherit forming the landscape which in turn forms us.

Suffice to say that the eschatology he aspires to must comprehend Vietnam and Ulster and the charnel-houses of Auschwitz:

> Air chall ann an aomadh na coille
> ìomhaighean iomadhathach ar spéis
> a chionn 's nach téid na sràidean ciùrrte
> 's a' choille mhaoth an cochur réidh.

(Lost in the decline of the wood/the many-coloured images of our aspiration/since the tortured streets will not go/in the wood in a smooth synthesis.)

At eleven years of age he had forsaken the ideology of the Free Presbyterians: he never has bound himself to uncritical acceptance of another. A native pessimism, strengthened by the early experience of the non-conformist has helped, at any rate, to make that an impossibility. *'Coilltean Ratharsair'* ends with these melancholy and exclamatory lines, resigned to the limitations of our symbols and our aspirations:

> Och a' choille, och a' choille
> dé na tha 'na doimhne dhoilleir!
>
> Tha eòl air slighe an t-snodhaich
> a' drùdhadh suas gu ghnothach,
> am fion sìor ùrar beothail
> gun fhios dha féin, gun oilean.
>
> Chan eil eòl air an t-slighe
> th'aig fiarachd cham a' chridhe
> 's chan eil eòl air a' mhilleadh
> do'n tàrr gun fhios a cheann-uidhe.
>
> Chan eil eòlas, chan eil eòlas
> air crìch dheireannaich gach tòrachd
> no air seòltachd nan lùban
> leis an caill i a cùrsa.

(O the wood, O the wood/How much there is in her dark depths! . . . The way of the sap is known/oozing up to its work,/the wine that is always new and living,/unconscious, untaught. There is no knowledge of the course/of the crooked veering of the heart/and there is no knowledge of the damage/to which its aim unwittingly comes./There is no knowledge, no knowledge/of the final end of each pursuit,/nor of the subtlety of the bends/with which it loses its course.)

(RC. 103)

Mention has already been made of the influence of the Metaphysical Poets and of the rhetoric of the Gaelic sermon and extempore prayer. The songs which he had been hearing since earliest childhood and which he has eagerly collected from singers all his life have also left their mark on what he has produced himself, both in terms of content and of rhetoric and metre. This is to be traced in the lyrics, like *'Fo sheòl'*, 'Under sail' (RC. 53), where one might expect to find it, but also for instance, in the third section of his Elegy for his brother Calum into which he weaves a line from a well-known lament for a drowned man, which Calum had collected from a singer in Benbecula.

The song from Benbecula begins with the foster-mother saying:

> 'S daor a cheannaich mi 'n t-iasgach;
> seo bhliadhna chuir as dhomh . . .

(Dearly I bought the fishing; this is the year that did for me . . .)

First it appears (RC. 177), in this altered form twice:

> Is daor a cheannaich thusa 'n t-uabhar
> a cheannaich sinne 'nad bhàs . . .

(You dearly bought the pride that we bought in your death)

and then,

> Is daor a cheannaich sinne 'n t-uabhar
> a mhiadaich le do bhàs:

(We dearly bought the pride/that increased with your death)

and finally, extending the image by deployment of the image of the salmon of knowledge and inspiration, he says:

> Is daor a cheannaich thusa 'n t-iasgach;
> Nuair a bha am pianadh 'nad fheòil,
> Nuair thug do lion a stigh na bradain
> Thàrr-gheala lìomhach 'nan stòr;
> Le lìon do cheithir bliadhna ciùrraidh
> Thug thu cliù dhuinn thar gach stòir.

(You dearly bought the fishing/when the pain was in your flesh,/when your net was taking in/the gleaming white-bellied salmon, a store; with/the net of your four years of agony/you gave us a pride beyond store.)

In the Introduction to *Nuabhàrdachd Ghàidhlig/Modern Scottish Gaelic Poems*, Donald MacAulay pinpointed Symbolism as being the most important influence upon Sorley Maclean and added: 'An understanding of the basic elements of this movement is essential to anyone who wishes to comprehend the complexity of Maclean's poetry' (pp 55–6). This is no doubt true.

What is also true is that within the corpus of his work each symbol is in constant movement.

It is, of course, of the very nature of symbols that they have a plain of denotation which is hard enough to delineate, but also a plain of connotation in which it is easy to go astray. The connotations operate both synchronically and diachronically: and it is in the diachronic that the person who is unfamiliar with the Gaelic tradition is liable to need most help.

The poem '*Hallaig*' (RC. 143–5), is set down under the rubric of a single line, 'Thà tìm, am fiadh, an coille Hallaig', which the poet himself has said came to him at an earlier time, but which serves as a key to the central preoccupation of the poem which follows. John MacInnes, in a short study of '*Hallaig*' published some years ago,[5] drew attention to the curious parallel between the deer (= time) image of '*Hallaig*' and the deer in Edwin Muir's 'The Road': 'There is a road that turning always/cuts off the country of Again./Archers stand there on every side,/and, as it runs, Time's deer is slain,/and lies where it has lain.'[6]

But behind Edwin Muir, and presupposed in any deepened appreciation of '*Hallaig*' must be the realisation that the deer as a symbol is not just plucked out of the air. This symbol has an ever-shifting place in the ecology, history and song-literature of the Highlands. The deer was chased by the nobility in great hunts involving several hundred beaters at a time. Understandably, therefore it comes, in the early songs protesting against the Clearances where the common pasture on the mountain was closed off to make sheep-runs, to represent a lost Golden Age:

> 'Nuair a chì mi na beanntan àrda,
> 'san fhearann àigh 's an robh Fionn a chomhnuidh,
> chan fhaic mi ann ach na caoraich bhàna
> 's Goill gun àireamh 'sa h-uile còdhail.[7]

(When I see the high mountains and the blessed land where Fionn was, I see nothing now but white sheep and Lowlanders without number in every gathering.)

In songs of the seventeenth century, a sort of love-hate relationship is often expressed between the hunter and the deer. So Domhnall mac Fhionnlaigh nan Dàn can say in a quatrain which Sorley Maclean himself praised in one of his essays long ago:[8]

> Gur gasda ruitheadh tu suas
> ri leacainn chruaidh is i cas;
> moladh gach aon neach an cù:
> molaim-s' an trù tha dol as!

(Nimbly you would run up/the hard steep mountain face;/let everyone else praise the dog:/I will praise the wretch that is getting away!)

Or the Ciaran Mabach (late seventeenth century) lying in bed with a broken leg in Edinburgh within ear-shot of the masons who are restoring Holyrood

Abbey in the early 1660s thinks of the hunt he may never participate in again. The deer he speaks of this way:[9]

> B'e mo ghràdh-s' am fear buidhe
> nach déan suidhe ma'n bhòrd,
> nach iarradh ri cheannach
> pinnt leanna na beòir;
> uisge-beatha math dùbailt
> cha b'e b'fhiù leat ri òl—
> b'fhearr leat biolair an f huarain
> a's uisge luaineach an lòin.

(My love is the brown man who does not sit down at table, who does not order a pint of ale or beer. A good double whisky you wouldn't touch: you'd prefer water-cress from the spring and the moving water of the streams.)

But in the nineteenth century all this changes in the face of a new threat—the crofters' own sheep-runs being curtailed to make room for deer forests for the hunting-shooting-fishing people. Now the deer becomes a symbol of a new and uncaring acquisitiveness. So the deer of Time in *'Hallaig'* (RC. 145), which is struck dead by 'the gun of Love' as it sniffs at the ruins of houses deserted by the people of Raasay whom Mr Rainy shipped off to the Antipodes, therefore carries within him layers of actual experience and suffering on that very site.

The symbol of the Cuillin has already been mentioned. It dominates almost every landscape in Skye and the adjoining mainland and, as the uncompromising symbol of the harsh constraints of life in those islands, contrasts with the woods already referred to. The mountains, different parts of which have been the summer-pasture of the shieling, sheep-runs, deer forests and the occasion of loss and tragedy come across very differently for one embedded in or familiar with Gaelic tradition from the way they will to one whose response to the mountains has been formed primarily by the Romantics. This is not to say that Sorley Maclean (who is a keen hill-walker) does not share this later relationship with Nature. He does: but, as John MacInnes has said[10] there is in him 'a blend of sensibilities that makes MacGill-eain the kind of poet he is: modern, sophisticated and Gaelic.'

For Sorley Maclean, as for Dr John MacLachlan of Rahoy in the nineteenth century, in that poem of his, *'Beinn Shianta'*, significantly so much admired by Maclean—nature has no significance apart from the people for whom it functions at various levels. This is clear in, for instance, the poem *'Fuaran'*, 'A Spring':

> Air latha thàinig mi le m' ghaol
> gu taobh a' chaochain iomallaich,
> chrom i a h-aodann sìos ri bhruaich
> 's cha robh a thuar fhein tuilleadh air.

(One day I came with my love/to the side of the remote brook/She bent her head to its brink/and it did not look the same again.)

But the poem ends with one of those (often slightly ironic or understated) couplets which in Maclean's poems often sum up what has gone before. The whole final quatrain is:

> Ach bha na glinn is iad a' falbh
> is calbh nam beann gun fhuireach rium,
> cha robh a choltas air na sléibhtean
> gum facas m' eudail ulaidhe.

(But the glens were going away/and the pillared mountains were not waiting for me/the hills did not look/as if my chanced-on treasure had been seen.)
(RC. 87)

The use of place-names must surely be understood in this context. The Gaelic tradition has always loved to repeat them in a kind of litany. But this is not only for the aural effect: the place-name gives the environment a greater than mere physical reality, though their repetition itself brings that cherished physical reality to expression. Their repetition in close proximity with those who lived there gives the ambiguous if not indifferent or hostile Nature a place in the history of Man.

There is all the difference in the world between the deserted but once peopled townlands of the East of Raasay—'Screapadal mo chinnidh/far robh Tarmad 's Eachann Mór' (Screapadal of my people/where Norman and Big Hector were)—and the anonymous, deceptively warm sand of the North African desert on which his six companions sit, 'dead and stiff—and frozen were it not for the heat—as if they were waiting for a message'. On this anonymous landscape, under 'the stars of Africa, jewelled and beautiful'/fo reultan Africa/'s iad leugach àlainn,—an anonymous and indifferent Election takes them and leaves him. Consistent with this is the fact that the poet far from the Island and every loved image of Scotland, far from Belsen and Dachau and bearing no rancour for the actual men in Rommel's army, on the way to fight them is buoyed up only by this:

> . . . biodh na bha mar a bha e,
> tha mi de dh'fhir mhór' a' Bhraighe,
> de Chloinn Mhic Ghille Chaluim threubhaich,
> de Mhathanaich Loch Aillis nan geurlann,
> agus fir m'ainme—có bu tréine
> nuair dh'fhádadh uabhar an léirchreach?

(. . . And be what was as it was,/I am of the big men of Braes,/of the heroic Raasay Macleods,/of the sharp-sword Mathesons of Lochalsh; and the men of my name—who were braver/when their ruinous pride was kindled?)
(RC. 116)

This is felt at a deep almost atavistic level, far from home. But back at home again, particularly in these last years one is conscious of a poetry populated with places and persons who are redolent of past conflict, of contemporary struggle and of a future which is harder to be sure of than at any

time in human history. MacCrimmon the piper, the Dall Munro, Maighistir
Ruairidh the evangelist have all come to play their part in a mythopoeia
which never has that contrived character which has sometimes marred the
work of twentieth-century writers in major languages. In the interview with
Donald Archie Macdonald (*Sorley Maclean: critical essays*, p 220) the poet
himself puts it thus:

> I came to maturity at the time of the great symbolist movement in European
> poetry . . . and my symbols came mostly from my environment . . . The
> Cuillins naturally became a symbol of difficulty, hardship and heroic qualities as
> against . . . the softness and relative luxury of the woods of Raasay with all
> their own contradictions . . . But, of course, that (the physical environment)
> was always affected, blended with what I knew of the history of my people.

At an early stage in his career, Sorley Maclean committed himself to the
view that the lyric is 'the summit of all poetry', and it has been argued that
it is as a lyricist he himself is most successful. But in *'Coilltean Ratharsair'*
(RC. 89–105), and in the unfinished longer poems *'An Cuilithionn'* and
'Uamha 'n Òir' and in the elegy for his brother Calum he has attempted
something longer which could stretch to hundreds of lines. Robert Calder
(*Chapman*, 30.68) has spoken of the lyrics as 'fragments' in that through their
depth of shared allusion 'the individual poems belong together for reasons
deeper than that they come from the same voice'. The two longer poems
referred to are themselves made up of partly independent sections rich in
shared allusion which invite the suggestion that we have to do here—not so
much with a long poem as with an extended cycle of poems such as is familiar
to us in the tradition from MacIntyre's *Moladh Beinn Dobhrain* and *Òran na
Comhachaig* back to the poems of the Cailleach Bhéara.[11]

Metrically, Sorley Maclean's work is innovatory, without being revolutionary. This aspect of his work has been discussed at length by D Thomson and J MacInnes[12]. He favoured fairly regular rhyming metres in his earlier
work and one notes a return to this in *'Uamha 'n Òir'* after a period in which
he appeared to move away from regular rhyme. It could be said that the poetry
gains its colour from the rhythm and changes of speed, in the movement from
the conversational to the lyrical from the lyrical to the declamatory.

NOTES

1 *See* Nan Milton, *John Maclean* (Pluto) 1973.
2 Quoted by J MacInnes, 'A Radically Traditional Voice' in *Cencrastus* 7, Winter
   1981–2, p 15.
3 J MacInnes, loc. cit. p 15.
4 Catalogue of Somhairle MacGill-eain exhibition of 1981, published by National
   Library of Scotland, p 14.
5 *Calgacus* 1.2. Summer 1975, pp 29–32.
6 Edwin Muir, *Collected Poems* (1960) p 61.
7 G Mac-na-Ceàrdadh (ed), *An tÒranaiche* (Glasgow, 1879), p 101.

8   W J Watson (ed), *Bàrdachd Gàidhlig* (Stirling, 1959), 6675–8.
9   J Mackenzie (ed), *Sàr-obair nam bàrd Gàidhealach* (Edinburgh, 1907) 2nd ed, p 60.
10   'Language, metre and diction in the poetry of Sorley Maclean' in *Sorley Maclean: critical essays* (Edinburgh, 1986), p 148.
11   G Murphy (ed), *Early Irish Lyrics* (Oxford, 1962), pp 74–82.
12   D S Thomson, *The new verse in Scottish Gaelic: a structural analysis* (Dublin: University College, 1974) (The Osborn Bergin Memorial Lecture, 4); J MacInnes, loc. cit.

FURTHER READING

COLLECTIONS

17 Poems for 6d. Somhairle MacGill-eathain and Robert Garioch (Edinburgh, 1940)

Dàin do Eimhir, agus Dàin Eile (Glaschu, 1943)

Four Points of a Saltire, the poetry of Sorley Maclean, George Campbell Hay, William Neill, Stuart MacGregor (Edinburgh, 1970). (Here abbreviated—4PS)

D MacAmhlaigh (deas.), *Nuabhàrdachd Ghàidhlig*/D Macaulay (ed), *Modern Scottish Gaelic Poems* (Edinburgh, 1976)

Reothairt is Contraigh, Taghadh de Dhàin 1932–72/*Spring Tide and Neap Tide, Selected Poems 1932–72* (Edinburgh, 1977). (Here abbreviated RC)

Chapter 11

Scottish Drama 1900–1950

DAVID HUTCHISON

Drama in Scotland is an under developed art form. Whereas the Scottish poetic tradition can be traced back to the medieval period and the Scottish novel is almost as old as the form itself, dramatic writing has only begun to establish itself firmly in recent times. Sir David Lindsay's *Ane Satyre of the Thrie Estaitis* is both a beginning and an end; such Scottish dramatic writing as followed it was both fitful and insecure. The reasons for this are well known. The open hostility of the reformed church to 'clerk-plays or comedies based on the canonical scriptures' made theatrical enterprise well nigh impossible outside the protective umbrella provided by the court of King James, and when that monarch hastened south to claim the throne of England in 1603, the theatre was fully exposed to the intemperate hostility of Calvinism. It was not until the nineteenth century that Scotland began to catch up with the provision which existed south of the border. In the first decade of the twentieth century theatre building accelerated—in 1900 there were 32 theatres in Scotland but by 1910 that figure had reached 53. Sixty years later the total had shrunk to 15, although it should be added that the growth in the 1960s and 1970s in the provision of multi-purpose venues in arts and leisure centres has ensured that far more than 15 stages are now used for professional performances.

It is a truism that writers cannot be expected to write for non-existent theatres, which is why such dramatists as appeared in Scotland before the present century sought London performances for their work. It might therefore be thought that with the expansion of theatrical provision in Scotland, which began over a hundred years ago, indigenous writers would at last have had the opportunities so long denied them. In fact the theatres which were opened in the nineteenth and early twentieth centuries were very dependent on the London based stock company system for their presentations. Scottish theatres were simply regional British theatres looking to the capital for the bulk of the plays which they offered. Traces of indigenous work can be found, but nothing of significance. However it is worth nothing the number of adaptations of novels by Walter Scott which appeared on the stage. These were also to be found on English stages but they had a longer life span in Scotland, and spawned other plays which took a romantic view of Scottish history.

That the general situation was unsatisfactory did not escape the attention of contemporary commentators.

163

> The appearance of a Scotch dramatist ought to be as likely an event as the appearance of a Scotch novelist. Unfortunately he would not be in so fortunate a position as regards 'aids to understanding'. The English devotee of the Kailyard School can, with the aid of glossary fight his way to a faint appreciation of what gives him so much joy. But a Scotch dramatist, however ably he might reproduce the humours of Bellahouston or Stockbridge, the passions of St Andrews or Millport, would be almost powerless without the backing of trained Scotch actors and actresses. These are days of decentralisation in fiction, as in other things, but decentralisation in the drama is as yet but the wildest of dreams.[1]

There is now no shortage of 'trained Scotch actors' but whether true 'decentralisation in the drama' has been achieved is another matter.

Paradoxically while the situation in the 'straight' theatre was far from encouraging, a native tradition was being developed in the music hall and its close confederate the pantomime. Although a fair number of performers on Scottish music hall and pantomime stages hailed from south of the border, a significant proportion were Scots, and sought to use Scottish experience as the raw material of their acts. This is particularly true of comedians and singer/comedians. Indeed given the nature of music hall and its fundamental dependence on a shared identity of experience between performer and audience it is hard to see how matters could have been otherwise. Recent work on the music hall in London by Gareth Stedman Jones[2] has explored the idea that its function in that city was to offer a kind of 'culture of consolation' to a working class which after the defeat of Chartism had concluded that capitalism and industrialisation were here to stay, and that amelioration not revolution should be the aim. Stedman Jones argues, furthermore, that in London, because of the absence of large industrial concerns and weak trade unions, the music hall fulfilled a function which in the heavy industrial areas was more likely to be fulfilled by work associated cultural institutions such as the unions themselves, the cooperative movement, brass bands, and male voice choirs. It offered opportunities for expression and creativity outside the constraints of work. It would be interesting to consider Scottish music hall in this light. The evidence from later recorded performances by such figures as Harry Lauder and Will Fyfe suggests that there was a much stronger element of escapist sentimentality in music hall in Scotland than in England but far more work is required before definite conclusions can be drawn on the matter.

Theatrical activity takes many forms, but it is usual to distinguish three broad categories. First of all there is the popular culture of music hall, variety and pantomime which has just been discussed. Then there is the high culture of drama which makes serious claims to the status of art because it seeks to examine experience from a critical perspective. In between there is a large area of theatrical activity whose form is that of high art, in that the presentations involved are plays rather than music hall turns, but these plays are essentially light weight, without any great ambition other than to provide a couple of hours' entertainment.

It is instructive to look at the varied fortunes of the three kinds of theatre distinguished above during the twentieth century. Popular theatre offers a picture of decline with a partial recovery in one area. Music hall quickly succumbed to the assault of the cinema in the early years of the century, and its largely working class audience transferred allegiance to the 'dumb show' of film. This represents a major cultural shift, for throughout the history of cinema in Britain the market has been dominated by American material rather than British, far less Scottish, material. Those music hall performers who survived did so largely by moving into the more respectable form of variety, the audience for which was a mixture of middle and working class, and by exploiting the opportunities presented by radio broadcasting which began in Britain in 1922 (in Scotland in 1923). Variety shows remained popular until well after the Second World War and could be seen not only throughout the year in the cities—the best example is perhaps the series of 'Five Past Eight' shows presented by Howard and Wyndham in Glasgow's Alhambra Theatre—but also during the summer season at various resorts such as Ayr, Rothesay, Arbroath and Dunoon. These shows were largely gone by the 1980s, although in Ayr the 'Gaiety Whirl' was still being mounted each year in the little theatre which gave its name to the show.

Variety's change of fortune can be largely attributed to television, for it was the growth of that medium in the 1950s and 1960s, coupled perhaps with the improvement in many people's domestic surroundings, which led to variety's decline, as it led to the catastrophic decline of the cinema. Television not only captured the working class audience, it captured a large segment of the middle class audience too. As far as the summer show is concerned, the growth in prosperity which led holidaymakers to Spain rather than the Clyde Coast is as inextricably linked to its decline as is the expansion of television.

Pantomine is the one great survivor in the area of popular theatre. Although it has had its shaky moments, the Scottish pantomine in the 1980s enjoys immense public support. It is also the case that by and large the Scottish pantomine has avoided the excesses seen south of the border where pop stars and the like have been cast in ludicrously inappropriate roles for which they are totally unfitted. In Scotland pantomime performers are basically actors, singers and dancers, rather than hit parade transients. The survival and indeed prosperity of pantomime in Scotland are to some extent due to this insistence on being true to the form itself. They are also due to the enlightened attitude of local authorities who have taken up the mantle of the professional managements which, with the exception of the Pavilion Theatre Company in Glasgow, have disappeared from the Scottish scene. But it cannot be a coincidence that pantomime is so successful at a time when a number of outstanding performers are at work, among whom must be mentioned Rikki Fulton, Jimmy Logan and above all, Stanley Baxter, whose extraordinary mimetic talent and linguistic versatility can light up a stage and lift a performance into a realm of its own.

Middle of the road theatre has also suffered a decline in the era of television, and when such plays appear, often as touring productions emanating from south of the border, they have actors known for their work in television in the principal roles.

It is in the area of high culture that there has been most development this century. Although in the early years it was the area which faced most difficulty, in the period since the war it is the one which has had most success. This is due to a number of factors, including the decline of other forms of theatre and the growth in public funding for 'serious' art, whether through Arts Council or local authority subvention. No one could claim that the current situation is one of rude health, but the subsidised theatre in Scotland is now *the* theatre. There is no equivalent of London's West End north of the border. With only one house in private hands, theatre has been nationalised. The customers continue to pay at the door, fund raising is a continuous process, sponsorship is significant and growing in importance, but it is public subsidy which keeps our theatres open.

In the early part of the century Scottish dramatists had to operate in a climate which was not particularly tolerant of the challenging or the radical. Indeed for most of the time the climate was distinctly conservative. The mainstream was represented by tours from south of the border and by the Scottish based repertory companies such as the Brandon Thomas Players and the Masque Players, whose programmes did not provide space for experiment or indeed for indigenous dramatists in any numbers. This meant that the Scottish writer had to look elsewhere for sustenance. With the exception of one brief spell before the First World War, throughout the period up until the 1940s the elsewhere in question was composed of companies of amateur actors. This presented the dramatist with a grim choice. Should he seek the support of such companies, the meagre financial rewards they offered and the attendant risk of mediocre, if sincere, performance, or should he look to London to have his work presented?

For James Barrie, the most financially successful Scottish dramatist to date, the choice did not really arise, for when he began working there was not even a native amateur theatre in Scotland worthy of attention. So Barrie went south and had his plays performed on the London stage. Most of these plays were not set in Scotland and those which were did not present their audiences with any great problems of comprehension. Something similar could be said of most of James Bridie's work. He had the bulk of his plays premiered south of the border, although he made some use of Scottish companies early in his career. But it was not long before Bridie realised that the only path to success for him was through the West End and that was where he turned his attention. As was the case with Barrie, Bridie did not present metropolitan audiences with problems of understanding, for he worked within tried West End forms and his philosophical and moral explorations rarely went too deep for comfort.

For Scottish dramatists who could not easily fit into the mould of Barrie or Bridie there was nowhere to go but the amateur theatre. The average member of an amateur drama club is always interested in enjoying himself, sometimes concerned to ensure high standards of presentation, but rarely committed to the development of a national dramatic tradition. Nonetheless the enthusiasm for amateur drama during the inter war period in Scotland was remarkable, with the number of entries to the Scottish Community Drama Association's one act play competition rising from 35 in 1926 to 307 in 1932. This was indeed the boom period of amateur theatre with the competition finals conducted in an atmosphere of intense rivalry. It must be added that by good fortune there were at the time a number of amateur companies which were much more serious about what they were doing than the vast majority of clubs. Several of these did seek to advance the cause of Scottish drama, the most important being the Scottish National Players, the Curtain Theatre and Unity Theatre. All three were based in Glasgow.

The Scottish National Players came into being after the First World War with the aims of producing 'plays dealing with Scottish life and character', and ultimately of founding a 'Scottish National Theatre'. The example of the Abbey Theatre in Dublin was very much in mind, and this was perhaps a fatal confusion, for Scotland was no underdeveloped country seeking to articulate its own identity and to throw off colonial rule, but a highly industrialised nation which had embraced the cause of Empire enthusiastically. For the twelve years or so of their active existence the Players mounted seasons of mainly new Scottish plays in Glasgow and elsewhere in Scotland. In addition they visited London on several occasions and made a fair number of broadcasts. Although the company was composed of amateurs, some of whom were later to turn professional, the Players engaged professional directors, the most distinguished of whom was the young Tyrone Guthrie. Guthrie stayed for a couple of years during which time he led a summer tour of the Highlands and directed *The Sunlight Sonata*, the first play by James Bridie to be performed on the stage. The company suspended operations in 1934 amid mounting financial difficulties, having decided two years previously not to take the risks involved in turning professional, although retrospectively it can be seen that only a professional company would have been able to attain the rather lofty aims which the Players had set themselves.

The Curtain Theatre was a more modest venture. It was founded in 1933 by a group of Glasgow amateurs who wanted to give new playwrights the opportunity to develop their craft. Initially performances were given in the drawing room of a large Victorian house and then later in the Lyric Theatre. For five years its work continued and it was through the Curtain that the writer Robert McLellan and the actor Duncan Macrae first came to public attention.

Unity Theatre was a much more radically oriented organisation than either the Scottish National Players or the Curtain. It was formed in 1941, as part of the national Unity Theatre movement, by amateurs from a number of clubs including the Workers' Theatre Group, the Transport Players and the Jewish Institute Players. Although it would be foolish to claim that Unity's members were all thorough going Marxists, the organisation itself had a commitment to proletarian drama which was clear in its choice of plays from the existing repertoire and from the kind of new work it presented. Conscious of the difficulties of making much progress as an amateur company, after the war Unity established a professional company which operated alongside the amateur one. The professional company played throughout Scotland, and like the Scottish National Players made a number of visits to London. Unity came to an end for the usual financial reasons, although for a time it had enjoyed the support of the recently established Arts Council, but that support was withdrawn, on account of alleged financial mismanagement. Several of the actors who began with Unity pursued successful careers in the Scottish theatre.

The efforts of these companies could be regarded as a continuation of the work of the Glasgow Repertory Theatre which had been established in that city in 1909. Under the directorship of Alfred Wareing a professional company performed challenging seasons of contemporary drama in the Royalty Theatre. The company, whose work was underwritten by public subscription, disbanded on the outbreak of war in 1914, but in the five years of its existence it performed over a hundred plays, almost a third of which were new to the stage and 16 of which were new Scottish plays. The company's most notable 'coup' was its presentation in 1909 of *The Seagull*, the first production of a Chekhov play in Britain. What the Glasgow Rep did for indigenous dramatists was to offer them what they most need, *professional* performance of their work alongside a strong contemporary repertoire. This the amateur clubs did not and could not offer. What they did do, however, was to make the presentation of Scottish plays central to their activities and the Scottish National Players and the Curtain made this their raison d'etre.

Towards the end of the inter-war period there were signs of the major shift from amateur to professional, which was in the offing. Perth Repertory Theatre was established in 1935 by David Steuart and Marjorie Dence who had met while studying in London, and by 1939 the company felt secure enough to mount a small theatre festival during which Bridie's *The Golden Legend of Shults* was presented. On the outbreak of war Robert Thornley, an English producer, took the lead in establishing a rep in Dundee, and during the war the tiny Byre at St Andrews was occupied by a professional company. In Glasgow the Rutherglen Rep (originally known as the MSU after its founder Molly S Urquhart) and the Citizens came into being in 1939 and 1943 respectively as did the smaller Park, in 1940. It was the forerunner of the theatre opened in Pitlochry in 1951 by the founder of the Park, John Stewart. Edinburgh finally caught up with the rest of the country when the Gateway Company took possession of the theatre of that name in 1953. What all of this meant was that by the end of the period under consideration the Scottish dramatist found himself in a situation where several theatres could and did offer professional presentations of new indigenous work. Several of the writers who had begun in the inter-war period were able to profit from this change which made the prospect of adequate performance more likely and the financial rewards of playwriting somewhat less miserable.

If the Scottish dramatist was working within a difficult theatrical situation, he was also working within a complex and fractured cultural context of which the issue of language can be regarded as a symptom. Scots had long since ceased to be the language of the educated classes, who had abandoned it for a version of English distinguishable from the standard form only in the matter of accent and occasional Scots words and expressions. Scots continued to be spoken but in rural areas and by the working classes. A further complication was that urban working class Scots was often regarded as in some way a debased form compared to rural varieties. For the Scots writer the desire to articulate his Scottishness through his choice of language was strong but for the dramatist the problem was more acute than for a poet like MacDiarmid. Unless he decided to use non-naturalistic forms, a hazardous course in an age when naturalism dominated the stage, he would be compelled to ensure that his characters spoke in ways which were recognisably close to reality. If he wished to use Scots rather than English then he would inevitably have to turn to rural or urban working class themes. Alternatively, he could turn to history, to periods when Scots was a viable language spoken throughout society. The linguistic situation was compounded by the existence of a Gaelic-speaking minority, whose experience historically has been different from that of their fellow Scots. But as a consequence of the great migrations southwards in the nineteenth century Scottish lowland culture has been imbued with memories of, and nostalgia for, a way of life radically different from that endured in the industrial slums and factories.

The responses of Scottish dramatists to this complex situation were varied. Barrie (1860–1937), as has been noted, worked in the English theatre, but his native land is not totally neglected in his plays. Scotland is the setting for *The Little Minister* (1897) Barrie's adaptation of his novel of the same name, the hero of *What Every Woman Knows* (1908) is the archetypal Scotsman on the make, and the strange island which has such a devastating effect on the eponymous heroine *Mary Rose* (1920) is somewhere in the outer Hebrides. It could be argued further that the very strong streak of sentiment in Barrie, which on occasion topples over into sentimentality, is the most Scottish thing about him. Such sentimentality, whose origins must be sought in the emotional distortions produced by Scots Presbyterianism and other factors fuelled the Kailyard School of novelists and continues to fuel an important strand of Scottish popular fiction.

Barrie, after initial disappointment, turned himself into a writer of well made plays in which the action is usually lively, the characters varied, and the wit pleasing. In *The Admirable Crichton* (1902) that wit is deployed to explore the case in favour of an aristocracy of nature as opposed to one of birth, when Lord Loam's butler, Crichton, takes command of the situation after his master's family and entourage are marooned on a desert island. Barrie is no radical, however, and when the party is rescued normal social relations are smoothly resumed as if they had never been interrupted. Social issues do not feature much in Barrie's work and when they do they are not explored very enthusiastically. It might seem significant that in *The Little Minister* the action begins in the middle of a weavers' strike, but the strike merely serves as the starting point for the romantic entanglement of the young minister of Thrums by a gypsy lady who is really the disguised daughter of a local aristocrat.

If there is one aspect of Barrie's talent which made its mark on a theatre dominated by naturalism it was his interest in the supernatural. His most successful venture in this sphere is of course *Peter Pan* (1904) which continues to hold a special niche in the repertoire. Although *Peter Pan* is essentially a story for children, in it can be seen Barrie's attraction to the power of a world beyond the material one, a world of dreams and fantasies. In *Dear Brutus* (1917) and *Mary Rose* this attraction is most clearly expressed. *Dear Brutus* is set in the country house of a rather mysterious gentleman called Lob—the name is a variation on Puck—on Midsummer's Eve. Lob has brought together a disparate collection of individuals all of whom have in common the desire for a second chance in life. Outside the windows a strange wood appears as if from nowhere, and the characters do indeed dally with what might have been before returning to the present with its unavoidable complications. The allusion to Shakespeare with its implication that we, not circumstances, are responsible for our fates, lurks behind the action. *Dear Brutus* is a play of considerable wit and some pathos, but lacks depth. Barrie goes so far and no further in his presentation of emotional and sexual conflict as if he were always on the edge of powerful feeling but never immersed in it.

Mary Rose is a more disturbing piece, which focuses on the strange experiences of a girl whose life is arrested when she steps on to a remote Hebridean island. The first time her parents 'lose' her for a few days, but on the second occasion she disappears for twenty-five years, leaving behind her young husband and their baby son. When she returns she has not aged at all—and Barrie does not quite know what to do with her. At the end of the play she re-appears as a ghost to her son, now a young man, and seems to be regressing even further back into childhood as she expresses the wish to 'go away and play'. As the curtain falls she is summoned to her final rest and walks into the night. For all the rather cloying quality of some of the dialogue, Barrie does succeed in this play in creating the sense of a world beyond the rational. *Mary Rose* is a piece which still has the ability to send shivers down an audience's spine.

The case of James Bridie (1888–1951) is more interesting. Bridie had early work performed in Scotland, by the Scottish National Players and the Masque Players, but almost two thirds of his plays were given their first performances in London or elsewhere in England. Towards the end of his career Bridie had his work premiered by Glasgow Citizens' Theatre, the company which he was instrumental in forming. It is clear that while Bridie was happy to turn to several of the professional companies which appeared in the latter part of the period under consideration, in their absence he was not prepared to be stuck in the amateur theatre. Nor was there any need for him to be so. Bridie ranged widely in his choice of subject matter, and while many of his plays are set in Scotland, others draw their material from the Apocrypha or from contemporary English life. Indeed his most commercially successful play *Daphne Laureola* (1949) is set firmly in the south. In this piece Bridie explores the relationship between an aristocratic lady and a romantic young man who is infatuated by her. When her husband dies, the lady opts not for her passionate suitor but for her chauffeur. It is a typical Bridie twist, for all through his work there is a recurring insistence on the danger of illusion and pretension.[3] Lady Pitts in *Daphne Laureola* informs the young lover whom she has spurned that she prefers 'a nice clean pig sty' to the romantic dreams which he is offering; the heroine of the very entertaining *Tobias and the Angel* (1930) is told by the angel Raphael, with whom she has fallen in love, that she must be satisfied with her human lot; and Jonah in *Jonah and the Whale* (1932) is forced to accept, after his activities as a prophet have not endeared him to his fellows, that he is 'only an ordinary man'.

Furthermore Bridie makes it clear that he does not regard ordinariness as unworthy. The eponymous hero of *Mr Gillie* (1950) for example, finds that the young people whom he has encouraged and of whom he has expected so much, come to grief in the world, but Bridie suggests that we should not therefore regard Gillie's life as a failure. However Bridie's insistence on the essentially limited nature of experience and on the ease with which aspiration and illusion can be confused, goes hand in hand with a curious admiration for men who ignore the boundaries of conventional morality and decency. The famous dissentor and resurectionist Robert Knox is presented in just such a light in *The Anatomist* (1930). He may be obtaining his specimens in a highly dubious way but there is more than a whiff of the end justifying the means in the dramatist's presentation of him. In another medical play, *The Sleeping Clergyman* (1933) Bridie presents us with several generations of the Cameron family. The first Charlie Cameron is a boorish medical student whose behaviour to all and sundry is devoid of any shred of decency, but we are told there is a spark of genius in Charlie. That spark is kindled to a flame in Charlie's grandson who at the end of the play is shown developing a vaccine which will save the world from some terrible epidemic. He too is a pretty disagreeable individual but the coexistence of genius with immorality apparently renders the immorality less heinous. While Bridie is clearly making an interesting observation here, for geniuses are not always the most virtuous of people, there does seem to be a less than grudging admiration on the dramatist's part for the characters he is presenting.

It might be concluded from all of this that Bridie is a writer interested in philosophical questions. But that would be to overstate the position. He is a writer who uses ideas, and plays with them on the stage, but he is in no sense a philosophical dramatist. *Mr Bolfry* (1943), is worth considering in this light. It appears to be a serious attempt to explore the relationship between good and evil in the context of Calvinism, and is set during the last war in a Free Kirk manse in the West Highlands. On a wretched Sunday afternoon two English soldiers who have been billetted in the manse ally themselves with the niece of the Reverend McCrimmon and take on her uncle in a debate about the true nature of Calvinism. The proceedings are enlivened when Mr Bolfry, an emissary of the devil dressed as a minister, is conjured up. Unfortunately the philosophical debate which ensues becomes hopelessly confused as Bridie's theatrical instincts ride roughshod over his dialectical enthusiasm.

Bridie has sometimes been compared with Shaw since both are writers who have used the theatre to explore ideas, but ideas always take second place to people in Bridie. He lacks Shaw's intellectual rigour and is more interested in other human beings. He is best regarded as a serious entertainer, a writer whose plays divert an audience with wit and skill but only rarely leave it with much to chew on or move it to great emotion.

A possible exception to this harsh judgement is *The Queen's Comedy* (1950) written towards the end of Bridie's career. It takes its material from the story of the Trojan Wars and presents it from a grim unheroic perspective. The ordinary mortals are seen as the victims of the unfeeling machinations of gods and generals. At the end of the play some of the mortals who have been killed, presented with the opportunity to confront the gods, seek an explanation for the terrible suffering which they have endured. But from the gods answers come there none. Bridie seems to be suggesting that there is no explanation for suffering and that to look for one is foolish. Far better to endure as best one can. *The Queen's Comedy* is an ambitious and challenging play. However it is not entirely successful: crucially, the dialogue of the more philosophical passages lacks the liveliness of the conversation between the ordinary mortals, and feels rather limp. Despite this the play is much more interesting than many of Bridie's other pieces.

Bridie's survival in the repertoire is uncertain, but he remains important. Quite apart from his efforts to develop theatre in Scotland, his initiation of the Citizens', his role in the establishment of the College of Drama in Glasgow, he demonstrated that it is possible for a Scottish playwright to work from a home base and succeed in the London theatre and beyond. Barrie's nationality was partially submerged in his plays, but Bridie's was not. He ranged widely in subject matter but he often presented Lowland Scotland on the stage, in such a fashion however that 'foreign' audiences had no difficulty in understanding, and since most of his characters were middle class, these audiences had no linguistic barriers to confront either. Bridie knew his own class and how to present it theatrically. The tragedy of his career is that perhaps because of the limitations imposed by his membership of that class he was not as good a dramatist as he could or should have been. How far he falls short becomes all too clear when we compare his work with that of Ibsen. Bridie is nonetheless the most notable writer of his generation who wrote about the lowland middle class. There were a few others, and indeed the Glasgow Repertory Company, whose performance had stimulated Bridie's interest in the theatre, presented work by two of them, G J Hamlen and Anthony Rowley. Rowley's *A Weaver's Shuttle* (1910) for example deals with the problems faced by a family firm which had not up-dated its production process—a rather modern theme—and although it is by no means a penetrating study it does have the merit of focusing on contemporary experience. It has to be said, however, that the two best plays which the Glasgow Repertory Company presented represent rather different strands in Scottish drama.

One of these, *Campbell of Kilmohr* (1914), is set in the Highlands in the period after the crushing of the 1745 Jacobite rebellion. It is a grim and skilful little piece about the attempt of a government official, the Campbell of the title, to wheedle out of a Jacobite prisoner the location of a rebel hideout, and in it the playwright is concerned to contrast the deviousness of the Lowlander with the integrity of the Highlander. The straightforward nature of this contrast is unfortunately indicative of the rather uncomplicated view of the nation's history which all too many Scottish playwrights have been inclined to take.

Campbell of Kilmohr takes place in the Highlands, and what is striking about the plays presented in the inter-war period is of how many of them this can be said. An examination of the output of the Scottish National Players— one act and full length plays—makes that clear. The most notable of the Players dramatists, John Brandane, set most of his plays on the island of Mull, sometimes in the past, sometimes the present. His best piece, *The Glen is Mine* (1923) explores the conflict between development and conservation in an entertaining if not particularly profound fashion, while *The Treasure Ship* (1924) gently satirises the attempts of businessmen in a West Highland town to stir up the interest of tourists in a Spanish galleon which is supposedly sunk in the vicinity. *The Spanish Galleon* (1922), a one act piece, relates the sinking of the Armada vessel in Tobermory Bay. Brandane does not offer any great insight into the nature of the Highland experience, historical or contemporary. His work is set firmly in the tradition of viewing the Highlands as a kind of Arcadia peopled by characters given to strange behaviour and lapses into the Gaelic.

The most distinguished dramatist who turned to history for his subject matter is Robert McLellan (1907–1984). McLellan's early work was presented by the amateur Curtain Theatre in Glasgow, but later in his career he benefited from the establishment of the reps, several of which performed his plays. McLellan is a dramatist who always seems to have been happier writing about the past than the present. Indeed on one occasion McLellan told the present writer that he felt that what he was doing was to create the kind of drama which would have been written in previous eras had there been a thriving Scottish theatre then. McLellan employs a vigorous Scots, which although archaic to the ear of a modern audience, is not so far removed from the rural Scots dialects of the early twentieth century as to make it incomprehensible. There is no question that with English McLellan's grip falters, and when his characters speak in that language they are less convincing than his Scots speaking characters. McLellan saw the resuscitation of the Scots language as a vital cultural project; indeed in one of his plays, *The Flouers o' Edinburgh* (1948) he satirises the eighteenth-century Edinburgh gentry who had enlisted the help of tutors from the south to assist them in their desire to acquire the civilised tones of English.

The play of McLellan's which shows most sign of surviving in the repertoire is *Jamie the Saxt* (1937). Set in the period 1591–94 when the young king was trying to stamp his authority on his country, and outwit the various factions ranged against him, the play offers an interesting portrait of James as a canny and perceptive individual who navigates his way through treacherous waters until he can look forward confidently to claiming the throne of England on Elizabeth's death. McLellan weaves a fairly intricate plot structure in which

Jamie is pitched against scheming lords, Edinburgh burghers, the Presbyterian Church and Elizabeth's government. The king survives not through
personal bravery, of which he appears to have a short supply, but through
the exercise of cunning and subtlety. The role of Jamie was originally played
by Duncan Macrae and the evidence suggests that his interpretation of the
part leant a little too much to the comic for McLellan's taste. As Ron Bain's
interpretation in the 1982 revival by the Scottish Theatre Company illustrated
there is no shortage of comic potential in the part, but there are other facets
to the character as well. *Jamie the Saxt* also provides ample evidence of
McLellan's skill in handling a complex plot and in the creation of lively
threatrical activity. The problem however with most of his work is that for a
modern audience the skill and liveliness do not compensate for a sense that
his plays have little to say to it. Furthermore, as time goes on McLellan's
Scots no longer seems like an attempt at the recreation of a language, but
more like a *cul de sac* up which other dramatists venture at their peril.

The presentation of rural lowland Scotland was also prefigured by the
Glasgow Repertory Company, since *Jean* by Donald Colquhoun (1910), the
other play presented by Wareing's company which has some call on our
attention, has just such a setting. But *Jean*, which presents the life of a farmer
in Lanarkshire as a constant struggle against adversity, is very different in
tone from the vast majority of the plays set in a similar milieu which appeared
in the inter-war period. This was the time when the 'Scots comedy' was turned
out in astonishing numbers to meet the insatiable demand of the amateur
movement. For all that the Scottish National Players set their sights far
higher than did the amateur movement in general, they too presented a fair
number of these plays. The archetypal Scots comedy is set in a village or
small town, the characters speak in the Doric and the action revolves around
misunderstandings, courtships and practical jokes, the basic ingredients of
comedy. The influence of the music hall sketch is clear in their construction.
Many Scots comedies are well written, most are derivative and eminently
forgettable. This might not matter were it not for the fact that there is
overwhelming evidence that in at least one case the amateur movement
destroyed a dramatist who had the potential to develop into a writer of
stature.

Joe Corrie (1894–1968) was a Fife miner who during the industrial conflict
of the 1920s turned to playwriting. *In Time o' Strife* (1928), his first full
length play, was performed by an amateur group in Fife made up mainly of
miners. The play explores the terrible hardships which striking imposed on
mining families, and brings out well the pressures which drive men to blackleg
on their mates. Corrie's commitment to justice and equality is clear enough
but he is too sensitive a writer to issue simple minded summonses to the
barricades. There are problems in the play: the central character wavers so
much in his attitude that he turns into an actor's nightmare, and Corrie's
undoubted ability to secure easy laughs gets the better of him all too often.
But there can be little doubt that *In Time o' Strife* signalled the arrival of a
proletarian dramatist of considerable potential. What happened to Corrie
thereafter was tragic. He had already had one act plays performed locally,

and two of these were taken up by the Scottish National Players, but despite the success of *In Time o' Strife*, which was toured on a semi-professional basis by the group which originally presented it, Corrie found it very difficult to continue working in this vein. The Scottish National Players refused to present *In Time o' Strife* apparently on political grounds, and lacking other outlets for his work, Corrie found himself turning to the amateur movement, which was only too happy to snap up the highly proficient Scots comedies which he produced. Corrie was living from his writing and he had to meet the demands of the market. If a company like Unity Theatre had been in existence at the time almost certainly he would have developed in a more interesting direction, but as it was, although he did manage to have produced a few one acters like *Hewers of Coal* (1937), which were much more radical in their political stance than his comedies, he became the toast of SCDA festivals and the star of publisher Brown Son and Ferguson's list of plays for amateurs.

With the arrival on the scene of Unity, Scotland had a company of some substance with a clear commitment to radical work. Unity's most commercially successful venture was Robert McLeish's *The Gorbals Story* (1946) which portrays the dreadful housing conditions in Glasgow and their human consequences. It is not a particularly impressive piece of writing, for McLeish is clearly learning his job as a playwright—alas he wrote only one other piece which was not a success—but is carried along by the author's concern for his characters. McLeish insists that these people matter, and, for all the deprivations they suffer, their lives are full of resilience and compassion. Unity presented a range of other new Scottish work, almost all naturalistic: George Munro who later had plays performed by the Citizens, began his career when Unity presented *Gold in his Boots* (1947) which is about a young man's attempts to escape poverty through pursuing a career as a footballer; James Barke wrote about the shipyards in *Major Operation* (1941); and Ena Lamont Stewart wrote about the realities of life in the nursing profession in *Starched Aprons* (1945), while in *Men Should Weep* (1947) she explored the tensions in a family under the stress of poverty.

Although *Men Should Weep*, with its emphasis on the sufferings of women, might seem to anticipate the more committed feminism of the 1970s and 1980s, what is very noticeable about the play is the even handed approach its author takes. Maggie Morrison's life is no picnic: her husband is unemployed and has only just managed to curb his alcoholic excesses; one of her children has tuberculosis; an older son has married a worthless wife. There is ample evidence of the struggle which women like Maggie have, but Stewart does not attack men as such. Indeed some of the nastier characters in the play, Maggie's daughter-in-law for example, and her 'greetin faced' mother-in-law, are women. It is also clear that Maggie's husband, John, although of little use to his wife, does try to find work, and that Maggie is still in love with him. Nonetheless the ending of the play when first performed was bleak in the extreme with every imaginable catastrophe befalling Maggie, culminating in her own death in childbirth. But Stewart later rewrote the last act and provided a much happier ending in which Maggie asserts herself decisively against her husband by insisting that the money, which one of her daughters is offering her parents to enable them to move to a better house, is accepted, despite the fact that her father decries it as a 'whore's winnin's'.

What remains striking about Unity's work is that it is unique in its sustained interest in contemporary social and political issues. The Glasgow Rep presented a few plays about the Scottish bourgeoisie, but in the output of the Scottish National Players and the Curtain there is only occasional engagement with political and social concerns. In its place there is an obsession with the past, with rural life and with the Highlands. In this situation Unity's emphasis on the contemporary and the committed is very important, although Unity's approach did not have a significant impact on the mainstream Scottish theatre until the 1970s and early 1980s.

It is clear from an examination of Scottish dramatic writing in more recent times that urban naturalism has become the dominant mode, so if there is a Scottish dramatic tradition then it can be traced back to writers who worked for Unity. Bridie's interest in the Scottish bourgeoisie can of course be paralleled in some of the work of Robert Kemp and his attraction to ideas in the plays of Tom Gallacher. The use of historical themes continued in the work of Kemp and Alexander Reid, though of more recent writers of note only Donald Campbell has frequently turned to history for his material. The Scots comedy is still alive and well, as are its practitioners in the amateur movement, but it is a pale shadow of what it once was and much less important than the subsidised reps. There, when signficant commitment to indigenous writing is to be found, and that is far from universal, it is the urban naturalistic play which has been presented most often.

The triumph of urban naturalism does of course have its dangers: themes tackled can be limited in range, as can the language employed in their exploration, and the more profound depths of experience can be neglected in favour of a rather easily won 'commitment'. Whether Scottish drama can reach a proper maturity when playwrights range widely in form and content remains to be seen. Whether the theatre in Scotland is genuinely and permanently committed to encouraging such a process of development is an open question.

NOTES

1   *Glasgow Herald*, 18 May 1895.
2   Gareth Stedman Jones 'Working class culture and working class politics in London 1870–1900' in B Waites *et al.* (eds) '*Popular Culture, Past and Present*' (London, 1981).
3   *See* Christopher Small, 'Bridie: the Unfinished Business,' *Scottish Theatre*, January 1971, for a discussion of James Bridie's resistance to pretension as also a defence mechanism against the philstinism of the middle-class into which he was born.

FURTHER READING

PLAYS

Both Barrie and Bridie were well served by London publishers, Hodder and Constable respectively. Gowans and Gray of Glasgow published several of the plays presented by the Glasgow Repertory Company, and William MacLellan of Glasgow several of Robert McLellan's plays. Calder and Boyars, London, brought out editions of *The Hypocrite* and *Jamie the Saxt* in 1970 and 1971 respectively. Brown Son and Ferguson of Glasgow published many of Joe Corrie's plays, and *In Time o' Strife* was the centrepiece of a selection of Corrie's work published by the 7.84 Theatre Company, Edinburgh, in 1985. Robert McLeish's *The Gorbals Story* has appeared from the same imprint as has Ena Lamont Stewart's *Men Should Weep*. John Brandane's plays were published by Constable.

CRITICISM AND BIOGRAPHY

Bannister, W, *James Bridie and his Theatre* (London, 1955)
Hutchison, D, *The Modern Scottish Theatre* (Glasgow, 1977)
Isaac, W, *Alfred Wareing* (London, 1951)
Low, J T, *Doctors, devils, saints and sinners: a study of Bridie* (Edinburgh, 1980)
Luyben, H, *James Bridie, clown and philosopher* (Pennsylvania, 1965)
Mackie, A, *The Scotch Comedians* (Edinburgh, 1973)
Tobin, T, *James Bridie* (Boston, 1980)
Wright, A, *J M Barrie. Glamour of Twilight* (Edinburgh, 1976)

Chapter 12

Reintegrated Scots: The Post-MacDiarmid Makars

TOM HUBBARD

The revival of poetry in Scots—as promoted by Hugh MacDiarmid in the 1920s—implied much more than is suggested by the terms 'synthetic Scots' or 'Lallans'. It is often remarked that the first term has unfortunate overtones of laboratorial artificiality and that the second evokes the douce babble of linguistic dilettantes drawn from the academic and other middle class professions: hardly encouraging images for the struggle to gain for Scots even that limited status which is now accorded to Gaelic. My alternative term 'reintegrated Scots' is offered for more than linguistic reasons. It suggests not only the reunification of a language which has fragmented into dialects, but also the reconnection of its unique culture to other cultures at home and abroad: implied in this is a determined response to the urgent questions of man in society and in the cosmos.

Such was MacDiarmid's example in *A Drunk Man Looks at the Thistle*, together with his other work in and about Scots. By his eightieth year he could be retrospective:

> To essay to write 'high poetry' in Scots after a lapse of centuries was no easy matter. It called for a knowledge of the whole range and potentialities of the Scots language, and a degree of intellectuality, by no means to be generally found, so it is not surprising that, while a few contemporary Scots poets have emulated the best of their medieval predecessors, and shown at the same time an adequate appreciation of the achievements and problems of modern life, the majority have been content to occupy a humbler rôle. (Introduction to Donald Campbell, *Rhymes 'n Reasons*, 1972)

Intellectuality; emulating the medieval makars; dealing with modern life. The following pages will concentrate on the poets who have most responded to these challenges.

As far back as 1923, in *The Scottish Chapbook*, MacDiarmid had claimed that the Scots vernacular was 'a vast unutilised mass of lapsed observation'. Scots could express whatever had been driven underground, lodged in the unconscious; it was appropriate that the first important makar after Mac-Diarmid should be a man with an instinct for archetypal symbolism and child psychology. William Soutar felt that 'if the Doric is to come back alive, it will come first on a cock-horse' and produced many bairnrhymes, riddles and

179

whigmaleeries beginning with *Seeds in the Wind* (1933, revised 1943). He thereby established a tradition, continued by J K Annand, 'Sandy Thomas Ross' and others, of writing poetry in Scots for children. In his adult poetry the symbolism, all too rarefied in his early verse in English, acquired a social and national toughness in his Scots work. He believed that the revival of Scots was related not only to 'the rediscovery of our national roots' but also to 'an alignment with the worker' ('Faith in the Vernacular', *The Voice of Scotland*, 1(1), 1938). Spoken Scots, albeit less dense than reintegrated Scots, remains strongest in the lower social strata—the 'driven underground' motif again—so the language is particularly appropriate to proletarian-cum-socialist themes. Soutar's ballad 'The Whale' certainly plunges the deeps, with the apparent rediscovery of MacDiarmid's Leviathan (itself appropriated from Herman Melville); nothing less is necessary for Scotland's renewal, for which Soutar had a powerful symbol in the unicorn:

> Owre ilka sound I hear the stound   [loud noise]
> O' the loupin' waterspoot,   [leaping]
> An' as it loupt the sea-baest gowp't   [gaped]
> An' the unicorn sprang oot:
> Aye, straucht atween the sinderin' chouks   [parting; jaws]
> The unicorn sprang oot.
>
> (*Poems in Scots and English*,
> selected by W R Aitken, 1975)

An even longer poem, 'The Auld Tree' (*Poems in Scots*, 1935), is resonant with references to Yggdrasil, the Nordic world-tree whose roots reach hell and whose branches reach heaven, and True Thomas's Eildon Tree, with its suggestion of mysteries revealed over a long period of time. The former is familiar from MacDiarmid's *A Drunk Man Looks at the Thistle* (indeed, Soutar's tree metamorphoses into the thistle); the latter will become the central motif in Sydney Goodsir Smith's *Under the Eildon Tree*. Scotland's roots are deep: its blossoms will range wide.

'The Auld Tree' is concerned with prophecy, with vision: as embodiment of this, Wallace, Burns and MacDiarmid all feature in the poem. In his panoramic *Sing a Sang o' Scotland* (1944) that underrated makar, Albert D Mackie, castigated the 'scribblin rhymesters' of his day and invoked the ambitious, large-scale qualities of Gaelic poetry and music. Interviewed by George Bruce in 1977 MacDiarmid declared his own high conception of the poet's task: 'The organic apprehension that can only be achieved through poetry seems to me sadly lacking. There has been a playing down . . . of the role of the imagination. The seer, the foreknower, has been displaced in a hierarchy of human beings. He requires to be replaced there.'

In due course it will become clear which two of MacDiarmid's successors, in my view, have most fulfilled this requirement as far as Scots is concerned. Most of Robert Garioch's work, however, is a great deal more circumscribed. Garioch evolved the persona of 'the wee man' whose *faux-naïf* speculations culminate in a witty put-down of the big yins. This is very much in the ironic, modern line of Charlie Chaplin and the Good Soldier Švejk; it is often remarked that Scots is as effective in its reductive idiom as in its visionary grandeur, and that Garioch excels in the former. The 'underground' motif modulates to those voices which are rarely heard in the councils of the great: the schoolteacher with the trauchles of his daily routine, his poetic aspirations effectively marginalised, as in 'Garioch's Repone til George Buchanan'; Embro urchins pursued by the polis in 'Fi'baw in the Street'; 'Brither Worm' very literally a creature from 'underground' as he snooves up throu a hole in the New Toun. Subterranean, yes; subversive, no. Sisyphus is condemned to a perpetual struggle with 'the muckle big scunnersom boulder'; far from challenging the Boss, though, he merely hopes he won't be caught having a fly tea-break. He is, after all, 'shair of his cheque at the month's end.' The railings of Dostoyevsky's 'underground man' were vehemently conservative; while we cannot find the Garioch persona guilty-by-association, it appeals more to populist sentiment than to democratic commitment.

Yet Garioch could also write 'The Canny Hen', a sardonic fable against industrial exploitation. He was a consummate verse-craftsman—especially in his versions of Belli's sonnets—and he speaks for craftsmanship generally. In 'Perfect' the wee man (a French polisher) acquires a degree of nobility in his stubborn preference, against the slick reliability of machine production, for the artisan's conscientious struggle with his materials. Garioch may have rejected the role of the bard (in the sense of the social poet offering direction to his people) and kept to that of the makar but a more ambitious quality is evident in at least two of his longer poems. 'The Wire' is a brooding, night-marish vision based on his memories of a POW camp, and in 'The Muir' a philosophical, theological and scientific argument amply fulfils MacDiarmid's demand for intellectuality in poetry. Garioch's own favourites among his works are his greatest achievement: the Scots versions of George Buchanan's Latin tragedies *Jephthah* and *The Baptist* (both 1959). The Prologue to *Jephthah* has an orchestral sonority:

> I come frae the Thunderer's throne in Hevin,
> his airborne herald, til Israel's hame
> promised to Jacob's seed as the centre o pouer . . .

In these works the populist cunning gives way entirely to the democratic intellect: together with Douglas Young's versions of Aristophanes (*The Pud-docks*, 1957; *The Burdies*, 1959) they reassert what Dr George Davie has called 'the vernacular basis of Scottish humanism', the once-proud relationship of mastery of the classics to mastery of Scots. In the late 1940s and early 1950s the democratic intellect was showing a decidedly working-class, left-wing character with T S Law's debut *Whit Tyme in the Day* (1948), the anthology *Fowrsom Reel* (1949), Alex Dow's *The New Rigged Ship* (1950) and (also in 1950) Tom Scott's discovery of his Scots voice while in Sicily: all this may prove to have had more long-term significance than the contemporary Lallans movement and its annual anthology, *Poetry Scotland*, edited by Maurice Lindsay who was later to desert the Scots cause.

Douglas Young was a prominent Lallans propagandist and his multifarious campaigns have distracted attention from his considerable achievement as a makar. He was that rare being, a university academic who was also a creative artist and a politico-cultural activist. His linguistic scholarship, together with his poetic gifts, made him one of our most accomplished translators of foreign poetry into Scots. He even tackled Lithuanian! In his version of Valéry's 'Le Cimetière Marin' ('The Kirkyaird by the Sea') the medieval Henryson–Dunbar tradition is nobly and movingly appropriate to a modern confrontation of the transience of human life. Tom Scott has remarked that in our over-individualistic and under-socialistic times there is a failure to take translation seriously as a creative activity: this may further explain the neglect of Douglas Young.

Young was the more universal because he was so local. His original poems—'Last Lauch', 'For a Wife in Jizzen [childbed]', 'Requiem', 'The Shepherd's Dochter' and many others—are the work not only of a Scot but of a north-Fifer. That strong sense of place in Scottish poetry eschews the sentimental and the picturesque. As a native of Tayport Young had the authority to claim that 'estuaries give you most markedly the feeling of being poised between two elements and two movements, the sense of the interaction of sea and land, of life and death and rebirth.'

His left-wing nationalism caused him to oscillate between the Scottish National Party (of which he was sometime Chairman) and the Labour Party. In parliamentary elections he was the SNP opponent, later a friend and supporter, of my grandfather who was Labour MP for Kirkcaldy Burghs between 1944 and 1959.

Fowrsom Reel, as the name suggests, carried the work of four poets, three of whom wrote in Scots—John Kincaid, George Todd and Thurso Berwick. It is curious that this 'Clyde Group' was writing in reintegrated Scots, given that Glaswegian dialect is less 'Scots' than other dialects and that today's Glasgow writers feel more at home in the conversational mode. John Kincaid was drawn to the poem of dramatic presentation, for multiple voices: a socialist counterpart to the medieval morality play. The line of descent is from Sir David Lyndsay's *Ane Satyre of the Thrie Estaites*. 'The Accuser' is 'a sort of cantata' for Alba, Worker and John MacLean, the legendary Clydeside Marxist. Glasgow is celebrated in the long poems 'Setterday Nicht Symphonie' and 'A Glesca Rhapsodie' which begins:

> Eh, ma citie o raucle sang [bold]
> ma braid stane citie wi dwaums o steel. [dreams]
> Eh, ma Glesca, ma mither o revolt,
> dauran the wunds in a raggit shawl.
> Eh ma hanselt hinnie wi scaurs o war, [darling]
> ma twalmonth lassock, ma carlin ages auld. [old woman]

In George Todd's 'Til ma Typewriter' the poet and his machine are in dialogue. The typewriter is more than just another commodity: made by workers, it can be an instrument of their liberation when used by the committed poet. Thurso Berwick (whose real name was Morris Blythman) contributes 'Brig o Giants' in which the Forth Railway Bridge, the Eiffel Tower and the Dniepro Dam are in symbolic solidarity; Blythman was born in Inverkeithing, the Fife town just north of the bridge.

In this immediate post-war period, radiant with poetry if otherwise drab, there appeared a Scots masterpiece by one whose sympathies were left-wing nationalist but whose background was anything but proletarian. In 1948 was published Sydney Goodsir Smith's sequence of love-elegies *Under the Eildon Tree*; it was revised six years later. Smith was born in New Zealand, the son of a future professor of medicine at Edinburgh University; he was educated at private schools and at Oxford. Yet he went on to become one of the most persuasive writers in Scots this century. Unlike the native working-class makars Smith had to *choose* his language. It was a matter not only of *individual* existentialism (the usual kind) but of *social* existentialism: that is to say, in order to find fulfilment as a creative individual he needed to seek fulfilment as a creative social being. 'Bein himsel' (as MacDiarmid might have put it) meant being part of the Scottish people and their culture.[1] For him the most authentic medium was Scots, although it might not always have seemed so at the beginning: in his early collections he was still awkwardly feeling his way. The promise was still there, and in *The Deevil's Waltz* (1946) he had clearly absorbed the example of the ballads and of the makars, particularly Dunbar: the harsh medieval grotesquerie suited his sensibility— and suits that of even later poets such as Alan Bold whose *Summoned by Knox* (1985) draws on the eldritch flavour of Fife folklore. This kind of thing can be 'modern' in a truer sense than any shallow trendiness. Our current poetic climate is dominated by the thin-lipped, the bland, the fear of going over the top; Smith, however, revelled in a Dionysian exuberance of language and life. He combined the personae of gangrel and scholar: *Under the Eildon Tree* juxtaposes the booziness and randiness of the howff with a grand allusiveness to world culture, as in elegy XIII, 'The Black Bull o Norroway'. Smith weaves quotations from foreign literatures into the texture of an already rich Scots; the European identity, so striking in Henryson, Dunbar and Buchanan, is reaffirmed. Europe, though, need not be the limit: more recently James Alex McCash, in his *A Bucolic Nickstick* (1983), includes Scots versions of Persian poetry; not unlike Smith, McCash offers us one verbal cornucopia after another. MacDiarmid, Smith and McCash have between them created the Scots neo-baroque.

Under the Eildon Tree is a 'quest' poem, seeking out the wildly varying experiences of love, both its 'follie' and its 'granderie'. The work is rooted in the myth of Thomas the Rhymer, in his way an outcast, a gangrel, as well as poet-seer. This archetype undergoes metamorphosis into Orpheus, Burns, Tristram and others—notably Oblomov. Thomas (Learmont) the Rhymer is the supposed ancestor of Lermontov, who helped to create 'the superfluous man' in Russian literature. Goncharov's Oblomov represents the degeneration of the superfluous man. In elegy V, Smith considers himself even worse than Oblomov.

> O, michtie Stalin in the Aist!
> Could ye but see me nou,
> The type, endpynt and final blume
> O' decadent capitalistical thirldom   [slavery]
> —It took five hunder year to produce me—
> Och, could ye but see me nou
> What a sermon could ye gie
>   Further frae the Hailie Kremlin
> Bummlan and thunderan owre the Steppes,
> Athort the mountains o' Europe humman
> Till Swack! at my front door, the great *Schloss Schmidt*
> That's Numéro Cinquante (ПЯТЬДЕСЯТ, ye ken) . . .   [pyat'desyat: fifty]

John C Hall has remarked on Smith's concern with transience, particularly the transience of love: in 'Credo' (*Figs and Thistles*, 1959) 'man must celebrate the progress of life itself, clinging to a personal ideal of truth as his only source of stability.' The existential vision again, applying also to *Under the Eildon Tree* and Smith's work generally. 'Luve and libertie are one' declares the makar in *The Vision of the Prodigal Son* (1960); in other words, individual and social freedom must be seen as interdependent; the quality of the struggle affects the quality of its outcome. In Smith's verse drama *The Wallace* (1960) the hero is doomed but we are exhilarated by his defiance of his mean-spirited captors. Others less exhilarated tend to damn this play with faint praise, pooh-poohing its alleged 'lumpen-nationalism'. For Sydney Goodsir Smith, Scotland was not an occasion for crude banner-waving but an extension of his own (and his Wallace's) full-blooded humanity: sound basis for a genuine nationalism and socialism. *The Wallace* is companionable with another verse-drama in Scots: R S Silver's *The Bruce* (1986; composed 1948–51).

'A very wide-awake and highly competent skilled man working in the coalfields of the Lowlands.' Douglas Young was referring, in 1952, to T S Law. Thirty-odd years later, Law has become an unperson of Scottish poetry, omitted even from the footnotes and indexes of the literary histories. Yet T S Law and Tom Scott, himself long slighted by the establishment, have in my view created the most impressive body of work in reintegrated Scots since MacDiarmid; indeed, more than any other makars they have striven to advance the MacDiarmidian tradition.

Law's Scottish socialism is uncompromising, and his Scots is dense, but his neglect may also be explained by his intense intellectualism. In the June 1947 issue of the *New Scot* he denounced 'certain tinpot enemies of intellectual poetry who know neither intellect from inkspots nor poetry from peever.' Such people are still powerful arbiters of taste. Yet the supposed 'difficulty' of Law's work can be exaggerated. His dialectical sensibility enables him to move with ease between sophisticated intellectual argument and illustration from folklore, as witness his many references to children's street-games and songs; like Hamish Henderson and Thurso Berwick, he has contributed directly to the folk tradition with his protest songs. His passion for music is itself dialectical, and has influenced the very structure of his poetry, for example in the use of 'hameil contarpynt' in *Moses at Mount Sinai* (unpublished; composed 1959–82). Law is no aesthete indulging in form for its own sake: the content of the poem concerns a dialectic of integrity and opportunism, of Moses and Aaron, of the former's trees of the Law and the latter's garden flowers of religious ritual. *Moses at Mount Sinai* shows that Law, like MacDiarmid, is involved with 'the tragedy of an unevolved people' and their potential evolution.

Licht attoore the Face (unpublished; composed 1966–78) is, like Tom Scott's *Brand the Builder* (1975), a profoundly moving meditation on Scottish working-class life and values. Law mourns his 'neebors' (workmates) killed in the Lindsay Colliery, Kelty, Fife, on 14 December 1957. He recalls how he learned of the disaster; on that day he was not in Fife but in Lanarkshire, and saw a newspaper lying by the footpath:

> and I boued ma hochs thare an luftit truith   [thighs]
> abuin the clert o cauld winter stoor   [dirt]
> tae pass the tyme amang the steer an sturt   [strife, trouble]
> o the ongauns o aa the wurld at hame   [ongoings]
> i the heidlynes. At hame, ay, at hame
> i thur lang hame for some.
>
>   Till then, never had
> I kent whit a stoond was, but this I kent then   [heavy blow, pain]
> that the Greeks never had a better wurd for it.

There is a poetry, then, that is 'underground' not only in relation to the generally-perceived poetry scene, but in its literal content. The Fife coalfields have also yielded the work of Joe Corrie, whose 'The Image o' God' is one of the most memorable poems on the miner's lot; the tradition has been continued by such younger makars as William Hershaw and Ian W King, both of whom display a mastery of the local idiom. Lanarkshire is the scene of Walter Perrie's *A Lamentation for the Children* (1977), composed in English and Scots sections, of which the finest is the lyric on arling, the ritual by which a child was bound to work in the pits for life. Most of the Scots poems in Ian Bowman's *Orientations* (1977) are concerned with the life—and death—of mining folk.

In *A Brawlik Makar* (unpublished; composed 1982–3), Law is moving in the direction of an epic of ideas. It is a study of MacDiarmid, distinguished from an academic treatise not simply by the fact that it is in verse, but by its author's passionate commitment to his argument and its implications. MacDiarmid's work embodies Law's conviction that socialism is not only an economic and political programme but a complex of intellectual, ethical and artistic values. A leading motif in Law's work is that the freedom of the people is dependent on the freedom of the poet; in consequence the latter is deliberately circumscribed by the powers that be. *A Brawlik Makar* contains this passage:

> Wurds are the freens o freedom. Daenae you
> forget that, you yersel incarcerate:
> they byde thur wheesht for you yersel tae free them   [wait in silence]
> as Hugh MacDiarmid freed Scots wurds whuin hame
> haed made a preison for them in the mynds
> o the jyler-Scots thursels whoe haednae thocht
> tae mak a benner cell athin the hert;   [inner; within]
> thon was the grun for gangerels an galliards!   [ground; lively young men]

Law refers not only to the release of the Scots language (and, by implication, the release of the Scottish people): in 1981 his South African niece, Barbara Hogan, was gaoled by the apartheid régime for belonging to the African National Congress.

Towards the end of *A Brawlik Makar* Law speculates that MacDiarmid's later English poetry 'may be mair tellin/in future Scots wrytin nor in future English/in Scotland.' His own work, if readily available, would present its own challenge to younger makars in terms of its depth and expansiveness. With one early exception, Law's published booklets have been issued by himself, and they represent but a fraction of his output.[2]

The poetry of Tom Scott may also 'throw a longer shadow as time recedes'.[3] This poet-seer is profoundly influenced by the medieval makars, even more than was Sydney Goodsir Smith. He despises fashion, but is contemporary in the most genuine sense: contemporary with the past, whose poets are his colleagues; contemporary with the present, for twentieth century world events affect him deeply; contemporary with a future threatened by capitalistic scrambling and nuclear insanity. He would, I think, endorse the credo of the veteran Norwegian poet Rolf Jacobsen: 'the poet has to walk ahead, bark, and signal danger.'

Scott was once described as 'a cross between Henryson and Keir Hardie'. His medievalism is not pastiche, but is rooted in a precapitalist ethic that is both humane (Henryson) and communal (Dunbar). In his book on Dunbar (1966) he commends that makar's attack on the new ideology of the Edinburgh merchants—'Singular proffeit so dois you blind,/The common proffeit gois behind'. In his Scots 'transcreations' of Villon—made at the behest of T S Eliot—it is clear that like his friend Goodsir Smith he is on the side of the gangrels, not so much for their roguery as their being 'agin the government' and flouting the manifold hypocrisies of bourgeoisdom. The 'Keir Hardie' side suggests a socialism that is not afraid to be utopian *as well as* scientific. Tom Scott grew up in Glasgow and St Andrews in the depressed 1920s and 1930s: he told me that he absorbed the idea that it was possible to be a socialist without being a Christian, but impossible to be a Christian without being also a socialist. Yeshua of Nazareth, Marx, Darwin and Jung have variously contributed to his world-view. He is a Scottish nationalist and internationalist 'for the very good reason that you cannot be one without the other.'

An Ode til New Jerusalem (1956) embodies an apparent paradox: a vision of socialist utopia composed in that aureate Scots style traditionally deemed to be aristocratic. The paradox, though, might well be glossed thus by T S Law in *A Brawlik Makar*: 'the yae great aristocracie o man,/the aristocracie o excellence/in ilka man, and at nae man's expense.'

> Open wide your diamant portals
> Let your twalfauld yetts gant open til us,
> Number us with your immortals
> And with holy meat and nectar fill us,
> That at last til our ain we may come
> Saikless and flawless, Jerusalem, frae all evil as free as a lamb.   [innocent]

After reading this, one would not be surprised to learn that Scott, like Law, is musically inclined: indeed he originally intended to become a singer. No-one in recent years has been more emphatic that 'poetry is verse that sings. If it's not verse, it's not poetry; if it doesn't sing it is verse that fails to become poetry. Poetry therefore is a musical art . . .'[4] When one talks of Tom Scott *composing* a poem one doesn't use the word lightly.

The Ship and ither Poems (1963) collects transcreations from Baudelaire, Villon, Dante, and the Anglo-Saxon. There are poems built round mythical archetypes from Homer to Melville (in 'Ahab' the title-hero has actually *survived* the struggle with Moby Dick: one thinks of Dante continuing the adventures of Ulysses where Homer left off! Indeed nine pages later we come to a Scots version of that very part of the *Inferno*). There is also 'The Bride' with its haunting first line—'I dreamed a luesome dream o ye yestreen'. 'Fergus' is a six-page epic taking us through Scottish history. Last, and certainly not least, there is 'The Ship':

> Sicna Ship the warld had never seen.
> To link the Auld Warld til the brairdan New   [burgeoning]
> We biggit up a haill pelagian toun,
> And spared nor men nor lands in makin her.

'The Ship' is more than an account of the building, voyage and wreckage of the *Titanic*: it also relates the development and the ultimate collapse, through capitalism, of European civilisation. This resonance of meaning from a specific reality to an expansive symbol exemplifies what Scott calls 'Polysemous Veritism'. Allegory broke up after the Middle Ages; poetry then took the twin lines of realism and symbolism. In modern times these two 're-integrate into a new polysemous art in which, instead of the abstract theology (or theory) of allegory proper, reality itself in the historical and scientific senses, becomes the adequate 'symbol' or allegorical term of a new vision.'[5] 'The Ship' is both vision and warning.

At the Shrine o the Unkent Sodger (1968) is a noble anti-militarist poem 'for recitation'—but *all* his poems are for recitation! On the day that America obliterates Hiroshima and Nagasaki, Albert Schweitzer is in the Congo healing the sick. Schweitzer 'avoids the hornet lest, in stingan him,/It kills itsel.' This reverence for life animates Scott's long nature-epic in English, *The Tree*

(1977). The full horrors of World War II, clearly unpurged by *At the Shrine*, are the object of his sorrow and anger in *The Dirty Business* (1986).

Creativity and destructiveness are twin themes of the autobiographical *Brand the Builder* (1975). The first section, 'Johnny Brand's Prologue' alternates between lyrical evocation of St Andrews and passionate denunciation of the destruction of its Cathedral and University by 'Reformers' and Anglicisers. Throughout the poem sex-hating Kirkians, anti-Scottish academics, smaa-toun philistines and assorted bourgeois parasites are contrasted with the real builders in what reads as a variation on Brecht's 'Wha biggit the seiven yetts o Thebes?' Malcolm Brand himself is a creator in stone: his son's materials will be words. Both will be adding something to the world. (Academicism is not confused with scholarship, which Scott admires—he is no mean scholar himself; Professor Étienne Swanson, a genuine scholar, is based on D'Arcy Thompson who encouraged the young Tom although he was not an official student of the University).

The Scots registers are appropriately varied according to omniscient narration or speech-based monologue, the first being more 'heightened', more 'literary' than the second. In 'Brand Soliloquises', the intelligent artisan considers the wider world of which St Andrews is an integral part, the world of the Hungarian uprising, genocide in Biafra, fascism in southern Europe; his own lifetime 'frae the horse-drawn cars in Glescae/Ti' space-ships and nuclear submarines.' The preceding section of the poem is the best known— 'Auld Sant-Aundreans: Brand the Builder'—with its unforgettable opening as Malcolm Brand, lowsed from work, makes his way home through the streets of the ancient town. Though somewhat answered by 'Brand Soliloquises', the last line of this section—'And this is aa the life he kens there is?'—has a power akin to that of the last line of Law's *Licht attoore the Face*: 'Paer fellas, that you deed thon wy.' MacDiarmid would have characterised such directness of utterance as having 'far greater poetic power than any of the contrivances of English verbalism . . . unadorned but passionate and penetrative as Hebrew eloquence . . . in keeping with our whole national Republican and Radical tradition'.[6] I have resisted the temptation to quote copiously from *Brand the Builder*, but here is the first stanza of the last section, 'The Death o Brand':

> Deid this day ligs the builder Brand
> But villa, hall, and steeple stand;
> His mell and chisel are useless lain,
> Yet nae tears coorse frae the hert o stane.

Branching out thematically from *Brand the Builder* is the work of John McDonald, both stonemason and wordmason, in his pamphlets *Zen Speug, Zen Tinker* (both 1985) and *Peeries an Stanes* (1986). Of Highland origin, he learned Scots from the speech of his workmates, supplemented by extensive reading. His poems are variously about the mason's darg, the Clearances and the continuing exploitation of Scotland, civil strife in Ulster and the abominations of apartheid. This amounts to a body of work which is often (but not always) angry, though (because?) composed by a gentle and courteous man; his philosophy is much influenced by Erich Fromm and he seeks a synthesis of the best of Marxism and oriental mysticism.

Brand the Builder's intense consciousness of Scotland's tragic history, and its visible evidence in Fife, pervade *Works in the Inglis Tongue* (1985) by Peter Davidson. Resident in Crail, Davidson is a young poet and composer with a passion for the culture of Renaissance Scotland. In his work we are aware of Fife as a microcosm of Scotland: castles, palaces, abbeys, many in ruins. 'Faa' on oor wastit citadels, my hairt/Faa' on lost Fife, owerwhelmit wi' the cauld'. Yet even the elegiac pieces are ultimately affirmative. No seller-out to the passing fashions of the 1980s, Davidson prefers, like Tom Scott, to be loyal to the 'ayebydan' values.

Going further north, two Aberdonians—Alexander Scott and Alastair Mackie—have made outstanding contributions to the 'reintegrated' tradition. Scots is at its least diluted in the North–East: written and spoken Doric do not seriously diverge from one another. This regional rather than reintegrated register is still practised by such younger poets as Alexander Hutchison and Sheena Blackhall. Scott and Mackie have in fact added to the rich word-hoard already available to them as children in working-class Aberdeen. 'Back to Dunbar'? Scott, former head of Glasgow University's Department of Scottish Literature, has further enriched his style by going—back to *Beowulf*. This is a perfectly proper procedure for a Scots poet: Scots is rooted in Anglo-Saxon, which should not be assumed a preserve of English Literature. The resulting hard, elemental tone is particularly appropriate for his long alliterative poem on Aberdeen, 'Heart of Stone', which opens:

> The sea-maw spires i the stane-gray lift   [gull]
> Owre sworlan swaws o the stane-gray sea,   [waves]
> Flaffers her wings—a flash o faem-white feathers—
> And warssles awa i the wake o the trauchled trawler
> That hirples hame hauf-drouned wi the weicht o herrin.   [limps]

Lyrics such as 'Continent o Venus' and 'Love is a Garth' emulate those of Scott's Renaissance namesake. As a young man, in 1945, he displayed great courage during his war service: 'Coronach' is a product of this experience, as are the 'Twa Images' with their expressionistic vision of battlefield horrors. More recent wars have called forth the bitter irony of poems such as 'Problems', concerning the use of science both to send astronauts to the moon and to devastate the population of Vietnam. The alienation of modern city life informs 'Haar in Princes Street' and 'Blues for *The Blue Lagoon*' but all too often Scott is less critical of contemporary decadence than fascinated by it. The tacky images of commercial mass entertainment—King Kong and so on—seem to interest him more than the broad European (and world) culture so evident in the other makars. Impressive technique—but trivial content: the sad result of a sensibility that is much too Apollonian at the expense of being Faustian (to borrow, via MacDiarmid, an antithesis of Spengler's).

Alastair Mackie, like Garioch, broods on the unheroic nature of modern life from the unheroic viewpoint of the schoolteacher. Whatever that may imply regarding the profession's image of itself—or (perhaps more significantly) society's attitude to the profession—early retirement from the chalkface releases time and energy for art. The poet can at last become a full-time one, with possibly years ahead of him or her. For that reason it would be premature to offer a definitive account of the work of either Mackie or another ex-teacher who is more prolific than ever, William Neill.

Given Mackie's 'wee man' starting point, there is all the more power in that dialectic of the expansive and the contractive which animates much of his work. 'I'm nae Ulysses and never will be' is a key line in the title poem of *Back-Green Odyssey and other Poems* (1980)—the very title expresses the contradiction—but Mackie is nonetheless obsessed by the epic (sometimes cosmic) voyage set against the domestic staying-put: 'A herbour is a tension atween twa pulls,/the beck o horizons and the rug o hame.' His ubiquitous pessimism about the future of Scots (contractive) is counterpointed by his determination to keep writing in that tongue (expansive). 'Châteaux en Ecosse' evokes the poet's grandmother singing by the fireside (a 'Dutch interior picture', as Tom Scott describes it), and concludes: 'Here's me blawin on the cauld ess o her tongue/to bigg, châteaux en Ecosse, thae bit poems.' Not unlike Tom Scott on St Andrews, Mackie on Aberdeen relates his immediate childhood environment to contemporary world events in the sequence 'In the Thirties'. Granite tenements; playing 'eetle ottle'; beyond that, the Nuremberg rallies and the strutting Duce. From Union Terrace Gardens the vision expands: 'aa Aiberdeen like black golochs [beetles] gaun their eerands/dottit past, to win to the Castlegate/Hizzelheid or the fower airts o the earth . . .' In 'Heart of Stone' Alexander Scott is sardonic about his native city; Mackie tends to be mellow. This mood is particularly apt in 'The Day-Book o a Death', an elegy-sequence for his late father, a former quarryman.

The reintegrating impulse—MacDiarmid's 'binding the braids' (*In Memoriam James Joyce*)—is magnificently embodied in the ability to write poetry in all three of the national languages. The work of George Campbell Hay and William Neill is in Gaelic, Scots and English; they were anthologised as two of the *Four Points of a Saltire* (1970). But the impulse in both cases also ventures furth of Scotland, and they have between them transcreated poetry from a wide variety of European languages. Such internationalism is indistinguishable from their nationalism: Hay's 'The Destruction of the Land' compares the fall of Troy with the Clearances. A people has vanished as if it had never been.

> An' us the lave—tae gang lik ghaists in a strange land?
> Stumblin steps an' unsiccar gait in oor awn glens;
> shuffle lik coos in ways that are waa'd on either hand;
> keep tae the causey, no' a fowk, but a flock o men.
> (*Wind on Loch Fyne*, 1948)

Across the Aegean, in 'The White Licht', Hay lovingly evokes the coast of Greece: how could a coastal Scot count this 'ane o the fremmit [foreign] lands?' 'Seeker, Reaper' is a sea journey, a vigorous celebration of the boat itself and of the whole coast of Scotland: emphasising that wholeness, that reintegration, the poem is macaronic, composed in Norse, Gaelic and Scots.

William Neill's Scots poetry, like Hay's, is refreshingly physical: more fashionable writers prefer to be *meta*physical, making or pretending to make demands on their own and their readers' cerebral gamesmanship and on nothing else. Neill has more pressing demands: the claims of Scotland both intellectual *and* material. His close relationship with the land (he has a farming background) leads to poems appealing to sharpness of sight, hearing, touch, taste and smell; his rigorous craftsmanship serves a clear political and philo-sophical vision of a Scotland no longer afraid to know itself. He admires Garioch, but his own satirical work has more sense of direction, is not satire for satire's sake. He is Scots makar and Gaelic bard, Gaelic makar and Scots bard. His recent *Wild Places* (1985) collects work mostly in English; a forthcoming 'selected poems' is to have a considerable Gaelic and Scots content.

Hay and Neill have gone beyond MacDiarmid's call for a *Grosstadtpoesie*, which itself was a necessary corrective to the old parish-pumperie. In our more ecologically minded times, the city may be as constricting of vision as the village or small town, in many ways more so; innovation can come from the peripheries. The poetry of Duncan Glen, Donald Campbell and David Morrison is enriched by their experience of both urban and non-urban environments. Many of the more recent arrivals are not based in Edinburgh or Glasgow (indeed Dundee can boast two fine female makars, Ellie McDon-ald and Kate Armstrong). Raymond Vettese is a prolific lyrist whose 'Mon-trose Poems' have appeared in magazines. The work of Harvey Holton, a Borders man now living in north Fife, is proof that the reintegrative impulse can animate a younger generation. He writes an alliterative Scots line which goes 'back to Dunbar' but which also rediscovers Celtic culture for a modern audience; he integrates his poetry with other arts, such as music and dance, as in his *Fionn* cycle, a performance of which I experienced in the appropriate setting of Rossend Castle, Burntisland, in June 1986. I felt that Holton and his colleagues were providing a positive answer to Ezra Pound's warning, in *ABC of Reading*: 'Music rots when it gets too far from the dance. Poetry atrophies when it gets too far from music.'

In a short essay it is impossible to do full justice to so many excellent makars, both late and living, both those whom I have discussed and those whom I have not even mentioned. The recent arrivals will in time require more than a mere postscript—but only if they distinguish themselves from the horde of unadventurous versifiers who continue to give Scots a bad name. Scottish poetry, Scotland and the world deserve nothing less.

NOTES

1   The existential quality of Smith's work was first pointed out by Thomas Crawford in his article 'The Poetry of Sydney Goodsir Smith', *Studies in Scottish Literature*

7 (1–2), (1969–70), pp 40–59 (41): 'Smith chose the Scottish tradition as Conrad chose the English tradition.' John C Hall goes further and argues from the poetry that Smith's politics were existential in nature: a dissenting stance was meaningful in itself irrespective of the success or failure of its objectives (John C Hall, 'The Writings of Sydney Goodsir Smith', unpublished PhD thesis, University of Aberdeen, 1982, *passim*).

2 After *Whit Tyme in the Day*, T S Law's booklets are *Abbey Craig tae Stirlin Castle* (1974); *Aftentymes a Tinkler* (1975); *Whyles a Targe* (1975); *A Pryle o Aces* (1977); *The NCO's* (1980).

3 As predicted by Thomas Crawford in 'Tom Scott: from Apocalypse to Brand', *Akros* 31 (August 1976), pp 57–69 (69).

4 Untitled article in *Agenda* 10(4)–11(1) (1972–3), pp 48–51 (48).

5 Tom Scott, 'Lament for the Great Music', in *Hugh MacDiarmid: a Critical Survey*, Duncan Glen (ed) (Edinburgh, 1972), pp 184–91 (185).

6 Hugh MacDiarmid, 'Robert Fergusson: Direct Poetry and the Scottish Genius', in *Robert Fergusson 1750–1774*, Sydney Goodsir Smith (ed) (Edinburgh, 1952), pp 51–74 (67, 71).

ACKNOWLEDGEMENTS

For entrusting me with unpublished material my warmest thanks go to Dr John C Hall, T S Law, William Neill and Dr Tom Scott. Both Dr Scott's collected poems and his history of Scottish literature remain unpublished.

FURTHER READING

You are invited to write to the Scottish Poetry Library, Tweeddale Court, 14 High Street, Edinburgh EH1 1TE, enclosing a stamped addressed envelope or international reply coupons. It can advise on both primary and secondary texts, and provide the most up to date information on the contemporary scene. Fuller biographical and bibliographical details of the older poets may be found in W R Aitken, *Scottish Literature in English and Scots: a Guide to Information Sources* (Detroit, 1982), and Trevor Royle, *The Macmillan Companion to Scottish Literature* (London, 1983). The main magazines publishing poetry in Scots are *Akros* (1965–83), *Chapman* (1970–), and (entirely in Scots) *Lallans* (1973–), but for a fuller list of Scottish literary periodicals see my Bibliography in *Twelve More Modern Scottish Poets*, edited by Charles King and Iain Crichton Smith (Sevenoaks, 1986).

Chapter 13

Thunder, Renaissance and Flowers: Gaelic Poetry in the Twentieth Century

RONALD I M BLACK

Sorley MacLean's *Dàin do Éimhir* of 1943 can be called the third great landmark of Gaelic publishing, the first two being Carswell's 1567 translation of Knox's liturgy and Alexander MacDonald's *Aiseirigh* of 1751. It was little known until after the War, however, and was in advance of its time; George Campbell Hay's *Fuaran Sléibh* was hailed in 1947 as the most important volume of Gaelic poetry for a century and a half, Hay himself as the best Gaelic poet since Alexander MacDonald.[1] Canons of taste were such that most of what was published during the first half of the century was not very good, and most of what was very good was not published. All this was to change in 1952 with the founding of *Gairm*; it is remarkable to reflect that before that year was out *Gairm* had already published Derick Thomson's gently disturbing picture of *Na Cailleachan* and Iain Crichton Smith's psycho-analytical 'You are at the Bottom of my Mind' . . . *'s mise slaodadh 's a' slaodadh air uachdar cuain*, 'and I hauling and hauling on the ocean's surface'.

An archaic keynote had been struck at the beginning of the century by the appearance of the traditional incantations that made up Carmichael's *Carmina Gadelica* (1900). Entrepreneurial Gaelic publishing collapsed after the First World War, and the best editions of Gaelic verse to appear in the first half of the century were those that harked back to the nineteenth century and beyond. The only anthology that gave due recognition to contemporary work was James Thomson's *An Dìleab* (1932). MacLean and Hay were seen about 1950 as the last gleam of the Gaelic sky;[2] it certainly seemed that Gaelic verse was all past and no future, so what happened after 1952 stands out the more as deserving the title of renaissance.

MacLean and Hay apart, then, the Gaelic verse of the first half of the century can conveniently be divided into what was published then (generally mediocre) and what has been published since (far better). On the one hand we have verse written for publication, or in pursuit of the Bardic Crown awarded from 1923 at the Mòd: a jealous, self-conscious verse designed to parade Gaelic riches according to alien ground-rules. Examples include Donald Sinclair's much-anthologised *Slighe nan Seann Seun*, Angus Morrison's *Dàin agus Òrain Ghàidhlig* (1929), Angus Robertson's eclogue *Cnoc an Fhradhairc* (1940), Angus Campbell (Am Bocsair)'s *Òrain Ghàidhlig* (1943) and Neil Ross's *Armageddon* (1950). Morrison attempted free verse and presented at length his *Smuaintean air Mòrachd Impireachd Bhreatainn* (Thoughts on the Greatness of the British Empire), but *Armageddon* is as close as Gaelic verse has come to McGonagall's; it describes in 1,152 extra-ordinary lines of Homeric blank verse the British Empire and its Nazi foe, the Battle of the River Plate, the Norway Campaign, the Fall of France and the Battle of Britain.

On the other hand there is verse made by soldiers who served in the trenches and by songmakers steeped in tradition. This is the unselfconscious verse of the real world, its purpose to communicate rather than to impress. Poets of the First World War include Lewismen John Munro and Murdo Murray,[3] and Donald MacDonald (Dòmhnall Ruadh Chorùna) from North Uist. Munro fell on 16 April 1918 after three-and-a-half years at the front, leaving thoughts on his fallen comrades in tortured free verse full of reminiscences-of-rhyme; 40 more years were to pass before free verse became widespread in Gaelic. However, Dòmhnall Ruadh Chorùna is probably the outstanding Gaelic poet of the trenches. In a remarkable series of ten compositions he describes what it looked, felt, sounded and even smelt like to march up to the front, lie awake on the eve of battle, go over the top, be gassed, wear a mask, be surrounded by the dead and dying remains of Gaelic-speaking comrades, and so on, all counterpoised with scenes of deer-hunting, a sym-bolically traditional pursuit of which he happened to be passionately fond. His versification is controlled yet ever-fresh, for unlike most of his con-temporaries he knew the virtues of brevity and variety. He lived to express his horror of weapons of mass destruction, in *Òran an 'H-Bomb'*, which stands in contrast to the gung-hoism with which a younger and lesser *bàrd baile*, the Skyeman Calum Nicolson, celebrated Hiroshima and threatened the 'atomic' on Molotov.

A polarity emerges here between the deep-rooted tradition of Uist and the more eclectic one of Lewis. The Uist verse tradition is strongly oral and sung, while Lewis poets are more likely to be literate in Gaelic and to write and declaim their work. The Uistman's tradition takes him back to the seventeenth century, the Lewisman's to the nineteenth. This has to do with a greater continuity of society in Uist than in Lewis, where history is popularly reckoned to begin with the coming of the evangelical gospel about 1800. The point is well underlined by Lewisman Ian C Smith's cheerful remark that 'the Highlands are very orderly and always have been'.[4]

These polarities could be well exemplified by a comparison of the work of two major poets who spent the Second World War as POWs—Angus Campbell (Am Puilean) from Ness in Lewis, and Donald John MacDonald of Peninerine in South Uist. Although they both published prose accounts of their experiences, it is the Lewisman who seems to have more to the point to tell us in his verse; his *Deargadan Phòland* (The Fleas of Poland) is vivid. The poets of South Uist and Eriskay, in particular, have a liking for aureate praise of nature, while those of Lewis prefer to concentrate, like Rob Donn, on people; this presumably reflects the influence of Alexander MacDonald and Duncan Bàn Macintyre on the south, and of the evangelical hymn-writers on the north. The large vocabulary of presbyterian discourse seems to give Lewis poets the edge in philosophical themes; the Peninerine bard's musical tradition seems to put him ahead on lyricism, but he has nothing that probes as deep as the Puilean's *Ciod E?* (Who is He?).

The influence of the psalms may be found in the curious tendency of some Lewis poets, notably Murdo MacFarlane, to relax normal word order. Lewis is the source of a great deal of the funniest, as well as the most serious, Gaelic verse; this is well seen in the work of George Morrison (Am Britheamh) and of Norman MacLeod (Am Bàrd Bochd), while the same dichotomy is visible in the work of Donald Grant from Skye. A systematic comparison of MacLeod's anthology of Lewis poetry, *Bàrdachd á Leódhas*, with John MacMillan's collections of South Uist poetry in *Gairm* 1968–80 would be instructive; between the two poles, the combination of the best of both traditions helped mould Sorley MacLean.

In the twentieth century, of course, place of origin is one thing, place of residence may be another. Such men's knowledge of the world was considerable, and tended to raise the most notable of them above the run of *bàird bhaile* (community poets): Murdo MacFarlane returned from the prairies of Manitoba, as he put it himself, 'nearly as poor as I left, but a little wiser' (*An Toinneamh Diomhair*, p 5). To be specific, Donald Macintyre (of whom more later) saw action in the First World War and lived for many years in Paisley. The Bocsair, the Britheamh and Donald Grant all lived many years in Glasgow; the Bocsair's most interesting poem is perhaps *Caithris nam Bodach* (The Old Men's Night-Watch), composed at Hawkhead Asylum, where he was a nurse. MacFarlane came back to Melbost, Lewis, to gain a reputation as 'the Cole Porter of Gaeldom' from his ability to set his material to original airs. He saw Gaelic verse into the pop age, but the label does little justice to his formidable intellect; the fresh wind of his imagination barks through his songs. Calum I N MacLeod emigrated from Lewis to Nova Scotia to work in Gaelic education there; in addition to his own output he collected and published much of the Gaelic poetry of the province, past and present. John Archie MacAskill emigrated from Berneray, Harris, to farm in Western Australia, where his nostalgia gained high colouring from storms, drought and troublesome aborigines. Western Australia also became the home of Hugh Laing from South Uist, one of a small number of Gaelic poets this century whose chief work has been in translating from other languages (others are John MacLean, William Neill and Christopher Whyte). Most remarkable of all, perhaps, was Duncan Livingstone, a stonemason from Mull who emigrated to South Africa in the aftermath of the Boer War. In a series of mould-breaking poems, notably *Feasgar an Duine Ghil* (The Evening of the White Man), he savaged the imperialistic ethos and surveyed its legacy throughout the world. As early as 1960 he used the words of 'A Black Woman Mourning her Husband who was Killed by the Police' in his poem of that name to warn his readers of the fruits of apartheid. This poem has the look and feel and rhythm of a Gaelic waulking-song, but a very un-Gaelic refrain which means 'Father, O Lord, Save Us'. It ends by threatening the men, women and children

An luchd ghil a bhuail ar daoine
Cuairt mu 'n amhaichean de 'n caolain
Baba Inkòsi Sikelele, Baba Inkòsi Sikelele

Of the white folk who struck our people/With a turn of their guts around their necks

Cuairt de 'n caolain an àite cneapan
Is siridh mi 'n sin taobh do leapach
Baba Inkòsi Sikelele, Baba Inkòsi Sikelele

A turn of their guts instead of beads/And then I'll seek the side of your bed.[5]

It is but a short step from Livingstone to George Campbell Hay. For 30 years our judgement of Hay's work was based almost entirely on his collections *Fuaran Sléibh* (1947) and *O na Ceithir Àirdean* (1952), and for many, that judgement was of a brilliant virtuoso: one who loved ideas well, but words more. However when *Mochtàr is Dùghall* appeared in 1982 the judgement had to be reversed. Africa had made the difference.

Hay grew up in Kintyre hearing English, Scots and Gaelic. Thanks to a linguist's ear, a phenomenal memory and a deep reading of the literatures of many periods, his verse is invested with rich lexical and metrical music. His nationalist verse is a cry for unity of purpose, straight from the heart, unsullied by ideology, and of a piece with its time. *Is i Alba nan Gall 's nan Gaidheal is gàire, is blàths, is beatha dhomh*: 'it is Scotland, Highland and Lowland, that is laughter and warmth and life for me'. *Meftah Bâbkum es-Sabar* (the Arabic for 'Patience the Key to your Door') is an argument against political fatalism which ends by warning that Scotland may be *rud suarach ann an cùil 'ga cheiltinn,/a thraogh 's a dhìochuimhnich sluagh eile* (a mean thing of no account, hidden away in a corner,/which another people drained dry and forgot). If it is his best patriotic poem, it is so for the 'wrong' reasons—above all, a supercharged North African beginning.

Four words from the same poem, *draoidheachd cheòlmhor fhacal liomhta* (the musical wizardry of polished words), sum up Hay's achievement as a poet of Kintyre and of nature. *Siubhal a'* Choire (The Voyaging of the *Corrie*) and *An Ciùran Ceòban Ceò* (The Smirry Drizzle of Mist), for example, have to be spoken for the full savour of their assonance and alliteration—the one declaimed, the other whispered. The *Corrie* was actually a yacht chartered by Hay and some friends in 1935 for a Clyde cruise, but he had spent many hours of his youth with the ring-net fishermen of Loch Fyne (only Dòmhnall Ruadh Chorùna, in his *'Motor-Boat' Heillsgeir*, has achieved the effect of buffeting waves to the same degree); *An Ciùran Ceòban Ceò* is a sustained celebration of still weather, introducing the name of a scrap of arable on the Kintyre shore which had been pointed out to him by the fishermen as one of their marks.

War broke out shortly after Hay had completed his degree at Oxford. After eight months on the run as a conscientious objector, and a few days in Saughton Jail, he joined up, spending 1942–5 with the RAOC in Tunisia, Algeria and Italy, and 1945–6 as a sergeant in the Education Corps in

Macedonia. Wherever he was he spent his free time mixing with the local community and soaking up their language. In *Atman* he introduces his friend ('brother') of that name, married, with five children, possessor of some goats, an ass, a cow and a plot of rye, who gave him wit, and tales, and praised the form and colour of Jebel Yussuf; stricken by hunger, Atman stole, lied to the judge to get off, and was reviled, whipped and imprisoned. But Atman, says Hay, is a man, and alive, two things which the judge is not; and he reminds us that Christ, who he refers to by the Arabic *Sidna Aissa*, was crucified with thieves.

> Nan robh thu beartach, is do chaolan
> garbh le caoile t' airein sgìth,
> cha bhiodh tu 'chuideachd air na mìolan
> an dubh phrìosan Mhondovì.

Had you been wealthy, and your gut/thick with the leanness of your tired ploughmen,/you would not be keeping company with the lice/in the black prison of Mondovi.

It is scarcely surprising that in Civil War conditions in Greece Hay was taken for a communist (which he was not, though certainly left-wing in an endearingly boyscoutish way). The result was tragic. A rightist gang made an attempt on his life, and a fierce fight ensued with knives and guns from which Hay emerged physically unharmed but mentally scarred. Like Sorley MacLean, then, who had the better fortune to be wounded but physically, he is a great pacifist poet. His most personal statement is *An t-Òigear a' Bruidhinn o'n Ùir* (The Young Man Speaking from the Grave), but his most praised composition to date is *Bisearta*.

Bizerta, in Tunisia, suffered intensive bombing. On night guard many miles away, the young soldier whose brother was Atman saw the sky ablaze, knew the sounds of it but could not hear them, knew the people of common blood who were struggling among stones and beams but could not see them. Humanity had become anonymous, and inhumanity began to take on human features as observed in the flames: *an t-Olc 'na chridhe 's 'na chuisle,/chì mi 'na bhuillean a' sìoladh 's a' leum e* (I see Evil as a pulse/and a heart declining and leaping in throbs). It is the very picture which Hay's father had painted in *Gillespie* of the burning of the fishing fleet in Brieston (Tarbert) harbour.

It took little imagination to see in Bizerta the image of Clydebank, to see in Atman the image of the Gael, to see in Tunisia or Algeria the colonial experience of Scotland or to find among the Arabs some of the lost world of the Highlands that was so dear to Hay. This is the inspiration of *Mochtàr is Dùghall*.

After the War Hay lived a largely reclusive life in Edinburgh, and the existence of a long poem begun in the 1940s was only discovered by Angus Martin in 1980 when interviewing Hay for the chapter 'Bard of Kintyre' in his *Kintyre: The Hidden Past*. Written mainly in Italy, and added to in Macedonia and Tarbert during 1946–7, it was published by Derick Thomson in 1982 (two years before Hay's death) under the sub-heading *Sgeula-Dhàn*

Fada Neochrìochnaichte (An Unfinished Epic Poem). Incomplete though it is, with over 1,200 lines it is longer than MacDonald's *Birlinn* and Macintyre's *Beinn Dobhrain* put together, and must stand with them as one of the great sustained achievements of Gaelic literature. It has philosophical depth, music, humour, atmosphere, colour, excitement, metrical variety, and a conceptual richness that takes the breath away.

Mochtàr represents the world of the Arab, Dùghall of the Gael. They have been killed together by a German soldier in the desert. Their two cultures are synthesised.

> Chan eil foirfeach no *marbat*
> A thearbas sibh le 'eòlas,
> Tàileab, iomàm no ministear
> Chuireas ioghnadh, crith no bròn oirbh.

> There is no elder or marabout/Who can estrange you with his knowledge,/ Taleb, imam or minister/To fill you with wonder, trembling or sorrow.

The bulk of the poem as we have it consists of a spectacular presentation of the heritage of Mochtàr—Mokhtâr, son of Obaïd the blessed prophet, son of Omar the traveller of the Sahara, son of Ahmad who was *am feachdan naomhaicht' Abd al-Cadar*, in the sanctified hosts of Abd el-Qader. The Dùghall section consists mainly of some vestigial sketches—The Wee Bay, The Fisherman's Wife, The Sea, The Woman Speaks. It is doubtful in any case whether the reader of Gaelic poetry needs to be told of Dùghall's antecedents. Mochtàr's genealogy offers in itself a telescoped image of Highland history, like this:

<pre>
Ahmad, the warrior   = the heroic age (till 1746)
      | |
Omar, the traveller = emigration (till 1846)
      | |
Obaïd, the prophet   = calvinism (till 1946)
      | |
   Mochtàr   Dùghall
</pre>

To get back to Culloden Hay would have had to give Dùghall a pedigree at least as long as the one which took his own descent back to Gaelic Galloway, *Seòras mac Iain 'ic Sheòrais 'ic Iain 'ic Dhonnchaidh 'ic Iain o Ghallaobh*. In fact he contents himself with a brief reference to Culloden and the decline of everything but tradition in Dùghall's father's and grandfather's day; more importantly, he asks his fundamental questions.

> Ciod e a th' annainn, a chlann mo dhùthcha?
> Ciod e a th' annainn is a bha 'n Dùghall?
> Ciod e tha an dualchas is an dùthchas?

> What are we, children of my country?/What are we and Dougall?/What are tradition and patrimony?

We are, he replies,

> Cainnt is eachdraidh, snàth nan glùinean,
> na ginealaich druim air dhruim a' cùrsachd,
> a' cas-ruith a chéile cleas nan sùghan.

Speech and history, the thread of generations,/generations coursing wave on wave,/swift-chasing each other like the billows.

And Dùghall, he adds, is a Gael, a Scot, and a man. (Hay's order.)

Hay experimented with two different endings for the poem, but his philosophical intention never varied. In his own English translation, one finishes: 'Two complex, priceless worlds were blotted out for ever before they had attained the fullness of their being, and were swept from the sky by a chance blow. Murder of the dead, murder of children never begotten—the end of two worlds.' And the other: 'There died the angry pride of regal Ahmed, the gentle meekness of Obayd and Omar's living heart—they died a second time along with Mokhtâr by the mortar.' It may be suggested that now that the old Gaelic world of the ring-net fishermen had died, Hay had found his soul in Algeria, and that this great but lopsided poem shows us that Hay was not so much a 'Bard of Kintyre' as a 'Bard of Africa'.

It might be contended that Hay did not bring Gaelic poetry forward, that he merely embellished it wondrously. On the other hand one might say that *Mochtàr is Dùghall* has permanently broadened the range of Gaelic verse. There are two poets, however, who brought Gaelic poetry forward in the twentieth century to the extent that one is at a loss to imagine how it might have looked without them. One is MacLean, the other Derick Thomson.

Thomson has been the long rumble of thunder to MacLean's brilliant flash of lightning. Born in Lewis in 1921, his work offers a commentary on the Gaelic experience in this century. He is the father of modern Gaelic publishing, and the founder (in 1968) of the Gaelic Books Council. His own first collection appeared in 1951, and his father James Thomson's collection *Fasgnadh* in 1953; *Fasgnadh* contains quiet reflections on nature, the gently experimental work of a mature poet. *Gairm*, founded by Derick Thomson and Finlay J MacDonald in 1952, began as a sort of all-Gaelic *Picture Post*; under Thomson's sole editorship it has increasingly stressed its rôle as a vehicle for new and experimental writing.

Two great paradoxes can be detected in Derick Thomson's work, one public, the other personal. The public one has to do with Thomson as teacher and propagandist. He has indefatigably put forward a modern, cosmopolitan view of the Gaelic world. He is extremely proud of his work in translating a biology textbook into Gaelic, and has expressed disappointment at the failure of others to follow this lead. His *Companion to Gaelic Scotland* has made Gaelic studies an open book where once they were closed, but presents a determinedly multicultural view of Gaeldom that seems to prefer castles to domestic architecture, painting to craftsmanship, Charles Rennie Mackintosh to the *céilidh*-house, Mendelssohn to the shieling. Yet there is none of this apparent élitism in his poetry, and for namedropping (albeit in the best possible taste) we must go to Sorley MacLean or Fearghas MacFhionnlaigh.

The personal paradox is the other side of the same coin. It is obvious from which end of the Lewis-Uist polarity Thomson springs; indeed he is Lewis's greatest poet ever, in precisely the way that Hay is the bard of Algeria rather than of Kintyre, for he celebrates not the landscape or seascape of Lewis but her people. But the people of Lewis will never fully embrace her secular poets and thinkers until their culture is in tatters, for it is nothing if not a spiritual culture; there are many in the island to whom 'a good book' means a religious one, and who would rather conceal social evils than expose them to light. Blinkered as such attitudes may be, they are representative of cultural values in Lewis in the past two centuries. Do away with such values, and you lose the linguistic and institutional props that have shored them up; what then is left? A tattered economy, the English language, materialism, the *Daily Record*, social security, television. That is surely why Thomson says of Bayble Hill and Hòl

> chaidh mise bhuap air taod
> cho fada 's a théid gaol bho fhuath.

I have strayed from them on my rope/as far as love can go from hate.

Both paradoxes are summarised, I think, in the little poem *Bùrn is Mòine is Coirc* (Water and Peat and Oats). These three words, spoken by a stranger in a city street, represent the first paradox, for they symbolise the Lewis Thomson loves, yet is estranged from. They bring him to this conclusion, the second paradox:

> An cridhe ri bacan, car ma char aig an fheist
> 's i fàs goirid,
> 's an inntinn saor.
> Is daor a cheannaich mi a saorsa.

(The heart tied to a tethering-post, round upon round of the rope,/till it grows short,/and the mind free./I bought its freedom dearly.)

The tethering-post, the round upon round of the shortening rope, and the freedom of Thomson's mind offer a paradigm of his work through five published collections. *An Dealbh Briste* (The Broken Picture, 1951) is the tethering-post. In it there is love and cultural patriotism, the apprenticeship of this master craftsman: metre-bridled, disciplined verse showing MacLean's influence. *Eadar Samhradh is Foghar* (Between Summer and Autumn, 1967) focuses more closely on Lewis and on the human condition, and loanwords begin to creep in. *Mu Chrìochan Hòil* (In the Vicinity of Hòl) is a Cottar's Saturday Night of a poem, Gaelic seasonal poetry in the best tradition of Alexander MacDonald, but in rhythmic free verse. At its best, Thomson's writing moves slowly, with an irresistible movement towards some inevitable truth or other. His picture of *Na Cailleachan* (The Old Women), for example, draws us inexorably through images of scarcity, and boredom, and evil (*tha 'n sileadh 'na ghlaodh dubh a' dlùthadh*, 'the molten soot's black gum comes closer'), and touches of deliberate banality, using that archetypal picture of a black house interior and its inhabitants that evades us in *The Companion to Gaelic Scotland*, to this ringing conclusion:

> O shaoghail, is goirid do chuairt, 's is lom an cridhe,
> is tana an sgàile, is dlùth oirnn nimh an fhuaraidh.

O life, short is your course, bare is the heart,/frail is the shelter, close to us is the venom of the cold wind.

In Thomson's third collection, *An Rathad Cian* (The Far Road, 1970), his style reaches its definitive form, the three-part lyrical allegory consisting of picture, thought and conclusion. *Srath Nabhair*, for example, is (by nineteenth-century default) our best poem of the Clearances: the picture is of *a' bhliadhna thugh sinn an taigh le bleideagan sneachda*, 'the year we thatched the house with snowflakes', the thought is of the other-worldly religion that allowed such things to happen, the conclusion is that this religion survives today, still seeking martyrs in preference to justice.

Thomson has patience, sensitivity, strength, and an all-seeing eye. In addition to large canvases teeming with life he paints brilliant portraits of groups like the herring-girls and of individuals like the cleaner at Bayble school where his father was head, and he leaves us little etchings like *Làmhan* (Hands), often adding intellect to observation as in *Teallaichean* (Hearths). When he breaks out of the bonds of self-discipline one knows that something has troubled him greatly; down through the years he has done this with increasing frequency. By 1970 he was moving towards puns, loanwords, throwaway lyrics, bitterness, descriptions of city life; in tune with the 1960s, the Gaelic literature of the past was placed at the disposal of humour, and he deliberately set out to shock. His fourth collection, *Saorsa agus an Iolaire* (Freedom and the Eagle, 1977) marks a shift towards ideology: the book is about his relationship with Lewis, as always, but also freedom of all kinds, North Sea Oil, drink, and religion. Three different poems offer three different allegories for Scotland resurgent (spider, thistle, eagle), while *An Crann* is a structure so multilayered in meaning that it is hard to believe it could get off the ground, yet it positively soars.

Another feature that emerges after 1970 is the influence of the public stage. There were now increasing opportunities for poets like Thomson to read their work in public. The result is verse of immediate impact—aural, in the case of alliterative poems like *Gaol is Gràdh* and *Fuaim-Dhàn*, and political, in the case of poems like *Earrach '74* and *Alba v. Argentina, 2/6/79*, in which the poet expresses his disgust at hearing the Central Station erupt with cries of *Sco-o-t-land, Sco-o-t-land* a month after Margaret Thatcher became prime minister:

> Alba chadalach,   sleepy Scotland,
> mìos ro fhadalach.   a month late.

Thomson's fifth collection is represented by the 23 new poems in his collected verse, *Creachadh na Clàrsaich* (Plundering the Harp, 1982). Of these, the sequence *Àirc a' Choimhcheangail* is the most important. Denotatively the title means the Ark of the Covenant, connotatively it means 'The Synthesis of the Relationship'. The relationship in question is of course with Lewis: in an incandescent sweep of his net Thomson echoes his best work of the past while surging forward to make new statements. Lewis religion, he realises, has confidence, strength, profound traditional and emotional roots; it has the virtues of sweetness and total familiarity, everlasting life, for example, offering

> . . . ìm is iasg,
> is carthannachd,
> laoidhean is sailm,
> coibhneas fo phlaide
> is lit 'sa mhadainn.

. . . butter and fish,/and good company,/hymns and psalms,/favours under the blanket/and porridge in the morning.

In an environment dominated by sea and rock, he can understand the pull on the Lewisman of one who recruited burly, honest fishermen to his cause, turned stones into bread and moved a huge rock from the mouth of his grave. Thinking back with the total recall that is one of his characteristics, he remembers what was good about the Sabbath. This he does principally in terms of sound: the clock strikes ten, his grandfather jabs words into the racket, a lark sings, rowlocks creak in the bay, eggs make a fearful din jumping in the pan. He describes the church, plaintively, conceding with mild embarrassment that it is its eschewal of beauty that set him against it. 'Why did you put me off?' he seems to say, 'you needn't have,' for

> bha corra dhuine ann
> a thug am bòidhchead innte 's aisde
> 's cha deach i 'na smàl.

there were occasional people/who took their beauty in and out of it/without its going up in flames.

And the beauty of Lewis is, of course, its people: some of those who got religion he proceeds to describe in an ineffable series of cameos, ending with the reflection that Glasgow was the Egypt from which Lewis folk in general were recalled to the Land of Promise, and thus he returns, uncomfortably, to himself:

> *Ùrnaigh*
>
> M' ùrnaigh
> nach lorgar mi
> là-eigin ann am éiginn
> air mo ghlùinean
> ag ùrnaigh.

Prayer/My prayer/that I be not found,/one day, in extremity,/on my knees,/praying.

So Thomson doubts doubt, while putting beyond doubt that his is the major voice of Gaelic poetry in the second half of the twentieth century. The development from traditional to modern styles and attitudes and thence towards a synthesis seems smooth enough in such a study of Thomson's work, but it would be a mistake to imagine that such a revolution was achieved across the board without letting of blood. During the quarter-century between the founding of *Gairm* and the appearance of *Saorsa agus an Iolaire* a holy war was fought between traditionalists and modernists for the soul of Gaelic poetry. However, the traditionalists were an ageing breed. They had already sold the pass by their refusal to understand the poetry of Sorley MacLean, even though he used traditional metres and traditional vocabulary, only his subjects and attitudes being new; their blindness was akin to that of the many Gaelic speakers who not only would not, but could not, read anything in English except the Bible. In the words of the modernists' guru, Donald MacAulay, they were

> . . . an fheadhainn a roghnaich
> boidhr' agus doille—
> 's a tha 'n aghaidh ris a' bhailbhe.

. . . the ones who have chosen/deafness and blindness—/and are facing dumbness.

Traditional poetry was thirled to rhyme and generally sung; its patterns were mesmeric, and at its worst it followed clichés like railway tracks. We may compare the traditionalist who called the South Uist burial ground *Cnoc Hàllainn taobh a' chuain*, 'Hàllainn Hill beside the sea', with the modernist who, with no loss of rhyme or rhythm, called it *machair ìosal do-shàsaicht' Hàllainn*, 'the low insatiable plain of Hàllainn'. The audience for traditional poetry knew what it liked—which, unfortunately, meant ditties in an increasingly limited vocabulary; above all, perhaps, it had ceased to be the living heritage of the generation brought up since the Second World War, as the *céilidh*-house died and its cultural rôle was usurped by secondary education and the media.

> Tha e nas fhaisge air Humphrey Bogart
> na tha e air Tormod Mór—
> o'n fhuair e an TV.[6]

He is closer to Humphrey Bogart/than he is to Tormod Mor—/since he got the TV.

MacAulay had observations to make, experiences to recount, and feelings to express, about poetry and language, Lewis, religion and exile, love and people, his period of national service in Turkey, peace, war and disarmament, and to do this he chose a style of verse which was as new to Gaelic as that of Pound to English 30 years before. It is uncompromising poetry, with few concessions to convention, sound, optimism or even humour; a theoretical linguist by training, he does not love words, but respects them greatly, selecting them carefully and with judicious use of blank space to represent the vagaries and deficiencies of his intellect as accurately as possible without pretending to resolve anything.

> Ghineadh dhomh faillean,
> á spàrn dhiamhair;
> dh'fhàs e tromham craobhach;
> chuir mi romham gu fàsadh e dìreach
>
> gus buil thoirt air slatan fiara.

A tree was for me engendered/by some mysterious striving;/its branches spread through me;/I decided that it should grow undeformed

to overcome deviant yardsticks.

He seems quite deliberately to eschew rhythm, rhyme and musicality, although capable of introducing any of these when it suits his purpose. Here, then, was a fluent Gaelic speaker with a very traditional poetic urge, whose work nevertheless demanded an entirely new definition of poetry.

A characteristic modernist trend was to point out that Calvinism is an alien aberration in Gaelic culture. MacAulay's well-balanced *Soisgeul 1955* (Gospel 1955) finds a psalm-tune as mysterious as the voyage of Maol Dùin, a prayer as his people's access to poetry, but a sermon to be so vicious, alien and embarrassing that he gets pins and needles in his feet. His *Féin-fhireantachd* (Selfrighteousness) talks in a nicely-sustained image of being drubbed in the washing-tub of alien philosophy and confidently hung out to dry in the heavens. Thomson's *Am Bodach-Ròcais* tells how the scarecrow of the title came into the *céilidh*-house with Middle-Eastern tales and Genevan philosophy, sweeping the fire from the middle of the floor and putting instead a 'bonfire in our breasts', while in Iain C Smith's *Coinnichidh Sinn* (We Will Meet) the pious man's view of an innocent heaven sounds to the woman like a frozen heaven and her bosom goes cold. The battle thus moved onto the classic ground of Gaelic dialectic, and it became difficult to stand simultaneously on traditional ground with regard to belief and on modern ground with regard to the medium of expression.

MacAulay's chief disciple was Donald John MacLeod, a Marxist from Harris who established his credentials by being crowned Bard at the 1964 Mòd, then went on to make a series of virulent attacks on traditional verse, religion and cultural attitudes. In *Ràithean na Bliadhna* (The Seasons of the Year) he turns a line of a simple ditty into a torrent of prose castigating his forefathers for knuckling under to capitalism, and finishes with the ultimate heresy: *An eilean mo luaidh, is fuath leam eilean mo ghràidh*, 'In the isle of my heart, I hate the isle of my love'. The Lewismen John Murray and Norman Campbell (a son of Am Bocsair) pulled the revolution in a more genial direction with verse which seemed profound more by accident than design. Murray's comic imagination sizzles in ferment in such poems as *Ar n-Airgead 's ar n-Òr* (Our Silver and our Gold), which satirises the traditionalists' pavlovian reactions, while Campbell's *Mi-fhìn agus a' Revolution agus mo*

Bhata-Daraich (Me and the Revolution and my Oaken Stick) conveys a glorious picture of traditional stanzas marching along Princes Street as the drunken poet, *cho dòigheil ri botal Parazone* (as happy as a bottle of Parazone), runs along behind the crowd and jumps up and down yelling suitably irreverent comments.

The Rt Rev T M Murchison, who presided over traditional taste in verse as the *Stornoway Gazette*'s Gaelic columnist and as editor of *An Gaidheal* and of the Gaelic supplement to *Life and Work*, mocked the new verse by writing a literary article backwards. MacLeod, reviewing Donald J MacDonald's traditionalist *Sguaban Eòrna* in 1974, spluttered that it was 'so . . . well, *Uibhisteach* (Uist)', and compared it unfavourably with Smith's work; when next year a poet of a still later generation (Duncan MacLaren) could find nothing good at all to say of Smith's brilliant *Eadar Fealla-Dhà is Glaschu*, we sense that a new era is dawning.[7] But by then the posthumous publication of the collected work of Donald Macintyre had provided an opportunity to assess the traditionalist case on its merits.

Macintyre was a South Uist man who worked as a bricklayer in Paisley. His work amounts to over 10,000 lines, and the subjects mentioned in his account of a traditional *céilidh* (*Thug mi 'n Oidhche Raoir glé Shàmhach*, 'I Spent Last Night very Quietly') amount to a degree course in Celtic Studies. His most popular pieces are not necessarily his best. He displays a huge and limpid vocabulary, and that uncanny facility of expression which has now died with the monoglot Gaelic world. His instincts are rooted in the seventeenth century. The return of the Stone of Destiny to the authorities in 1952 reminds him of the collusion between Covenanters and Cromwellians that led to the massacre of Highland troops at Inverkeithing in 1651, and he describes a Glasgow pub in *Bùth Dhòmhnaill 'Ic Leòid* (Donald MacLeod's Bar) as if he had just fallen through a time-warp. Such a seventeenth-century view of the twentieth is in direct contrast to the twentieth-century view of the seventeenth that we find in Derick Thomson's *Introduction to Gaelic Poetry*, in which, for example, it is suggested that the reputation of Màiri Nighean Alasdair Ruaidh has been greatly inflated.

Macintyre revels in the violence of Mussolini's death in a way which would have turned even Iain Lom's stomach. This demonstrates how the furthering of a poetic tradition can involve the perpetuation of outdated philosophies. Yet his *O, Faighibh Suas an Cogadh* (O, Get Ye Up the War) ranges over international politics with a gently left-wing irony that eluded even his editor. He declares himself against racism, yet is persistently anti-semitic; intellectual inconsistency like this was one of the principal charges levelled by the modernists, university-trained as they were, against the less sophisticated traditionalists. Not that intellectual slackness is easy to find in Macintyre's work. *Nuair a Thàinig am* Buroo *do Dhùthaich nam Beann* (When the Buroo Came to the Land of the Mountains) stands in critical contrast to generations of verse that romanticise the past.

> Gum b'e 'n t-ùrlar am poll
> Air a stampadh fo 'm bonn

> Ach gun crathadh iad tonn ghainmhich air,
> Agus fraighnigh 'na sruth
> Leis na ballachan dubh'—
> An rud 's lugha orra 'n diugh ainmeachadh.

(The floor was just mud/Stamped underfoot/Save that they'd shake a dash of sand on it,/And dampness streamed/Down the sooty walls—/Which they're most loth to mention today.)

Poems like *Fàilte an Diabhail Droch Dhuine* (The Devil's Welcome to the Bad Man) offer symbolism as profound and thoughtful as any in modern verse, and only a lyrical imagination of startling originality could see Gaelic

> Mar churra chnàmhach air mullach fàsaich
> 'S nach fuiling càch dhi bhith tighinn 'nan ceann.

(As a bony heron on top of a wilderness/That no others will allow near them.)

Macintyre's subject-matter is so varied that it offers fecund comparisons with modern verse. If we set his study of a chair (*Òran na Cathrach*) against Thomson's *Làmhan* (Hands) we find that the former is longer, funnier; both are equally vivid; both have a powerful sting in the tail; Macintyre's message is social (the power of Jewry), Thomson's psychological (the power of memory). Looking at Macintyre's *Aoir an Luchd-Riaghlaidh* (The Satire of the Ruling Class) and John Murray's *An t-Acras* (Hunger) we find that both note the contrasting eating habits of the rich capitalist and the soldier who fights his wars for him; Macintyre sketches in the political and social context at great length, however, and touches on solutions, while Murray offers only some carefully-balanced central imagery with hints that both men may be equally unhappy. Finally, if we compare Macintyre's *Aeòlus agus am Balg* (Aeolus and the Bellows) and Ian Crichton Smith's *A' Ghaoth* (which looks as if it was influenced by a characteristically quiet poem of the same name by James Thomson), we have two poems about wind, one huge, one tiny; but while Macintyre offers words and pictures on a cosmic scale, including damage to property and a religious message, Smith just paints the same picture in a line or two then asks six unanswered questions which make the wind sound like an unruly adolescent. The balance of clarity favours Smith.[8]

While MacAulay plays his scrupulous game of Russian roulette, Smith fires poems like machine-guns, spraying symbols and images everywhere. Some hit a target (wounding, never killing), some ricochet around, some fall to the ground and are lost forever. This success rate is much the same as that of many traditional poets, the difference being one of scale (the more different modern verse is from traditional, the more it is the same): he expresses in a word what formerly took a stanza, being a master conductor who blends images, memories and ideas into an effortless symphony. *Orchestra mo ghaoil . . .* (The orchestra of my love), he writes, and calls up tradition with a nod to woodwind: *èiridh camhanaich no dhà* (a dawn or two will rise), or

Co-dhiù thug e gu m' chuimhne
cruachan-mònach, muir is teine,
etcetera.

Anyway it brought to my memory/peat-stacks, sea and fire,/etcetera.

The twenty poems in *Bùrn is Aran* (Water and Bread, 1960) demonstrate the fundamental tone and technique of a Smith poem. He rejoices in rhyme and rhythm but is no slave to them. Vocabulary is simple, ideas complex. His world is of the interior as Duncan Bàn's was of the exterior, and he observes and cherishes the intricacies of human behaviour as Duncan Bàn did that of the deer. Even the moon is likened to an indoor phenomenon, *truinnsear air balla* (a plate on a wall). He retails experience not directly, like Thomson or (sometimes) a camera, but as filtered and distorted by mind and memory. A church opens, and *Shuidh mi sìos innte 'nam inntinn*: 'I sat down inside it in my mind'. He is capable of a lyric peak like *lainnir a' chuain mhóir 's a ghàire* (the gleam of the great ocean and its laugh), yet shrugs it off, almost as if this were MacLean talking and not himself. He has a slightly manic faculty for picking the most unexpected word or phrase. He employs the symbolism of stark colours, and opposes static symbols of order and stability to dynamic symbols of disorder and instability. In a poem like *Aig a' Chladh* (At the Cemetery) these are mixed and balanced to a degree reminiscent of the doctrine of the humours: *cuan a' seinn* (ocean singing), *bioball a' losgadh ann an làmhan/gaoithe 's gréine* (bible burning in the hands/of wind and sun), *grian a' dòrtadh, cuan a' dòrtadh* (sun pouring, ocean pouring), *adan dubh' gu dorch a' seòladh* (black hats darkly sailing), and so on, paint a dynamic picture of a static scene to express the unity of the cosmos with private grief.

Smith's second collection, *Bìobaill is Sanasan-Reice* (Bibles and Advertisements, 1965), presents a consistently serious and deromanticised view of a world increasingly confused, monocultural, monolingual and materialistic. His best poem is perhaps *An t-Òban* (Oban), which paints an atmospheric picture of the litter-strewn, rain-soaked promenade while exuding faint whiffs of Gaelic tradition. Everything seems reduced to paper, to advertisements— lions and tigers on circus posters, the town, the sea, and the Gael (himself) who appears on the street now the tourists have gone, and is turned red and green by the traffic-lights until his bones appear as if in an X-ray. The circus posters make him feel that the Gael and his culture is being swallowed up by the modern world as surely as the Christians were fed to the lions in Palestine. He may never excel this now, having declared his intention to write no more 'big' verse (*Na h-Eilthirich*, p 25).

Smith's insights on the human menagerie are complemented by his free-verse studies of animal personality for children in *Na h-Ainmhidhean* (The Animals, 1979). His previous two collections, *Rabhdan is Rudan* (Rhymes and Things, 1973) and *Eadar Fealla-Dhà is Glaschu* (Between Joking and Glasgow, 1974) show his increasingly humorous bent. The latter is full of cartoons in words, such as a delightful picture of when the Jehovah's Witnesses came to call (*Aig an Doras*, 'At the Door'); words themselves often take a major rôle, as when he visualises proverbs as *baile de shiùil dhonna* (a city of brown sails), and *Mas e Ghàidhlig an Cànan* (If Gaelic is the Language) is no less an important poem for being gentle, amusing, and in rhyme.

Na h-Eilthirich (The Emigrants, 1983) is a quiet collection of no great complexity, in which Smith reflects on youth, memory and the passage of time. The stimulation of foreign travel and of the poetry-reading circuit is reflected in verse about places, including Australia, the USA and Canada. The best of all, however, is in praise of Lewis, which he sees through fresh eyes, and the explanation is supplied by a poem on parting in which images of departure and return are neatly transposed:

> Nuair a dh'fhàg am bàt' an cidhe
> thill thu dhachaigh,
> do bhonaid air cùl do chinn . . .

When the boat left the pier/you came home,/your bonnet on the back of your head . . .

In 1985 the Scottish Poetry Library counted 40 living poets writing in Gaelic; the full total is more like double this, but probably not over a hundred. In 1900 there would have been thousands. Poetry of all kinds continues to be written, and on all subjects, including for example Jock Stein, Page Three mamillaries, the Falklands War, and the Prince and Princess of Wales' visit to Scalpay in 1985. New poets continue to appear (and disappear), the most clear and representative voice being perhaps that of Myles Campbell from Skye, whose collection *Eileanan* (Islands, 1980) offers a convenient typology of contemporary Gaelic verse, being divided into (1) *Cànan is Dùthchas* 'Language and Patrimony', (2) *Na Boireannaich* 'Women', (3) *Creideamh is Mì-chreideamh* 'Religion and Irreligion' and (4) *Cridhe is Eanchainn* 'Heart and Brain'. This begs the question of where political and social concern fit in, so it is instructive to find outstanding political poems like *An Referendum airson Pàrlamaid ann an Alba 1/3/79* at (1), and poems of social concern like *An t-Aran* (Bread) at (3). On this typology we will hang our concluding remarks.

Category (1) provides what amounts to a definition of modernism in Gaelic verse. If a poet does not touch on *cànan is dùthchas*, he must surely be a *bàrd baile*: he does not discuss it because in a way he *is* it. The *bàrd baile* tradition is now very attenuated: hymns, elegies (Mgr Neil MacKellaig of Daliburgh was elegised in 1982 by two different poets), lovesongs, popsongs, praise of places, and the odd little squib like Torquil MacRae's 1986 piece on his fellow-oilrig-workers at Arnish. Some good *bàrdachd bhaile* is still taking a long time to reach print, however, an example being Donald MacDonald of Eriskay's definitive verse account of the 'Whisky Galore' saga of 1941, published in his enjoyable *Rannan á Eilean na h-Òige* of 1981.

For some modern poets, like Ian MacDonald (Grimsay) and Norman MacDonald (Lewis), relationship with the native place continues to be of prime importance in their work; others, like Aonghas MacNeacail and

Fearghas MacFhionnlaigh, offer a refreshingly global outlook. Two very comparable modern poets who have reflected their life and times in a discursively autobiographical, relaxed yet highly musical way have been the Rev John MacLeod and Angus Peter Campbell; between them they span the twentieth-century experience, and would be memorable even if only for insights like MacLeod's

> Cur shìthean ar litearachais
> Aig bonn clach cuimhn' ar cànain.

Putting the flowers of our literature/At the foot of our language's memorial.

Of category (2) it may be said that it is remarkable how often sexual desire makes an appearance in contemporary verse. MacNeacail in particular has made the subject his own; his verse is built on love and nature, indeed if we had a word that meant both love and nature, that word would decribe his verse. Sea and land teem cosmically with life in *Sireadh Bradain Sicir: Seeking Wise Salmon* (1983) and *An Cathadh Mór: The Great Snowbattle* (1984), while *An Seachnadh: The Avoiding* (1986) exudes the electric quality of hard-won personal experience more than has any other collection of Gaelic verse since *Dàin do Éimhir*. Darwin and Frazer are his heroes, not Marx or Christ, and as for Freud, *cha d'fhuasgail e càil nach robh 'nam leasraidh*, 'he unlocked nothing that was not in my loins'. Emotion is both whetted by nature and reinterpreted in terms of it. In *Acras* (Hunger) the woman is the sea, rising red-lipped at dawn to offer food before retreating; in *An Eilid Bhàn* she becomes a white hind, loved by him but stalked and gralloched by others like the deer of Duncan Ban's *Beinn Dobhrain*. A passionately committed writer of robust, sensuous verse that owes something to the past for its imagery while uncompromisingly modern in form, MacNeacail may be said to have succeeded Hay as the leading nature poet in Gaelic.

As for women poets, after the death in 1928 of Katherine Grant they became almost invisible for a while except as hymnwriters, but emerge later in the traditionalist personae of Mary MacLean from Grimsay, Kirsty MacKay from South Uist, and two Christina MacLeods from Bayble in Lewis (having also produced Thomson and Smith, what village in Europe has given more to literature this century?). *A' Choille Chiar*, the collected poems of Catriona and Morag Montgomery (two sisters from Skye), shows very strongly the influence of Sorley MacLean, with much fine craftsmanship and attention to detail. Mary Cameron (née Montgomery, from Lewis) has written on language, culture and nationalism, while Mary MacDonald from Grimsay has produced a sensitive little collection, *Mo Lorgan Fhìn* (My Own Footprints, 1985), full of the ghosts of the past and of the future. But all in all the female contribution to Gaelic literature has been less than in any previous century.

The liberalisation—some would call it collapse—of Highland society is further reflected in category (3). We are moving on from the polarised anticalvinism of MacAulay, MacLeod, Smith's *adan dubha* and the early Thomson to a religious viewpoint which is at once more complex and more positive:

religion is no longer sealed up by church, ministers, elders, elect, sermons and sabbaths, but is exposed to view on open shelves. Donald John MacIver's verse is as guilt-ridden and tortured as his short stories, but not as morbid— *An toir thu dhomh mathanas/airson sireadh mathanais,/eadhon airson mathanas/ mathanais?* 'Will you give me forgiveness/for seeking forgiveness,/even for forgiveness/of forgiveness?' Like Thomson, Myles Campbell sees himself as

mise air a bheil eagal	I who am afraid
a bhith 'na mo Chrìosdaidh,	to be a Christian,
air a bheil eagal	who am afraid
a bhith 'na mo pheacach.	to be a sinner.

The writing, translating, circulating and publishing of spiritual verse has proceeded apace throughout the century, a new ecumenical hymn-book, *Seinnibh dhan Tighearna*, appearing in 1986.

Category (4) is well represented by Myles Campbell's *Do Chròcus air a Shlighe a Nèamh* (To a Crocus on its Way to Heaven), a poem of pellucid sensitivity. But we must use it mainly to consider a couple of the trends that have left the end of the century so different from its beginning. Firstly, the gap which yawned in the 1960s between modernists and traditionalists appears to have closed. Poets like MacLean and Hay who once seemed *avant garde* can now be seen to occupy various parts of the middle ground. Even the subject of a poem like Callum Graham's modernist *Daoine bha an Leódhas Uair-eiginn* (Men that were in Lewis Once) of 1966 can be traced back through John Smith of Iarshader to Alexander MacDonald. As Donald J MacDonald of Peninerine cast off the *bàrd baile*'s mantle by expressing serious global concerns in stately but varied metres, Derick Thomson picked it up by playing to his new-found gallery and sparking off delightful modernist ditties on trivial-sounding events. The Bardic Crown stimulated some good experimental work (Norman MacLean's *Maol Donn* of 1967, for example, synthesises pipe music and literature) before being gradually abandoned in the 1970s. Some poets, like Colin MacKenzie, John Paterson, Neil Brownlie and Donald R Morrison, have quietly tilled a small patch of middle ground over many years and grown not a few roses on it, while others, such as Kenneth Ross, Duncan MacLeod and Roderick MacDonald, have preferred to stand with a foot in each camp.

The other major trend has been the increasing prominence of learners of Gaelic. Such people learn as they write, and their verse can grow steadily in assurance. The early Gaelic work of the doyen of the group, William Neill, for whom the learning of Gaelic was the expiation of guilt, seems unduly preoccupied with symbols of Scottish unity and disunity (kilt, haggis, Edinburgh, politicians, landlords, grouse moors, city Gaels, mythology), while after about 1980 the virtues of simplicity, modesty, humour and unpredictability appear as his eye focuses on real individuals and concrete objects. Another learner, Duncan MacLaren, has written memorably on his native Clydebank. Yet another, Fearghas MacFhionnlaigh, is an explosively good poet with a totally distinctive voice; his is the Gaelic of the computer age, the extension of medieval scholasticism and Thomson's biology textbook, full of compounds, assimilated loanwords and international scientific terms. He makes no concessions to lexical tradition (in this he stands diametrically opposed to Donald Macintyre and Sorley MacLean). An art teacher by profession, his work has instant visual impact: a typical beginning is *sièt-phleun a' sàthadh* 'a jet-plane thrusting'; an allegory about de Bohun at Bannockburn starts *thàinig e oirbh mar shrònadharcach 'na dheann* 'he came at you like a rhinoceros in full tilt'; a poem on Humpty-Dumpty ends laconically with the English words *eggshell finish*. Flowers are described in such poems as *An Geiréiniam* and *Flùraichean* as *neon-dhearg* 'neon-red' or *factoraidhean foto-cho-chur a' beò-ghlacadh na gréine* 'photosynthesis factories seizing the sun alive'. His principal field of reference is art, his cultural background cosmopolitan, his reading wide. His passions are God and nationalism; these themes and many more are examined in *A' Mheanbh-chuileag* (The Midge, 1980), a 708-line philosophical treatise of considerable depth and power. A midge is caught in a spider's web; the poet is fond of small things—like Gaelic, like Scotland—so, in God's name, he releases it, concluding that the dynamic of the universe is

> So-leòntachd agus cumhachd;
> agus tròcair.
>
> Vulnerability and power;/and mercy.

There is meat and music in *A' Mheanbhchuileag*, and it is undoubtedly one of the major Gaelic poems of the century.

Other learners include California's Gaelic poet Dennis King, who expresses the instability of his environment with great sensitivity in poems like *Tro-cadero Transfer, San Francisco*, and Victor Price, whose view of the Highlands is that of the most kindly and intelligent type of tourist. What else does such a tourist do but learn the language? Would that all incomers could further Gaelic literature like this

> . . . tha a' bheatha dol air adhart
> Ach tha sùilean a' ghliocais
> Air cùlaibh a chinn.
>
> . . . life goes forward/ But wisdom's eyes are/At the back of its head.[9]

NOTES

1 *O Na Ceithir Airdean*, dust jacket quotations.
2 Dr John MacInnes, writing in *Gairm* 87 (Summer 1974) p 279.
3 *See* Murray's *Luach na Saorsa* for both these poets.
4 I C Smith, *Towards the Human* (Edinburgh, 1986), p 101.
5 Livingstone's work was published in *Gairm* 1955–65 and assessed by Derick Thomson in Gairm 119 (Summer 1982), pp 257–68.

6   I C Smith, *Eadar Fealla-Dhà is Glaschu* (Glasgow, 1974), p 43.
7   The source for everything in this and the preceding paragraph is *Gairm* 1964–75.
8   This refers to the poem *'A' Ghasth'* beginning *Tha a' ghasth a' seideadh anns an t-simileir*, in *Eadar Fealla-Dhà is Glaschu*, p 37, and not to Smith's poem of the same title in *Chapman* 42 (1985), p. 69.
9   Examples of the work of most of the poets mentioned in this chapter will be found, untranslated in *Gairm*, that of MacFhionnlaigh in Gairm 1973–85. In recent years Gaelic verse, with translation, has begun to appear with increasing regularity in other magazines, notably *Chapman* and *Lines Review*.

FURTHER READING

Campbell, Angus, *Moll is Cruithneachd* (Glasgow, 1972)
Campbell, Angus, *Bàrdachd a' Bhocsair* (Edinburgh, 1978)
Creighton, H and MacLeod, C I N (eds), *Gaelic Songs in Nova Scotia* (Ottawa, 1964)
Grant, Donald, *Tìr an Àigh* (Glasgow, 1971)
Grant, Katherine, *Aig Tigh na Beinne* (Oban/Glasgow, 1911)
International Poetry Review vol 5, no. 1 (Greensboro NC, Spring 1979). Scottish issue
Laing, Hugh, *Gu Tìr mo Luaidh* (Stornoway, 1964)
MacAskill, John A, *An Ribheid Chiùil* (Stirling, 1961)
MacAulay, Donald, *Seóbhrach ás a' Chlaich* (Glasgow, 1967)
—— (ed), *Nua-Bhàrdachd Ghàidhlig* (Edinburgh, 1976)
—— 'On Some Aspects of the Appreciation of Modern Gaelic Poetry', in *Scottish Gaelic Studies* vol 11, pt. 1 (1966), pp 136–45
MacDonald, Donald, *Dòmhnall Ruadh Chorùna* (Glasgow, 1969)
MacDonald, Donald J, *Sguaban Eòrna* (Inverness, 1973)
MacDonald, Norman, *Fàd* (Stornoway, 1978)
MacDonald, Roderick, *Leth-Cheud Bliadhna* (Glasgow, 1978)
MacFarlane, Murdo, *An Toinneamh Dìomhair* (Stornoway, 1973)
MacFhionnlaigh, Fearghas, 'The Midge', in *Cencrastus* 10 (1982), pp 28–33
Macintyre, Donald, *Sporan Dhòmhnaill* (Edinburgh, 1968)
MacKinnon, Lachlan (ed), *Bàird a' Chomuinn* (Glasgow, 1953)
MacLeod, Calum I N, *An t-Eilthireach* (Sydney NS, 1952)
—— (ed), *Bàrdachd á Albainn Nuaidh* (Glasgow, 1970)
MacLeod, Christina, *Ceòlraidh Cridhe* (Glasgow, *c.* 1943)
—— *An Sireadh* (Stirling, 1952)
MacLeod, Duncan, *Casan Rùisgte* (Glasgow, 1985)
Meek, Donald, 'Land and Loyalty: The Gaelic Verse of George Campbell Hay', in *Chapman* 39 (Winter 1984), pp 2–8
Morrison, George, *Òrain a' Bhritheimh* (Glasgow, 1985)
Murray, Murdo, *Luach na Saorsa* (Glasgow, 1970)
Nicolson, Calum, *Bàrdachd Chaluim Ruaidh* (Glasgow, 1975)
Orbis no. 58–9 (Nuneaton, Autumn–Winter 1985. Scottish issue.
Poetry Australia no. 63 (Sydney NSW, May 1977). Gaelic issue.
Rankin, Robert A, 'George Campbell Hay as I knew him', in *Chapman* 40 (Spring 1985), pp 1–12
Thomson, Derick, *The New Verse in Scottish Gaelic* (Dublin, 1974)
—— 'Tradition and Innovation in Gaelic Verse Since 1950', in *Transactions of the Gaelic Society of Inverness* 53 (1982–4), pp 91–114
—— 'An Anthology of Recent Gaelic Verse', in *Akros* vol 11, no. 31 (August 1976), pp 3–45
—— 'New Gaelic Writing' in *Cencrastus* 7 (Winter 1981–82) pp 34–5
Whyte, Christopher, 'Derick Thomson: Reluctant Symbolist', in *Chapman* 38 (Autumn 1984), pp 1–15

Chapter 14

The Later MacDiarmid

ALAN RIACH

For Hugh MacDiarmid (C M Grieve), 1935 was a critical year in which long-standing conditions of personal stress, extreme poverty and public estrangement culminated in a severe nervous breakdown. We may date the later MacDiarmid from this year, although the kind of poetry MacDiarmid wrote extensively after 1935 was already in evidence in volumes published or written before that year. *Stony Limits* (1934) is clearly the pivotal volume in this regard. Here we find the signs of what was to follow in poems such as 'In the Caledonian Forest', 'Song of the New Economics' or 'The Progress of Poetry'. These all share one characteristic which distinguishes them from Mac-Diarmid's later long poems: they each attempt a structurally coherent and balanced argument. But already arguments and ideas in MacDiarmid's work are beginning to multiply their cross-references and the dynamic of the poetry is beginning to strain against the limitations of unified texts. 'On a Raised Beach', the crucial poem of the volume, may be read as a critique of the idea of unity coming at exactly the point in MacDiarmid's career where his mastery of unified structure was beginning to collapse.

MacDiarmid had been planning to co-ordinate his entire poetic output through the structure of one poem on an epic scale since the early 1930s, and had published an architectonic blueprint in 1931 for a work to be entitled *Clann Albann*. This was never completed, and there was no planned structure for the epic poetry he did write, so a different notion of the 'fitness' of the parts comes to hold sway. The design-governing principle of the later MacDiarmid is one of critical inclusiveness, and this is evident in both the compositional procedure of the poetry and the philosophy which informs it.

> One loves the temporal, some unique manifestation,
> Something irreplaceable that dies.
>
> But one is loyal to an ideal limit
> Involved in all specific objects of love
> And in all co-operating wills.
>
> Shall the lonely griefs and joys of men
> Forever remain a pluralistic universe?
> Need they, if thought and will are bent in common interest
> In making this universe *one*? (p 958)[1]

MacDiarmid invokes the requirement of cosmic adjustment in a vision with deep moral significance, but there is simultaneously a pragmatic commitment

to social reality even in his most esoteric work. And this constantly underwrites any 'merely literary' reading of his later work. *The Battle Continues*,
from which this extract is taken, is a 4,000 line response to the Spanish Civil
War, and Roy Campbell's approval of Franco's victory. The temperature of
the poem ranges from passionate condemnation to rational, cool but committed speculation, as in the above. The mode of the poem is traditionally
Scottish: it is a flyting, determined to oppose Campbell's reactionary and
pathological stance. It was conceived of as separate from MacDiarmid's epic
enterprise, and though written in the late 1930s was not published in book
form until 1957, with no quarter given to Campbell's corpse.

The 'Third Hymn to Lenin', published in book form with the First and
Second Hymns also in 1957, was similarly intended to be a poem unified by
its pitch, argument and sense of address; but, as with *The Battle Continues*,
outreaching and transforming visionary apprehension characterises this and
all MacDiarmid's later work. The corpus of this work includes a staggering
number of books besides books of poetry. *Scottish Eccentrics* (1936), *The
Islands of Scotland* (1939), his autobiography *Lucky Poet* (1943), the unpublished *Red Scotland*, anthologies, translations, critical work—all contribute
towards MacDiarmid's breadth of achievement and command, and help to
define his stature, not simply as a superb lyricist, which he certainly was and
continued to be, but as an epic national poet. This rôle is particularly evident
in such singularly Scottish work as the *Dìreadh* poems or 'Island Funeral',
and it was one he developed into, and dedicated himself to maintaining. Ruth
McQuillan succinctly describes a clear symptom of this development: 'Hugh
MacDiarmid, especially the older, post–1935 MacDiarmid, wrote not individual books but a life's work, and it is entirely suitable that the margins of
his unpublished, and even his published volumes should remain blurred: one
book shading into another, as in *In Memoriam* he frequently postulates the
kind of poetry he wants—which is the governing theme of the volume that
apparently succeeds this book.'[2]

Passages from both *In Memoriam James Joyce* (1955) and *The Kind of
Poetry I Want* (1961) appeared in *Lucky Poet* in 1943, but these two works
remain of central importance to an understanding of the later MacDiarmid.
Both were intended to form parts of an epic which, like *The Cantos* of Ezra
Pound or *The Maximus Poems* of Charles Olson, became a continuous 'work
in progress'. One common procedure in all MacDiarmid's later work is the
way in which analogies and metaphors are multiplied, not to make hierarchical comparisons nor to diminish the particularity of any single thing or
event, but to assert or announce correspondences and relations which, taken
altogether, affirm the indivisible totality of existence, and provide a dynamic
Weltenschauung. In its original etymological form, metaphor means a transport of language, and in much of MacDiarmid's later poetry, the verse
simply becomes the movement through a kaleidoscope of lists, examples and
instances:

> As subtle and complete and tight
> As the integration of the thousands of brush strokes

In a Cézanne canvas . . .
Alive as a bout of all-in wrestling,
With countless illustrations like my photograph of a Morning Dove
Taken at a speed of 1/75,000 of a second,
A poetry that speaks 'of trees,
From the cedar tree that is in Lebanon
Even unto the hyssop that springeth out of the wall,'
And speaks also 'of beasts, and of fowl,
And of creeping things, and of fishes' . . . (p 1019)

The celebration of artistic genius, human vigour, technological development
and the natural world in this passage is a condition of the 'poetry' these
separate items are representative of. And MacDiarmid's celebration is zestful.
It is true that in reading allusive poetry you need to know what is being
alluded to, but MacDiarmid's later work is full of information which is
allowed to convey its own value and fascination to a far greater extent than
information in the work of Pound or Olson, for example. MacDiarmid is
generous; he allows things to speak for themselves, and it would be wrong to
undervalue the sense of serendipity, the lucidity and delight which runs
through so much of MacDiarmid's later work. It demands to be read quickly
as well as attentively, for the enervating quality of its sustained energy to be
fully appreciated.

> —And all this here, everything I write, of course
> Is an extended metaphor for something I never mention. (p 745)

This process, as the title *The Kind of Poetry I Want* suggests, is both a
method and a purpose. While it implicates its readers in its enactment,
MacDiarmid's later poetry displaces them as consumers. This should qualify
Tom Leonard's description of MacDiarmid's 'life-long advocacy of, and
concentration on, lexis itself: anti-existential in its insistence on the validity
of the naming process'.[3] Leonard's conclusion is highly critical: 'In [Mac-
Diarmid's] insistence on the primacy of name and category, he is still fundamentally using language as an instrument of appropriation, as a means of
"possessing reality".' Yet there is more going on in MacDiarmid's later poetry
than self-aggrandisement, and its form and movement suggest other qualities
than those of a narcissistic cultural and linguistic monopoly capitalist, which
is what Leonard suggests MacDiarmid may be. To respond to the later
MacDiarmid at all is to be required to register the fact that to experience
language as signifier is to affirm the existence of desire. That affirmation can
be a steely and useful instrument in the struggle in which, MacDiarmid
understood, language is embroiled. Art, Edwin Morgan pointed out, was
considered by MacDiarmid to be

> a metamorphosing force in its own right, with a duty to advance, and in
> advancing to advance man's spirit. That this should happen particularly
> through *language*, and that the poet should be its most convincing exponent,

follows naturally from the fact that language is man's most distinctive evolutionary instrument.[4]

Kenneth Buthlay has also observed: 'With MacDiarmid, one finds that one is always returning to questions of *language*.'[5] What MacDiarmid returns to most frequently in *In Memoriam James Joyce* is indeed language. He addresses Joyce:

> So this is what our lives have been given to find,
> A language that can serve our purposes,
> A marvellous lucidity, a quality of fiery aery light,
> Flowing like clear water, flying like a bird,
> Burning like a sunlit landscape. (p 822)

The 'language that can serve our purposes' is poetry, in all its various forms and functions, and keen with the sense of the cultural dominance of traditional bourgeois English poetry within Britain. It would misrepresent the later MacDiarmid not to emphasise that he continued to write a diversity of different kinds of poem, lyrics, satires, rhapsodies, meditations, jokes, epigrams, love poems, portraits, elegies, publicly celebrative poems (such as the one written to toast a Glasgow production of Brecht's *The Good Woman of Szechuan*), and so on. But as with the range of books of prose he produced, these can all be seen as serving what he calls above 'our purposes'.

These purposes are inevitably not only literary. MacDiarmid is aware of an 'indispensable distinction between language and speech' and is vitally concerned with the political implications this raises. He is accurate, as well as impassioned, when he calls: 'Speech. All men's whore. My beloved.' The kind of poetry he wants depends upon a particular kind of social development:

> —All dreams of 'imperialism' must be exorcised,
> Including linguistic imperialism, which sums up all the rest. (p 790)

His millennium is Marxist; his vision of world language is a communist one. It is exactly in keeping with the situation proposed by Stalin (or Stalin's writers, for that matter) in *Marxism and the Problem of Linguistics* where we read that in 'the epoch *after the victory of socialism* on a world scale,' the imperialist policy of suppressing and assimilating languages will no longer exist.

> Here we shall have not two languages, one of which is to suffer defeat, while the other is to emerge from the struggle victorious, but hundreds of national languages, out of which, as a result of a prolonged economic, political and cultural co-operation of nations, there will first appear most enriched unified zonal languages, and subsequently the zonal languages will merge into a single international language, which, of course, will be neither German, nor Russian, nor English, but a new language that has absorbed the best elements of the national and zonal languages.[6]

This is the situation implied in the original Author's Note to *In Memoriam James Joyce* where MacDiarmid claims that the only situation in which such a unification of diversities as that he envisages can be achieved is 'a society which I naturally envisage as Marxist'.[7]

Poetry, of course, is not simply what it says and statements in any language are changed by their presence in a poem. But *In Memoriam James Joyce* does not merely exhibit a number of inserted statements; it is almost entirely constituted by quoted material. 'Plagiarism' is really too small a grenade to throw against work like this. MacDiarmid's use of other people's writings is part of the rebellion against the traditional notions of authorship and originality, immured in laws of copyright and based in the consciousness of print, property and class. This rebellion itself was a major component of modernism, and among its objectives was a renewal of perception and revaluation of the functions of language. Break down the context of bodies of words and you can allocate a new purpose to them. The artifice of linguistic construction in MacDiarmid's later work helps us to question the linguistic ordering of the world, to challenge a normal or normative ordering and to consider alternatives. MacDiarmid himself was clear that the method by which his later work was constructed should be taken into account: 'The multiplicity of quotations, references and allusions . . . must be completely understood, since they constitute the *language* in which it is written . . .'[8] There is a revealing analogy in Joyce's career. When Valery Larbaud, translating *Ulysses*, asked him if quotations should go in quotation marks, Joyce replied in a letter dated 4 June 1928, 'the fewer quotation marks the better' because even without them the reader 'will know early in the book that S D's mind is full like everyone else's of borrowed words.'[9] MacDiarmid, unlike Joyce, provides no mediating fictitious characters, no Stephen or Molly or Bloom. In his later work there is only the mediating fiction of the poet and his unconcealed and intervening practice.

Conventional literary criticism assumes poetry is to be read as the work of the poet, the expression of the author. But 'the poet' can never be more than an effect of language. The 'poet' corresponds to a real figure, but that person is never satisfactorily the entire source of the homogeneity (of style, stance, dynamic)—or indeed heterogeneity—of their works. Identity is only ever possible as misrecognition and you can only ever identify yourself by speaking of yourself from somewhere else. A characteristic which Kenneth Buthlay discerned in *Annals of the Five Senses* (1923), the first book by C M Grieve, was 'an obscure but poignant sense of [the author] being an entirely different person to himself.'[10] The later MacDiarmid shows this sense in more radical ways. Gestures of what might otherwise seem outrageous extravagance are therefore important and viable forms of challenge:

> There is no language in the world
> That has not yielded me delight. (p 818)

> I have known all the poets of the world, I think. (p 1032)

An author's name is not a simple reference; it has other than indicative functions. It describes a work, an *oeuvre* or part of a strain in a work. A splendid example of this is the poem 'Perfect' which caused some controversy when it was shown to have been reconstituted from part of a short story by the Welsh writer Glyn Jones. The suggestion was made that the poem, which Kenneth Buthlay has shown to be remarkable in itself,[11] should have been published under the joint signature of MacDiarmid and Jones. This would certainly have altered the significance of the name-function, and altered the emphasis which we give to that function. (For instance, taking the poem as *MacDiarmid*'s, Buthlay can with ease refer to other parts of MacDiarmid's *oeuvre* to further his argument, and suggest that there is a specifically Scottish Celtic significance in the connection between the poem's location—'On the Western Seaboard of South Uist'—and the Celtic name which C M Grieve adopted.) The 'author-function', to use Michel Foucault's term, is characteristic of the mode of existence, circulation and the functioning of certain texts within a society. The author is the principle of thrift in the proliferation of meaning. There is certainly something peculiarly apposite in this, since 'MacDiarmid' is, in a sense, all that holds the proliferating later work together, and he was evidently aware of the singularity of his poetic enterprise and his own unique qualifications for it. In a note at the beginning of the *Disjecta Membra* manuscripts of the never published or completed *Impavidi Progrediamur* he wrote:

> Write this poem as things are today
> is like cornering a car at high speed
> on a mountainous road and
> suddenly seeing
> an obstacle offering only
> one chance in a million of clearance
> Write this poem—but it could never have been
> thought of, possible at any other time
> since the world began
> or by and to any other
> man.[12]

However, there is also in the later MacDiarmid a sense that given historical modifications in society, this author-function may well disappear in such a manner that polysemic texts may once again function according to another mode. The changes which would effect such an alteration in literature are what MacDiarmid calls for in *In Memoriam James Joyce*: 'At this moment when . . . as never before,/The creation of the seamless garment,/Is the poet's task . . .' The system whereby the seamless garment of polysemic texts is restricted to any specific meaning or direction is that which allows the name 'MacDiarmid' its author-function. In other words, the millennial vision of MacDiarmid's later work has a material analogue only in culture, specifically in literature and most specifically in itself. This is what Brecht suggests when he says that the great writers behave as though the class struggle was already over, and 'deal with the new situation, conceived as collectivist, which is the aim of the revolution.' MacDiarmid's later work is therefore transitional. Its achievement is the extent to which it dares to be experimental, while its project remains unconcluded. If the notion of a 'work' is traditional and thought of in a Newtonian fashion, concrete, occupying book-space, the 'text' is something else. Its method is a *traversal*; it can cut across a work or several works. Etymologically the text is a cloth; *textus*, from which text derives, means 'woven'. The texts of the later MacDiarmid traverse not only his own later poetry (and prose) but the works of many others. To understand this is not to seek for his 'sources' or 'influences' in order to satisfy the myth of filiation. It is, rather, to comprehend the effective confluence of how the poetry works *and* what it is saying.

It would be wrong to suggest that that confluence takes place without turbulence or discomfort. The later MacDiarmid is not an omniscient perfectionist. His understanding of particular vocabularies and his grasp and application of ideas and arguments are not commensurate with a full empirical knowledge of a number of languages. Consequently, the sense of accommodation one finds in Joyce is less evident in MacDiarmid. The superabundantly numerous references are acquired centripetally: the poetry spins them into itself and holds them in a constantly altering but stable equilibrium. MacDiarmid's writing is, moreover, didactic, and avows definite strategies and preferences. In his later work, he engages in direct espousals of political positions while posing new questions about the relation between the reader and text. But he explicitly refuses both the helplessness of the pessimistic intellect and the nirvana of play; he subscribes to the Nietzschean affirmation of the chaotic potential of the world, the pleasure and necessity of becoming in a world of signs there for the use of an active intelligence. But he is never so genteel as to forget the material conditions of struggle and change through which words are dependent:

> —If the book's ultimate realisation
> Is the impotence of language
> In the face of the event,
> This abdication is announced
> With a power of words wholly inaccessible
> To those never overpowered and speechless. (p 776)

Yet, while this was intended to generate argument, it was also a poetry of advocation and direct address, and as it ran to thousands of lines over many books, it was bound to be daunting to readers not yet familiar with Joyce or Brecht. T S Eliot, in fact, appreciated this aspect of MacDiarmid's later work, commenting on a large section of *In Memoriam* in a letter to MacDiarmid dated 24 April 1941, 'It is . . . a very fine monument to Joyce though I am afraid that it gains no advantage from the association until such time as Joyce's later work is properly appreciated.'[13] With a few notable exceptions, critical and sympathetic reading of the later MacDiarmid has been slow to arrive, both in Scotland and in the Anglo–American critical establishment. But we need no longer defer our appraisal of the function of MacDiarmid's later poetry as the creation among its readership of a kind of Brechtian audience.

This is not to idealise or revise his work. His nationalism should be understood historically as well as theoretically. The idea that Scotland was culturally distinct, with separate literary and artistic traditions from England, he took to its literal conclusion: that the country should therefore be politically distinct. He saw the old Celtic civilisation as a source of spiritual authority and, while scorning 'The Celtic Twilight' school, accepted the example of heroism shown in the Irish literary movement. Consequently he adapted the Victorian–Romantic crusade which had been the legacy of Padraic Pearse and Daniel Corkery, against the spiritual atrophy involved in the spread of middle-class culture. The fictive nature of these ideas of social and national regeneration did not, however (and does not), render them futile. Not only can they suggest persuasive variations in the reading of history, but they can continue to exercise their subversiveness because they are—and MacDiarmid understood them to be—volatile and dangerous ideas. His nationality is imaginatively useful in placing his artistic endeavour in an implacably hostile world. But history, he knows, can't finally be reduced to metaphor and his understanding of Scotland is founded on material reality and personal experience as much as visionary apprehension. Being Scottish, certainly for all of C M Grieve's lifetime, entailed a constant self-critique which continuously deferred the sense of achieved cultural and political identity. In this way, his national and communist commitments are fundamentally allied. He is not content (as Yeats was) with the essences of self, community, nationhood, racial theory and *Zeitgeist*, but insists upon considerations of class, economics, modern science and technology, social and governmental organisation and ideology, the ethos of imperialism and the linguistic variety of the peoples of the earth. He claimed that his political interests were primarily aesthetic: 'my real concern with Socialism is as an artist's organised approach to the interdependencies of life.' (*Lucky Poet*, p 241) But he was also a committed member of the Communist Party of Great Britain from 1934 to 1938 and from 1956 until his death in 1978, and his poetic career shows a growing commitment to the practice described by Walter Benjamin in 1936:

> '*Fiat ars—pereat mundus*,' says Fascism, and, as Marinetti admits, expects war to supply the artistic gratification of a sense perception that has been changed by technology. This is evidently the consummation of '*l'art pour l'art*'. Mankind, which in Homer's time was an object of contemplation for the Olympian gods, now is one for itself. Its self-alienation has reached such a degree that it can experience its own destruction as an aesthetic pleasure of the first order. This is the situation of politics which Fascism is rendering aesthetic. Communism responds by politicising art.[14]

In this sense, the art of the later MacDiarmid is thoroughly politicised. When, for example, MacDiarmid uses the first person plural, he is ordering a solidarity which retains potential because it remains unsatisfied.

> Have we not travelled all over
> What the Arab geographer Al–Aziz
> Called Daghestan's 'Mountain of Languages,'
> Kumyk, Avar, Lezghin, Lak,
> Darghin and Tabasaran? (p 795)

At the same time, there is an energetically irreverent and infectious comic sense in the later MacDiarmid, as when he says that he dreams 'of poems like the bread-knife/Which cuts three slices at once'. Another example:

> Other masters may conceivably write
> Even yet in C major
> But we—we take the perhaps 'primrose path'
> To the dodecaphonic bonfire. (p 758)

C major is the traditional romantic note of triumph and achievement in melodic music. The dodecaphonic reference is to Schoenberg's twelve-tone system of composition. MacDiarmid is emphasising that his work is 'Simultaneist' and not merely linear in development; but we also recall the Porter in *Macbeth*:

> Knock, knock, knock! Who's there? Faith, here's an English tailor come hither for stealing out of a French house: come in, tailor. Here you may roast your goose. Knock, knock; never at quiet! What are you? But this place is too cold for hell. I'll devil-porter it no further. I had thought to let in some of all the professions that go the primrose way to th'everlasting bonfire. Anon, anon! I pray you, remember the porter.
> (Shakespeare, *Macbeth*, II, iii)

MacDiarmid is certainly pleased to introduce as many 'of all the professions' as he can in the course of his dodecaphonic progress. Even the solemn Sanskrit with which T S Eliot closes *The Waste Land* is obliquely suggested by the last line of *In Memoriam James Joyce*, a colloquial Gurkhali phrase to the effect that 'Everything's really all right'—despite all appearances to the contrary. Like Brecht (and indeed, like Pound), MacDiarmid championed oriental art and philosophy as a means to criticise and oppose the Western tradition, and to reject bourgeois liberalism.

> For unlike you, Joyce, I am more concerned
> With the East than the West and the poetry I seek
> Must be the work of one who has always known
> That the Tarim valley is of more importance
> Than Jordan or the Rhine in world history. (p 801)

The Tarim valley, in the Sinkiang Uighur Autonomous Region of China, has at least two claims to major importance in world history. It contains the sites of some of the earliest human habitations in China. But more immediately relevant to MacDiarmid's purposes is the fact that the ancient imperial highways of the Han and later dynasties, the chief old land routes by which Chinese silks went to Rome and Buddhism came to China, ran through the Tarim valley. It was, quite literally, the place of 'The Meeting of the East and the West'.

Such examples could be multiplied. At any given moment in the poetry of the later MacDiarmid, an underlying contradiction or an implicit correspondence may be suggested, a serendipitous discovery may be made, and take on a particular importance, and be given expression. But this practice doesn't exhaust the poetry's resources nor does it amount to a final, fixed interpretation of reality. The imperatives are never abandoned while newly-prompted ideas and contradictory impulses take their space. The certain boundaries of Cartesian or Platonic thought are not completely lost but denied the supremacy they more usually exert (especially in discussions about languages). We can draw out meanings from the texts, but they will slip surely back into the poetry's transformative flow.[15]

There is, then, a fundamentally celebrative extension of selfhood involved in the later MacDiarmid. Far from resulting in the dissolution of identity, MacDiarmid's later poetry extends the self without the anxiety born of a desire to escape from it. In *Stony Limits*, the forbidding austerity of that carefully poised and concentrated poem 'On a Raised Beach' enclosed an axial confrontation between the atheist poet and the logocentric universe. In the later works, themes, ideas, facts, names, languages, cultures, sources and quotations are let loose from any imperial centrality and occur in a free, but not directionless movement.

If that movement involves correspondence through more than a simply horizontal plane, then the complexity of the texts need not blind us to the fact that they have such purposive direction.

NOTES

1 All page references to MacDiarmid's poems are to *The Complete Poems of Hugh MacDiarmid, 1920–1976*, Michael Grieve and W R Aitken (eds), 2 vols (Harmondsworth, 1985).

2 Ruth McQuillan, 'The Complete MacDiarmid', in *Studies in Scottish Literature*, G Ross Roy (ed) (Volume XVIII, Department of English, University of South Carolina), p 202.

3 Tom Leonard, 'The Locust Tree in Flower, and why it had Difficulty Flowering in Britain', in *Intimate Voices: Selected Work: 1965–1983* (Newcastle upon Tyne, 1984), pp 95–102 (pp 97–8).

4 Edwin Morgan, *Hugh MacDiarmid* (Essex, 1976), p 28.

5 Kenneth Buthlay, *Hugh MacDiarmid* (*C M Grieve*) (Edinburgh and London, 1964), p 43.

6 J V Stalin, *Marxism and the Problem of Linguistics* (Moscow 1954; repr Peking 1972), pp 51–2.

7 Hugh MacDiarmid, 'Author's Note', in *In Memoriam James Joyce* (Glasgow 1955, repr 1956), p 17.

8   Hugh MacDiarmid, 'Reply to Criticism', *The Voice of Scotland* 7, 1 (April 1956), pp 19–25.
9   James Joyce, *Letters*, Stuart Gilbert (ed) (Volume 1, London, 1957), p 263.
10   Kenneth Buthlay, op cit p 18. The phrase is quoted from *Annals of the Five Senses* (Montrose, 1923; Edinburgh, 1930), p 13.
11   Kenneth Buthlay, 'Some Hints for Source-Hunters', *Scottish Literary Journal: MacDiarmid Memorial Number*, 5, 2, December 1978.
12   Manuscript in private collection.
13   Quoted in *The Letters of Hugh MacDiarmid*, Alan Bold (ed) (London, 1984), p 454.
14   Walter Benjamin, *Illuminations*, Hannah Arendt (ed), trans Harry Zohn (London, 1973), p 244.
15   I am indebted here to T J Cribb's discussion of *Finnegans Wake* in 'That Old Mimesis', *LTP: Journal of Literature Teaching Politics*, 3 (Cambridge, 1984), pp 71–8 (p 76).

FURTHER READING

Stony Limits and other poems (London, 1934)

Lucky Poet: A Self–Study in Literature and Political Ideas (London, 1943) 'Scottish Poetry 1923–1953', *Lines Review*, 4 (January, 1954)

In Memoriam James Joyce (Glasgow, 1955; repr 1956)

The Battle Continues (Edinburgh, 1957)

The Kind of Poetry I Want (Edinburgh, 1961)

David Hume—Scotland's Greatest Son (Edinburgh, 1962)

'The Return of the Long Poem', in *Ezra Pound: Perspectives*, Noel Stock (ed) (Chicago, 1965)

'Scotland', in *Celtic Nationalism* (London, 1968)

Selected Essays, Duncan Glen (ed) (London, 1969)

'Scotland: Full Circle', in *Whither Scotland?*, Duncan Glen (ed) (London, 1971)

The Threepenny Opera, Bertolt Brecht, trans Hugh MacDiarmid (London, 1973)

'Foreword', in *Poets to the People: South African Freedom Poems*, Barry Feinberg (ed) (London, 1974)

Metaphysics and Poetry, a conversation with Walter Perrie (Hamilton, 1975)

Aesthetics in Scotland, Alan Bold (ed) (Edinburgh, 1984)

The Letters of Hugh MacDiarmid, Alan Bold (ed) (Edinburgh, 1984)

Chapter 15

The Industrial Novel

MANFRED MALZAHN

Industrial Scotland was largely created in the nineteenth century, when the country's central belt underwent a transformation as rapid as it was drastic. The result—apart from the obvious economical and sociological consequences—was a further cultural division added to the Lowland/Highland dichotomy. In the mid eighteenth century, the Scottish population was still fairly evenly spread out; by 1820, over half the people were crowded together in the central regions.[1] Statistically speaking, the average Scot had become an urban dweller, directly or indirectly dependent on industry for a livelihood, in an environment essentially alien to that of his ancestors, or his contemporaries in other parts of the land.

Scottish literature was notoriously slow in reacting to these changes. While for instance in Germany, poets such as Freiligrath and Heine, and later, playwrights like Hauptmann, and while in England novelists like Dickens, Disraeli, Eliot and Gaskell confronted their readers with the new reality and its pungent problems, Scottish writers would turn to history or to provincial life for their material. The industrial milieu features only marginally in the work of authors regarded as major figures on the Scottish literary scene in the nineteenth century, e.g. John Galt or John Gibson Lockhart; for more, one has to go to writers generally held in less esteem, e.g. Henry Duncan or George Mills.[2]

Until well after World War One, there was no significant alteration of this state of affairs: Kailyard and Anti-Kailyard ruled, and the experience of life shared by a majority of the Scottish people still seemed to be excluded from the house of Scottish fiction, with its shutters allowing only odd glimpses of furnaces, factories, or tenements. But there was at least an indication of the fictional potential inherent in working-class life, particularly in a Glasgow setting. A case in point is John Joy Bell's *Wee Macgreegor*, first published as a serial in the *Glasgow Evening Times* in 1901, and subsequently in book form in 1902.

In its immense popularity, coupled with some critical disdain—Maurice Lindsay, grudgingly acknowledging the sale of more than 250,000 copies, insists that 'it has nothing to do with literature'[3]—Bell's book must be seen as a landmark. It proved that there was a market for stories which were set in a world which the potential urban readers could recognise as a projection of their own, however far from a comprehensive and adequate portrayal. The minor scale of incidents reported (there is no greater tragedy than the breaking of Mum's teapot, and no greater bliss than sharing a boiled egg with 'Paw') justifies Moira Burgess's classification of the Glasgow urchin's adventures as 'Urban Kailyard',[4] but Bell at least created a self-sufficient and coherent working-class setting without having to resort to Victorian formulas for melodrama or moralising, Girls Taking to the Streets, Men Taking to Drink, or Poor Boys Becoming Wealthy.

In place of the appeal to voyeurist and capitalist wish-fulfilment inherent in these constellations, Bell merely pitched the attraction of the world of childhood, coupled with a strong sense of locale, and succeeded in establishing working-class Glasgow as a viable location for fiction. This comes close to saying the same for working-class Scotland, for the one is the epitome of the other. There are Scottish industrial novels which are not set in or near Glasgow, but most of the type-casting ones are; and the Glasgow types which literature helped to create or perpetuate, have at least to a certain extent come to represent Scotland itself. While most of the world still mainly draws on the visual cliché of the Highlander In Full Regalia, to the other inhabitants of the British Isles and some English-speaking people elsewhere, the standard image of Scottishness is grounded on patterns of speech and behaviour, and those of a Billy Connolly rather than of a Harry Lauder.

This is also true of Scottish self-perception, in which working-class features are important because they are more identifiably Scottish than their more anglicised urban middle-class counterparts. Consequently, the assertion of a working-class identity in a Scottish context is likely to appear also as the assertion of a Scottish identity, in spite of the cosmopolitan aspect of industrial culture, which favours a kind of basic global uniformity.

The Scottish Renaissance with its propaganda for the concept of a truly national literature thus seemed to generate the most opportune climate for an emergence of the Scottish working-class novel on a large scale, but there was a delayed effect. In the 1920s and early 1930s, fiction with a working-class concern was still thin on the ground, and such as there was, as, for example, John Cockburn's *Tenement* or Dot Allan's *Hunger March*, did not create enough of an impact to be remembered by more than just a few. Those novels that are still widely recalled, though not necessarily also widely read, stem from the mid 1930s, and are frequently grouped together under the heading 'proletarian'. This term must be seen as highly debatable, however, as one of the authors concerned conceded in retrospect at least with regard to his own work. A trendsetter for the genre, George Blake, looked back in embarrassment about 20 years later, at the period and his own merits:

> the 'proletarian' novel did begin to emerge in Scotland during those exciting 1930s. The movement may have been sparked off by George Blake with *The Shipbuilders* . . . Since its appearance Blake has confessed in public print that he now thinks it unworthy of its epic subject. He pleads guilty to an insufficient knowledge of working-class life and to the adoption of a middle-class attitude to the theme of industrial conflict and despair.[5]

This disclaimer adds to the confusion with which one could well be left at the end of an attempt to sum up critical opinion of the book. Wittig praises it,[6] Hart regards it as a failure;[7] Burgess and Bold find a major difference between bourgeois and working-class characters, viz., Burgess thinks the latter more convincing than the first;[8] Bold finds the first more so than the latter,[9] while both agree that the disparity is a considerable flaw. This is not the place for an additional, let alone a final opinion, but it is interesting to note that once again—as in Bell's case[10]—it is a commercially successful, and, through its popularity, widely influential book which causes the critics some headaches. The field of working-class literature and its criticism seems ideally suited to showing up the contradictions between populist and élitist notions of culture which can be found in some extremity in the Scottish Renaissance movement, and in its legacy to present generations.

The question as to what weaknesses *The Shipbuilders* (1935) has, and to what extent these can be attributed to Blake's social background, may safely be left open. In this context, however, the book appears as noteworthy for two further reasons which are interrelated: the historical content, and the constellation of characters. Firstly, it deals with a dying industry, a way of life that is on its way out, i.e. shipbuilding on the Clyde in the 1930s. The central figures in the plot are boss and worker, an odd couple branded by history as anachronistic remnants in a changed environment. The way the bond between master and man is described has echoes of D H Lawrence, while the incongruity of the two survivors thus linked recalls J F Cooper's tales of the American West. The parallel can be carried further: what is lamented is the passing of a pioneer age, a world that had scope for heroic achievement, giving way to a kind of progress that seems as unpalatable as inevitable.

In both instances, the question 'Was the glory ever real, except as a story told to a child?'[11] is merely rhetorical. The function of myth—and *The Ship-builders* is an attempt at myth-creation—is to provide patterns for the ordering of experience. It appears that the industrial experience could only be fitted entirely into the Scottish pattern when it had some similarity to other instances of lost glory. Historical truth—whether the Celts were really such an admirable people, for instance, or whether life in Scotland was really freer before the Reformation—is, to put it blandly, irrelevant to somebody interested in contemporary Scottish culture, its inherent features and possibilities. What is important, is the recognition of myths, and their possible functions as a hindrance or a help to the appreciation of reality, as defeatist apologies for, or creative challenges to the reality we find ourselves in.

All told, trying to come to terms with the industrial world through myth, as in the case of Blake, is doubtlessly more laudable than the escapism prevalent before his day. A similar task, and on a grander scale, had been attempted shortly before Blake, by James Leslie Mitchell. The last volume of his *Scots Quair* trilogy, *Grey Granite*, comes within the scope of this survey, as it is set in a fictional industrial town. Nevertheless, the full meaning of the narrative can only be seen in the context of the whole trilogy, which follows the heroine Chris Guthrie through different stages of her life, each associated with a specific setting (country, small burgh, and industrial town) and different men: father, three husbands, and son. They are the victims of ideas, of obsessions or causes, of which the son Ewan's is communism; ostensibly the most solid in the succession, as the lithic image in the title indicates.

The tone of the narration in *Grey Granite* (1934) is much more subtle than in a book such as *The Shipbuilders*, where heavy-handed authorial comments stick out among passages of plain narrative, dialogue, and above all, inner speech. Mitchell uses point of view with such artistry that the reader is almost led to believe he is given an objective account of events. But the novel is not a realist one, though there is realism in it, especially in the description of industrial labour itself:[12]

> Hardly anything to do with the others at all, stroking his shot in the Furnaces, stripped to the waist, he stripped brown, mother's skin, and tightened his belt over shovel and barrow, cleared out the clinkers and wheeled up a load and flung it deep in the whoom of the flame, the Works kittling up as the morning woke, bells snarling hell if the heat now and then went low in one fire or another. In an hour or so Ewan'd be dripping with sweat, and drink and drink from the tap in the rear, water that gushed out again from him, a spongelike life and tremendous fun.
>
> (p 372)

There is a good deal of admiration in this description of a youthful Stakhanov who has a good time while working twice as hard as all the rest, but one does not have to know that country boy Mitchell had no great love for farm work and never even tried industrial labour, to sense the underlying suspicion.[13] If Ewan appears in a heroic light, the superhuman feat is closely linked to something inhuman, which transforms even the solid granite in Ewan into something 'darker and coarser . . . in tint antrin queer'.[14] In retrospect, this endows a passage like the one quoted above with a touch of the supernatural, or, if one will, moral allegory. Good and evil are mixed up in the fight for communism, and the true tragedy lies in the fact that the evil is inevitable because the fight is part of history, which to Mitchell was in its entirety a product of man's fall from the blessed state of classless primitivism. Even if his sympathies lie with the workers' cause, Ewan cannot feel any sympathy for them as human beings, nor expect any in return:[15]

> they weren't heroes or gods oppressed, or likely to be generous and reasonable when their great black wave came flooding at last, up and up, swamping the high places with mud and blood. Most likely such leaders of the workers as themselves would be flung aside or trampled under, it didn't matter, nothing to them, THEY THEMSELVES WERE THE WORKERS and they'd no more protest than a man's fingers complain of a foolish muscle.
>
> (p 481)

Again, Ewan's stance invites both admiration and fear. The cool acquiescence in the necessity of self-sacrifice without any illusions to glorify this action, and the gradual relinquishing of human ties and considerations that goes with it: this is the classic dilemma of the revolutionary, and could have made for a prime example of a tract on partisan morality. However, Ewan is only one out of four men who fall by the wayside, eaten up by a frenzy of ploughing and digging, devoured by war, or swallowed in religious clouds. His Moloch is the last, as the focus of the novel shifts back to Chris, whose way of mixing with the world of history and yet forever staying outside its reach seems to be the only chance for the salvation of moral and psychological integrity. Given the heroine's identification with 'the Land', the existence which precedes as well as survives the accidentals of history, this could suggest the existence of a bypass for the evasion of the historical process, were it not for the fact that Chris has to go through the various phases of her country's history as 'Chris Caledonia', before finding final fulfilment and rest in solitary union with 'the Land' itself.[16]

Myth, symbol, allegory: these are the devices of writers who are dealing with big issues, who are using fiction as a means of transcending the limits of individual experience. This is a characteristic feature of Scottish Renaissance writing. One can also see such attempts at making sense of a working class reality involving individuals in social contexts beyond their control and understanding, against the background of Socialist Realism, which became official doctrine in the Soviet Union in 1932. It demanded, beside the accurate rendering of reality in literature, also a transcendence in the prediction and exploration of future possibilities. However, the overriding directive from Lenin was for partiality, and that ambiguities should be resolved within a work of literature is maybe a bit much to ask of any writer; it was certainly too much to ask of Scottish writers in the 1930s, whose main task it was to keep alive the consciousness of the important questions of identity, and a life worth living. To bring Mitchell,for instance, completely in line with Socialist dogma can consequently prove to be nothing else but an uphill battle.[17]

That some of the classic working-class novels in Scotland were written in the 1930s, can be related to the growth of Scottish Nationalism, the Literary Revival, the triumph of Socialist Realism: but also, first and foremost, to the effects of the worldwide economic depression which hit Scottish industry particularly hard. Thus, a large part of the working class became the unemployed, who were less likely to see organised class struggle as their main concern, and more liable to concentrate on individual techniques of survival. Historians have expressed some doubt as to whether, in spite of the reputation of Red Clydeside, Scottish workers ever developed a consciousness of their class status that gave them a real sense of unity, or whether they were prevented from that by 'a range of attitudes that were never wholly of industrial mass-society,'[18] handed down by craftsman and crofter to the industrial worker. What is meant is a certain sense of pride, of human equality in spite of class distinctions, 'for a' that and a' that'. Industrial workers were bound to find that their economic position, especially under the threat of unemployment, held little warrant for such Burnsian sentiments, and to find they had to look for different ways to prove that a man was a man.

This introduces a new variant to the theme of survival, a new kind of working-class hero who does not fight in solidarity with his comrades, who does not fight against exploitation or anything in particular, who does not fight for anyone or anything, not even himself; a hero who fights because it is the only way of life he can choose to lead. The prototype of this kind is Johnnie Stark the 'Razor King', in *No Mean City: A Story of the Glasgow Slums* (1935), written by Alexander MacArthur and H Kingsley Long, the latter in the rôle of editor. Here is another embarrassing best-seller, which has to date clocked up more than twice as many copies as the quarter of a million quoted for *Wee Macgreegor*. Predictably enough, it gets attacked twice as severely in literary criticism, if not entirely left out, as in F R Hart's *The Scottish Novel*.

The criticism is mostly justified, but the omission is indeed curious, especially in a study written in America. Given his astute insights into Scottish culture, one would have expected Hart to realise that the resulting gap is as wide as one that would appear if one left the Leatherstocking novels out of the history of American fiction. In a survey of working-class literature, it would be, for various reasons, even more unthinkable to ignore *No Mean City*. First, one would practically dismiss the possible inclusion of a working-class readership, besides the origin of the author, the subjects dealt with, and the perspective of the narration, as a criterion for the constitution of the genre. Secondly, the book has had widespread and long-lasting repercussions, a considerable number of epigones, and there are even more writers who provide evidence of a conscious rejection of the formula it offers, recognising the dangers of the stereotype, using it in a distanced, ironic fashion, or in brief references which are enough to conjure up a whole cluster of images taken for granted.[19]

At the centre of this set of images is the hard man, a character who is not particularly evil, but capable of extremely violent behaviour because that is the obvious road to recognition, to status, to an individual identity. In *No Mean City* Johnnie Stark does not consciously reject bourgeois morality or capitalist society: in fact, he respects the hierarchy of power, both physical and financial, as do the other characters in the book, who are portrayed as obsessed with class distinction—not that of Capital versus Labour, but distinctions within the working class itself. Ambition appears as futile, and political action as self-destructive, both exemplified by Johnnie's brother Peter, a social climber who merely by accident becomes a sufferer for socialism. The only escape routes offering a touch of glory are careers as professional dancers, or indeed the excitement of gang fights, although the escapes offered are temporary, and the glory is short-lived.

This gloomy scenario is described in a condescending tone, the reader being constantly reminded of the characters' lack of self-awareness, moral values, and resolve to act for an improvement of their conditions. On top of the style of the narrative, the dialogue—used very sparingly—is not too convincing. At least to a modern reader, lines like 'Nit the jorry . . . Nark it!'[20] would seem to have their origin in Lewis Carroll's wonderlands, rather than in Glasgow's Gorbals. Why, then, is *No Mean City* still one of the most popular Scottish books ever written? One possible explanation is that it still strikes a familiar chord: readers will still recognise the macho ideal, the drinking, the fighting, the attitude to women; and the deprivation, the lack of purpose, and the fatalism, in Scottish life today—while at the same time they can distance themselves from these familiar phenomena in contemplating the fictional slum dwellers like an alien tribe, following a hero whose actions they can savour without having to condone them.

It is worth noting that at the time this anti-hero was let loose, a very real Scottish working-class hero was still alive, though he had by then already become a character of folklore, well enough known for Peter in *No Mean City* to say no more than 'Ah don't want to be a John MacLean'[21] to make his meaning clear. This Glasgow schoolteacher had become a leader of the Glasgow workers, and a Bolshevik consul, before he was imprisoned and became 'a saint and a martyr.'[22] Here was the ultimate model to graft the hero of a novel on, but this did not happen, whilst in poetry, song, and drama, the MacLean figure was duly celebrated.[23] That the novel did not have a share in the shaping of the legend could well be seen as evidence for popular doubt about the rootedness of the genre in Scottish culture.

One of the closest approximations to a John MacLean figure in fiction is the character of Jock MacKelvie in James Barke's *Major Operation* (1936), from the same decade as the novels previously discussed. Although he is just a local leader of the workers, MacKelvie is almost superhumanly just, considerate, sensible, tolerant, resolute, intelligent, educated: in short, a champion of the people, but not the hero of the novel in a narrative sense. This is a coal-merchant called George Anderson, who winds up by accident in the same hospital room as MacKelvie. He becomes a complete convert to the workers' cause before his release, finds that he cannot shake off his background to blend in completely with his new comrades, and dies in self-sacrifice for the protection of the man in whom he believes even more than in the cause he stands for.

Major Operation demands some believing on the part of the reader, too, but it is, on the whole, cleverly enough executed to make the allegory of the failed marriage between the classes digestible. The dramatic irony of the ending is matched by the ironic tone of the narration at the beginning. Before the plot sets in, the reader is taken on a kaleidoscopic tour of Glasgow, a city which is itself a patient undergoing a major operation under 'the scalpel of class.'[24] Barke is even more overt, although also a bit diffuse, about his attempt to create a mythological overtone: like Blake, he uses a male couple whose fortunes are tied up together, but whose union is not made to last, mainly because of Anderson's weaknesses; MacKelvie, on the other hand, is as nearly faultless as he could have been without actually appearing as a saint. The propagandistic intentions behind his portrayal are not always kept sufficiently at bay to prevent a backfiring of the defence of the working-class character, as in this description:[25]

> MacKelvie liked his mates. They were raw but they were genuine—when you got to know them. They weren't angels of course. Razor slashers, wife-beaters, incestmongers, adulterers, blackmailers, gangsters . . . But a man, morally rotten, didn't work long with MacKelvie.

If the intention of creating a positive counter-image to that which appears in

No Mean City is a worthy one, the apologetic zeal results, at least in this instance, in absurdity. However, between these two extremes lay the range of contemporary representations of the Scottish working class in fiction: this was the legacy of the 1930s, which at the same time opened up new possibilities and possible trappings for those who followed.

Indeed, most of the books that did follow, right up to the present day, can be delineated against those dealt with so far. This is no derogatory statement, as many authors have searched for, and found, their own paths between the Scilla of condemnation, and the Charybdis of glorification of working-class manners, and have made creative use of the set of characters, plots, and images at their disposal. Still, it took some time before the 1930s found their match; for two decades, there was not much that was truly remarkable in the genre, and still less material that was written by new authors.

One of these new writers was Tom Hanlin, whose novel *Once in Every Lifetime* appeared posthumously in 1945. It introduces a first-person working-class narrator, who tells the story with a humble presumptuousness, or arrogant modesty that is very direct in its appeal to the reader. While claiming total innocence—'I don't know any writing tricks. I just tell things as they happened.'[26]—Frank Stewart proceeds with the story of his life in a mining community, his love for a girl called Jenny Dewar, and his analysis of what went wrong in their lives, plus his reason for telling the tale:

> This story is for you, written in your language, and the happenings in it happen every day in your life. Nobody has ever written this way before and, though I'm telling you the oldest story in the world, the way I tell it you'll get the same sensation you get reading the ink-wet stop press.[27]

Direct approach and a tone of urgency pervade the book, and make for intense reading. The general issue is the relationship between the environment's influence, and individual freedom to dictate the course of one's life. The narrator acknowledges the former, but his whole story is one earnest entreaty to the reader not to forget that the latter also exists, even if those times when one can actually influence one's own destiny can pass very quickly. The *carpe diem* motif recalls the wartime situation in which the book was written, although this is not directly reflected by the plot.[28]

The Second World War did not leave much of a mark on Scottish working-class fiction. The country's being at war on an all-out scale had pushed the class war out of the limelight; there had been a certain levelling of class distinctions in military service, in the rationing of supplies, and the belief in a common cause. This had been of course much less so in the First World War, and it is not insignificant that one novel that appeared in 1948 dealt with that bygone mass slaughter instead of the one that had finished more recently. Edward Gaitens's *Dance of the Apprentices* has a hero who goes to prison as a conscientious objector, feeling that his cause is that of the working man, and that this war is not his war. He meets with some support, some non-comprehension, and some people who think he is simply a cop-out;

an opinion that might well be voiced about the author who dodged the more contemporary and more fundamental aspects of the issue.[29]

As Britain moved from the austerity of the war years towards the security of the Welfare State, even such traditional Scottish industries as the shipyards experienced a development that looked like a revival, in the continuation of the boom in production caused by the wartime effort.[30] Thus, a novel dealing with working-class life in the 1950s could safely centre on an aspect of mass culture which had previously been neglected in favour of the more obviously important issues. The subject is football, and the novel that gave it its full fictional due was *The Thistle and the Grail* by Robin Jenkins. It deals with a small football club's pursuit of the Scottish Junior Cup, the Grail of the title, and the effect this has on the people involved with the fortunes of the club— ultimately, the whole community. Football in Jenkins's book is an integrative factor, providing a sense of identity and communal achievement; but the competitiveness has its corrupting influences. The attainment of the grail is tarnished by the means: a formal protest against a lost tie, put foward by the president who earlier on had found such actions distasteful and unsporting, but suddenly appears as 'reformed'.[31] Jenkins's novel acknowledges the rôle of Scotland's most popular and most proletarian sport, but portrays its redemptive qualities in a rather ironic light.

Jenkins was over forty, when his football novel was published in 1954; in the 1960s, the dawning age of youth, novelists were getting younger, and so were their heroes. The key theme was growing up; the key term for a working class hero going through adolescence was escape. In Hugh Munro's *The Clydesiders* (1961), set between the two Wars, Colin Haig runs away to sea when he finds he can not marry the girl he wants because of different religions, but mainly because there is nothing to stay for but a life modelled on that of his father, a shipyard worker sacked because he could not keep his pride and his mouth under control, violent when drunk, and bitter when sober. To become like him is the one thing Colin does not want, but he has the suspicion that nobody 'can ever really change what they've been born with.'[32]

Despite the physical escape, the conclusion is fatalistic: it is even more so in Gordon M Williams' *From Scenes Like These* (1968), a psychologically rich study of adolescence which has similar ingredients: a father/son relationship based on hatred, a rejection of all that parents stand for, and a resolve to avoid their mistakes; the absence of any goal within reach and worth striving for, and finally, the hero's capitulation and escape towards the lifestyle of 'a real moronic working man'[33] just to get away from the constrictions of respectability, and the demand for an education that seems of no practical value. Primarily, Dunky Logan runs away from a domineering mother and the task of being grown-up, for a male Never-Neverland of drink, football, and sexual fantasy.

Education is rejected in both novels, because it does not offer a realistic chance of escape. The representatives of education who might serve as model personalities can give no more guidance than the parents. Sadistic, cynical, frustrated: that is very much the standard image of the teacher in Scottish fiction, and this is a shameful testimony indeed for a country which has for centuries prided itself on the beneficial character of its educational system.

Apart from casting a different light on some traditional assumptions about education, another positive influence of working class fiction that challenges the 'hard man' image and all that goes with it, is the demand for more openness to physical contact as essential to all close human relationships. Williams's hero wonders about movies:[34]

> Funny how in the pictures you often saw kids give their mothers a kiss or a hug. He could no more have done that than shagged a horse.

The sentiment underlying this rather extreme statement is recognisable as belonging to a cluster of behavioural patterns and underlying values which has a special significance in Scottish working-class fiction, though by no means being the exclusive property of the working classes. However, the persistence of the image and the way the resulting cliché is still exploited are telling. A recent paperback edition of *The Big Man* (1985) by William McIlvanney for instance, one of the best contemporary writers in the genre and certainly no mere sensation-monger, is advertised with a picture of a mean unsavoury-looking man that can obviously be expected to have an instant sales appeal, although the hero of the book is not a Johnnie Stark at all.

Neither is the hero of *Docherty* (1975), McIlvanney's best-known novel. It has more of a concern for community than the books of the 1960s discussed here, portraying the hero Tam Docherty as representative of the way of life that has as a major weakness and as a major strength a kind of solidarity based on an individual sense of right and wrong, a solidarity strong enough to keep the social network functioning, but not sufficiently strong to win the contest for a major improvement of living conditions. Similarly, Tam Docherty is not strong enough to enforce his commonsense, secular but almost missionary morality, on a changing world. Neither is he able to adapt to changed circumstances, and he is as stubborn at his death as ever before; but none of those that are left behind have any better sets of values to offer, neither his son Mick the Communist, nor Angus who wants to get on in the world. Only the youngest son Conn, who provides the point of view for large parts of the narrative, seems likely to carry on where his father left off.

The childhood perspective is consistent in the narration of *The Magic Glass* (1981) by Anne Smith, one of the few female authors who have come to the fore in this particularly male-dominated corner of the Scottish literary scene. If this on the whole reflects the state of Scottish society, then working-class fiction represents an extreme side of this reality. On the one hand, women are depicted as victims, at the receiving end of a brutal society; alternatively or simultaneously, they are domestic tyrants, adding pressure from within to the external hardships imposed on families. Women of an impressive stature

are rare, and rarer still are rebel figures: ironically, one of the most eman-
cipated versions of the working-class hero's sidekick (for a working-class
heroine is all but absent) is Lizzie, wife of the notorious 'Razor King' of *No
Mean City*, even if is she is not endowed with the awareness which is the
precondition of fundamental rebelliousness.

Anne Smith's heroine Stella possesses that kind of awareness. She finds
herself constantly at odds with the patterns and values of society, and its
demands on her, the issues being much the same as in the other novels of
adolescence described, but with an added poignancy, and a greater deal
of reflection within the consciousness of the focal character. One survival
technique that is important to Stella is her imagination, the hope that the
adult world does include 'mysteries and miracles'[35] hidden behind the dull
face of reality. A similar technique is employed by the hero of James Kelman's
The Busconductor Hines (1984), which in a stream-of-consciousness narration
follows the rambling thoughts of its hero, as he tries to cope with the hassles
of everyday life, a rebel more out of bewilderment than commitment. A recent
article has praised Kelman's book as a superb achievement in realism,[36] but
such a statement calls for some qualification. The main narrative technique
is the transcendence of reality through the hero's imagination, and thus the
amount of realistic detail—bus routes, timetables, figures—acquires a similar
status as the description of ships, whales and whaling in Melville's *Moby
Dick*. The realism is deceptive, as it operates mainly on a surface level, above
all that of language. Scottish working-class fiction has always had a linguistic
problem with the conflicting demands of gentility and realism, and Kelman—
besides many other merits of his book—has found a convincing solution in
letting the story be told in the language of the central character, even if
not in first-person narration, thus avoiding the potentially disturbing stylistic barrier between dialogue and narration evident in so many other
novels.

Lastly, there is another recent book that has shown a possible way out of
the trappings of the genre. Alasdair Gray's *Lanark* (1981) has a hero with a
working-class background who tries to become an artist: another possible
escape route which features in working-class novels such as Archie Hind's *The
Dear Green Place*, mostly with autobiographical references, and reflections on
the rôle of the artist in Scottish society in general. To this theme, Gray brings
an unusual narrative technique, supplementing the conventional, largely
realistic story of his hero Duncan Thaw's life with a fantastic tale of his
afterlife as Lanark, in a city called Unthank which is a projection of Glasgow
onto a different plane of existence, as Lanark is a projection of Thaw. The
transcendence of reality allows the experimental realisation of positive or
negative possibilities inherent in the reality described, and makes for a complex and inspiring book, which is firmly rooted in the real world, in spite of
the flights of fancy in the story. Recent publications such as this have shown
that the Scottish working-class novel offers both models to draw upon,
formulas to use and to play with, clichés to satarise, and room for invention.
As William Power said fifty years ago in his reflections on *Literature and
Oatmeal*, the freedom to draw an honest image of Scotland which will clash

with the 'conventional "idea" of Scotland . . . to which Scots writers must conform,'[37] is maybe still least restricted in the industrial novel.

NOTES

1   Cf. Bruce Lenman, *An Economic History of Modern Scotland 1660–1976* (London, 1977), p 103.
2   Cf. Moira Burgess, *The Glasgow Novel. A Survey and Bibliography*, second edition (Motherwell & Glasgow, 1986), pp 21ff.
3   Maurice Lindsay, *History of Scottish Literature* (London, 1977), p 372.
4   Cf. Burgess, *The Glasgow Novel*, p 39.
5   George Blake, *Annals of Scotland, 1895–1955. An Essay on the Twentieth-Century Scottish Novel, Related to a Series of Programmes with the Same Title to be Broadcast by the BBC for Winter Listening, 1956–57* (London, 1956), pp 31f.
6   Cf. Kurt Wittig, *The Scottish Tradition in Literature*, facsimile of 1st edn (Edinburgh, 1978), p 323.
7   Cf. Francis Russell Hart, *The Scottish Novel, A Critical Survey* (London, 1978), p 213.
8   Cf. *The Glasgow Novel*, p 56.
9   Cf. Alan Bold, *Modern Scottish Literature* (London, 1983).
10 Cf. *The Glasgow Novel*, p 39.
11 Hart, *The Scottish Novel*, p 217.
12 *Grey Granite*, Part I.
13 Cf. Douglas F Young, *Beyond the Sunset. A Study of James Leslie Mitchell* (*Lewis Grassic Gibbon*), (Aberdeen, 1973), pp 2f.
14 *Grey Granite*, Part IV.
15 Ibid.
16 Cf. *The Scottish Novel*, pp 234f., *Beyond the Sunset*, p 3.
17 Cf. e.g. Ian Carter, 'Lewis Grassic Gibbon, *A Scots Quair*, and the Peasantry', *History Workshop* 6 (Autumn 1978), pp 169ff.
18 Christopher Harvie, *No Gods and Precious Few Heroes*, The New History of Scotland, Vol 8 (London, 1981), p 133.
19 When, for instance, in Alasdair Gray's *Lanark*, the hero refers to 'a music-hall song and a few bad novels' which represent the imaginative use of Glasgow in writing, the reference is as plain as the irony.
20 *No Mean City*, Chapter I.
21 Ibid., Chapter 16.
22 Ibid.
23 Cf. Josef Raszkowski, 'Battlepost of the Poor: The Legend of John MacLean', *Cencrastus* 1 (Autumn 1979), pp 9ff.
24 *Major Operation*, Part II.
25 Ibid., Part I.
26 *Once in Every Lifetime*, Chapter 2.
27 Ibid.
28 Hanlin was killed in 1944.
29 As dealt with, for instance, by Robin Jenkins in *A Would-be Saint* some forty years later.
30 Cf. Lenman, *An Economic History of Modern Scotland*, p 237.

31 *The Thistle and the Grail*, Chapter 19.
32 *The Clydesiders*, Chapter 25.
33 *From Scenes Like These*, Part I.
34 Ibid., Part II.
35 *The magic glass*, Chapter 2.
36 Frederic Lindsay, 'The Glasgow Novel: Myths and Directions', *Books in Scotland* 21 (Summer 1986), pp 3f.
37 William Power, *Literature and Oatmeal. What Literature Has Meant to Scotland.* (London, 1935), p 194.

FURTHER READING

Gray, Nigel *The Silent Majority. A Study of the Working Class in Postwar British Fiction* (London, 1973)

James, Louis, *Fiction for the Working Man* (Harmondsworth, 1974)

Bulmer, Martin (ed), *Working-Class Images of Society* (London, 1975)

Chapter 16

Compton Mackenzie and the Scottish Popular Novel

GAVIN WALLACE

Somewhere within the lexis of most critics, reviewers, writers and teachers of modern Scottish literature exists a well-rehearsed classificatory phrase labelled 'Kailyard', 'Tartanry' or 'Scottish popular culture', denoting a reflex ranging in tone from cynical bemusement to vituperative disgust, which is activated all too frequently in the face of those features of national identity which have become, for most Scottish intellectuals, an obdurate impasse to literary self-confidence and adequate self-definition. In spite of several noteworthy attempts since the 1970s, most notably by Tom Nairn in *The Break-Up of Britain*, to determine a means of understanding—if not redeeming—Tartanry's notoriety as the intolerable flaw in Scottish national authenticity, critics find themselves trapped between acknowledging the weight of Scottish popular culture and outdoing each other in finding suitably reductive epithets to denote the extent of its vulgar enormity: a complex which characterises even the initiative displayed by Nairn himself.

Establishing a satisfactory account of twentieth-century Scottish popular culture and its relationship to the impact of the Kailyard school of the late nineteenth century as the source of what Nairn dubbed an entire 'cultural sub-nationalism'[1] has been fraught with contradictions and problems. A major reason for this, as Nairn is careful to stress, is the fact that the legacy of the Kailyard has become intertwined with sources of Scottish representation existing *outwith* the confines of literature which infect the entire arena of a mass-culture from which the majority of educational institutions prefer to keep the function of literary criticism immune. These sources have conspired to create 'the tartan monster', Nairn's now-celebrated generic term for a material sub-culture of pervasive magnitude, compounded by the vast image-making processes of the press and the electronic media, the latter invariably outwith Scottish control and seemingly dependent on Kailyard sentimentality and tartan fetishism as the major sources for marketing a Scottish image.

'Kailyard' (except for the strictly academic specialist) and 'Scottish popular culture' have become virtually synonymous, interchangeable and invariably pejorative terms in the approach of many commentators on Scottish literature which signify—often somewhat vaguely—the paradigms of a false historical and cultural consciousness. As early as 1951, the novelist George Blake in his perceptive but too condemnatory *Barrie and the Kailyard School* connected

243

Kailyard fiction with the newspaper empire of D C Thomson, attacking its publications on the grounds of a 'careful cultivation of the Kailyard strain'.[2] More recently, contemporary novels of Scottish working-class life drawn from the industrial west have been faulted for their overtones of 'urban-Kailyard' values, indicating a term become so flexible that it can be applied to those very novels based on urban naturalism whose origins lie in the antithetical realism of anti-Kailyard fiction of the early twentieth century.

As such generic blurrings and contradictions suggest, the vast scope of the Kailyard/popular culture 'false consciousness' means that labels are far more frequently and indiscriminately applied in dismissal and dismay than actually investigated as valid critical concepts. The seldom-questioned view of Kailyard and tartanry as joint ideologies exercising a fierce stranglehold on imaginative potential has persisted. In the course of the twentieth century, Scotland—more so than is the case within other European cultures—has experienced an increasingly acute, and morbidly self-conscious, polarity between the values of its 'high' and its 'popular' culture. George Blake himself betrayed his fear of this divide when he described the case of the popular novelist and journalist Neil Munro as 'painfully' expressing 'the dreadful *dichotomy* in the soul of the gifted Scot'.[3] Critical study of Scottish literature in the past 50 years is replete with this antisyzygy-like imagery of fissure between populism and creative integrity, and figures like Robert Burns and Walter Scott, whose academic status as major writers co-exist uneasily with their populist image as national icons, falsely-honoured or otherwise, show that this schism is no illusion.

Francis Russell Hart refers generally to 'the haunting possibility that Scottish culture has features inimical to the novel';[4] one might easily invert the observation to claim that the Kailyard has come to be castigated for engendering not only a school of writing, but also a broad mentality, displaying features inimical to the interests of Scottish culture. In a general sense the Kailyard and counter-Kailyard climate of the early decades of the twentieth century was important in that it heightened a new sensitivity in Scotland to problems concerning the relationship between its culture, politics and society more anxiously explored than in other countries, England in particular. The resultant defensiveness concerning a valid national literature— so vital to the achievements of the Renaissance—has been of equal importance in sustaining a critical awareness equipped to realise fully the substantial achievements in Scottish writing since MacDiarmid. Nonetheless, it can be argued that this defensiveness, and its corresponding wariness of the popular, has also been counter-productive in that much has been expelled from what has been deemed to constitute the nation's valid literary inheritance. Given the hard struggle there has been against marginalising influences to promote even an elementary understanding of Scottish literature, this is very understandable, but if the process of understanding is to be built upon it is vital that several neglected factors receive urgent attention.

By far the most substantial lacunae of this sort is represented by the sociological dimensions of literacy within a new mass-reading public in Scotland which played such a vital role in the success of the Kailyard. Critical preoccupation with Kailyard fiction itself, and neglect of the character of the society consuming it, has meant that it was not until the mid 1980s that a startling discovery of popular, high-quality vernacular fiction in the Scottish press—flourishing alongside the heyday of Barrie, Crockett and Maclaren—demanded revision of the accepted picture of nineteenth-century Scotland swamped by a popular literature symptomatic of provincial decline.

Challenging and innovative research of this kind has been limited and occasional. The failure to evaluate fully such vital sociological considerations is closely bound up with the fact that Scottish culture as a whole has never received the benefit of detailed analyses of reading habits and literacy among twentieth-century reading public. There is no Scottish equivalent of pioneering English works in this field like Hoggart's *The Uses of Literacy* (1957) or Q D Leavis's *Fiction and the Reading Public* (1932), let alone the continuing efforts which have revised the methodology and perspective of such works, most of which remain unhelpfully specific to English social characterisics. Furthermore, the initiative displayed in the recent emergence of cultural and media studies in England is equally inappropriate to peculiarly Scottish experience, while similar and very innovative analysis of Scottish film and television in recent years has posed problems in the applicability of its findings to the sphere of literature, for reasons which will be suggested later. More generally, new approaches in Scotland to mass-culture are often frustrated by the unsuitability to a Scottish context of the definitive ideology of 'culture and society' as established by the English New Left since the 1950s.

This yawning gap within Scottish literary studies may be taken to represent both symptom and cause of a larger failing: failure to acknowledge the simple fact that in one very real sense, while critics have agonised endlessly over the rights and wrongs, implications and manoeuvres, of the Kailyard perspective and furthered an instinctive distrust of the popular, the Kailyard—in its original form as accessible and popular fiction—has continued to flourish and flourishes still. The success of the Scottish popular novel with its indigenous reading public has continued throughout the course of the twentieth century with an endurance which is remarkable, and while its purveyors may have long eschewed the values of Kailyard fiction, sales figures and popularity indicate an analogous saturation level, making the popular novel a substantial component of that Scottish popular culture whose omnipresence has been frequently lamented but never adequately explained as an inescapable feature of the nation's life.

Popular fiction in Scotland in the twentieth century falls into three distinct phases. It can be taken to begin with Neil Munro's short-lived attempts to continue the Kailyard strain in the early twentieth century, soon superseded by his respected and successful historical romances, *John Splendid* (1898), *Doom Castle* (1901), and *The New Road* (1914). Journalistic success as eventual editor of the *Glasgow Evening News*, however, led to his flirtation with Blake's 'terrible dichotomy' and the creation of the alias 'Hugh Foulis', through which Munro created the vastly more successful stereotypical Scottish comic figures of the waiter *Erchie* (1904) and the commercial traveller Jimmie Swan (1917) and, more famously still, Para Handy and the quaint crew of the Clyde puffer 'The Vital Spark'. Munro's sterteotypes have proved an immensely enduring influence on subsequent Scottish comedy, comic writers and comedians, so much so that his more earnest work has been eclipsed. In this regard he is the first twentieth-century Scottish writer to fulfil a persistent pattern.

The period 1920–1950, which embraces the creative and political challenge of MacDiarmid and the Renaissance and the beginning of its second wave, also spans the huge success of popular sagas like A J Cronin's *Hatter's Castle* (1931) and *The Citadel* (1937). The second important phase of the popular novel, however, is dominated by the long careers of a closely related triangle of novelists who won an immense public affection and lasting popularity— John Buchan, Compton Mackenzie, and Eric Linklater. In the latter half of the century, the predominant strain and the third phase within the Scottish popular novel, alongside the post-Mackenzie Hebridean novels of Lilian Beckwith in the 1960s, has been a genre which boasts a distinguished pedigree: the historical romance as 'invented' by Walter Scott. Drawing on the seemingly limitless gallery of famous and infamous Scottish historical personages, forensic attention to period detail and elaborate plotting has sustained the productive careers of Nigel Tranter and Dorothy Dunnett and a host of imitators. The persistence of the historical saga has been accompanied by the spy-thriller and high-suspense, high-adventure novel, a genre in which Scotland has excelled in producing two of its most famed exponents, Ian Fleming and Alistair Maclean.

It is with the middle group of writers, however—Buchan, Mackenzie, and Linklater—that the issues surrounding popular Scottish fiction since the Kailyard are implicated most strongly and urgently. All three novelists managed, with varying degrees of success, to cultivate a profile of literary seriousness yet remain best-selling authors through careers distinguished by prodigious output, rigorous professionalism and the achievement of considerable oeuvres. Despite this comprehensive body of work, however, all three have continually failed to attract the full-scale critical attention they deserve, though Linklater has fared a little better in recent years. There are reasons for this lack of critical initiative, the most important of which rests in the unusual position occupied by the novelists themselves. However separate in terms of background, creative personality and fictional priorities, Buchan, Mackenzie, and Linklater are connected in that they remain prominent Scottish writers whose genuine affiliation to a national culture remains questionable, while their claims to be engaged with authentically Scottish preoccupations and themes can often appear dangerously spurious.

In questioning the claims of these writers to the influence of what the novelist Muriel Spark has detected in her own work as 'a Scottish formation', commentators have alluded to the fact that the creative character of all three is marked by a tendency to indulge in an interplay between English and Scottish personae, a willingness to participate in the cultural, creative and political issues surrounding the Renaissance while indulging in the identifiably English mannerisms and overtones, in narrative style and lifestyle, against which so many Scottish writers of the time were reacting. Thus the reflection of the themes of Presbyterianism and Calvinism which can be found in the accomplished, Stevensonian adventure novels of John Buchan (explored more explicitly and earnestly in *Witch Wood* (1927)) must be seen in the context of Buchan's equally important, and equally close, identification with the Oxford ethos of the pre-1914 Edwardian generation and his immersion in the peculiarly English values of Parliamentarianism and colonial duty, aspects of which appear conspicuously throughout Buchan's autobiography, *Memory Hold-The-Door* (1940). His declaration, following a visit to the Cotswolds, that 'the essential England could not perish',[5] and other frequent anglocentric gestures, jar strongly with equally heartfelt testimonies to the powerful influence of Scottish history and landscape—that of the Borders especially—on the writer's imagination, and forces one to ask if Buchan's Scottish persona served merely as a vital yet shallow component absorbed within an essentially British patriotism of 'national' unity and imperial mission.

A similar though more ironically felt political ambivalence underlines the life and novels of Eric Linklater, who towards the end of his life declared proudly that he was perhaps the only Scottish writer who was 'both a Scottish nationalist and an imperialist'.[6] As its title suggests, *The Lion and the Unicorn* (1935), Linklater's contribution to Gibbon and MacDiarmid's *Voice of Scotland* series, rehearses his discernibly patrician view of Scotland's claim to autonomy through conservative symbols and institutions, and is politically circumspect. The extent of his commitment to the national movement in the 1930s—his contribution was short-lived, tokenistic and disastrous—finds its fictional corollary in his finest novel, *Magnus Merriman* (1934), in which an ironised portrayal of Scotland's political and cultural regeneration in the late 1920s is conveyed through a hero whose very name symbolises the juxtaposition between the author's archaic Orkney inheritance, 'Magnus' signifying the ascetic profundity of sainthood, and the shallow and cynical contemporary values with which 'Merriman' must endeavour to reconcile his mock-heroic quest for the fulfilment of authentic cultural roots. The farcical deflations, fragile delusions and comic ambiguities of conduct which characterises Magnus's life are instructive about the uncertainties the author perceived in his Scottish status, while even more revealing is the ease with which Linklater could adapt his adroit command of farcical exhuberance and urbane voice to the seemingly alien terrain of the comedy of English manners, most notably in *Poet's Pub* (1929) and *Ripeness is All* (1935), where satirical energy co-exists with a sense of complicity between author and subject-matter.

Linklater's friend and fellow-novelist Compton Mackenzie possessed greater fluency as a writer of comic fiction, and an even wider scope of farcical invention. Linklater's late comedy *Laxdale Hall* (1951) is clearly indebted to Mackenzie's long series of Highland comedies, and the achievements of both novelists demonstrate the important degree to which popular fiction in twentieth-century Scotland was for a considerable time dominated by comic and farcical perspectives. Yet even Hugh MacDiarmid, the last figure one would have expected to tolerate Scottish writers who had 'sold out' through a flirtation with anti-intellectual and frivolous comic capering, acknowledged the genuine influence and status of this Scottish school of 'wit':

> It is very pleasant to think of men like Norman Douglas, Hector Munro, Compton Mackenzie, and a few others when one is oppressed by the terrible lack of wit in Scotland today and particularly—save for the blessing of Eric Linklater—in Scottish authors today, and disfigured by the antics of Sir Harry Lauder and the other Scotch 'coamics' . . . it is not so pleasant to think of how the brainless buffoonery and 'chortling wut' of the latter are accepted as particularly Scottish, while the brilliant sallies of the few such as I have mentioned go for nothing and entirely fail to leaven the sad dough of modern Scottish '*moeurs*'.[7]

Lauder plagued MacDiarmid's mind, as he haunts the sensitive Scottish mind still 40 years on, as the diabolical high priest of Nairn's 'tartan monster' of commercialised Scottishness, the comedian whose image served as the envoy of a denigrating cultural stereotype exported all over the world. For MacDiarmid, Lauder's falsification of the Scots in his promotion of a music-hall version of Scottish 'wit' represented the exploitation of a genuinely innate national characterisic deployed to the full, if not adequately recognised, in writers like Mackenzie and Linklater. MacDiarmid's preparedness to accept rather than scourge such writers indicates a relaxation of his widely-suffered fierceness in imposing the severe political and creative parameters within which a Scottish literary consciousness was to be forged, and this is even more surprising in view of the peculiar cultural duality and discernible 'Englishness' manifest in Linklater and Mackenzie referred to earlier. His moment of tolerance further emphasises the unacceptable paucity of attention such writers have received since.

The reputation of Compton Mackenzie in particular bears this out, for his career vindicates the observation that an excess of popularity in Scotland breeds an intensity of intellectual contempt, especially so in the case of a writer who through the tactics of comedy attempted to undermine the grim pragmatism and defeatism so often bemoaned as the most stubborn feature of the Scots' attitude to their history and culture. Mackenzie attained his most popular successes in Scotland, towards the end of his career, through his comic fiction, at the expense of an already fragile critical reputation. His long series of interconnected Highland comedies—*The Monarch of the Glen* (1941), *Keep the Home Guard Turning* (1943), *Whisky Galore* (1947), *Hunting the Fairies* (1949), *The Rival Monster* (1952), and *Rockets Galore* (1957)—is more readily classified with MacDiarmid's contempt for the commercialised mendacity of Lauderesque tartan parody than any claim they might have to represent an authentic contribution to Scottish humour. The resultant failure to reconcile Mackenzie's status as both an intellectual and a popular influence in Scottish writing makes him uniquely and valuably illustrative of the wider implications in that pronounced schism between a high and a popular Scottish culture in which Mackenzie's achievements have been disfigured and trapped for many years. This process has misrepresented not only his more ambitious work but the comedies themselves, frequently dismissed as glib and patronising money-spinners based upon a spurious Scottish subject-matter. There is a case to be argued which might justify both the success of these comedies and their contribution, albeit limited in relevance, to Scottish themes and issues.

In 1933, in a memorable phrase, Mackenzie identified the way in which the Kailyard movement had 'mortgaged Scottish literature to indignity'.[8] It is an irony peculiar to the nature of a fractured Scottish culture that Mackenzie's pursuit a decade later of a similarly accessible comic Scottish fiction—which betrays little of the condescension which underwrites the Kailyard—effectively made him a victim of the process he had so accurately summarised and mortgaged his own reputation to obscurity and misunderstanding. This is nowhere more evident than in the underestimation of Mackenzie's self-conscious repatriation to Scotland in the 1920s, and his exploration of an English-Scottish creative and cultural duality of perspective which is a good deal more sincere, and ultimately more redemptive, than the troubling ambivalences which have been detected in the like cases of Buchan and Linklater.

Mackenzie was one of the first creative writers to identify with the resurgence of national and cultural activity in Scotland, ending a long process of growing disaffection with the Edwardian English cultural ambience which fostered his highly achieved pre-War novels. The finest of these, *Sinister Street* (1913–14), reveals not only a distinctive and crafted stylistic voice but also a disquieting thematic preoccupation, manifest in the spiritual restlessness of its semi-autobiographical hero Michael Fane, with the stifling and alienating effects of English culture and values upon the potential artist. By 1929, a year after he had helped to found the Scottish National Party, the new priorities of the writer found blunt and uncompromising expression:

> Let us turn to our own background and forsake utterly the enticement of an alien and for us unnatural culture. We have grafted ourselves upon the rich rose of England. It has flourished on our stock. We have served it well. But the suckers of the wild Scots rose are beginning to show green underneath. Let them grow and blossom, and let the alien graft above, however rich, wither and die. You know our wild Scots rose? It is white, and small, and prickly, and possesses a sharp sweet scent which makes the heart ache.[9]

Mackenzie's new-found and regenerative orientation became an ideological condition of his writing, a condition he expressed in terms which clarify the unusual position of a novelist who would attempt to reconcile the English narrative paradigms reflected in his earlier fictional personality with identifiably Scottish preoccupations: 'an English voice and a Scottish heart is a better combination than a Scottish voice and an English heart'.[10] The aphorism is simultaneously personal and universal, apologetic and assertive, and provides the 'heart' of the significance of Mackenzie's status within Scottish culture and its attendant strengths and limitations.

Enjoying for a time a close working relationship with MacDiarmid, who respected his views and welcomed his contribution, Mackenzie made consistent efforts on behalf of the new nationalism through the various roles of public speaker, broadcaster and journalist to popularise and disseminate the aims and rationale of the culturally-oriented drive towards Scottish political autonomy. These efforts culminated in his election in 1931 as the first Nationalist Rector of Glasgow University, an event which made him the epoch-marking figurehead of an entire political movement and the natural successor of prominent nationalist personalities like R B Cunninghame Graham.

More importantly, Mackenzie's nationalism was also to bear creative fruit in a work representing not only the author's major fictional achievement, but an ambitious experiment displaying affinities with the ideologies explored by the major novelists of the Renaissance. *The Four Winds of Love* (1937–1945), a vast excursionary odyssey based on a narrative of forensic intellectual and philosophical debate between its characters, is also a subtle exploration of the politics of peripheral nationalism as it has influenced the history of Europe in the twentieth century. Throughout its extensive European canvas the ideologies of Marxism, nationalism and Catholicism form a matrix of interpretative orthodoxies assessing the dynamncs of twentieth-century change. The novel's most intriguing thematic departure, however—from the point of view of the modern Scottish novel—is a subtle inner pattern devoted to the nature of the British state, exploring through the perspective of the hero John Ogilvie the decline of England's imperial status and her continued domination of the Celtic peripheries, Ireland and Scotland in particular. The author's sophisticated grasp of complex intellectual and political dilemmas entirely germane to Scottish preoccupations is a consistent strength of this *roman fleuve* which makes the work's continued obscurity very regrettable, though it would be wrong to underestimate the novel's serious technical deficiencies, most of which are attributable to the author's reliance on an idealised pedagogic hero as authorial surrogate on whose shoulders the awesome totality of the narrative somewhat precariously rests.

Mackenzie, however, was to enjoy a public image as the author of *Whisky Galore* and its stablemates which earned him a popular profile as enduring as that created by J M Barrie, while the graver and philosophical authorial persona of *The Four Winds of Love* was pushed further into obscurity. This denotes an inevitable mechanism in reputation-making, determined, it would seem, by the blatant antisyzygy of sorts between the intellectual density and scope of Mackenzie's long novel and the seeming flippancy of his Highland comedies. This is precisely why the apparent conflict between the priorities in Mackenzie's career is of such value, for this tension encapsulates the paradoxical character of Scottish culture which has been outlined above. Within the 'high' cultural endeavour of creating the definitive fictional statement of *The Four Winds of Love* as an expression of Renaissance aspirations, Mackenzie foresaw and exploited the potential for popular and accessible fiction, with a distinctively Scottish appeal, that might transcend the limited currency of more ambitious work.

The Four Winds of Love owes its uniqueness, in part, to its systematic and comprehensive exploration of twentieth-century European nationalism as a dialectic between national self-determination and fascistic or imperialistic aggression. Yet it was in 1941, as Mackenzie was in the midst of writing the sequence and focussing the novel's action on renascent Scottish nationalism in the 1920s and 1930s, that he interrupted composition to write the first of his Highland comedies, *The Monarch of the Glen*. The apparent antithesis can, properly read, effectively be taken to signify a complementarity. *The Four Winds* celebrate through its extended development the narrative of historical evolution impinging on cultural and social upheaval, whereas the comedies—in a mirror-image parody—play games with the cultural blinkering and distortion arising from a 'domesticated' conception of history through characters who inhabit an idealised Scottish historical past as a refuge from acknowledging the realities of the present.

This thematic polarity is anticipated in *The Four Winds of Love*, for Scottish nationalism there is interpreted in terms of a dialectic between ideology and mobilisation. This theme is declared within the masssively extended debate between the hero John Ogilvie and a young radical nationalist, Alasdair McPhee, which opens *The North Wind of Love* and provides the prelude to the novel's final shift of thematic attention to Scotland. The very ambience of the Highland hotel in which Ogilvie and McPhee stage their debate suggests a banal contradiction of Ogilvie's impassioned political sincerity:

> On the wall opposite the door hung a large steel-engraving spotted with brown mould which represented a mythical Fitzgerald saving an almost equally mythical King Alexander from the antlers of an infuriated stag and thereby gaining the favour on which the fortunes of Clann Choinnich were supposed to have been built up . . . Under the engraving was a diminutive and ill-executed watercolour of Dunvegan Castle . . . On either side of the engraving hung a seatrout in a glass case, to both of which time had given a somewhat kippered appearance. The rest of the pictures showed the stock sentimentalised scenes of Highland life—sheep, shepherds, plaided lassies, shaggy cattle, hills, lochs, birds, and sunsets.[11]

As McPhee recognises, this *kitsch* decor is far from unconnected with the intractable Scottish political issues which he and Ogilvie seek to confront. The room amounts to a catalogue of the cliched symbols and icons ossified in the popular Scottish imagination as the falsified and sentimental version of a historical past in which no reconciliation with the present world of a distintegrated culture and history is made possible.

Although Mackenzie's critique of modern Scotland throughout *The North Wind of Love* is somewhat limited to the author's knowledge of the Highlands—unlike, for instance, the wide-ranging polemic and satire found in MacDiarmid and Gibbon in *The Scottish Scene* (1934)—Mackenzie was able to deploy his Highland-orientated conception of Scotland to very different ends. The attitudes towards the Scottish past enshrined in Ogilvie's hotel lounge, and the disparity between those attitudes and present reality, contain a potent irony which would form the terrain of the comic version of Scotland promoted in the comic sequence. The *kitsch* decor becomes the mentality which his comic characters inhabit, a mentality which the author was prepared to popularise further but also to question through the discrete conflicts in values which inform the plots of the novels themselves.

Of the six connected novels, three are centred around the anglified Highland laird Ben Nevis and his castle and estate of 'Glenbogle', and three on the two 'Todday' islands, Mackenzie's idealised rendering of the Hebrides and the Catholic community of Barra in particular, where the author lived for the ten most productive years of his career. The farcical energy of the Glenbogle world gradually gives way to the gentler sentimental realism of the Todday books. This culminates in *Rockets Galore*, in the author's own words 'a bitter farce', which stands apart from the remainder. The political implications of the actual events which inspired the novel—the threat of establishing guided-missile bases on South Uist in 1955—pervade the novel so insistently that a new and cynical realpolitik threatens to undermine comedy confronting realities proof against the comic perspective. This tension was very real, since *Rockets Galore* was the last comic novel with a Scottish relevance Mackenzie was to write.

The series begins more innocently: in *The Monarch of the Glen*, boisterous irreverence is the keynote. Mackenzie invites the reader into his newly-conceived Scottish world with an all-important gesture. The narrator immediately concedes his task of scene-setting to the voice of an imaginary pseudo-Celtic Twilight 'topographer' Hector Hamish Mackay, excerpts from whose books like *Faerie Lands Forlorn* and *Summer Days Among The Heather* punctuate the remaining comedies at regular intervals. Mackay's platitudinous prose is adopted as a parodic shorthand for misrepresentative Highland romanticism, the literary equivalent of that hotel *kitsch* in *The North Wind*, the mentality exhibited by the landed gentry who own the landscape Mackay describes and a condition which incomers to this world attempt to assimilate. Although throughout the course of the comedies Mackay's authority is gradually weakened by more cynical purveyors of Scottishness (by the time of *Rockets Galore* he has disappeared altogether), in one sense the perspective of the novels depends upon his presence. Through Mackay's glaring artificiality, the author exhibits the self-consciousness with which he accepts the parameters of cultural attitudes he knows to be mendacious, but within which the novels must endeavour to operate. The precise intentionality of this device is demonstrated in the fact that Hector Hamish Mackay's prose represents Mackenzie's astute parody of the once-ubiquitous works of Alasdair Alpin Macgregor, now largely forgotten as the author of books on the Highlands and Western Isles replete with the Gaelic sentimentality and Celtic Twilight nebulosity Mackenzie lovingly exaggerates in his surrogate author. This internalised rejection of popular Highland romanticism is a cunning ruse on Mackenzie's part, for by mimicking the voice and values of another, he partly absolves himself from the responsibility of opening the gate to the Kailyard, as it were, and stepping through himself.

Indeed, like the archetypal Kailyard village, Ben Nevis's 'Glenbogle' represents an ahistorical country of the mind, while the character of Ben Nevis himself—as stubborn as his namesake is high—is based on the conservative prejudices necessary to the challenge of resisting and denying intrusion or change and defending the imagery of an antique Highland past already destroyed in the evolution of the present world from which he seems so securely immune. Mackenzie would seem to suggest, therefore, an ambivalence in the flouting of Highland symbols as an identity already anachronistic but which express a genuine, if myopic, source of Scottish consciousness. This tension allows for the novel's mock-heroic and satirical dynamic—the bloody past of clan conflict or Jacobite rebellion becomes the absurd confrontation between the anglified Scottish gentry and arrogant, trespassing Cockney hikers. Ben Nevis possesses all the force of his own blustering yet genial innocence, while his conception of Highland and Scottish history is as absurdly anglocentric as Mackay's is patently romantic. Imperialist, arch-conservative, epitome of the Tory Unionist, as an anglicised laird he embodies a phoney cultural interdependence which guarantees inexhaustible satirical and comic scope. Everything his Scottish pretensions encounter is inscribed with his upper-class English accent and mannerisms. Playing the role equivalent to Linklater's Magnus Merriman, Ben Nevis signifies something of a fantastic farcical inversion of the perspective of the English voice and Scottish heart which Mackenzie had stated as the nature of his position within Scottish culture.

Ben Nevis's sinister alter-ego in the series, Paul Waggett, is the source of the comedies' darker thematic intent, and the author's most thoroughly developed comic character. In his pretensions as latter-day English colonialist, accidentally finding himself in a position where he can indulge in his bureaucratic fatuities and play Governor General off centre-court, Waggett remains entirely oblivious, until *Rockets Galore* and the demise of Mackenzie's comic world, of the native values measured against which he is found ridiculous and finally dangerously dictatorial by the islanders, and of course in turn by the reader. His increased aggressiveness, provoking the only real violence in the series, cracks an already flimsy comic mould.

In *Rockets Galore* the striking co-existence of ideological declamation by the island's leaders, closely related to the eloquent politics of John Ogilvie, and the farcical ploy through which the island's destruction is deflected, is final indication of the almost symbiotic relationship between the two roles Mackenzie played in Scotland. Discussing the problematic posed by similar Scottish writers, Alan Bold suggests that 'the distinction between the artist and the entertainer is a Scottish schism that has resulted in an excessively moralistic art and an extremely idiotic level of entertainment. Scots have seldom been able to combine artistry and entertainment; writers who do so are rare and remarkable'.[12] Bold and several other critics have acknowledged the fact that Mackenzie contributed to Scottish culture as an intellectual and an entertainer, but none has investigated the further implications of his achievement or the extent to which this 'schism' is illustrative of general problems in cultural production in Scotland as a whole.

Perhaps it is time for the severity of Bold's paradigm to be tempered, since it reveals a tendency to view the roles of intellectual and entertainer as mutually exclusive functions, and there are serious presuppositions at play in thus partitioning any writer's motives that call into question the values by which literature is defined and adopted for the purposes of education. It has been the very success of his popular reputation which has so handicapped the means to a satisfactory critical appraisal of Mackenzie's complementary fictional tactics. There is a specific need to reconcile these conflicting images of Mackenzie as two priorities of a career which qualify—rather than invalidate—each other. Recognition of this in Scotland is a priority in the context of a twentieth-century literature illuminated by writers who have attained great public following at the expense of critical and academic attention.

Mackenzie's evident refusal to regard the rejection of reconciling art and entertainment as essential to Scotland's cultural dignity is further illustrated in an equally important and neglected facet of his 'populism': his insights and contributions to mass media. As an accomplished broadcaster, founder of *The Gramophone*, television presenter and above all in his critical shrewdness in founding the innovative radio review *Vox* (1929) in the infant days of broadcasting, Mackenzie possessed an impressive and perceptive familiarity with the role and potential of the British media from the late 1920s until his death. This is a qualification unparalleled in any other Scottish writer of the period, and his manipulation of radio broadcasts as a means of extending his contribution as nationalist activist contrasts strikingly with the indifference of MacDiarmid to these vital developments in communications. Mackenzie's offering of the editorship of *Vox* to MacDiarmid is revealing; that the latter's period in control was short-lived may have been one of the great opportunities lost to the Renaissance.

The first number of *Vox*, in a stroke entirely characteristic of both men, carried in its opening pages an editorial in English translated into Scottish and Irish Gaelic, Welsh, Cornish, and Manx—a remarkably punctual statement about the implications of the metropolitan, centralising character of the then-fledgling BBC. This early awareness developed, as is demonstrated in the content of the later Highland comedies—*The Rival Monster* and *Rockets Galore* especially—which acknowledge the significant advent of television and the growth of the British film-industry, the mechanisms of which the author carefully parodies. In 1949, of course, Mackenzie had experienced personal involvement with the film-industry in the famous Ealing Studios production of his most famous work, *Whisky Galore*, although the finished product left the author dissatisfied as an example of the ability of cinema to translate fictional material faithfully. Ironically, the huge success of the film—despite the misinterpretations and omissions which irritated the author—still forms the basis of Mackenzie's image as a Scottish writer for many, and has doubtless supplanted knowledge of the novel itself for many more.

The manoeuvres behind the film and others like it with a Scottish relevance (including the films based on *Rockets Galore* and Linklater's *Laxdale Hall*) have been the object of attention within a welcome upsurge in media analysis in Scotland during the 1980s. Colin McArthur's *Scotch Reels* (1982) symposium attempted a bold demystification of the severe distortions promulgated in representation of the Scots and Scotland in cinema and television, and the lessons such analyses offer have yet to be fully appreciated by the indigenous literary establishment. The need for cross-cultural reference of this kind is all the more urgent, since the excursion into a 'deconstruction' of the systematic imagery of Scottish film by McArthur and others has so far failed to take into account the complex issues surrounding literary reception and production in the Scottish novel which have contributed to the illustrative disparity between the film of *Whisky Galore* and the fictional text from which it derives.

With the D C Thomson newspaper empire still producing its diet of post-Kailyard journalism, Munro-esque cartoon stereotypes in 'The Broons' and 'Oor Wullie' and pawky Scottishness in general, the novel *Whisky Galore* shares the honours as one of Scotland's most conspicuous popular classics; a frequent subject of amateur theatricals, synonymous with the Hebrides, repeatedly cited as a reach-me-down metaphor for that most enduring of Scottish myths—whisky—a novel which answers perfectly those who would associate whisky and its mystical liturgy with some innate truth about the Scottish psyche. Most readers will be familiar with the images, on the covers of at least one of innumerable editions, of Lauderesque red-nosed and bekilted Highland worthies genially soused from half-empty bottles of 'Stag's Breath' dangling from sporrans, staggering in picturesquely Celtic fashion before a background of Hebridean sea and moonlight. Recent paperback editions of *Whisky Galore* and its companions confirm that Mackenzie's image has without doubt found its niche within what might be generally described as the 'iconography' of popular Scottishness, the phenomenon which provided the starting point of this discussion.

Taking his iniative from Tom Nairn's attempts to tame the tartan monster, the media analyst Murray Grigor's *Scotch Myths* project (which also provided the impetus for *Scotch Reels*), with its vast assemblage of popular Scottish imagery, represented a timely and valuable attempt to establish a means of decoding this system of icons, and the salutory lesson it taught was that however distasteful the commercial solidity and enterprise which can produce a material culture of such awesome diversity within sameness, the imagery sustaining it represents an inescapable sphere of cultural consciousness whose close relationship with, and derivation from, sources of high culture simply cannot be ignored. The case of Mackenzie can help us to see why.

It might be argued that by attempting to redeem relatively lightweight fictional material by assimilating it within the upper strata of a culture's achievements, one is guilty of a spurious aggrandisement of the essentially unworthy and ephemeral. Like the Kailyard phenomenon, however, Mackenzie's comic novels bear out the truth that it is often through lesser literature that issues of cultural identity and consciousness are highlighted in clear and instructive ways. More importantly, there is the lesson in the way in which

Mackenzie counters the frequency of creative exile in Scottish writers of distinction into seemingly less intractable cultures, a condition which has further exaggerated the unease felt by critics in claiming a Scottish native influence on writers no longer native, and in some cases even those who remain native, as Linklater did. Mackenzie effectively acted out in reverse the classic symptoms of Scottish creative exile, especially as they were displayed in the assimilation to metropolitan English cultural values in J M Barrie, the father of Kailyard. For Mackenzie, assimilation to the values of the Scottish political and cultural regeneration of the 1920s expressed the disquiet he felt within the values implicit in his onetime status as one of England's most celebrated writers.

NOTES

1 Tom Nairn, *The Break-Up of Britain*, 2nd edn (London, 1981). Chapter 3, 'Old and New Scotish Nationalism', p 160.
2 George Blake, *Barrie and the Kailyard School* (London, 1951), p 85.
3 Ibid, p 14.
4 Francis Russell Hart, *The Scottish Novel: A Critical Survey* (London, 1978), p viii.
5 John Buchan, *Memory Hold-The-Door* (London, 1940, repr 1984). Chapter VII, 'Inter Arma', p 168.
6 Stated by Linklater in the filmed interview with Ian Grimble *A Stone in the Heather*, directed by Laurence Henson, written by Jeremy Bruce-Watt. Produced by International Films (Scotland) Ltd, for Films of Scotland and the Scottish Arts Council, 1974.
7 Hugh MacDiarmid *Lucky Poet* (London, 1943), p 151.
8 Compton Mackenzie *Literature in My Time* (London, 1933), p 238.
9 Compton Mackenzie 'What's Wrong With Scotland? (The Soul of the Nation)', *The Scots Independent*, Vol III, December 1929, pp 19–21, p 19, Edited version of radio broadcast given on 5 November 1929.
10 Ibid.
11 Compton Mackenzie *The North Wind of Love* Book One (London, 1945, repr 1968), pp 8–9.
12 Alan Bold *Modern Scottish Literature* (London, 1983), p 165.

FURTHER READING

Of the few discussions of Mackenzie's fiction available, the best is to be found in Hart's *The Scottish Novel*. In addition to the works cited in the text and notes, readers are directed to the following as useful background material on Scottish popular fiction and culture from the Kailyard to the present.

Campbell, Ian, *Kailyard* (Edinburgh, 1981)

Campbell, John Lorne, *Our Barra Years*: (1) 'The Friends at Suiheachan', *Scots Magazine*, August 1975, Vol 103, no. 5, pp 494–504; (2) 'Fields of Battle', *Scots Magazine*, September 1975, Vol 103, no. 6, pp 613–24

Chapman, Michael, *The Gaelic Vision in Scottish Culture* (London, 1978)

Craig, Cairns, 'Visitors From The Stars: Scottish Film Culture', *Cencrastus* no. 11. New Year 1983, pp 6–12

Donaldson, William, *Popular Literature in Victorian Scotland: Language, Fiction and the Press* (Aberdeen, 1986)

Harvie, Christopher, *No Gods And Precious Few Heroes: Scotland 1914–1980*, Arnold New History of Scotland, Vol 8 (London, 1981)

Linklater, Andro, *Compton Mackenzie: A Life* (London, 1987)

McArthur, Colin (ed), *Scotch Reels: Scotland in Cinema and Television* (London, 1982); 'Breaking The Signs: *Scotch Myths* as Cultural Struggle', *Cencrastus* no. 7, Winter 1981–82, pp 22–5

Malzahn, Manfred, *Aspects of Identity: The Contemporary Scottish Novel (1978–1981) as National Self-Expression* (London, 1985)

Parnell, Michael, *Eric Linklater: A Critical Biography* (London, 1984)

Watson, Roderick, *The Literature History of Scotland*, Macmillan History of Literature Series (London, 1984)

Chapter 17

Four Novelists of the 1950s and 1960s

GLENDA NORQUAY

'If you don't go you can't come back'

Towards the end of Alan Sharp's novel, *A Green Tree in Gedde* (1965), one of the novel's central characters, John Moseby, is shown reflecting that: 'The mind is God striving to create Eden in order to live there'. Moseby is on the point of leaving his constrictingly conventional marriage and is also contemplating the move away from what he perceives as an equally sterile environment: Scotland itself. His situation is not uncommon in novels written in Scotland in the 1950s and 1960s in that it indicates a desire for escape, for flight from a country seen as restrictive in its morality, petty in its politics and unable to provide any kind of fulfilment, or sense of identity. It has been argued that twentieth century Scottish fiction in general has been characterised by this sense of stasis, the absence of both a significant past and a meaningful present.[1] And Mosbey's position epitomises that general sense of disaffection. The image he uses to define his reactions, however, is more clearly representative of a small group of novelists working within the 1950s and 1960s: the escape from circumstance is envisaged essentially in theological and philosophical terms. Four writers in particular share this obsession with the metaphysics of transcendence and liberation. James Kennaway, Alan Sharp, George Friel and Robin Jenkins, unlike contemporaries such as William McIlvanney and Archie Hind who are primarily concerned with the depiction of Scottish proletarian experience in their work, do not confine themselves to the social sphere of Scottish life; instead they explore what may be termed a cast of mind and the restrictions it creates when manifested in social morality. This cast of mind they present as being characteristically Scottish and, in many ways, much more difficult to escape than urban deprivation or cultural inferiorisation.

Moseby's description of the human mind with a desire for Eden echoes a phrase used by the writer Campbell MacLean to describe the Scottish Reformation: 'the attempt to create the kingdom of God on earth.'[2] Nor is the impetus behind his thoughts dissimilar, although the desires which shape them are rather different. From the Reformation onwards one of the dominant factors in Scottish thought is that of Calvinism, with its stress on both the fallen nature of the world (the inevitably flawed character of humanity), and the 'Elect' individual's potential for transcendence through the grace of

God. And this double stress becomes an important contributory element in any idea of a Scottish psyche. Tom Nairn describes the Reformation and its effect in a Scottish location by distinguishing it from the economically linked European Reformation described by Weber: 'originally the reformation movement was an absolute attempt at a moral and religious order, isolated from the very conditions that would have made it an integral part of history . . . Just because it could not be the veiled ideology of a class, the Scottish Reformation was bound to be an abstract millenial dream . . . The Scots wanted, and needed, Salvation in the most total sense imaginable. Scotland's Reformation gave it them neat.'[3] In Moseby's comment, and in the works of the four writers under consideration, the same complex balance of the desire for escape and transcendence combined with a recognition or fear that such escape might not prove possible is to be found.

This religious emphasis may appear unlikely in relation to writers of the mid twentieth century, an age which is usually perceived as moving towards a rejection of God; and, paradoxically, a general characteristic of these writers' works would appear to be their alienation from and dislike of a religious perspective. This does not mean, however, that they are unaware of the impact of Calvinism; nor that they can shake themselves free from a structure of feeling which is presented in their novels as part of the Scottish cultural inheritance. The impact of the Reformation in Scotland, the desire for a Kingdom of God on earth when all social, cultural and historical forces appear to be operating against its realisation, becomes the subject matter of their novels. Nor is the complexity of their attitude wholly new: writing on Byron, Angus Calder has described him as victim to: 'a Calvinist hunch that the world is not suffused with love, delight and pure morality—it is *either* a fallen world of carnal snares and delusions, *or*, God not existing, it is mere stone and dust.'[4] For the twentieth century writer, in a world where God may be more easily rejected, the latter option would appear to be the more attractive.

This view of the world as mere stones and dust has, moreover, found ample reflection in twentieth century philosophy, and in particular in the ideas of existentialism. Terry Eagleton describes the outlook of existentialist writers in these terms:

> Man is stripped of society and has no reality beyond the self; character is dissolved to mental states, objective reality reduced to unintelligible chaos . . . Individuals are gripped by despair and *angst*, robbed of social revelations and so of authentic selfhood, history becomes pointless or cyclical, dwindled to mere duration.[5]

To a certain extent this would appear to be the dominant feeling and attitude in the novels under consideration; in a world without God the desire for Eden must inevitably remain unfulfilled. But in none of these writers' works is this outlook presented as totally satisfactory; there is an acknowledgement of, but dissatisfaction with, the existentialist outlook—a desire for 'something more', combined with a recognition that this is unlikely to be forthcoming. Allan Massie summarises this attitude neatly when he states:

> What do we mean by Calvinism when we speak of Scotland? . . . it is God felt as the wind of pure Reason and also as something beyond reason. It makes an intellectual appreciation of the existential position and adds 'and yet'.[6]

It is this element of 'and yet' which Sharp, Kennaway, Jenkins and Friel appear unable to leave behind. A similar point is made even more forcefully in Sharp's novel, when Moseby's tutor at University suggests to him that the Scots are a race of 'existential mystics. Passionately concerned with the world as their domain yet obsessed with the dream of transcendence.' He then goes on to argue that the main problem for Scots has been 'that all our avenues of transcendence have been Calvinist.'

This concept of limited escape has significant implications for the novels under consideration. The characters in them are represented as being positioned within a dual process: on the one hand they are shown as searching for escape from personal, cultural and ideological limitations, seeking any form of transcendence; in so doing they are attempting to break away from all that they perceive as constrictive and, usually, by implication, all that is Scottish. On the other hand, their departure consists of a movement towards and through extremes of attitude and behaviour. And their definition of what presents an alternative to their society, to its moral and behavioural codes, what they perceive to be 'extreme', is then expressed in terms of absolute good and absolute evil. Escape then may only be envisaged in terms of polarities which are already part of that cultural identity from which they seek release: the extreme polarities of Calvinist thought. They cannot 'create Eden' except in their own terms—and what they are finally confronted with is not the opportunity for escape but the recognition of the extent to which they are trapped within assimilated ideas and within their own national history and identity.

Ironically, then, although the four writers under consideration may each appear to present a reaction against the Scottish background which constrains them, it is the same Scottish inheritance which creates the ideology determining their conceptualisation of an alternative. In their polarisation of an elusive Eden and a petty, sordid or restrictive 'reality', they create a dichotomy not dissimilar to the 'fallen world' and promised 'heaven' of Calvinism.

JAMES KENNAWAY

Of the four writers considered here, James Kennaway appears most easily categorised: a 1950s rebel, the exile from Scotland. Born in 1928, the son of a Perthshire solicitor and of a doctor, Kennaway went into the army for a spell after leaving University, but then moved into the worlds of literary

London and the film industry after the success of his first novel, *Tunes of Glory* (1956). From then until his early death in a motoring accident in 1968 Kennaway published a series of novels, bitter explorations of individuals who are pushed to extremes through circumstances or who test themselves against circumstances by creating extreme situations. His novels become increasingly minimalist in approach with the final novel published after his death simply called *Silence* (1972). Although it is only in his first two novels that social and moral codes are presented as forces which must be continually tested and challenged, his juxtaposition of petty, domestic morality with savagery, cruelty or fanaticism continues throughout his work. In this respect his works deal with that complex of ideas which Alan Sharp has usefully defined as: 'the protestant paradox of total predestination and the importance of outward forms.' Kennaway's own, most successful, description of the paradoxes he sees as inherent in Scottish character may be found in *Household Ghosts* (1961):

> A glance at their history or literature . . . reveals what lies underneath the slow accent, the respectability and the solid flesh. Under the cake lies Bonny Dundee.
> (p 174)

Underneath the cosy couthiness represented by Dundee Cake may be found the history of the Covenanters and the butchery of Claverhouse. Domestic parochialism and the attempt to create the kingdom of God on earth are juxtaposed in Scottish history—and also in the philosophy of Calvinism with its emphasis on the work ethic and the appearance of being 'Saved', but with its darker aspects lying in that essential uncertainty as to whether one is saved or damned, so skilfully explored in 'Holy Willie's Prayer' and Hogg's *Confessions of a Justified Sinner*. As historians have recognised, the Scottish Reformation leads to an emphasis on outward form, the proof not only of moral respectability but also of Election/Salvation: this, however, also conceals the deeper uncertainties created by the notion that the mind of God cannot be known and the fact of one's election may never be wholly confirmed in this world. As Gordon Marshall describes it:

> The insistence on assurance made the religion an easy prey to hypocrisy—such as that of 'Holy Willie' . . . Any cessation from the continual strivings for proof and assurance itself became synonymous with lack of proof of election. It is the insistence on never-ending sanctification and regeneration that gave Calvinists their seemingly unlimited strength under the most arduous of circumstances and, likewise, prevented them from easily becoming complacent when times were good.[7]

And it is this paradoxical combination of a surface emphasis on appearance and respectability combined with a much darker apprehension of polarities of good and evil, heaven and hell, which Kennaway, along with the other writers considered, explores in his work.

In *Tunes of Glory* it is on the apparently superficial parochialism of Scottish military life that Kennaway concentrates. The novel opens with parody of Scottishness and its potential claustrophobia: in Campbell barracks, located in a Perthshire town surrounded by snow, a dance takes place in the officer's mess as the regiment awaits the arrival of its new Colonel. The cold weather outside, the isolation of the scene, the warmth, drink, bagpipe music and dancing inside, appear exaggeratedly Scottish, and are enjoyed as such by 'Jock' Sinclair, the regiment's acting Colonel and the man who many expected to have been given that post permanently. Irascible, sentimental, possessing the 'common touch' in his ability to communicate with his men, Jock also has a reputation for valour and fierceness: like the scene, he too appears larger than life. The surreal quality of the occasion is exposed by the entry of the mild Colonel Barrow and his reaction of alienated bemusement. The novel follows through the subsequent struggle between Jock's notions of heroism and leadership, his power of personality, with Barrow's official authority and desire to be accepted. Reluctantly placed in the position of bringing down a man whom he admires as an opposite to himself, Barrow finally gains control; the 'victory' is, however, too much for him and he commits suicide. But in the end it is Jock whose ideals are most completely destroyed: after Barrow's suicide he is seen dressed in full military regalia, realising that the appearance, the uniform, is all that is left of the 'tunes of glory', and that his own sense of 'glory' has been maintained at the cost of turning valour to brutality, strength to bullying. As Jock realises: 'A soldier does not just need a brain to think with, nor yet an arm to strike with; he needs teeth to hang on with.' Jock's sentimentality and sense of national identity can only flourish upon a concealed base of brute force and sense of struggle; again, under the cake lies Bonnie Dundee.

Tunes of Glory is a succinct and self-contained study of a Scottish tragic hero; it was some years before Kennaway was to publish another novel and *Household Ghosts*, although sharing some of the earlier novel's concerns, and moving in the same upper-middle class milieu, is very different in character. The emphasis on dialogue that was increasingly to become a feature of later novels is already present and the novel focuses even more clearly on the relationships between a small group of individuals. But it is also in *Household Ghosts* that Kennaway most fully explores various forms of 'Scottishness' and their implications.

The 'household' of the title is the home of a decaying aristocratic Perthshire family, the survivors (or 'ghosts') of which consist of a retired, widowed Colonel, over whom the shadow of some past disgrace still hangs, and his two adult children, Mary and Pink, along with Mary's husband, Stephen. It is around the relationships between Mary, Pink, Stephen and the man with whom Mary is in love, David Dow, that the novel centres. In their childhood bright, brittle, vivacious Mary, and gentle but inadequate Pink, created a private world for themselves with their own language and characters. At moments of tension, created through Pink's increasing reliance on drink, and Mary's turbulent and unhappy love life, they return to this world which is both a parody and a tribute to the claustrophobic Scottishness they see around them. This world is best captured by the Young Conservatives dance with which the novel begins: 'The gymnasium at Dow's Academy that night was a monumental patch-up of ugliness and joy' (p 7): a world both of banality and extremes. It may also be found in Mary and Pink's 'Belle and Bun, the Kelvinside spinsters', routine:

'A little of what you fancy, Belle—it'll do you the world of good.'
'Is that a fact, Bun?'
'That's a fact.'

And through this routine, familiar and mockingly cosy, yet also anarchic, they may both live within and escape, through parody, the limits of their narrow world. It is only when others refuse to play their games, calling them children as Stephen does, or liars, as David calls Mary, that their world crumbles. David, son of the local headmaster, who has escaped to London and become a scientist, the character who has apparently rejected most in terms of his Scottish background, is shown, however, to be much more in thrall to the residual influence of Scottish morality than any of the others. It is David, described as a 'mixture between a second-class pugilist and Deacon Brodie on the prowl', who most clearly notices this dimension of his own personality in relation to his affair with Mary: 'They christened her Mary, I cast myself perversely as Knox'. (p 174) Pink and Mary's relationship with their own idea of religion is far less problematic; God they refer to as 'Moo' and Pink freely acknowledges: 'We've an awful lot of Moo tucked away'. (p 110) Likewise Mary and Pink discuss quite openly why they should feel guilt when they say 'Stuff Moo'. And Pink both conceals and displays his own sense of fear through the parodic cry of 'I am afraid. Yippee!' (p 117)

It is David, in contrast, who is afraid to acknowledge the extent of his own fears, metaphysical and personal; David who is forced to the point of recognising that: 'We are the most dangerous of all, the prematurely immature.' (p 178) Moreover, it is David, crushing others to establish his own power and superiority, who is most afraid of recognising either the existence of God or the meaninglessness of a universe without God:

We look into the dark, and there's always someone there. We look into the dark and see the faces of those we have already destroyed, by our own ignorance of ourselves; our immaturity.
We look into the dark, sweet cousin, and no wonder we are afraid.

(p 187)

By the novel's conclusion it is David who has gone back to a world of fears, recreating within his own Londonised and scientific mind—the very mentality from which he sought escape, while Mary, content to settle for less, retreating into her marriage, the estate and 'normality', emerges as a survivor. Pink is less fortunate in that his process of normalisation must take the form of a 'nursing home' in which he may be dried out. Nevertheless he too avoids having to face the recognitions of self and of cultural identity by which David is confronted.

In *Household Ghosts* Kennaway presents alternative perspectives: two responses to the idea of Scottishness. In none of the novels which follow is this balance maintained. Instead his later novels penetrate deeper into the darkness, testing human reactions in extreme situations, or finding situations which produce extreme reactions. In *Some Gorgeous Accident* (1967), the central character, Link, describes his life as 'the wild pursuit of pain for pain's sake'. The triangular relationship in which Link finds himself reinforces his sense that the world is a place of cruelty, and without meaning: Link experiences reality as a 'decontrolled nightmare, as if he had no strength to guide his own concerns.' And Link's reaction to this is an anarchic acceptance and assimilation of nightmare: 'So go with random, baby!' (p 39) As if to parallel this sense of randomness the novel models itself on the cross-examinations of the trial scene with which the novel ends, adopting a question and answer format for much of the time and with a narrative which parodies its own ommniscience with an extreme cynicism. Sections within the novel have headings which develop both readers' identification and anticipation, such as '*Carefully, Link. Tune into the evidence, old man . . .*' or '*And about Fiddes? Describe, for Christ's sake. We all know what the story's about.*' The narrative itself adopts a similarly colloquial tone, and makes an overt identification with Link, the character whom the novel would appear to condemn most severely in terms of behaviour: 'Link, be it observed, doing pretty well so far, definitely doing good.' And the novel ends with the narrator giving advice to the character:

> Come on, Linky: on. Too much going for you to be a moral rheumatic yet. Don't turn round. Don't get drawn back into all that; nor be bugged by the forty reasons that led you to it . . . Not got to be no pillar of salt. To forget is to be wiser. It is wiser to be sane. So head for the sunset, Link, and vanish in the fog. (p 194)

Once again the character is shown seeking escape, in this instance in true movie fashion, by vanishing into the sunset; but the narrator's bitter tone also acknowledges the impossibility, or at least, unlikeliness, of this as a solution, mocking both Link's stance and the position adopted by the novel itself.

The Cost of Living Like This (1969), is a novel about an eminent scientist, Julian, dying of cancer and having an affair with a much younger, working-class girl, to the despair of his wife who has tended him through his illness. Julian's main concern seems to be to match pain with pain, as if emotional pain will not only detract from the physical agony but also reassure him that he is still alive. Self-destruction becomes a means of avoiding other forms of destruction that are in store, in a process of continually outwitting 'fate'— even if the novel's cry of 'O look down, God. Is there never an end to your twists?' (p 10) would seem to indicate that this is a game it is impossible to win. Again the novel relies mainly on dialogue, evading any demands on the narrator to make sense of the world described and providing the minimum of control. In Kennaway's case the increasing brevity of style represents in itself an anarchic refusal to be controlled, in many ways more successful than the rebellions of the characters within his work.

ALAN SHARP

The novels of Alan Sharp also manifest a defiant attitude to literary conventions; and like Kennaway's characters, those of Sharp are also shown to be searching for fulfilment and a valid sense of identity. For two of the characters, Moseby and his friend, Harry Gibbon, this search begins in Scotland but for all the characters the search for Eden takes them far beyond its boundaries.

A Green Tree in Gedde (1965) was written by Alan Sharp as the first novel in a proposed trilogy. The second novel of the trilogy, *The Wind Shifts*, published in 1976, is generally agreed to lack the strength of the first. The proposed third volume never appeared. *A Green Tree in Gedde* is, nevertheless, a considerable achievement. Written in a self-conscious style which it labels 'codjoycery', the novel examines the search for Eden and the ways in which its central characters attempt to transcend the limitations of their lives, to create their own form of paradise—in most cases either with little success or with dangerous consequences.

The novel is structured around sections which move between the thoughts and experiences of four characters: Moseby, Gibbon, Cuffee and his sister, Ruth. John Moseby, living in Greenock and taking a teacher training course at Glasgow University, longs to escape both from his marriage, his studies, and what he sees as the negativity of west of Scotland attitudes: too much religion and too little sex.

> And it was about now he began to understand what being West Coast Scottish meant, with its preoccupations with guilt and sex and sin and its image of man as a monster . . . And most characteristic was the disguise, you must never cry your foulness aloud because no one would admit it as common. (p 94)

Moseby's response to his disgust with his own respectability is to 'cry his foulness aloud'—and in the most extreme way possible. Within his home location, however, he can only achieve this by having a sordid affair with a married ex-girlfriend. Realising fairly quickly that this is not enough, that the banality of the environment will still triumph—'You don't have lovers in Partick—only fancy men'—he decides to seek escape further afield. The end of the novel shows him, unconcerned with the possible break up of his marriage, deciding to leave Scotland. And that moment of realisation is described in terms close to the image of David Dow, afraid, peering into the dark:

> He shivered, afraid, emptily afraid as night covered the land from end to end in pure dark, faintly stained by towns and cities but rising always above their yellow scars into the regions of silence and still, the high hang, the vast vault

of other than earthly space, where the moon does not shine to light nor guide but in purposeless perpetuance exists, where stars no longer twinkle their blinter to yearning watchers but burn aeon-old holes in time.   (p 380)

Again the world is described as an alien universe, apparently without concern for humankind, a world existing time without end—and without purpose. In some respects this world is that of existentialism: without determinants or significance. The image of humanity dwarfed by an alien and alienating universe is also, however, very similar to that of the relationship between the individual and God emphasised by Calvinism, a religion in which it is stressed that humanity has no way of knowing or understanding the mind or decisions of the Creator. In attempting to escape, therefore, Moseby reproduces the same impulses which underlie that surface morality of which he complains: the dark recognition of moral polarities and disgust with a fallen world. Moseby himself expresses his disgust with existence, and with sexuality in particular, in an image of 'the alpha and the omega of Durex and frogs' (p 100), of beginnings and ends, of teleological extremes. Any attempt to impose a pattern of significance upon his existence would appear to lead inevitably into a recreation of terms, polarities and oppositions—good and evil, beginning and end, Eden and Hell—which dominate that very way of thinking from which he is trying to escape.

In his desire to escape, Moseby compares himself with his friend, Harry Gibbon, the same age and also from Greenock but, as the novel begins, getting ready to leave Scotland behind and embark upon a series of adventures with his English friend, Cuffee. Gibbon is the character most at ease with his roots, possessing a strong sense of family identity and in particular identifying with the figure of his granduncle, the itinerant preacher Robert Gibbon, whose religion appears to offer an alternative to the rigours of Calvinism, and from whose extraordinary writings the novel's title, epigraph and vision of Eden is taken:

> A great tree there is in Gedde growing, and in its branches the hawk it perches with the dove; fruit there is for all to eat, golden and silver globes and purple plums, and all abloss with bloom its brondes. No perdifol is there nor foliomort, and hallards none but green leaf everlasting.
>   Know ye not this halidome, this greenheart axletree; know ye not Gedde. Its seed lies within us each.

Gibbon, then, does have a sense of his past, of a meaningful history and identity, but to assert its existence he feels this identity must be tested, even called into question, by placing himself in less familiar circumstances.

The other two major characters are a brother and sister, Ruth and Peter Cuffee. Cuffee is the most anarchic figure in the novel, the one who appears to offer the best chance of escaping and who most obviously challenges conventions in his extreme behaviour. As Cuffee takes Gibbon to London, to Paris, and finally sets off himself through the Black Forest with a strange German woman who fascinates him, Cuffee makes things happen. This is in marked contrast to his sister Ruth. Like Cuffee she is attempting to leave behind the incestuous relationship they had established many years before, but remains rooted in one place, feeling both the static environment and her own loneliness closing in on her. Escape is offered for Ruth, at least temporarily, by her beginning a relationship with Harry Gibbon after his return from travel, but in terms of the novel's logic this would not appear to be a permanent solution. Indeed, in *The Wind Shifts* this relationship breaks down and Ruth has an affair with Moseby.

Nevertheless it is Harry Gibbon who sets out the logic which governs the novel and the problematic with which all the characters are faced; explaining his reasons for leaving Greenock, he quotes a comment of his uncle's: 'If you don't go you can't come back.' What may be seen as escape is, in fact, not a leaving behind but simply an act of revision; no new Eden is created. An old man whom Gibbon and Moseby meet in their local, early in the novel, laughs with them at the idea of the Great War being a 'war to end all wars', as a futile search for Paradise. He goes on to tell them the story of a young soldier, disturbed by the war, who commits suicide by suffocating himself in his own kitbag hanging in the kitchen—a story which Moseby feels has a significance for him he is afraid to acknowledge. This incident has been given a convincing reading by Cairns Craig in terms of Scotland and its historyless past:

> Two antithetic meanings flow from this image. For the old man it symbolises a historical experience so horrific, so overwhelming, that it cannot be escaped even in the safety of one's own home . . . To Moseby, however, the image has a resonance of a completely different kind: it is the claustrophobic kitchen the melancholy Tommy has tried to escape from, it is the experience of history, however brutal, he seeks. After knowledge, no matter how horrific, of that other realm, the enclosed domestic world is unacceptable, and wrapping himself in his kit bag he asserts significance that has been offered and then withdrawn by history.[8]

But it is also possible to see this image relating to the novel's themes in another sense. In order to escape the limits of his world, the soldier climbs inside an even more limited and enclosed world, unable to think beyond the boundaries which circumscribe his world he retreats further into them in his search for Eden; likewise the characters in the novel are presented as unable to think themselves outwith the limited terms in which they see the world and in which they imagine Eden.

GEORGE FRIEL

George Friel was a writer who had great difficulty in getting his work published in his lifetime, and whose work has largely been misunderstood since his death in 1972. His settings are urban Glasgow and the often bleak and limited lives of working class people in the tenements and housing estates. The gritty realism of books like *The Boy who Wanted Peace* (1964), *Grace and Miss Partridge* (1969) and *Mr Alfred MA* (1972) made it easy to identify Friel with the traditions of Glaswegian social realism. But Friel was, in fact, a devotee of James Joyce's writing, and each novel is a carefully constructed experiment in parable, symbol and narrative style, full of wordplay and allusion. The subject matter of his works is that which has found its most common expression in the realist mode, but his style is modernist and experimental.

Coming from a Catholic background, Friel does not share the Calvinist presuppositions of his contemporaries, but the disjunction in modes— between realism of content and artifice of style—mirrors the conflicts which his characters suffer, trapped between their imagination of an ideal world and the banal realities of making do with the actual. Like many of Joyce's characters, they strive towards a higher plane of human experience and imaginative purity, and find that their feet are trapped in the mire of a physical world they can only regard as failed. The conflicts of the calvinist inheritance which continue to obsess novelists such as Sharp and Jenkins, become conflicts of the spiritual and the social in Friel, who seems to have been unable to rconcile himself either to the faith of communism (espoused, for instance, by his brother, a cartoonist for the *Daily Worker*) or to the traditional faith of the Church.[9] The spiritual becomes a purely aesthetic mode which struggles weakly with the forces of an insistent and ugly reality.

Thus Percy Phinn, hero of *The Boy who Wanted Peace*, is trapped between the wish to escape into a world at one with his poetic ambitions, and the desire to impose himself on the world and make it conform to his imagination. In Percy's efforts to dominate a group of boys in their basement hideout, Friel constructs a miniature of the history of magic and religion, of the eternal return of the savage upon the civilised. In *Grace and Miss Partridge*, Miss Partridge's desire to save the child of her neighbours from sin, to retain in her the 'grace' which her name betokens, becomes a drive to destroy the child before she can have the opportunity to betray her innocence and Miss Partridge's ideals.

With each novel, Friel's ability to fuse realism and allegory became more subtle and assured. In *Grace and Miss Partridge*, for instance, it is only slowly that we realise that the narrator has, in fact, married Grace, and is, therefore, involved in a very personal way in his reconstruction of Miss Partridge's obsessions. And it is only in the last chapter that we discover that much of his information has come from Miss Partridge's diaries, but that his mother has kept the last and most important diary from him. These final revelations dissolve the whole texture of the previous presentation, unravelling the surface of the story and revealing new potentialities which the novel itself will neither affirm nor deny. It is a structure of endless trapdoors through which we fall from the security of the real into the glamour of the fancied and back again.

Friel's final novel *Mr Alfred MA* focuses all of these issues in his most assured work. The central character, Mr Alfred, an ageing schoolmaster, becomes increasingly disillusioned with his job, with the city of Glasgow, vandalised, neglected, decaying, and with what he sees as an equivalent spiritual deadness in Scottish life. Mr Alfred's means of escaping this world of decay and nightmare is to wander the streets of Glasgow at night, drinking in unsavoury pubs, seeking out companions to alleviate his loneliness. The world appears increasingly alien to him until he finds a spiritual companion in one of his young female pupils at school. When his relationship with the one person who seems to offer an alternative to malice and cynicism is discovered, hoewever, the eyes of the world, viewing the relationship as perverse, soon turn it into a thing of shame and corruption. In an increasingly alien world, with this chance of Eden gone, Mr Alfred turns in his bewilderment to the streets of Glasgow, trying to decipher the slogans scrawled upon the walls: 'Ya Bass' in particular. Who, or what, he wonders, is 'Ya Bass'. The answer comes to him in a scene towards the end of the novel in which a world of fantasy—a nightmare or the beginnings of mental breakdown—takes over. Attacked in the street and seeking refuge in a nearby tenement, Mr Alfred is confronted by a character calling himself 'Tod', who claims not only to be an ex-pupil of Mr Alfred's but also the person responsible for 'Ya Bass' and much much more. Tod explains, 'I believe in the dialectic. The unity of opposites. Law in anarchy. That's what I'm after . . . Badness is all.' His anarchy and love of extremes is seen not only as indicative of the coming society but also in a perverse way as both a solution to and a product of Mr Alfred's anxieties and desires. Tod explains: 'All I've did is to reduce human conflict to its simplest terms.' And Mr Alfred in despair adopts Tod's solution: at the end of the novel he is found spraying grafitti on walls, attempting to participate in the world of extremes before declining into the safety of senility.

The philosophy set out by Tod—'Badness is all'—may be seen as representative of the extremes which the three novelists so far considered explore. Moving in the moral direction of what is conventionally labelled 'evil', they appear to be motivated by a dual and conflicting impulse: by proving that evil exists and may flourish, they show the inadequacy of social and moral codes as a means of structuring existence. However, they may also be seen as pushing moral definitions to extremes as a perverse means of proving their existence. By exploring the nature of evil they are also testing the concept of damnation: in Baudelarian fashion trying to prove the existence of God or good by demonstrating that evil does and can exist.[10]

ROBIN JENKINS

Of the four writers considered here, Robin Jenkins is by far the most prolific, having published over twenty novels. Within this essay only novels in Scottish settings will be considered but he has written fine novels, set in Malaya, Afghanistan and Spain, which explore similar themes although obviously within a different context. Jenkins, born in 1912, is also of a slightly older generation, and although his novels may on first impression appear more conventional in terms of realism and outlook, his exploration of issues similar to those of Kennaway, Sharp and Friel is equally sophisticated. If they show the inadequacy of moral codes as a way of structuring existence while simultaneously trying to prove the existence of God by proving that such a thing as 'evil' may and does exist, Jenkins moves in an opposite direction. In his work he tests extremes of 'good' instead of evil, creating situations in which human reactions to the concept of good may be explored, and the concept of 'goodness' itself held up for examination.

For Jenkins the human condition is defined by a double awareness, both of the limitations of human potential in moral terms, and the desire to transcend these limitations which might—and his novels continue to question rather than assert this possibility—be of value in itself. A similar duality may be found in Sharp's work and in *Mr Alfred MA* but concentrated within the one character. In Jenkins' fiction, however, the characters tend to be more overtly polarised, representing one side or other of the issue. In so doing he creates for himself as a novelist a problematic which parallels the metaphysical speculations of his work: is it possible for the writer of fiction to create a credible and wholly good character? Jenkins' novels, then, are distinguished by a series of characters who are presented either as seeking extremes of good or, more rarely, represent extremes of evil, but who are themselves trapped within a relative and conditional universe which apparently denies the polarities they epitomise. Novels such as *A Toast to the Lord* (1972) and *A Would-be Saint* (1978) present characters who are so 'good' or 'holy' as to be unbearable to those around them; more importantly, however, the novels also present the readers with a question as to whether this goodness does, in fact, exist, or is not simply a sophisticated form of hypocrisy and attention-seeking. This is reinforced by the novels' narrative technique: in each the reader is denied complete knowledge of the characters so that we too have to contemplate the possibility that we might be the victims either of an authorial hoax, or of our own desire to believe that goodness does exist.

A Would-be Saint is particularly interesting in this respect. Gavin Hamilton, a typical 'lad o' pairts', adopts from an early age a stance of extreme goodness which those around him view as a denial of all his talents; his intellectual abilities, his footballing skill, his charm for women, are all cast aside as he grows to realise that they will hinder his achievement of 'goodness'—the sainthood of the title. As the novel progresses Gavin moves from his role as hero, a character with whom the reader may identify and sympathise, to a figure who, in his uncomfortable and 'ruinous goodness' remains an enigma:

> It was noticed how, though Gavin was very friendly, and never failed to stop you in the street and ask with undeniable sincerity how you and your family were, you always felt a bit awkward talking to him . . . Some said it was because Gavin, without ever saying a word that could be called preaching, made you feel that there were lots of good deeds you should have done and lots of bad deeds you shouldn't. He was, alas, the genuine article and the last person to talk to if you wanted to feel satisfied with yourself.   (p 97)

By the end of the novel Gavin's own existence, his personal motivation, becomes less of a source of speculation for those around them as they realise that he is necessary to them as a symbol of goodness; representing an ideal moral position but not one which they themselves are either desirous or capable of attaining:

> Thinking about Gavin gave them faith. They were prisoners, he was still free. Finding the burden too heavy or too shameful, they had long ago put down their idealistic protest against the war. Gavin still carried his.
>
> Like me, thought MacMillan, they lie awake at night despising themselves for adding to the world's falseness and hypocrisy, then they remember Gavin and feel instantly absolved. (p 192)

The theme of someone set apart from society, either through innocence or unbearable goodness—or a combination of goodness and naivity—is common to the majority of Jenkins' novels. And in many of his novels it is this combination of unfriendly world and isolated individual which leads to destruction of some kind or another. In *The Cone-Gatherers* (1955), for example, the two central characters, the brothers Calum and Neil, are given the task during the war of collecting cones for seeding from the estate of Lady Runcie-Campbell. The brothers soon fall foul of the estate's gamekeeper, Duror, a man whose own dissatisfaction with his existence has led to a view of the world as a place of malignancy and evil. In particular his dislike is focused on Callum; gentle, simple, dwarf-like. The combination of his innocent nature and deformed body becomes a torment to Duror. Ironically the novel shows that the entrance of true goodness—in Calum—into the apparently edenic world of the estate, is the force which leads to its destruction, although this is achieved through the actions and evil intent of Duror. The novel contains elements of fable—an isolated, slightly unreal setting, vivid symbolic imagery—and shows Jenkins embracing with relish the confrontation between polarities of good and evil, and the effect this has on the more 'moderate' characters who witness it.

Above all Jenkins appears to abhor spiritual lassitude: for him the polarities of good and evil present a more stimulating, if ultimately untenable, means of constructing a moral reality. Perhaps most interesting for Jenkins are characters who through extremes in their behaviour reveal the relative and conditional nature of the rules for moral behaviour. The three novels most striking in this respect are *A Very Scotch Affair* (1968); *Fergus Lamont* (1979); and *The Awakening of George Darroch* (1985). In each of these novels the characters are aware of—even exploit—the contingent nature of their societies, breaking the moral rules which conceal this. In each case too their awareness of contingency and conditionality comes into conflict with their search for ultimate values or extremes which will allow them to break free from this relative world.

A Very Scotch Affair focuses on Mungo Niven, a man who, in middle age, decides to leave his wife, family and native Glasgow in order to exploit a newly-acquired, wealthy, mistress and to achieve what he sees as a better way of life. Like Moseby, Gibbon and David Dow, Mungo believes himself to be leaving behind the attitudinal 'ghetto' that is Scotland. Like them too, however, he discovers he is taking that mentality with him: 'The trouble with you, Mungo', his mistress Myra tells him, 'is that you're too scotch. You enjoy letting your conscience torment you.' (p 7) And Mungo himself is shown realising that 'the unrelenting morality of his native Glasgow would not be shaken off.' (p 14) Mungo too, then, 'goes' but 'comes back'. However, to the disapproval of those within the ghetto, his return for his wife's funeral is only a brief one, even if his affair has come to an end. Those in Glasgow do not disapprove of Mungo's aspirations and ideals; indeed they are shown to be quite interested in his 'daft' ideas, as his neighbour, Nan Fraser reveals: 'more than once he had amused her and Alec by telling them that he would like to live in the country, with trees round his house'. (p 19) What they do resent, however, is the fact that, even if only briefly, he does succeeed in effecting his escape, leaving behind 'the innumerable coils of sheer commonplace habit' (p 24) which Mungo sees Scotland as representing. After the death of his wife Mungo realises that the 'responsible' thing to do would be to return to his family; nevertheless he decides not to stay 'back'. And in a sense this decision is shown to be as challenging, and as heroic in its refusal to be trapped by moral codes or by circumstances as shouldering the burden of moral responsibility. Mungo's daughter Peggy, usually more critical of her father than anyone, realises that she understands his decision: 'She knew that she too was a traitor, ready to escape when the time came.' (p 85) Even the local minister appears to justify Mungo's actions by arguing that 'A man can commit a great sin because there is greatness in his soul.' (p 119) And Mungo's determination to push as far as possible in the direction of creating his own Eden, like his capacity for self-destruction, is described as being characteristically Scottish. At the beginning of part two, when his affair is about to collapse, we are told: 'The ultimate disruption was waited for, as if predestined. It was a very scotch dissolution to a very scotch affair.' (p 137) Once again the influence of Calvinism is brought into play, trapping the mind and governing behaviour, even if in a self-destructive manner.

It is not surprising then, that the first, and to date, the only historical novel written by Jenkins is about the Disruption of 1842. *The Awakening of George Darroch* concentrates on the life of a minister, his family and friends around the time of the Disruption—the division within the Church of Scotland and the secession of the Free Church. George Darroch himself, whose procrastination on the decision as to whether he should secede structures the novel, is in many ways a similar character to Mungo Niven: fallible, flawed, apparently self-seeking. Yet he also has surprising affinities with Gavin Hamilton of *A Would-be Saint*, appearing to undergo some kind of spiritual experience which leads to an ambiguous transformation. The reader, again, is not allowed sufficient information to say whether Darroch's final decision, and his courage in carrying it into effect is the result of a spiritual insight, a shrewd assessment of where his future lies, or a spontaneous and self-dramatising response to a particular moment. Our only response must be that of the ministers who debate the pros and cons of secession with him: 'They could not make up their minds whether they were dealing with a booby or with someone who, through Christ's favour, knew things that they, for all their erudition, never would'. (p 244) This theme of the inspired fool is one common to all Jenkins' novels. Even when Darroch is the first minister to follow after the leaders who are leaving to form the Free Church, his actions are open to various interpretations, even by his own son, James:

> He knew what had happened: given the best opportunity of his life to show off his father had not been able to resist it. For the sake of a minute's vanity he had sentenced his family to years of hardship. (p 266)

Similarly, the Disruption itself may be seen as both a triumph of independence and the refusal to compromise, the epitome of a Scottish religious spirit, or an act of self-destruction and vain stubborness:

> James felt like screaming that they were all wrong; what they had seen was a demonstration of the disastrous divisiveness of the Scottish nation which had kept it materially and spiritually impoverished in the past and was still doing so today. (p 267)

Thus the historical moment which could be viewed as a triumph of the Calvinist desire to maintain religious independence and rigour, its final chance to 'create the Kingdom of God on earth', is also presented as a moment of destruction brought about by high minded desires for the impossible, but fuelled by personal ambition and self delusion. And yet, even after James's outburst, the ambivalence of the moment is maintained in the text, as the actions of the Disruption remain a potential symbol of both folly and heroism.

This blurring of the divisions between the foolish and heroic, the selfless and the self-seeking remains a central interest in Jenkins' work. Mention must be made therefore of the novel which deals with such a juxtaposition of motives with specific reference to a Scottish context. *Fergus Lamont* differs from other Jenkins' novels in the sophistication of its time scheme and the experimental use of first person narrative, but the west of Scotland setting is familiar. The 'hero' and narrator of the novel, Fergus, is brought up in the slums of 'Gantock'. By a mixture of talent, egoism, ruthlessness and duplicity, however, he succeeds in leaving his background behind, asserting a somewhat dubious claim to aristocratic parentage and becoming an officer, gentleman and, more surprisingly, a poet. In his later years Fergus finds these successes increasingly unfulfilling and retreats to a remote Scottish island where he discovers happiness with a strange type of Celtic goddess—the strapping, pipe-smoking, golden-haired Kirstie. Until the death of Kirstie, Fergus thus lives in his own version of Eden, a golden world relying on a particularly Scottish myth. And Fergus, who throughout the narrative castigates the Scots for the narrow-mindedness, parochialism and self-seeking, is himself the most 'archetypal' Scot of all. Dressing in a kilt all through his life, sentimental yet a social climber, hypocritical yet shrewedly ironic, Fergus does 'go' and 'come back'. At the end of the book his return to Gantock is shown, a return made possible not only by his going away but also by his retreat further into a

Scottish identity and set of cultural myths on his island. With typical Jenkins irony, of course, this return to Gantock is not wholly successful. The few friends he finds there have changed considerably and even fewer past acquaintances recognise him. Yet of all the characters considered, Fergus, the apparently undeserving, is perhaps the most successful in effecting a return to Scotland, even if his 'Eden' is temporary and, by the novel's conclusion, elusive once again.

A shared characteristic of the novels considered is the dissatisfaction of their central characters with contemporary Scotland. All seek some form of escape from the restrictions they perceive its society and spirit as embodying. In each case, however, the escape they envisage is not simply into an alternative world, but into a world which offers perfection: flight must lead them into Eden. Because of the elusiveness, indeed impossibility, of such an ideal their desires inevitably remain unfulfilled. And this failure serves in turn to maintain the edenic concept as ideal and symbolic, fuelling their desire for it. Likewise, it could be argued that the four novelists considered here all attempt the escape from—through a critique of—a Scottish cast of mind, its religious and cultural inheritance. Yet in so doing it is the same cast of mind, Calvinist in origins, metaphysical in nature, which both determines their flight and ensures their return.

NOTES

1   Cairns Craig, 'The Body in the Kit Bag: History and the Scottish Novel', *Cencrastus* no. 1 (1979), describes: 'an underlying pattern in many twentieth century Scottish novels which oppose a static community, by-passed by the mainstream of history to a world beyond whose essential meanings are defined by history'. (p 18)
2   'Only a people who took themselves seriously could have embarked upon so ambitious a programme. For it was nothing less than the attempt to dedicate the whole life of a nation to a single end. In theological terms it was the attempt to create the Kingdom of God on earth.' Campbell MacLean, 'Who is their God', in *Alistair MacLean Introduces Scotland*, A Dunnett (ed) (1972).
3   Tom Nairn, 'The Three Dreams of Scottish Nationalism', in *Memoirs of a Modern Scotland*, K Miller (ed) (1970).
4   Angus Calder, 'Byron and Scotland', in *Cencrastus* no. 15 (1984).
5   T Eagleton, *Marxism and Literary Criticism* (1976), p 31.
6   Allan Massie, 'Retrospective', in *Jock Tamsons' Bairns*, T Royle (ed) (1977), p 66.
7   Gordon Marshall, *Presbyteries and Profits* (1980), p 63.

8 C Craig, ibid., p 18.
9 Details of Friel's political ideas and his family background can be found in Iain Cameron, 'George Friel: an introduction to his life and work' (unpublished M.Litt thesis, University of Edinburgh, 1986).
10 'Baudelaire . . . constructed a scheme of things for his own use. This scheme embraced not only an "artificial paradise" but also an artificial hell—both necessary elements in his attempt to control by form, of which he was the master, the nauseating spiritual anarchy which otherwise would have overwhelmed him.' G Brereton, *An Introduction to the French Poets* (1965), p 148.

Chapter 18

Muriel Spark

VALERIE SHAW

'I wish to inform you that your housekeeper fills me with anxiety like John Knox. I fear she is rather narrow.'
(from the 'love correspondence' of Miss Jean Brodie)

Suppose this to be ane Fabill,
And overheillt with typis figurall
(Henryson)

In *The Prime of Miss Jean Brodie* (1961), the only novel by Muriel Spark with a Scottish setting, young pupils at the Marcia Blaine School for Girls receive a fairly haphazard literary education. They recite poetry to suit Miss Brodie's personal taste—Tennyson's 'Lady of Shalott' is a favourite—and in the stricter atmosphere of Miss Gaunt's class the punishment for talking is 'A hundred lines of *Marmion*'. Yet Miss Brodie's talent for quotation ensures that the girls are constantly hearing snatches of literary language, for her speech is rich in allusions. Sometimes, she raids the past for lines to express a mood suited to the season, as when she quotes 'Come autumn sae pensive' or describes her 'warrior lover' Hugh (who seems to have borne quite a resemblance to Burns himself) as 'one of the Flowers of the forest, lying in his grave'.[1] Miss Brodie apparently has a touch of what George Blake called 'the chronic Scots disease of nostalgia'.[2] But she also believes in the practical worth of proverbial wisdom, instructing her pupils with well-worn maxims like 'Speech is silver but silence is golden', presumably for the same reason as Fleur Talbot in *Loitering with Intent* (1981) who finds that popular sayings 'may lack the grandeur of the ten Commandments, but they are more to the point'.[3]

A more oblique type of guidance is involved, however, on the occasion when Miss Brodie reads to her class from James Hogg's ballad 'Kilmeny'— 'Kilmeny was pure as pure could be'—and then provides her own acerbic gloss: 'Which is to say, she did not go to the glen to mix with men' (pp 47–48).[4] In context, both the quotation and Miss Brodie's pointing of it merely illustrate her facetious compliance with the genteel standards of the school where she works; only through 'veiled allusion' (p 47) could she possibly talk about sex to little ten-year-old Edinburgh girls in the 1930s. But if the reader is led deeper into Hogg's poem, which was introduced in *The Queen's Wake* as the work of a religious bard, the quoted line actually offers an enigmatic statement of what is Spark's central theme in the novel. Based on a Border

277

tale about a farmer's daughter who mysteriously vanishes for several days and then returns, unharmed but incapable of explaining what has happened to her, Hogg's 'Kilmeny' is all about an escape from the human world into 'a land where sin had never been' (1.45). Kilmeny was chosen by the supernatural beings who took her away, because she was, in a phrase which itself anticipates the title of Spark's novel, 'a virgin in her prime' (1.78). Kilmeny embodies a cherished rarity, a reply to the question posed by the Biblical text which is displayed, underlined in red, beneath the imposing portrait of the worthy Edinburgh bookbinder's widow who endowed Marcia Blaine School in the mid-nineteenth century: 'O where shall I find a virtuous woman, for her price is above rubies'.[5] In Hogg's profoundly Christian myth, Kilmeny is rewarded for her virtue by being released from the sore burdens of guilt and time: 'I have brought her awae frae the snares of men/That sin or death she never may ken' (11.83–84). The unworldly state of mystic joy attained here is precisely what Sandy Stranger in *The Prime of Miss Jean Brodie* hopes to attain when she becomes a Catholic nun. But Sandy is never allowed to settle peacefully in 'the land of thought' (1.170) to which Kilmeny is magically translated. Ironically, her intellectual accomplishment as the author of a surprise bestseller entitled *The Transfiguration of the Commonplace* drags her back into the messy realm of the emotions—her own as well as other people's.

The allusion to Hogg in *The Prime of Miss Jean Brodie* is of course both too brief and too isolated for it to mean that Spark is counting on her reader to pursue the line beyond its fleeting occurrence in one comic scene. In fact the power of this particular allusion and of others like it in her work is that the author does not elaborate upon them or even allow characters who make—or hear—them to realise their full weight or significance. The effect is to concentrate in unstated ways what an unfolding plot more explicitly displays and to enrich atmosphere subtly without spoiling the lightness of comic touch. It is left to the reader to reflect and amplify, or to perceive the similitudes and parallelisms which give Spark's work a proverbial quality quite different from Miss Brodie's style of teaching. Miss Brodie's utterances are often 'proverbs' in the sense of pithy sayings which have won popular acceptance through their obvious correspondence to the facts of human nature and practical experience; but Spark herself comes closer to the type of wisdom offered by the Old Testament book of Proverbs from which that bracing text on the school lectern is taken. Composed by thinkers, Proverbs uses figurative discourse to offer guidance in the practical morality which might be expected to have mattered most to Marcia Blaine in Victorian Scotland, but while in many ways a prudential work, it is religious in spirit and gnomic in its method. The reader of Proverbs is from the outset called upon as someone with a taste for riddles and an ability 'to understand a proverb, and the interpretation; the words of the wise and their dark sayings' (1.5). In very much the same spirit and with similar aims Spark uses the secular form of the novel to instruct her readers obliquely in the art of living well and simultaneously to convey deeply religious meanings through 'dark sayings'.

What holds for the single example given of Spark's literary allusiveness and the power with which a quotation like the one from Hogg can penetrate an entire novel's meaning, may be extended to the wider, and more problematic, question of Spark's relationship with her native Scottish culture. Just as an exploration of the line from 'Kilmeny' discloses suggestive affinities and contrasts between Hogg's chaste heroine and Sandy Stranger, so can Scottish likenesses be caught in Spark's work without these having to be claimed as decisive sources or even influences. It is all a matter of atmosphere. Specific debts are in any case hardly to be expected of a writer who, although born and educated in Edinburgh, chose to begin her career as a professional artist in England, and then only after a period spent even further away from Scotland, in Central Africa. Since the 1940s Spark has made her home in large metropolitan centres, living at various times in London, New York and Rome. No doubt this is why she is so often seen as an exile whose art is built upon a conscious rejection of her Calvinist homeland. But the picture is not quite so simple.

Spark's reputation as a novelist dates from her conversion to Roman Catholicism in 1954, an event which she has described as the finding of a location for the rather diffuse religious feelings she had experienced up until the early 1950s. Although she does acknowledge that the 'God-building atmosphere' of her childhood was a conditioning factor, the precise nature and extent of any influence exerted by Presbyterian Scotland can only be guessed at. Spark herself has gone no farther than saying it was a matter of general colouring and predisposition; she has talked about the 'very peculiar environment' produced by the part-Jewish origins which gave her childhood 'a kind of Jewish tinge but without any formal instruction', and a schooling which was Presbyterian but not churchgoing. Like David Daiches in the 1920s she was a child of Jewish background living in a non-Jewish environment, but whereas Daiches was the rabbi's son she had no devotional structure to contain the 'strong religious' feelings she recalls having as a girl. The result was a characteristically adolescent fusion of art and religion; diffuse spiritual emotions were channelled into art and poetry, and Spark remembers appreciating Christ more as 'a romantic, moving figure' than for his divinity.[6] Between her schooldays and 1952, when she did begin to turn towards specific religious beliefs and practices, she was not undergoing conflict but rather a period of complete indifference to religion. Significantly, it was during the time when Spark was actively making herself into a poet and critic that this religious neutrality became dissatisfying, almost as though in both artistic and spiritual spheres she was experiencing that 'craving for discipline' which has been said to constitute the recognisably Calvinist strain in the Scottish temperament.[7]

All of Spark's fiction certainly displays a fascination with authority of diverse kinds and forms. This is equally apparent in technically experimental pieces like *The Driver's Seat* (1970) and *Not to Disturb* (1971), where questions about authority and authorship overlap, and in novels where the settings—the school in *The Prime of Miss Jean Brodie*, for example, or the convent in *The Abbess of Crewe* (1974)—emphasise the already prominent theme of obedience to established rules. The problem of how to reconcile the desires of the individual to the needs of the community at large is recurrent, linking novels which at first seem totally dissimilar: Spark's desert-island novel, *Robinson* (1958) is a fantasy which actually shares with the far longer realistic novel *The Mandelbaum Gate* (1965) a concern with the way a search for personal identity is bound up with the forms designed by society to regulate behaviour.

Not that the theme of authority and its counterpart guilt is pursued by Spark through abstractions. In fact she gives it presence, so obvious as often to go unnoticed, by including numerous policemen in her stories. Sometimes they have genial walk-on parts, as in the opening chapter of *Loitering with Intent*, but on other occasions they represent something more aggressive and sinister, which is how the New York police appear in *The Hothouse by the East River* (1973), or the 'grey-clad policemen' in *The Driver's Seat*, advancing in formation with tear-gas satchels and gas-masks 'at the ready'.[8] It is notable too that Sandy Stranger, who regrets not having been born into an authoritarian Calvinist background she could discard, quite abandons her previous hero-figures, Alan Breck and Mr Rochester included, and appropriates through fantasy a female ideal in the person of a 'wonderful policewoman' (p 87). She creates for herself a surrogate identity as Sergeant Anne Grey's trusty 'right-hand woman in the Force', dedicated to 'eliminate sex from Edinburgh and environs' (p 89). The pre-adolescent phase of creating fantasies and role-models is well observed by Spark who gives it a special edge by associating it with self-distrust and so recalling the long tradition which sees the Kirk in Scotland occupying the function carried out elsewhere by a secular police force.[9] In *The Prime of Miss Jean Brodie* representatives of the Kirk mount surveillance on poor Gordon Lowther's sexual escapades, forcing him eventually to retire from his dearly-loved offices of choir-master and Church Elder. The phenomenon that Willa Muir designated 'McGrundyism' is clearly evident in 1930s Edinburgh as it is depicted in this novel.[10]

But although Spark's upbringing may have given her particularly keen insight into the fusion of materialism and piety in middle-class Scottish Presbyterianism, her scorn for the way people observe external forms while neglecting inward spiritual matters is not confined to her one Edinburgh novel. It can be seen on one hand that the increasing cosmopolitanism of her fiction reflects her own travels and the deepening of her acquaintance with European literature and culture, but what is just as remarkable on the other is her sheer consistency of attitude. The forms taken by human subservience to carnal aims have undergone changes during the time Spark has been writing, that is all. Consequently, her picture of genteel—and profoundly hypocritical—respectability in *The Prime of Miss Jean Brodie* is transformed and supplemented, but not displaced, by the slavish trend-following she satirises in later novels, particularly those written in the 1970s. This is hardly surprising, since from the perspective of a believer in Roman Catholicism as the One True Church all other faiths are shadowy and unreal, often grotesquely so. For East Coast America in the 1970s 'religion' becomes the cult of psychoanalysis, and *The Hothouse by the East River* shows so-called

'Guidance Leaders' taking over from priests; earlier, in *The Driver's Seat*, Europe had been depicted as the site of an evangelising 'macrobiotics' mission originating in America and which is only distinguished by its totally commercial motives from another American character's naive confidence in the tenets of the Jehovah's Witnesses: different periods and places yield the false priests they deserve, and there is never any want of a gullible congregation. Affluence and the rise of consumerism are seen in these books as widening the opportunities for pseudo-spiritual exploitation, but in essence the human perversity of clinging to life is the same as it was in *Momento Mori* (1959) where Henry Mortimer, a retired detective whose methods bring him closer to Spark's authorial persona than any of her uniformed policemen-figures, voices an objection to worldliness on grounds which are as much aesthetic as they are spiritual: Death, he says, 'should be part of the full expectancy of life. Without an ever-present sense of death life is inspid. You might as well live on the whites of eggs.'[11]

Tenacious views like Spark's favour the satirical mode and make her more a writer of parables that a speculative inquirer into human nature. Yet it would be wrong to see her Catholicism as merely opposing her Edinburgh background. A more useful approach is suggested by Cardinal Newman's observation that Calvinism's 'sharp separation between the elect and the world' contains much that is 'cognate or parallel to the Catholic doctrine'. It is common knowledge that Spark is thoroughly familiar with Newman's *Apologia Pro Vita Sua*. At one point in that work Newman brings out the likeness between Calvinism and Catholicism and then goes on to discuss how the Calvinist proposition that, 'the converted and the unconverted can be discriminated by man, and that the regenerate cannot fall away' actually differs from the more nerve-wracking Catholic emphasis on 'the possibility and danger of falling away'. For the Catholic, Newman explains, the dogma of 'the awful antagonism between good and evil' is 'shaded and softened' by the notion of 'different degrees' of justification: 'there is no certain knowledge given to any one that he is simply in a state of grace'.[12] Uncertainty of this sort frequently distinguishes the Spark characters who can be called seekers, from those who, like Miss Brodie, are convinced of their own election to grace: and the same principle can be said to characterise the novelist's dealings with her readers, who are often left with radical doubts about which (if any) of the fictional characters is in a state of grace, even in the non-theological sense of simply earning the novelist's and reader's approval and goodwill.

The common ground discerned by Newman between Calvinism and Catholicism may be partly what allows Spark to write recognisably Catholic fiction while drawing on an artistic tradition which took specific forms in earlier Scottish fiction. The legacy is apparent in her choice of themes, though here as in all other areas she transforms and disguises what she begins with. Perennially Scottish, according to Alan Bold, are themes of the divided personality; the concept of childhood as idyllic; the clash of father with son, embodying a conflict between authority and imagination; and the absence of any moral middle ground.[13] All of these are to be found in Spark's work, though she subverts the motif of happy childhood by making her child-characters unnervingly manipulative and knowing, like the ones in her short story 'The Twins' (*The Go-Away Bird with other Stories*, 1958); and she highlights the absence of parents more than their tyranny, forcing her heroines to seek models of authority outside of the family. It is the fatherless state of January Marlow in *Robinson* or Caroline in *The Comforters* (1957) that makes them adventurers more in the mould of a Stevenson orphan than a young Gourlay and connects Spark with writers of romance rather than with Scottish realism. More recently her interest seems to have taken her even further behind the surface of the parent-child relationship to the artistic quest which aims to create its own imaginative authority, as Fleur Talbot's in *Loitering with Intent* does; and in *The Only Problem* (1984) her attention goes to the implications of an all-powerful father apparently deserting his own creation in the manner of Job's God.

Among the themes enumerated by Bold it is undoubtedly the split self which is most prominent in Spark's fiction, particularly when justification and self-justification are associated topics. Kinship with Scottish predecessors is demonstrable in these cases, and never more clearly than when there are elements of the Gothic, or when supernatural effects are assimilated into realistic narration. *The Ballad of Peckham Rye* (1960), with its refrain-like repetitions, delight in the grotesque, and silence about motivation, recalls the Border Ballads which Spark openly admires. There are echoes too of the famous nineteenth-century blend of the Gothic and the theological, Hogg's *Private Memoirs and Confessions of a Justified Sinner*. Dougal Douglas has a demonic ability to change his shape at will, and his actions resemble those of Hogg's Robert Wringhim in springing from a conviction that he is immune to all authority as it is enshrined in civic or moral laws. Simultaneously attractive and repulsive, Dougal projects his own insubordination onto everyone around him and anarchically undermines the stability of life in industrial Peckham. Like Hogg, Spark exposes the fragility of contemporary society's civilised facade and shows at the same time the outcome of actions performed by people who elect themselves to grace. Dougal takes himself far less seriously, is less suicidally enchanted by a feeling of his own superiority, than either Wringhim or Miss Brodie, and this is appropriate to the spirit of black comedy conveyed by the entire book. If Dougal's choice of tennis courts as the rendezvous for a fight has traces of the tennis-match scene described by the Editor early on in Hogg's novel, then it is as a passing joke embellishing the grave parallel between Wringhim's underhand tactics in a brawl and Dougal's. Spark's setting is insistently modern, showing the care she always takes with topography, but within this the forces at work are atavistic ones.

Reminiscent of Hogg too is the impression of predestination given by Spark's disclosure, right at the start, of how her plot will end, something she does again and again in her novels. And although pervaded by a sense of evil combatting good, no more than Hogg does she allow her work to sustain any clear allegorical interpretation; the reader of *The Ballad of Peckham Rye* may hope for some indication that a spiritual world with genuine power and meaning exists beyond what is depicted, but this never comes. The result is that no matter how frenetically the characters dance and gyrate they remain fundamentally passive, imprisoned like Wringhim thrashing about in the 'little hell' of the weaver's web, and like countless other figures in Gothic romance.[14] Connected with this, and making it apt to remember that Hogg originally intended *The Private Memoirs and Confessions* to remain anonymous, is Spark's detached manner which gives the narration a ballad-like impersonality. Hogg's purpose was greatly assisted by his use of multiple narration to subvert any expectation of consensus perception or decisive interpretation and to turn the relationship between author and text into something playful, however grim the subject-matter. Meaning becomes multiple and unstable. Because there is no single authoritative voice in Hogg's novel, the narrative segments stand apart from one another and so give a total impression of indefiniteness, despite the wealth of naturalistic detail offered. This effect is also to be found in *The Ballad of Peckham Rye* which proceeds by scenes, each seemingly complete in itself, built up out of fully dramatised action and dialogue—stage directions, almost—yet still appearing fragmented in relation to other scenes.

Spark's method of making her readers uneasy by presenting portions of narrative which uncannily double one another might be said to bring her work closer to the international development of post-modernist literature than to any nineteenth-century example. But beyond the dream-like sense of arbitrariness and the acknowledgement that no narrative can possibly encompass all of reality, there is at work a confidence in the mythic power of fiction that is comparatively rare among her twentieth-century contemporaries. Even at those moments when her work recalls Beckett's more than Hogg's or Stevenson's—and it often does, especially when pointless or downright crazy behaviour is being described—there is an unmistakeable moral interest which gives even her most outlandish experiments a traditional flavour. One instance is the way she uses the motif of the double. Her tendency is not to concentrate on the twentieth-century successor to the doppelgänger, the divided self, or to invoke post-Freudian psychological explanations, but rather to maintain the vividly dualistic vision expressed so memorably by Stevenson. Polarities and extremes are asserted, with the greatest challenge to the unified self coming from the coexisting good and evil within man. Sir Quentin Oliver in *Loitering with Intent* differs from Stevenson's Dr Jekyll, not in the degree of moral shock or the pitch at which human ambiguities are registered, but in his social context. So, for example, to note that what took the form of sexual repression in *Dr Jekyll and Mr Hyde* becomes in Spark's fiction the blurring of boundaries between heterosexuality and homosexuality is to see the nineteenth-century doppelgänger splitting into multiple selves while the capacity for evil remains constant.

It is a common occurrence in Spark novels that an observant character, most often an artist-figure, begins to notice weird resemblances between one person and another, and then for nothing to be made of this in the plot. Superficially, the perceived likenesses underline the impression that in an artist's eyes we are all types, but in Spark they also hint at the mysterious connectedness of all visible phenomena, and supplement the more conventional satiric theme of false appearances. Spark treated the division between public and private selves explicitly in *The Public Image* (1968) but since then she has intensified the feeling that perhaps the most difficult human task is to locate the moral essence which distinguishes one man as good, another as inherently evil. The problem is as great for her heroines as it was for Hogg's Wringhim or for David Balfour in Stevenson's *Kidnapped* who startles Ebenezer by asking if he and his brother were perhaps twins and later has to work out for himself that Hoseasons 'was neither so good as I supposed him, nor quite so bad as Ransome did; for, in fact he was two men.'[15] The axiom that man is not one but two runs through all Spark's writing and produces various tones and moods, baleful in *Momento Mori* but merrier in *Loitering with Intent* where Fleur Talbot informs us: 'At that time I had a number of marvellous friends, full of good and evil' (p 9).

The reality of evil which transcends any specific place is what paradoxically justifies the fantastic, exaggerated quality of Spark's novels—or romances as they might better be called. A transaction within the writer's imagination that brings moral absolutes into the range of artistic treatment is actually set out for us in *Loitering with Intent* when Fleur reflects on a condition quite distinct from the mixed natures of her 'marvellous friends'. Every artist, she observes, at some time in life, encounters 'pure evil, realised as it may have been under the form of disease, injustice, fear, oppression or any other ill element that can afflict living creatures' (p 169). What this means is that although anybody can perceive evil and suffer its effects, only the artist can connect the experience with the question of what sort of truth art can and should offer: 'I think it true that no artist has lived who has not experienced and then recognised something, at first too incredibly evil to seem real, then so undoubtedly real as to be undoubtedly true' (p 169). Evil 'realises' itself in various ways, which is why the artist's materials are never exhausted and Spark herself can become a social chronicler at the same time as a mythmaker. The Eichmann trial in *The Mandelbaum Gate*; political chicanery along Watergate lines in *The Abbess of Crewe*; terrorism as a secondary theme in several novels and then becoming a leading subject in *The Only Problem*: each new manifestation of man's terrible capacity for error calls for a different type of fictional treatment, a varying degree of ridicule or gravity of manner, but all of them can be made to pass from the initial stage of being 'too incredibly evil to seem real' into a province where they are 'undoubtedly true' *because* 'undoubtedly real'—and made real for us by the artist's very special brand of lies.

Spark's description of her novels as 'fiction, out of which a kind of truth emerges' is commonly invoked, but it is not often noticed how close this brings her to the writers of the central text of the Christian myth—the Bible.[16] Holy Writ is frequently echoed in her prose, either through direct quotation or fainter allusions and traces. In keeping with both her mixed Scottish-Jewish inheritance and her satiric intentions, by far the largest number of open references come from the Old Testament. When the Gospels do come into play the purpose seems to be less the striking of an optimistic note than a warning about the high cost of total religious commitment. Listening to a handsome young Anglican curate preach the evening service, Joanna in *The Girls of Slender Means* (1963) has derived from the Sermon on the Mount a decision to be 'maimed' as a human being so that she can enter the Kingdom of Heaven.[17] She interprets Christ's personal message to herself as a directive to relinquish earthly love and happiness, and in the climactic scene of the novel, while the other girls huddle together waiting to be rescued from the burning May of Teck Club, she calms them by reciting Psalms from the Book of Common Prayer. Her voice penetrates the 'din of demolition' (p 163), and it is the sound more than the meaning of 'the strange utterances of Day 27 in the Anglican order' that holds the girls and Joanna too, fixed, 'as if hypnotised' (p 162). We have already been told that Joanna does not usually 'quote anything for its aptitude' (p 8), and here she is only obeying her 'habit' of 'the words for the right day' (p 164), seeming oblivious of the peculiar appropriacy of the Psalms she intones: Psalm 126, a song of redemption from exile and a hopeful prayer for those who have not yet returned; Psalm 127, which warns against over-anxiety in work and endeavours; Psalm 129, rejoicing in the overthrow of the wicked; and the De Profundis, Psalm 130, which she has only just begun when her turn comes to clamber up the ladder to the window from which the girls are escaping. It is deeply ironic that the whole house collapses into its centre, 'a high heap of rubble' (p 167), before Joanna (whose surname is Childe) even reaches Psalm 131 which should conclude the litany of the day with a song of child-like resignation and commitment to God in time of trouble. Instead, the first line of the De Profundis—'Out of the deep have I called'—is left dangling, severed from the confident assertion of ultimate redemption, not only from the consequences of sin but from sin itself, which the whole Psalm expresses. The 'ungodly' have not been destroyed, as is made evident in the novel by Selina's escape and Joanna's death, and the allusions broaden out to an inclusive vision which is conveyed by a prophetic authorial voice, reminding us that the Anglican litany is, 'held to be applicable to all sorts of conditions of human life at that particular moment, when in London homing workers plodded across the park . . . the Labour Government was new-born, and elsewhere on the face of the globe people slept, queued for liberation-rations, beat the tom-toms, took shelter from the bombers or went for a ride on a dodgem at the fun-fair' (pp 162–3). Against any new hope must be set the continued existence of fear and frivolity.

Outside of the Book of Common Prayer, it is on what is known as the 'Wisdom Literature' of the Jews that Spark draws most heavily. The 'Jewish tinge' imparted to her early environment may partly account for her attraction to the Old Testament and in particular to Proverbs, where people are decisively rewarded or punished during their earthly existence. In *The Girls of Slender Means* Selina escapes and Nicholas Farringdon is martyred, but in *Momento Mori* and *Loitering with Intent* the hopeless condition of fools and sinners is dealt with as roundly and justly as it is in Proverbs. Comedy demands that rewards and punishments take effect in the present life, and so Spark kills off many of her wicked characters with great ease, and at the end of several of her novels she offers summaries of what happened to the characters left alive when the story closed. Here the author goes beyond being a preacher in the image of a nineteenth-century realist like Trollope and becomes a divinity who administers law and governs all of the affairs that can be encompassed by a single narrative. A paradoxical effect arises of characters behaving wilfully, even hysterically, within plots so tightly controlled that inevitabilty is beyond dispute. Most striking in this respect are *The Driver's Seat* and *Not to Disturb*: Lise's death is preordained—indeed, self-ordained—and so is the murder which will make the servants their fortunes. Even when it is definitely a higher force that is moving everybody towards death in *Momento Mori*, human invention cooperates and the supernatural is perfectly at home using the modern telephone.

Spark resembles the writers of Proverbs in declining to express any clear belief in the reality of life after death, though she does seem to be counting on the implied presence of spiritual values which will assert themselves within the reader's understanding of the diverse Vanity Fairs she depicts. In *The Hothouse by the East River* a future dispensation which would provide a redeeming Christian perspective is utterly denied: first, the characters are dead from the very outset, and secondly, Spark makes them inhabit the earthly Inferno of modern New York, 'home of the vivisectors of the mind, and of the mentally vivisected still to be reassembled, and of those who live intact, habitually wondering about their states of sanity, and home of those whose minds have been dead, bearing the scars of resurrection'.[18] The last word alone mocks the corrupt secularism of the society presented in the book. The creator-figure, named Paul to point the irony, instead of situating himself on a road to conversion panics when circumstances force him to realise his own guilt: 'Come back to Manhattan the mental clinic, cries his heart, where we analyse and dope the savageries of existence' (p 89). New York in *The Hothouse by the East River* is an extreme version of the intellectual anaesthesia which debases entirely the conjunction of sanity and virtue promoted by Proverbs. It is dire in comparison with the silent and sedate Puritan Sundays which Paul recollects spending while working for British Intelligence in wartime England; or with Sandy Stranger's prim but mysterious and ever-changing Edinburgh.

Absurdity is carried so far in *The Hothouse by the East River* that the appropriate presiding text is Ecclesiastes. The Preacher who reveals the countless vanities he has seen under the sun is recalled not only by the mood of this novel but more exactly by the motif of Elsa's shadow—or rather the uncanny phenomenon of her casting no shadow at all. And perhaps the most famous lines of all from Ecclesiastes are parodied when the authorial voice remarks: 'One shoud live first, then die, not die then live; everything to its own time' (p 142). The monotony of life; the dark sides of human nature; the fragility of such good things as are attainable in life, and, most of all, the lack of any clearly prophetic element, connect Spark's novel with the biblical text. No vision is offered of a better life yet to be brought to light in the future, and accordingly man's dealings are separated from the control of a God, and of his surrogate, the novelist. The effect of a plan concealed which distinguishes Ecclesiastes from other Old Testament books is achieved in Spark's novel by a variety of means, notably her well-judged use of the present tense.

Structurally as well as philosophically Ecclesiastes, with its frequent breaks and repetitions, deviations and fragmented thought-patterns, may have been especially congenial to her at this stage of her career. It gave the weight of venerable tradition to narrative devices of a kind which the example of many of her contemporary post-modernists shows can degenerate readily into mere game-playing. The same principle of 'personation' that is evident in the writer of Ecclesiastes claiming to utter the counsels of Solomon himself is to be found in Spark, though it should be noted that she doubles the personation device by making her characters interweave quotation and colloquial idiom in their own speech. Lister the butler in *Not to Disturb* is a fine instance of this. He alludes to a wealth of authors, including Webster, Marvell and (particularly aptly in view of the international atmosphere of the book's setting in Geneva, 'the Protestant Rome') Henry James. These references are plainly explicable in the terms of *Not to Disturb*'s central themes, but more puzzling is Lister's recitation from the Book of Job during the bizarre press-conference he holds in the pantry after the murder of his employers. From the third chapter of Job he selects verse 25: 'For the thing which I greatly feared is come upon me, and that which I was afraid of is come upon me. I was out in safety, neither had I rest, neither was I quiet'.[19] Like Joanna in *The Girls of Slender Means* he does not complete or conclude, leaving out the words which in the original announce how Job's agitated forebodings are realised and his prophecy fulfilled: 'yet trouble came'. The frenzy which characterises Job's mind at this point and, in Spark's novel, the entire scene, is considerably heightened. Snatches from the interviews being given by the other servants intervene before we hear Lister's voice again, this time summoning up the image of the fearless warhorse which plays an impressive part in God's humbling instruction of Job in Chapter 39. It is certainly not easy to decide what Lister is trying to convey to his listener, let alone to the reader, and the whole scene has a nonsense quality about it, like something out of a comic opera. Covertly, however, Spark is encouraging the reader to think about divine justice in the context of the servants' anarchic behaviour and also drawing attention to the likeness between her own practice and the insoluble riddles with which God tests Job. Her interest is in the mysterious relationship between the creator and his creations, and there is no sign of that interest waning. Far from it; the baffling ideas contained in Job are the major subject of her recent philosophical novel *The Only Problem*.

Philosophical reflections blend with playfulness in all of Spark's writing, very much in the spirit of Ecclesiastes, which proposes an alternation of wholesome effort with relaxation as the way to contentment. Spark also resembles Stevenson in her ability to unite art and entertainment; she never slights the power of fiction to take readers into the domain of play. Her adventurousness is by no means restricted to matters of form and technique but passes directly into the plots she devises and then joyfully fills with elements that would be at home in adventure stories of the kind developed by Stevenson and Buchan. Secrecy, espionage and disguise feature in many of her books, and it seems likely that the appeal of pre-modernist writers has been stronger for her than anything she would have found on the con-temporary Scottish literary scene while she was growing up. Affinities are again in the form of glimpses and echoes, as when the topic of betrayal in *The Prime of Miss Jean Brodie* has shades of *Kidnapped*, which Sandy reads so avidly; or when the topographically exact description of the man-shaped island in *Robinson* is reminiscent of Stevenson's rendering of Treasure Island like a fat dragon standing up. More intriguingly, the qualities conventionally associated with the boy-hero of turn-of-the-century adventure stories— 'Women were excluded', said Stevenson firmly of his plan for *Treasure Island*—are transferred to the girls who were kept out of such fiction in its early days.[20] When she scrambles through the precipitous tunnel January Marlow in *Robinson* is a modern-day reincarnation of David Crawfurd in Buchan's *Prester John* as well as being a heroic figure making a mythic descent into the underworld. Spark even gives the likeness an extra twist by drawing attention to January's conventional femininity at the stages of theadventure when being deprived of make-up seems as great a disaster to her as the plane crash itself.

As might be expected, Spark takes the figurative implications of adventure-story elements much further than either Stevenson or Buchan. So much further in fact that the only thing she leaves completely unveiled is her scorn for the literal-minded or anyone who sets store by facts. Her characters are made to transform experience into interpretation and sometimes they earn spiritual insight as a reward equivalent to the fortune granted to the adventure-story boy-hero. Understanding is never complete, however, and usually the heroine, along with the reader, is brought to a final mood, not an intellectual posture. Spark exposes the relativity of all formulations, using a number of contrivances among which her emphasis on linguistic diversity is particularly interesting. On the simplest level, this is a matter of her wonderful ear for accents and speech mannerisms, including those of genteel Scots, but increasingly it has corresponded to her use of foreign settings. Frequently, English is not the first or only language of her major characters, and in *The Driver's Seat* Lise's proficiency in four European languages is merely an exaggerated version, with perhaps hint of the demonic, of what is already to be found in other Spark novels. Spark's sense of cultural pluralism is in itself a move against provincialism, and it has served to detach her entirely from the debate about the Scottish writer's linguistic position which was going on while she was being educated in Edinburgh. She has been able to break completely free from the polarised situation described by Edwin Muir in *Scott and Scotland* (1936); for her the question is not, which of two alternative languages the Scottish writer should employ, but how to make her prose style reflect the linguistic multiplicity produced by modern communication-systems while safeguarding standards of excellence in English prose-writing. She eludes all attempts to appropriate her as Scottish in terms of place, language, or subject, though as has been suggested this does not mean that her imagination has not been moved by the culture into which she was born. It should not, after all, be a matter of regret that her Scottish roots are only hazily discernible within her panoptic vision or that she does not fit comfortably into what Karl Miller calls 'the Northern Pantheon'.[21] As Miss Brodie assures her girls, quoting from Proverbs (29.18) words which incidentally formed the motto of the Poetry Society when Spark was General Secretary and editor of its magazine, 'Where there is no vision, the people perish' (p 4).

NOTES

1 *The Prime of Miss Jean Brodie* (London, 1961), pp 73, 59, 13. Further references to this edition are given after quotations in the text.
2 *Barrie and the Kailyard School* (London, 1951), p 18.
3 *Loitering with Intent* (London, 1981), p 151. Further references to this edition are given after quotations in the text.
4 *Selected Poems* Douglas S Mack (ed) (Oxford, 1970), p 32, 1.4. Further line references to this poem are given after quotations in the text.
5 Proverbs, 31.10.
6 'My Conversion', *Twentieth Century*, 170 (Autumn 1961), p 58. *See* David Daiches, *Two Worlds: An Edinburgh Jewish Childhood* (Sussex, 1957).
7 Tom Nairn, 'The Three Dreams of Scottish Nationalism', in *Memoirs of a Modern Scotland*, Karl Miller (ed) (London, 1970), p 44.
8 *The Driver's Seat* (London, 1970), p 109.
9 *See* Nairn, op cit., p 37.
10 *Mrs Grundy in Scotland* (London, 1936).
11 *Momento Mori* (London, 1959), p 166.
12 *Apologia Pro Vita Sua*, Longmans Pocket edn (London, 1907), p 6.
13 *Modern Scottish Literature* (London, 1983), p 103.
14 *The Private Memoirs and Confessions of a Justified Sinner*, John Carey (ed) (London, 1969), p 215.
15 *The Works of Robert Louis Stevenson*, Tusitala edn (London, 1923), VI, 38.
16 Interview with Frank Kermode, in 'The House of Fiction: Interviews with Seven English Novelists', *Partisan Review* 30, no. 1 (Spring 1963), p 80.
17 *The Girls of Slender Means* (London, 1963), p 25. Further references to this edition are given after quotations in the text.
18 *The Hothouse by the East River* (London, 1973), p 12. Further references to this edition are given after quotations in the text.
19 *Not to Disturb* (London, 1971), p 153.
20 *Works*, Tusitala edn (London, 1923), II, xxvi.
21 'Romantic Town', in *Memoirs of a Modern Scotland*, p 118.

FURTHER READING

Bold, Alan (ed), *Muriel Spark: An Odd Capacity for Vision* (London, 1984)
Kemp, Peter, *Muriel Spark* (London, 1974)
Lodge, David, *The Novelist at the Crossroads* (London, 1971)
Malkoff, Karl, *Muriel Spark* (New York, 1968)
Massie, Allan, *Muriel Spark* (Edinburgh, 1979)
Smout, T C, *A Century of the Scottish People 1830–1950* (London, 1986)
Stanford, Derek, *Inside the Forties* (London, 1977)
—— *Muriel Spark: A Biographical and Critical Study* (Fontwell, 1963)
Stubbs, Patricia, *Muriel Spark* (London, 1973)

Chapter 19

Twentieth-century Women's Writing: The Nest of Singing Birds

JOY HENDRY

The ratio of mentions, men to women, in critical tomes and anthologies is perhaps not the most definitive of literary yardsticks, but it can be revealing to discover in these volumes the degree to which the contribution of women in twentieth-century Scottish writing has been minimised and marginalised, particularly in poetry. In fiction, women have done better in that one or two are accepted as mainstream, important writers. Muriel Spark and Naomi Mitchison, and, more recently, Joan Lingard, Jessie Kesson and Elspeth Davie are now regarded as worthy of more than scant attention.

It is a widely held assumption in feminist thinking that in the male-dominated world, poetry as queen of the literary arts was clutched more lovingly to the male bosom. Like the role of the priest or mage, the role of poet or bard was reserved for men, and women were kept at arms length, their poetic efforts, if any emerged, dismissed as either 'song' or 'verse'. Fiction, being more entrenched in the social and domestic sphere, and unburdened by poetry's pseudo-mystique, was more suitable *a priori* for women as a literary medium. In this respect, Scotland is no different from England or America in that it does shyly admit to the odd nineteenth or twentieth-century female fiction-writer, but the relative scarcity of Scottish women writers has led to an even greater lack of female models for the emerging writer. I doubt if any Scottish woman writer has felt that her environment was encouraging, sympathetic or favourable to her achieving the full extent of her potential. Those who succeed are those who thrive in an adverse climate. Indeed, I invented the image 'the double knot in the peeny'[1] to describe the double disadvantage suffered by Scottish woman writers in being firstly Scottish and secondly female. Essentially, Scottish women writers, of all forms and genres, have had a pretty raw deal. Kurt Wittig, in *The Scottish Tradition in Literature* is typical when he describes Susan Ferrier as having written three novels 'in which an occasional secondary character is all that "gets across" to a modern reader'. Twentieth-century novelists do not fare much better at the critics' hands. Even in such a recent volume as Roderick Watson's *The Literature of Scotland*, the treatment of Naomi Mitchison, for instance, can only be regarded as inadequate.

So even with fiction, too many of our writers disappear from print and from critical attention. Only in 1977 did Jessie Kesson's *The White Bird Passes* re-emerge, and now she is considered one of Scotland's finest novelists.

Recently we have seen the re-issue of two of Naomi Mitchison's best novels, *The Corn King and the Spring Queen*, and *The Bull Calves*, the original edition of which met with almost total silence—astonishingly, since it is a twentieth-century masterpiece. Mitchison's sheer prolificacy ensures her a place in the public eye, but with those whose output is not so conspicuous, we find important women writers who have not just fallen from favour, but dropped out of sight altogether. Neil Gunn's correspondent and friend, Nan Shepherd, is a classic example; her novels are scarcely mentioned in any critical volume. Even W R Aitken's bibliographical work, *Scottish Literature in English and Scots*, lists only her articles on male poets, neglecting her creative work entirely.[2] Willa Muir is mentioned in Alan Bold's *Modern Scottish Literature*[3] only with reference to the support she gave to her husband, Edwin: Bold ignores altogether Willa Muir's own writings. Rarely do eminent male writers achieve so perfect an obscurity.

With poetry, the situation is even worse. In the period to 1975, only three names readily spring to mind: Violet Jacob, Marion Angus and Helen B Cruickshank, who are largely dismissed as minor versifiers by the critics. Wittig gives Jacob credit for 'strong feelings' in her poetry, remarking that 'though the background is rural, she *does try* to give it a more universal meaning'. (p 277–8) [Italics mine]. Alan Bold makes jokes about home-made Marions and shrinking Violets, comparing them to Lewis Spence, 'a man who put his patriotic ideals to a public political test'. (p 25) Of Helen B Cruickshank, Wittig comments with surprise on her power of abstraction, and her ability in some poems to employ symbolism to good effect (p 278–9). The most positive response to Jacob and Angus comes from Maurice Lindsay, who credits them with having restored emotional honesty to Scots poetry.[4] The response of Janet Caird, concluding her article on Violet Jacob and Helen Cruickshank in *Cencrastus* is to describe them as 'true artists, worthy members of that nest of singing birds—the neglected women poets of Scotland.'[5]

Looking backwards one finds that in the Lowland, Scots or English writing tradition, earlier periods seem almost blank, producing little apart from the aristocratic song-writers. (The Gaelic tradition is comparatively rich in women poets, and respectful towards their works.) But many women have contributed to the oral tradition, and their work is identifiable among the anonymous contributions of the time. It's worth remembering that both the Gaelic and Scots traditions pay little heed to distinctions between song and poetry so beloved of critics. The poets Jacob, Angus and Cruickshank are the direct descendants of the song writers like Lady Nairne, and of the anonymous writers of poems and songs. Their use of a less-debased Scots than was common in the Kailyard period of the nineteenth century was important in the development of the Scottish Renaissance.

Popular opinion has it that only the poetry of Violet Jacob deserves to be remembered, although, ironically, she was first appreciated as a prose writer. Her poetry reveals an innovative use of Scots as a medium for serious poetry. Jacob's command of North-east Scots came from being, as a child, 'aye in and oot amo' the ploughman's feet at the Mains o' Dun'.[6] She herself was upper-class, but, like her aristocratic predecessors, her poetry is closely linked to the folk tradition, and the great ballads of Scottish literature. Her poems are supremely human, with clever use of dialogue and character, wit and satire. Rarely does she speak directly to her readers, but assumes the persona of a recognisable, rural type, through which a particular situation, or feeling, or attitude is explored.

Her ability to create a sense of landscape in poems like 'Craigo Woods' provoked Helen B Cruickshank to write in her *Octobiography*: 'I now feel Craigo Wood is sacred to Violet Jacob and I have never used the name in my own verse, although this was our nearest and dearest woodland Sunday walk.'[7] Poems like 'The Neep Fields by the Sea' evince a sentimentality and descend to a level of rusticity which is a hallmark of some of her poorer, though popular efforts. Some poems achieve a lyric expression indicative of high poetic achievement, like her description of the aftermath of Culloden in 'Cairneyside':

> And I socht the place at my mither's hairth
> Whaur a broken lad micht hide—
> There was naucht left standin' but nakit wa's
> By the water o' Cairneyside.

Her finest poetry balances sentiment on a knife edge to create a statement of sometimes heart-rending poignancy: 'The Wild Geese', is on the well-worn theme of exile, but seldom has the longing for the country left been so well expressed.

Her Scots has a remarkable lilt to it, a feel for rhythm and cadence. Only in certain passages in Grassic Gibbon's *A Scots Quair* are the rhythms and idioms, the thrust and flow of Scots speech better captured. This quality in her writing has not been fully appreciated, but it is perhaps the reason behind the recent discovery of a new potential in her poetry as lyrics for folk song. Jim Reid of Angus has recently set 'The Wild Geese' to his own melody and Sylvia Barnes has made similar use of 'The Last O' The Tinkler'. The ballad quality and the simple diction of Jacob's poetry lends itself to such use.

Even if we accept Janet Caird's assessment of Jacob as 'a minor poet' (although she is a good minor poet) who 'at her best speaks with a very individual voice',[8] it is with posterity's dismissal of her as a prose writer that I most disagree. As the publication of *The Lum Hat & Other Stories*, her later short fiction, shows, she is a considerable prose writer and story-teller with an effortless and almost faultless prose style. She wrote four novels: *The Sheep Stealers*, *The Interloper*, *The History of Aythan Waring* and *Flemington* and several novellas. *The Sheep Stealers*, her first novel, set in the Anglo-Welsh border country, is an adventure story, but depth is provided by the background of political and economic exploitation, with ordinary people taking to riot in protest against excessive tolls on turnpike roads. Her characterisation avoids the obvious. The hero is neither handsome and dashing nor wicked and irredeemable, but a complex character whose disregard for personal safety appeals but whose selfishness and irresponsibility make him at times quite dislikeable. The conclusion of the novel is felt as truly tragic. Although marred by occasional mannered phrases and stilted, conventional expression, it is gripping, well worth reading, and reveals an open-mindedness about life, including a sexual frankness, which characterises all Jacob's writing.

The Interloper, the first of her two novels set in Angus, is a romance with a complex plot, in which love triumphs just in time, after an extremely rough passage. It is typical of Jacob's originality of imagination that the heroine, Cecilia, is finally rescued from an unwanted marriage by a motley combination of her real lover Gilbert, and his unlikely accomplices, Granny Stirk, Queen of the Cadgers, the travelling fisherfolk, her grandson Jimmy and a horse! This social mixing is a typically Scottish feature, and she makes the most of the potential inherent in such strange alliances and connections— and not just to comic effect. *The Interloper* is intensely readable, and in the creation of characters such as Granny Stirk, truly memorable. In his introduction to *The Lum Hat & Other Stories*, Ronald Garden quotes the *Spectator* reviewer, who comments, 'Mrs Jacob is no devotee of the Kailyard cult, following in regard to the use of dialect, the excellent example set by Sir Walter.'[9]

Writing in *Chapman 27–8*, Marion Lochhead describes *The Interloper* as 'a strong tale, told with restraint and economy', and indeed the stylistic excesses which marr *The Sheep Stealers* are now absent, and the prose style is fluent, well controlled and understated. Lochhead claims that Jacob's last novel, *Flemington* 'has even more strength and integrity . . . This almost forgotten novel has a quality bordering on genius . . . it is a truly great historical novel, both in narrative and background and, even more, in character study.'[10]

Marion Lochhead is not overstating the case. It is an adventure story in the best tradition of Scott and Stevenson. John Buchan described it as 'the best Scots romance since the *Master of Ballantrae*'.[11] In my view, it surpasses the best of Buchan, invites direct comparison with Stevenson's already cited novel, and makes *Kidnapped*, which it also resembles, look Enid Blyton-ish. Set against the background of the Forty-Five Rebellion, the novel steers an exciting course through the complex of loyalties and political cross-currents with a masterly objectivity which emphasises the tragedy of those times. Jacob's fertile imagination provides us with a successor to Granny Stirk in the form of Skirling Wattie, a legless piper and singer, loyal assistant to the hero, Archie Flemington, in his spying activities. Ironically, Wattie's loyalty leads him to betray Archie, and in the end leads to his own death, as well as Archie's. Like Naomi Mitchison's *The Bull Calves*, *Flemington* transcends politics without, like Scott and Stevenson, compromising its version of events and undermining its characters, and makes a statement about the importance of loyalty, integrity, the sancity of human life itself, and, by inference, the need to achieve political integration in Scotland. It is a very female vision.

Jacob's short stories are also compelling, fatalistic and interesting. Several critics compare her novels, particularly in their employment of atmospheric setting, with Hardy. While Hardy's stories have an obsessive, insistent pessimism, drawn from his vision of an indifferent God and an indifferent universe, Jacob's pessimism is quiet, drawn instead from her awareness of the difficulties, the ironic complexities and the loneliness of human existence. Christina, heroine of 'The Lum Hat' is unable to throw off the sexual oppression in her background to take up an independent life as wife of a man who would clearly be a good husband to her. Old Jimmy Strachan's life is lonely and frustrated, dominated by his unsympathetic niece, Maria. Fifty-eight swans land in the neighbourhood, and remind him of purpose in life, of beauty, of an unspoken ideal, but the effort of going to see the swans kills him. The story is told with simplicity, great economy and control. Violet Jacob the prose writer is long overdue for critical re-appraisal.

MacDiarmid's verdict on Jacob in *Contemporary Scottish Studies* is revealing. He attributes her 'failure to achieve greatness' to the fact that she was furthering an English, not a Scottish tradition, and laments 'the divided and, in the last analysis, ineffectual nature of her prose work—as in her apparent obliviousness to the vital problems confronting Scottish nationality today, which a better-oriented spirit with her raciality of character could not have refrained from addressing. In other words, the present position of Scotland as a nation has deprived us of all but a shadow of the Mrs Jacob whom in less over-Anglicised circumstances we might have had.'[12]

It would appear that he was not referring to *Flemington*, which he appears not to have read. Grieve's low opinion of the historic novel as 'a bastard form' must also be taken into account. It is, in fact, the double knot in the peeny referred to earlier. All things considered, Jacob's achievement, in real terms, was considerable.

Helen B Cruickshank, in *Octobiography*, refers to 'the gnomic charm' of Marion Angus, and says: 'On the whole, I rated Marion's poems higher than Mrs Jacob's. Their work was in some respects much akin but Marion had an element of the old ballad magic and a rarer quality, a feyness, that was foreign to Mrs Jacob.'[13] Cruickshank also laments the general neglect of her work.

Cruickshank's verdict is astute. If we can rid ourselves of our modern smug rationalism and pseudo-scientific prejudice, we might be able to appreciate the fey, supernatural quality in Angus's work, instead of regarding it as a sign of simpleminded backwardness. The rhythms of her poems are quieter and less varied than Jacob's, but her musical ear, her sensitivity to the sound of words is more acute. In her poems in English, she achieves a more genuine note than Jacob. I wonder if her poem, 'The Mourners' inspired William Soutar's 'Babylon':

> She was one a fine lass;
> All flesh is grass.
> We go down, every one,
> In sorrow when our day is done.

or if 'The Can'el' is behind his 'The Tryst', arguably one of his best poems.

There is a purity and simplicity about Angus's poetry, in Scots and English, which is rare indeed. Of her English poems, 'The Captive', 'Heritage', 'Cotton Grasses' are intensely appealing. Nor is her world always sweet and attractive: Scots poems like 'The Broken Brig' combine feyness and archetypal imagery, drawing on the elemental power of 'Lyke Wake Dirge' to create a profoundly disturbing picture of the helplessness of humanity against the blows of fate. In poems like 'The Turn of the Day', her use of natural images reverberates, suggesting more than could be encompassed by literal interpretation:

> Under the cauld, green grass,
>   Wee wakenin', wanderin' burn,
> Sing your ain sang.
>   The day's at the turn,
> But simmer's lang, lang.

'Alas Poor Queen' has been over-anthologised, when other poems might have been just as suitable: 'Ann Gilchrist', for example, which powerfully evokes our sympathy on behalf of a woman ostracised as a witch. The poem ends:

> An' I wuss the whins wis nae sae shairp
>   Nor the muckle moss saw weet,
> For wha wull gie Ann Gilchrist fire
>   Tae warm her clay-cauld feet?

At its best, her work is very fine indeed, and, like Jacob's, could provide lyrics for modern folk-song. She should not be ungratefully dismissed because of her supernatural themes—the supernatural remains a real part of many people's lives; nor should her writings be seen as the wistful meanderings and longings of a woman who never married. She led a sheltered life, which no doubt affected her poetry. But her achievement is real and worthy of appreciation.

Helen B Cruickshank is another woman whose poetry has never received its due. The twenty or so years between her and Jacob and Angus made an enormous difference. While their formative years were in the late Victorian period, Cruickshank's young life coincided with the growth of the suffragette movement and the First World War. Yet her life, and her development as a writer was restricted. Like many of her sex, she was left responsible for the welfare of an ageing mother. Aged 36, she had to bid 'farewell to my free and easy Bohemian life' in her studio flat and 'goodbye to my hopes of being able to wed my penniless artist' (at that time women civil servants had to resign their posts on marriage).

Cruickshank's poetry reflects a more modern sensibility, someone who, despite restrictions, participates in life on an equal basis with men. MacDiarmid referred to her in a radio tribute as a 'catalyst' in the Scottish literary renaissance.[14] Writing with equal facility in Scots and English, she uses a greater variety of forms, including blank verse and prose-poetry, but was not innovative technically. She has greater range of tone and mood than Jacob or Angus, but is not such a careful craftswoman. Like Angus, she is a presence in her poetry; indeed, one special quality is her frankness about her life and its frustrations. There is also a playful quality counterbalanced with a gravity and seriousness not found in the older poets. Cruickshank writes about the world around her in a way that neither of them did.

There are the anthologised favourites, like the wonderful 'Shy Geordie', which evinces a freedom from conventional moralities all three poets have in common. She too can adopt a character or persona, and dramatise it with skill and subtlety. Independence of mind and spirit are always present: 'Keepit In' is itself a powerful indictment of Scottish educational methodology, and 'Comfort in Puirtith' has an outspoken combativeness typical of Mac-Diarmid's work. Her sympathy for the suffering of others is found in poems like 'Ealasaidh', addressed to an exiled Gael and written in cadences deliberately echoing Gaelic rhythms:

> And here the ancient speech
> You loved essaying,
> Rising and falling like the wave-borne birds,
> The cadences that wind and tide are weaving
> Of Gaelic words.

Perhaps her ability to empathise enabled her to bear her sorrows with such courage, and to turn these to positive effect. This is what makes 'Prayer', in which she considers her childlessness, so moving: 'Help me always to choose,/To comfort and to bless,/And in Man's service lose/My fruitful barrenness'. Many poems express her love of nature in all its forms. Political themes also occur regularly: 'Lines Written For The Scottish Watch' declares against tenement poverty 'O how can grace or peace or health abide/such poverty'. Many poems reflect her love of Scotland, like 'The Bracelet':

> No bracelet of bright hair about the bone
>   Is emblem of my life's enduring passion,
> But semi-precious gem or polished stone
>   Declares my love of Scotland in my fashion.

She has, unlike Donne or Dowson, 'but a simple tale/Of symbols of true love in Scotland's stones'—maybe one of her most memorable lines. That poem is typical of her humility, but perhaps 'At the End' is the most moving of all, in which she anticipates death and what might follow.

Yet again, more attention should be paid to Cruickshank, her work, and her other contributions to literary life, through PEN, and her literary friendships. Hers is a very natural, unselfconscious and selfless voice, her poetry rich, varied and exceptional in its humanity.

Alice V Stuart's earlier poetry is mostly conventional. There are religious devotional poems, pieces on standard classical themes, full of classical allusions; the style is essentially Victorian. Yet obviously the author is an intellectual with ability as a verse-maker and a grasp of the poetic forms and techniques of the English tradition. There are signs of genuine lyrical quality in poems such as 'Hope', but this is spoiled by over-blown diction. Oddly, the moment Stuart returns to her Scottish roots, she comes to life, as in 'The Seal Woman', a poetic retelling of the folk-tale, which, although stilted, has an energy that her more aureate poems lack. A true note is also sounded in 'Without'—a response to virginity. The title poem, 'The Far Calling' is straight out of the Celtic Twilight and Fiona MacLeod. She has a tendency to be preoccupied with poetry and poetic mystique, and to resort to exaggerated romanticism in poems such as 'Petition'. Her second volume, 'The Dark Tarn' is largely unremarkable, apart from a rather sprawling poem, 'The Patchwork Quilt' about a dying woman reliving parts of her life—a new departure for Stuart, in theme and form.

Alice Stuart's later poems are more interesting and genuine in their inspiration. Her themes become the changing seasons, nature, education, ageing, people and places. 'In the Wood of the World', one of her best poems, she uses the nursery tale of Little Red Riding Hood to explore the possessiveness of maternal feelings:

> So she must go.
> Mothers must learn to let their darlings walk
> the wood of the world, nor cherish them too closely.
> Love can imprison; and if there are wolves,
> are there not wood-cutters too?

While Stuart has technical facility, she fails except in rare moments to capture the reader's imagination: the tendency to the romantic is seldom quite overcome. On balance too, the poems lack a discernible original voice, the sense of a unique centre from which the poetry proceeds. Part of Stuart's difficulty is that she looks for inspiration to the nineteenth century English tradition and fails almost totally to interact with the Scottish tradition, and, inevitably for a Scottish writer in such circumstances, writes in a vacuum. There are no poems in Scots, no signs of influences of Scots or Gaelic speech, except superficially in the Celtic Twilight poems. In her last volume, there are well-turned lines, memorable ideas, unusual poems like 'The Hour of the Visit', a supernatural tale of how the Brahan Seer came by his power of prophetic vision, and 'The Tale of the Hazel Tree', a sequence based on The Grimm original of the Cinderella Story, which merits more attention than I can give here. The four poems published in *Chapman 27–8* not long before she died are sensitive meditations on the passing of time, on ageing, evidence that there is work still to be published, and that critical attention is merited.

Bessie J B MacArthur produced a few small pamphlets of poetry. Her poems in English are indifferent in quality, lacking in originality and conventional in theme. Her writing in Scots has much more vitality, and at her best, there are some well-turned pieces in Marion Angus vein. Two poems stand out: 'The Braw Thocht', an imaginative piece about mental processes, set out in ballad/story form; and 'Nocht o' Mortal Sicht'—a grim account of the effect of war:

> For nocht o' mortal sicht I see—
> But warrin tanks on ilka hand,
> And twistit men that lie sae still
> And sma', upon the desert sand.

The quality of the poem justifies its place in *The Oxford Book of Scottish Verse*. Agnes Hall writes in both Scots and English, essentially conventional pieces, with a higher degree of achievement in the English poems, but again the most conspicuously successful poems are in Scots, this time more in the Violet Jacob style of adopting the pose of various different characters. 'The Light Gone Out' makes an impact in its portrayal of a loveless existence, but it is marred by self-pity. The verse-making is competent, but the range limited.

Kate Bone is a surprising figure writing in Scots and English who is to my knowledge unpublished outside of single items in newspapers and three volumes published under the same title, *Thistle By-Blaws*, although each is different. Her writing is fairly conventional in form, but quite unpredictable in content. Robert Garioch, in an introduction, remarks: 'Now it is up to the critics and anthologists to place [these poems] firmly among the half-century's literary movement'. Garioch welcomes their 'quiet good sense, good humour and deceptively penetrating wit, all well under control'. Poems which begin predictably suddenly develop in unforeseen directions: in 'Is This the Lass', a man laments changes in his loved one, but has, despite himself, to recognise unattractive changes in himself. The Scots poems are racy, humorous, sometimes lyrical and haunting: 'The Last Fire' ends: 'the lowe is deid, the branch is brunt awa'/Ashes tae ashes, cauld finality,/But in the hert an immortality'. Some of her English poems are highly achieved pieces of weight and dignity; 'Constancy' concludes; 'Do not reproach me with inconstancy;/I am not made of stable stuff like stone/But all my many selves are yours alone.' Wendy Wood should also be mentioned as someone who has written entertainingly and well.

Valued she may be as a novelist, but Naomi Mitchison is largely ignored as a poet. Much of her poetry remains unpublished, but one volume, *The Cleansing of the Knife* is currently available. In conversation recently, Mitchison said that she felt her poetry comes from a deeper source inside herself than her other writing, even the best of the novels. Her poetry is engaged with the real world, the actions and objects of everyday life, but not limited in range to practical existence. In such poems as 'The Alban Goes Out: 1939', the title poem, 'The Cleansing of the Knife', and 'The Talking Oats' and the introductory poem to *The Bull Calves* Mitchison attempts to articulate a vision of Scotland, past, present and future. While mindful of the disintegration endemic in Scottish history, she aims towards an integrated, wholesome, fulfilling future. The poems are largely 'spoken' by involved observers; often her own voice is heard, sometimes in the background, sometimes speaking directly. Nancy Gish, reviewing 'The Cleansing of the Knife'[15] accuses Mitchison of speaking in her own voice *about* Scotland, and lapsing therefore into sentiment and moralising. But the voices used are of someone directly caught up in the events described, and Mitchison is too concerned with the need to understand and *act* to allow sentiment to blunt the vision. Her central message is of loyalty, responsibility, of the debt owed by each to the community, local, national, world-wide:

> Even at most alone
> We are more than merely ourselves;
> Our souls are not our own.

Her own community of Carradale provides the setting for these poems, acting as a microcosm for Scotland as a whole. In her short poems, too, are fine achievements, 'Adoption of a Parliamentary Candidate, Lochgilphead: 1939', 'Comfort', to name but two. The time is ripe for the re-evaluation of her work, including her poetry.

In his essay 'Literary Lights', Lewis Grassic Gibbon acknowledges Muriel Stuart as 'one of the very few great poets writing in non-experimental English. She has a comprehension and a lyric beauty almost unknown to this English day.' He adds, 'she is as little Scots as Dante'.[16] In the same essay, he places firmly within the English, not the Scottish literary tradition, such figures as Neil Gunn and Naomi Mitchison. However, MacDiarmid waxes lyrical about Stuart's poetry, which, he claims, 'is almost always on the major plane', and, in contrast to Gibbon, perceives a 'fundamental relationship' between Stuart and the Makars. His confidence that, if his contemporary Scotland didn't much value her work then posterity would, seems so far to have been misplaced.[17]

Stuart's writing is noteworthy by any standards. Her analysis of the situation of women bites deeper and ticks at a more universal, elemental level than any other writer I can think of to this day. One of her most powerful poems is 'Andromeda Unfettered', a long poetic dialogue between Andromeda, the spirit of woman, Persens, the new spirit of man, and two choruses, the first of women who desire the 'old thrall', and secondly of 'women who crave the new freedom'. Stuart's note prefacing the poem claims that it is not 'a study of the economic struggle of women, but of the deep-rooted antagonism of spirit which constitutes the eternal sex-problem.' The poem lives up to this intention. Andromeda says:

> I have been
> All that man has desired or dreamed of me.
> I have trodden a double-weary way—with Sin,
> Or with Sin's pale, cold sister Chastity.
> I am a thing of twilight. I am afraid.

In response, the second chorus gives this very memorable verdict:

> Not love, not love! Love was our first undoing,
> We have lived too long on heart-beats . . .

Outspoken and forthright as she is on the subject of women, she is equally bold and passionate as a poet of love in all its various guises. 'The Bastard', a monologue to an unborn child, is astonishing in its open-minded insight into the conflicting feelings of a woman in such a situation, as well being an outright condemnation of a society which so stigmatises people. It is difficult to believe that the poem was written around the time of the First World War. In 'Indictment', she inveighs against men's double standards about sex, asking them 'In women is it Chastity you prize'. . .

> Can Chastity cool your kisses slake your sighs?
> And when, at last, o'ertaken and embraced,
> We give you burning lips, wild words and eyes,
> In your arms lying, would you have us chaste?

As MacDiarmid saw, it was perhaps too strong for its time. The poems on religious themes equally challenge and explore territory about which respectful silence is kept by better-mannered writers. Her psychological insight and power of imagination recalls Browning, especially in poems like 'The Tryst' which remind us of 'Porphyria's Lover'. Muriel Stuart is a writer who addresses major issues and whose courage and writing ability should at last be recognised. She is the most unjustly ignored poet of this period.

Another neglected singing bird is Olive Fraser. The publication of *The Pure Account* went largely unmarked. Writing both in Scots and English, her purity of lyricism and gentleness of touch conveys an exquisite lightness and sensitivity to her work. A sense of potential unachieved remains: the difficulty of her life, which was unsettled and dogged by mental illness, prevented her from developing her poetic talents. Early poems like 'The Vikings' which won the Chancellor's Medal in Cambridge University, 1935, demonstrate technical virtuosity of a high order. In 'The Unwanted Child', she confronts her own conviction that her birth was not welcomed, particularly by her father, with brave straightforwardness and devastating simplicity of utterance:

> You could have had them all,
> The dust, the glories too,
> But I was the wrong music
> And why I never knew.

One of her finest poems, 'The Glen of the Clearance', counterpoints the tragedy of the Clearances with lines from the Latin Mass. This imaginative stroke creates a distance from the subject which allows the impact of the disaster to be conveyed without indulgence or sentimentality. Olive Fraser has left us with a very worthwhile body of poems and a prize-winning play, *The Road to Glenlivet*, and more which remains unpublished.

Also largely unpublished is Ann Scott–Moncrieff, although a sequence of poems in *Chapman 38*, shows her as a lively poetic presence with a strong, individual voice. Her early death at 29 deprived us of a gifted writer of both prose and poetry, but proper assessment of her contribution cannot be undertaken until more of her work is available.

A word should be said about Doric poets Flora Garry and Mary Symon. Garry's collection *Bennygoak and Other Poems* was immensely popular. Her grasp of Doric is sure, exploiting the onomatopoeic potential of the dialect and its biting, dry wit. The tendency of her work is towards pawky humour and her range limited to the couthie portrayal of rural life, but her eye can be sharp, as in 'To Suffie, Last of the Buchan Fishwives': 'A fish creel wi a wife aneth't/Steed at wir kitchen door'. Mary Symon also has fluency in Scots and an ear for its rhythms. While she can produce couthie humour, there is a serious strain in her work, especially in her war poems, some of which, like 'The Soldiers' Cairn' are very moving indeed. Garry and Symon are ultimately minor figures, similar to but far outshone by Jacob and Angus.

Kathleen Raine is one of the major poets of this century. Her work ranges across the spectrum of intellectual and spiritual life and gives testimony to the view of poetry as a medium through which to assert eternal values. Her poetry is genuinely philosophical and meditative, without losing its grip of the real world. She has an extraordinary ability to recreate landscape in a way which implies both history and culture. It is not possible here to do justice to her work, as the emphasis is on women whose work has been neglected, but it should be said that her poetry belongs clearly to the Scottish tradition. Raine herself is half-Scottish and lives in London, but draws her chief inspiration from the Scottish landscape, history and culture. Her own statement that she sees herself as Scottish should be taken at face value.

Turning now to two neglected women novelists, Willa Muir and Nan Shepherd, some of whose novels have recently been republished. Neither was prolific in output: Nan Shepherd wrote three novels, Willa Muir two, but the quality of their writing is extremely high. Yet Francis Hart doesn't even mention Shepherd in *The Scottish Novel*, when such as Lillian Beckwith are afforded generous, if not uncritical coverage.

Despite that, Willa Muir's literary offerings are weighty. During the 1920s she collaborated with her husband to produce translations of Hauptmann, Feuchtwanger, Broch and Carossa and, most famously, Kafka's *The Trial* and *The Castle*, when none of these writers were available in English. After Muir's death in 1959, she fulfilled a commission given to him to produce *Living with Ballads*—an imaginative and perceptive study of the ballad tradition. Her record of her life with Edwin is published in *Belonging*, which appeared two years before her death. A book of her poems, *Laconics, Jingles and Other Verses*, was privately issued in 1970.

Mrs Grundy in Scotland is a most original and witty analysis of the social, political and religious threats to healthy living in Scotland, past and present. The original Grundy character comes from Thomas Morton's comedy *Speed the Plough*, and testifies to the essentially hierarchical nature of English society. Mrs Grundy embodies our secret fears, personifies our inferiorities, and in her conservative, static view of society, teaches us to accept these as inevitable. The egalitarian strain in Scottish life prevents Mrs Grundy (who came to Scotland with Queen Victoria) from achieving the same elevated place within our national psyche, but a Scottish equivalent, Mrs MacGrundy rejects outright the snobbism Mrs Grundy represents but is a Calvinistic,

Scottish Presbyterian equivalent, achieved by whisking Mrs Grundy up to heaven. Mrs MacGrundy, and 'the growing power and influence of London and increasing wealth raised a tempest of inferiority complexes in Scotland'. As far as the Gaidhealtachd is concerned, she 'set herself earnestly to wean the Highlanders from their wicked ways, and succeeded, beyond all expectations in smashing up the fabric of an ancient and gracious culture.' The book is an appeal for a reappraisal of women's roles, and of the relation of the individual to the environment. Although written more than fifty years ago, it contains much of contemporary relevance.

Imagined Corners is a remarkable first novel, although Muir comments that 'it had enough material in it for two novels, which I was too amateurish to realise at the time'. Francis Hart rightly compares it with *Middlemarch* in structure, range and conception. Set in the fictional north-east Scottish coastal town of Calderwick, the novel explores the tensions within a Scots community attributable finally to social mores and religion, and to restrictions on individual freedom, the effect of sexual repression, and particularly the effect on women of living as second-rate citizens in such a world. The central symbol, equivalent to the web in *Middlemarch*, is of a glass, into which elements are precipitated. The development of the novel, which is fundamentally concerned with the necessity of change, is determined by the effect of precipitating new elements into the solution, by means of which all is changed, the original solution or situation, and the new elements themselves.

The necessity for change comes from the flawed and unhealthy nature of the community itself, and the novel may be seen as the struggle for independence of mind and action in a conventionally determined environment. The analysis of the situation of women is acute: the assumption is that 'the female sex was devised by God for the lower grades of work and knowledge and that it was beneath the dignity of a man to stoop to female tasks'. (p 29) And yet only female characters, Elizabeth Shand and Madame Mutze particularly, are capable either of imagination in thought and action, and of participating in intellectual life. Elizabeth has a strong visionary sense, is able to live up to difficult ideals and has the strength to stand out against popular disapproval and established behaviour. Yet we see how the narrowness of the community, and the agency, ironically, of the fifth column inside herself of her love for her husband Hector, leads Elizabeth to try to turn herself into the figure of the noble wife (like Virginia Woolfe's 'woman of the house') and to deny her essential nature. Only the precipitation of the final element into the solution, Madame Mutze, Elizabeth's notorious sister-in-law, saves her from spiritual death, and Madame Mutze, Lochinvar-like, sweeps her off back to Germany with her. Calderwick is not big enough for either of them to live in and be whole.

That is but one strand, if the central one, of a very complex novel, one full of insight into Scottish life. Perhaps Muir was right in her own assessment that it contains enough for two novels, yet she manages to sustain and develop all the different strands, combining them into a very satisfying, stimulating whole. Of her second novel, *Mrs Ritchie*, she says: 'I cannot now tell how I managed to finish a second novel, but it does not surprise me that I lost control of it in the second half, although the first half is quite good'.[18] Out of her memoirs, that is the extent of her comments about her own creative efforts—an extraordinary indication of the low priority she gave to her own writing.

Mrs Ritchie in many ways resembles Douglas Brown's *House with the Green Shutters* in its ruthless sweep towards the inevitable destruction of something profoundly unhealthy. It traces the stages by which Annie Rattray degenerates from being a bright young scholar whose intellectual ambitions are early stifled by her mother. From that point on, Annie, caught up in a grim process of self-preservation, mercilessly attacks all life whenever it attempts to assert itself. Her creative instincts are stifled, twisted, and turn instead to obsessive religiosity, which, as she grows older, oppresses the humanity out of husband and family, driving her son to fling himself under a train and her daughter to leave for good to preserve both body and mind. The faults of the novel resemble those of *Green Shutters* also in that, particularly in the second half, as Muir herself observes, the characters become two-dimensional, stereotyped, and the picture painted almost too extreme and horrific to be vaguely life-like. Nevertheless, just as Douglas Brown's novel has many virtues, so *Mrs Ritchie* presents Scots with a vision of the negative side of themselves, one which may only be half true, but which needs to be articulated nonetheless. Perhaps had she not been so pressurised, she could have gone on to write a novel which expressed a more integrated vision, one which could look to the future without having to secure the permanent exile of all worthwhile characters as their only salvation. These valuable novels should not have been kept from us for so long.

One link between the novels of Willa Muir and those of Nan Shepherd, is that they recurrently emphasise that mystical experiences, the spiritual side of existence, and intellectual endeavour as a whole, is as much if not more a part of women's life as men's. Indeed, by contrast, men's spirituality and intellectuality is portrayed as (often) ego-ridden and shallow. Shepherd in particular shows how women are forced to make compromises, for emotional and social reasons, which they often do unselfishly, if not without frustration or regret, as a result of which they, unlike their frequently less gifted male counterparts, fail to realise their potential. Both novelists share a general open-mindedness, and a frankness about sex in particular.

Martha Ironside, heroine of Shepherd's first novel, *The Quarry Wood*, has to run the gauntlet of almost all the problems or traps which can determine or twist the development of intelligent young women, and anticipates Grassic Gibbon's Chris Guthrie. Set in the north east of Scotland, the novel centres around Martha's conflict between the pull of the land and the lure of education, between her own intellectual ambitions and her social and family duty, as the only one willing and able to nurse grand-aunt Josephine, and the tension in values and life-style between her father's essentially peasant sensibility and her mother's more middle-class, socially conscious background. Like many able women whose instinct it is to minimise their own abilities, she projects her own idealism onto her married, student friend Luke, whom she idolises and falls in love with. Gradually, through the experience of nursing Aunt Josephine (the most impressive character in the novel), she resolves these difficulties, realising that neither she nor Luke are what she had believed, that the nature of her feelings towards him are an externalisation of her own spirituality. 'Dependent on a man to complete me! I thought I couldn't be anything without him', she thinks indignantly. 'I can be my own creator'. (p 266)

That insight remains a goal still to be achieved at the end of the novel. She also has to learn how much she has in common with her peasant, uneducated father, and as she watches him plough the earth, she thinks, ' "I've come from him." ' (p 295) The conclusion seems flat, but it closely approximates to real life: 'Life was stranger than they had supposed'. (p 304) The realisation achieved, as indicated at the beginning of the novel, is that wisdom comes not from books, not from individuals like Luke, whose contact with reality is tenuous at best, but from human beings like Aunt Josephine, and like Martha's father. *The Quarry Wood* is (amongst other things) one of the most insightful and truthful account of the development of a woman it has been my pleasure to read.

The other novels, *The Weatherhouse* and *A Pass in the Grampians* deal with similar themes, centred around the development of a young girl. In the latter, it develops into a tremendous battle for the soul of the heroine, Jennifer, whose individuality, strength of character and vitality enables her in the end to choose what is valuable from the sources attempting to influence her, but still to keep to her own light. She has 'glimpsed now the wild, lonely stormy things that stir and pass', and must live now 'not for the anticipated certainty—ploughing, seed-time, harrowing and harvest—but for the incredible fugitive approaches of an order whose laws she may not fathom.' (p 243) The novel also deals with the conflict of changing times and, like *Sunset Song*, the establishment of a new order. The central insight of the novel is contained in the symbolism of the title: the pass is the way out into the world, but it is equally a way back. The reciprocity is crucial. Of course, it also signifies a crisis. *The Weatherhouse*, while in some ways too diversified a work, best illustrates Shepherd's ability to capture the range and depth of Scots character, in this case especially of older women. Her grasp of dialogue, particularly in Scots, shows a keen ear for the rhythms and turns of Scots speech. Why there were no more novels from Shepherd's pen is beyond the scope of this essay, but in those lying out of print, there is a treasurehouse awaiting discovery.

The space available here forces me to be highly selective, to ignore writers whose work is currently in print and recognised. With the emphasis on poetry here, it is not possible to deal with novels like Jane Duncan's Reachfar books, Catherine Carswell's highly idiosyncratic Lawrentian novels, Nancy Brysson Morrison, Margaret Thomson Davis, Catherine Gavin, Margaret Hamilton, Dot Allan and Moira Burgess's Glasgow novels, and the historical novels of Dorothy Dunnett, at least some of which will be considered elsewhere in this volume. The contribution of women in shorter fiction also requires examination: the short stories of Elspeth Davie, Jessie Kesson, Dorothy K Haynes, Una Flett, Deirdre Chapman, Eona Macnicol and others.

Within drama, attention should be directed to Ada F Kay, author of *The Man From Thermopylae*, to the work of Joan Ure, whose *oeuvre* includes prose and poetry, and the major talent of Ena Lamont Stewart, whose play, *Men Should Weep*, recently published and performed by 7:84 Theatre Company (Scotland), was among the first attempts in Scottish drama to portray working class life as it was, and certainly the first to do this from a woman's point of view. The discouragement of neglect prevented Ena Lamont Stewart from persisting in her writing, and deprived us of what might have become a major dramatic voice.

To return finally to my main theme, poetry, something must be said about more recent times. My period ends with 1975, at a time when new voices of women both young and old were just beginning to emerge. From the older generation, we have poets like Janet Caird, who is also a fine novelist and short story-writer, but whose poetry is perhaps her most notable achievement. Her two volumes, *Some Walk a Narrow Path* and *A Distant Urn* testify to a talent still developing and becoming more confident. Her grasp of form, the employment of *le mot juste*, her precise placing of image and symbol, can rarely be faulted. She handles extended metaphor with relaxed ease, her nature poems reverberate with symbolic significance, but the poet's touch has a gentleness and intimacy seldom visible in the work of a male poet.

Also just emerging at the end of this period are poets Liz Lochhead and Tessa Ransford, two very different figures, Lochhead's *Memo For Spring* was a great success, but the poems tend to be preoccupied with the problems of adolescence, and to provide verbal cameos of life. Strongly influenced by American writing, Lochhead's poems explore the possibilities inherent in everyday speech, particularly in colloquial slang, and probe into those areas of intimate detail which we often prefer to leave unexplored. Her later work takes her into drama, where her preoccupation with everyday speech has scope for development, and into the writing and performing of entertaining monologues of everyday life. Her later poetry explores the realms of mythology and social mores, and recent achievements in drama include a highly acclaimed translation of Moliere's *Tartuffe*. Ransford's poetry is concerned to explore the possibilities inherent in traditional forms. Like Kathleen Raine's, Ransford's poetry has a highly metaphysical bias, her themes the world of religion and the spirit. She is also fundamentally concerned with the realities of life, in particular to deal with the nature of woman's experience. The outstanding quality in Ransford's work is its ambitious treatment of highly intellectual themes.

Many other women are beginning to emerge as poets and writers: Jenny Robertson, Valerie Gillies, Gaelic writers Catriona and Morag Montgomery, Ellie MacDonald, Joy Pitman, Mary Gladstone, Kathleen Jamie and playwrights Marcella Evaristi, Rona Munro, novelist Ros Brackenbury, a recent comer to Scotland, and too many others to name. In the hands of these writers, women's writing in Scotland is certainly no longer preoccupied with rural or small town existence. Almost all the writers mentioned are united by an ability to transcend restrictions of sex and class in the writing and an anxiety to do more than simply accept and replicate judgements and ideas from male writing, or from time past. As women come gradually to take their full place in the world, and gather the confidence to feel that all experience is open to them, the limitations we have seen operating in some of the writers dealt with here will gradually vanish. It is certainly true that fate and a male chauvinist society, and the habit of women to devalue their own importance creatively has deprived us of possibly several major women writers, and that the restriction of the female voice in Scotland is a just source of sorrow and disappointment. But even when, as with Willa Muir, Nan Shepherd and Ena Lamont Stewart, their experience has not been conducive to the production of a substantial corpus of work, their output, limited though it may be, is important both historically and critically, and we must not be content with the critical evaluation of the past which has tended to dismiss or ignore them. Their work must be re-evaluated, and pressure put on critics (still largely male) to do more than simply perpetuate the critical opinion of the past, bearing in mind that they are to some extent still the ones with the power to decide such matters as which novels merit republication and which do not.

The nest of singing birds now harbours quite a diverse throng, and sufficient momentum is beginning to be generated to ensure that their songs will not continue to fade unheard into the silence of obscurity.

NOTES

1   Joy Hendry, 'The Double Knot in the Peeny', in *In Other Words: Writing as a Feminist* Gail Chester and Sigrid Nielsen (eds) (London, 1987).
2   W R Aitken, *Scottish Literature in English and Scots*, American Literature, English Literature and World Literatures in English, Information Guide Series, Vol 37 (Michigan, 1982), pp 210, 244.
3   Alan Bold, *Modern Scottish Literature* (London, 1983), pp 59, 60.
4   Maurice Lindsay, 'Scottish Poetry in the Forties', in *Akros*, Vol 10, No 28 (Preston, 1975), pp 36–53 (p 39).
5   Janet Caird, 'The Poetry of Violet Jacob and Helen B Cruickshank, *Cencrastus* 19 (Edinburgh, 1984), pp 32–4 (p 34).
6   Helen B Cruickshank, *Octobiography* (Montrose, 1976) p 135.
7   Helen B Cruickshank, *Octobiography*, op.cit., p 14.
8   Janet Caird, *Cencrastus*, op.cit., p 33.
9   Ronald Garden, introduction to *The Lum Hat and Other Stories*, (Aberdeen, 1982), p xvi.
10 Marion Lochhead, 'Feminine Quartet', *Chapman* 27–8, *Woven by Women*, Vol VI No 3-4 (Edinburgh, 1980), pp 24, 25.
11 John Buchan, vide Ronald Garden, op.cit., p xvi.
12 Hugh MacDiarmid, *Contemporary Scottish Studies* (Edinburgh, 1976), p 9–10.
13 Helen B Cruickshank, *Octobiography*, op.cit., p 76, p 135.

14 Hugh MacDiarmid, quoted by G Gordon Wright, in Preface to *More Collected Poems*, Helen B Cruickshank (Edinburgh, 1978).
15 Nancy K Gish, Chapman 27–8, op. cit., pp 120.
16 Lewis Grassic Gibbon. *A Scots Hairst: Essays and Short Stories*, Ian S Munro (ed) (London, 1967), pp 151–2.
17 Hugh MacDiarmid, *Contemporary Scottish Studies*, op.cit., pp 49–50.
18 Willa Muir, *Belonging* (London, 1968), p 163.

FURTHER READING

Angus, Marion, *Sun and Candlelight* (Edinburgh, 1927)
—— *The Singin' Lass* (Edinburgh, 1929)
—— *The Turn of the Day* (Edinburgh, 1931)
Bone, Kate, *Thistle By-Blaws* (West Linton, 1971): (the other volumes give no other
    publication details)
Caird, Janet, *Some Walk a Narrow Path* (Edinburgh, 1977)
—— *A Distant Urn* (Edinburgh, 1983)
Cruickshank, Helen B, *Collected Poems* (Edinburgh, 1971)
Fraser, Olive, *The Pure Account* (Aberdeen, 1981)
Garry, Flora, *Bennygoak and Other Poems* (Preston, 1974)
Hall, Agnes, *Who Will Open Instead* (Dunfermline, 1954)
Jacob, Violet, *The Sheep Stealers* (London, 1902)
—— *The Interloper* (London, 1904)
—— *The History of Aythan Waring* (London, 1908)
—— *Flemington* (London, 1911)
—— *The Lum Hat and Other Stories, Last Tales of Violet Jacob* Ronald Garden
    (ed) (Aberdeen, 1982)
Kay, Ada F, *The Man From Thermopylae* (Glasgow, 1981)
Kesson, Jessie, *The White Bird Passes* (Edinburgh, 1980)
Lochhead, Liz, *Memo for Spring* (Edinburgh, 1972)
MacArthur, Bessie J B (Edinburgh, 1939)
Mitchison, Naomi, *The Cleansing of the Knife* (Edinburgh, 1978)
—— *The Corn King and the Spring Queen* (London, 1983)
—— *The Bull Calves* (Glasgow, 1985)
Muir, Willa, *Mrs Ritchie* (London, 1933)
—— *Imagined Corners* (London, 1936)
—— *Mrs Grundy in Scotland* (London, 1936)
—— *Living with Ballads* (London, 1965)
—— *Belonging: A Memoir* (London, 1968)
Shepherd, Nan, *The Quarry Wood* (London, 1928)
—— *The Weatherhouse* (London, 1930)
—— *A Pass in the Grampians* (London, 1933)
Stewart, Ena Lamont, *Men Should Weep* (Edinburgh, 1985)
Stuart, Alice V, *The Far Calling* (London, 1944)
—— *The Dark Tarn* (Oxford, 1953)
—— *The Unquiet Tide* (Edinburgh, 1971)
Stuart, Muriel, *The Cockpit of Idols* (London, 1918)
—— *Poems* (London, 1922)
Wood, Wendy, *Astronauts and Tinklers* (Edinburgh, 1985)

Chapter 20

Internationalising Scottish Poetry

RODERICK WATSON

'Scotland small? Our multiform, our infinite Scotland *small?*'

The modern Scottish Renaissance declared an international outlook from the very start when MacDiarmid's *Chapbook Programme* set out in 1922 to 'bring Scottish Literature into closer touch with current European tendencies in technique and ideation', The theme was developed the following year with 'A Theory of Scots Letters', and the movement's international aspirations have been cited ever since to refute those who would maintain that its more obviously Scottish concerns must be merely parochial when set against the revolution which this century has seen in the contemporary arts of Europe and America.

In fact it was characteristic of many writers of this period to find or to seek universal truths in the most specifically local features of their own background or upbringing. Thus, for example, Joyce's *Ulysses* presented a microcosm of all human life, art and history in the mundane and grubby details of Dublin streets: William Carlos Williams sought the same for his home town of Paterson, while MacDiarmid hoped for a glimpse of 'timeless flame' and its 'eternal mood' in Auchtermuchty and Ecclefechan. In this sense a redefinition and a vindication of 'provincialism' was a notable motif in early modern literature, and although by no means simply a matter of regional or national pride, Scottish writers have been particularly active in this field with an extraordinary diversity of voices ranging from Neil Gunn to Alasdair Gray, from George Mackay Brown to Tom Leonard. This essay will look at the 'second generation' of Scottish poets who were born between 1900 and 1930, and how they tackled matters of personal, national and international awareness in their work in English.

If the Scottish literary renaissance rose from the aftermath of the First World War, there can be little doubt that the Depression years and the Second World War were equally formative experiences for many of the older 'second generation' writers.[1] Thus the last section of Sidney Goodsir Smith's collection *The Deevil's Waltz* (1946), visualised the whole world in the grip of some ghastly halloween dance whose evolutions swung hundreds of souls from the frozen gloom of arctic convoys to war in the heat of the desert. Indeed, the North African campaign saw an extraordinary concentration of Scottish poets, and at one time or another this theatre was visited by Sorley Maclean, George Campbell Hay, Hamish Henderson, Robert Garioch, G S Fraser and Edwin Morgan. Their sense of being Scots was not swallowed up in the larger conflict of world war, and indeed such awareness is often the indirect theme of many poems from this period.

The passionate verses in Sorley Maclean's *Dain do Eimhir* testify to his indignation at the suffering of the poor and the oppressed coupled with fears about the rise of Franco in Spain. The poems are suffused with an intense questioning about whether such political commitments can ever be balanced against more personal and intimate demands. Maclean went on to serve in the North African campaign, and some of the best poems from the Second World War were written by him in Gaelic. No-one could hate fascism more, and yet what Maclean found in the desert was the democracy of death in 'taghadh', a grim Calvinist 'election' which spelled out a moral that was more existential than political. (*See* 'Latha Foghair'/'An Autumn Day'.) More than that, the Second World War became a mirror which threw light on his own roots and the nature of his own culture at home, so that 'Curai-dhean'/'Heroes', for example, is as much an examination of traditional Highland pride and the ambiguities of heroism on either side, as it is a recognition of how modern wars are fought.

This reflective response was shared by many of the Scottish poets who found themselves in action. Hamish Henderson, as fierce a socialist as Maclean, made the most active political and personal commitment to the overthrow of fascism, but in the end this is not what his war poetry is about. Instead he wrote *Elegies for the Dead in Cyrenaica*, poems for all the working men, German, English, Scottish, Italian, who found themselves dying among the rocks on behalf of systems over which they had no effective control. Henderson's scepticism is less ironical than Maclean's, however, and he does not hesitate to call up the old Highland war-cries and the vaunting of traditional Gaelic Brosnachadh, 'incitement' poems: 'Sons of the hounds/come here and get flesh. Search, Bite!' ('Fifth Elegy'). Yet the two poets still have reservations in common. They both come, after all, from a culture which has a long tradition of military recruitment for foreign wars, and an equally telling tradition of absentee landlords, land clearances and broken promises. Death may be dealt out by the vagaries of fate, but Henderson is still disturbed by the easy assumptions of those in command, 'born to command', whose inheritance is to handle the cards and choose the game:

> On one point however there is unanimity: their sacrifice
> though hard and heroic was on the whole 'necessary'.
> I too have acquiesced
> in this evasion: that the unlucky
> or the destined must inevitably fail
> and be impaled on the basalt pinnacles of darkness.

> Yet how can I shame them, saying that they
> have died for us: that it was expedient
> a generation should die for the people?
>
> ('Sixth Elegy')

Such scepticism is very much the prevailing spirit of Robert Garioch's poetry, and although he wrote few verses directly about the desert campaign, his autobiography as a prisoner of war, *Two Men and a Blanket*, makes it clear that the experience was central to his way of viewing the world. He has spoken on behalf of humble troops and the powerless—Henderson's 'swaddies'—ever since. There were others who would not add to such suffering at any cost, and Norman MacCaig became a conscientious objector, while Douglas Young refused to serve for political reasons to do with Scotland's sovereignty. Both learned, not without cost, what it was to swim against the tide.

George Campbell Hay saw Bizerta in flames only to make a deep identification with Arab culture and its traditional values which, like his own, had so little to do with the pace of modernity and materialistic goals. A bitter vision of how the war played midwife to a different sense of international brotherhood can be found in his polyglot poem from 1947, 'Esta Selva Selvaggia', ('this savage wood', from Canto I of Dante's *Inferno*.)

> The swaying landmines lingering down
> between Duntocher and the moon,
> made Scotland and the world one.
> At last we found a civilisation
> common to Europe and our nation
> sirens, blast, disintegration.[2]

Written in English, the poem uses Arabic, French, German, Greek and Italian as if in snatches of conversation picked up from the '*perduta gente* of this world'—the lost ordinary folk, trampled, tortured and exploited, who swear that 'only the great make wars', and then reveal an enduring racism in themselves when they speak of different peoples and religions.

Although not written from personal experience (he was 17 when the war ended), James Burns Singer's long poem 'The Transparent Prisoner' (1957), is a most moving evocation of suffering and inner courage. Written from the point of view of a captured soldier sent to slave labour in a Nazi coal mine, the poet comes to an ambiguously mystical experience of tender innocence and the 'transparency' of all being. These intimations return to haunt him in later years, after he has killed a guard and escaped to a freedom which has left him strangely empty. Burns Singer was brought up in Scotland, but as an American citizen with a Polish-Jewish father and a Scottish-Norwegian mother, it seems likely that his own feelings about his identity and allegiances helped to make 'The Transparent Prisoner' an imaginative *tour de force* on behalf of all those who disappeared into the concentration camps or the Gulags of a post-war world.

Not all responses dealt directly with the battlefield. Ruthven Todd's first substantial collection, *Until Now* (1942), stands witness to a general apprehension shared by many in late 1930s Britain. Todd was born and brought up in Scotland, and although he moved to London as an adult, and returned to America at the end of the war (he was of American parentage), his early work was undoubtedly influenced by the landscape and the weather of the North. In poems such as 'Northward the Islands' and 'In September 1937', he evokes 'the otter trapped beside the burn', or the island of Mull where 'the hills/Were brown lions, crouched to meet the autumn gales', as images of value. These become a touchstone for what the poet can believe in, and yet they also belong to an atmosphere of dread, violence, and uneasy beauty:

> In the hard rain and the rip of thunder,
> I remembered the haze coming in from the sea
> And the clatter of Gaelic voices by the breakwater,
> Or in the fields as the reapers took their tea;
> I remembered the cast foal lying where it died,
> Which we buried, one evening, above high tide:
>
> And the three rams that smashed the fank-gate,
> Running loose for five days on the moor
> Before we could catch them,—far too late . . .
> In September, I saw the drab newsposters
> Telling of wars, in Spain and in the East,
> And wished I'd stayed on Mull . . .
>
> ('In September 1937')

The poet's distaste for fascism and his sympathies with Spain and China may be understated, but they are no less effectively present in the tension of such lines.

'Personal History: For My Son', and 'An Autobiography', speak for Todd's ironic recognition of how his personal background might relate to the broader forces of history. He recognises, however, that 'I cannot return/To scythe the corn or build a stack'; for while 'the islands stay the same', 'the difference has grown in me' ('Northward the Islands'). This leaves him resenting 'the imminence of the future', especially when such a future presages global war. As the poems in this collection unfold—they are dated from 1938 to 1941—there is a sense of increasing desperation. Hence, at 26, 'Nostalgic for a world I never knew' ('Elegy'), Todd produced notably powerful poems of dread and rage. Such pressure seems to have released in him a fountain of ambivalent feelings for the historical processes which have somehow brought the world to such a pass–including the 'Scottishness' of his own upbringing. 'I was born in this city of grey stone and bitter wind,/Of tenements sooted up with lying history':

> In Charlotte Square let me hear Sir Walter Scott droning,
> Drivelling a dream of history, and let me meet Burns,
> Outside the Tron Bar, drunk with disgust as much as whisky.

Todd's position has something in common with Edwin Muir's in 'Scotland 1941', but the younger poet is driven by a more general and apocalyptic disgust. He visualises himself walking 'among the cities of the weeping world':

> [I] stumble among the ruins of Madrid and lean on the framework
> That once was Warsaw, look at Oslo and Copenhagen,
> And at that latest city, Paris, where dreams are tough as steel.
>
> ('In Edinburgh, 1940')

Although not directly connected with the poets of the 'New Apocalypse', the scarcely focussed rage of Ruthven Todd's feelings at this time, reveals much, I think, about the social and historical roots of that movement. And in specific 'war' poems such as 'During an Air Raid' (set in London) or 'Imagination', his imagery moves into an overtly Apocalyptic, and sometimes overblown intensity: 'The eagle's talons, today's tattered token,/Tear tomorrow; and thunder is the trampling/Of the pedestrian past . . . The dove of your love will never return/To the proud past . . .' Finding the same sense of confusion, pain and rage in Picasso's *Guernica* and Kafka's prose, Todd wrote sonnets about them. He evoked the work of Joan Miro, Paul Klee and de' Chirico as emblems of what was at risk in war-torn times, even as his sonnets reinterpreted their painterly images as prophetic of terror and destruction. In looking for fellow spirits in the past, he found Blake, Fuseli, Melville and Rimbaud—all conceived as being in sympathy with his own feeling for the violence of the times, best conveyed through the intensities of expressionistic distortion, abstraction and surrealism. Faced with the rise of fascism, this particular Scottish poet drew on the resources and the implications of artistic modernism to speak for what he valued and what was under threat.

Not all were so inclined to the *avant garde*, for G S Fraser's poetry from the 1940s reveals a neo-classical perspective on life. Despite being the theorist of the New Apocalypse and greatly enthusiastic about his young fellow writers in that group, Fraser's own verse is markedly conventional in technique. Indeed, he valued what he saw as an Horatian balance in both art and life, which he conveyed with his self-deprecating tone and a charitable eye for human folly. Entirely aware of his Scottish roots (he was born in Glasgow, graduated from St Andrews and began his career as a journalist in Aberdeen), Fraser did not lay claim to the tortured heather-stems of a Hugh Mac-Diarmid:

> Since Poverty for me has never sharpened
> Her single tooth, and since Adversity
> So far has failed to jab me with her hair-pin
> I marvel who my Scottish Muse can be.
>
> I am Convention's child, the cub reporter,
> The sleek, the smooth, conservatively poised:
> Abandoned long ago by Beauty's daughter;
> Tamed like a broncho, and commercialised!
>
> ('To Hugh MacDiarmid')

From such a wry point of view, self-innoculated against pretension, Fraser's poems from the war period begin to establish their own kind of political integrity. He speaks as an observer (he was posted to Cairo and Eritrea as a staff writer for the Ministry of Information), and some of his best poems take the form of epistles home—nostalgic, decent, reflective, charitable, sometimes weary, and always wary of the assured rigidities of ambition, ideology and absolutism which might be said to have brought the world to such a pass. In 'Exile's Letter' he chose a metaphor of exile to convey a 'whole age . . . exiled from the realities', only to conclude that the old have always been exiled from the young, just as he, himself, was now exiled from 'Scotland's winter sleets' and 'the studious boy/With books and gardens for his toy'. His conclusion is entirely different from Ruthven Todd's rage against the past and a Scottish inheritance seemingly thirled to tartan when Europe was in flames. Fraser's style is more modest, and typically generous—'So exiled from ourselves we live/And yet can learn to forgive/The past that promised us so much . . . ' ('Exile's Letter').

The poets of the New Apocalypse movement, associated with three anthologies edited by J F Hendry and Henry Treece,[3] were less quick to forgive the past. Espousing a 'liberation of feelings that are breaking down the old social fabric', Hendry conceived a fluid combination of Freudianism, Marxism, proto-feminism and surrealism under the conviction that 'social palliatives are useless until the psychological factors are treated correctly'. In this essay for *Poetry Scotland* in 1945, Hendry also cited D H Lawrence's late study *Apocalypse* (1931), as a key document for the Apocalyptics, because of its emphasis on mystery, power, and a projection of the spirit towards organic unity between self and universe. The Dionysian, Nietzschean drift of this rather foggy case is evident enough, but it contained a species of political impetus too, in that it visualised a transformation of the masses through internal psychological revolution, and a triumph of the power of symbols over capitalism and industrial society. The movement conceived itself in international terms, and J F Hendry called up Rimbaud, Appollinaire and Mayakovsky as forerunners, if only to conclude that the Celtic nations might be particularly potent in such a field, because they have always stood for spiritual values against 'the intolerable tyranny of industrialism, commerce, and generally mechanically imposed order.'

This latter view of the Celtic ethos, with parallel cases pursued along different lines by MacDiarmid, Maclean and Hay, has turned out to be lastingly influential in how Scottish culture has come to define itself in modern times. Certainly Scots were prominent enough among the Apocalyptics, with theory from G S Fraser and the art critic Robert Melville, and poems from Hendry himself, Tom Scott and the young Norman MacCaig. Hendry noted a sympathetic voice in the early work of Maurice Lindsay and W S Graham, and claimed connections, too, with A S Neill's radical thoughts on education.

Hendry ended the *Poetry Scotland* essay by quoting from Yeats's 'The Second Coming'. If the great Irish poet could see only nihilism and despair in 'the blood-dimmed tide' which had been loosed upon the world, then that was a challenge to the new Apocalyptics to find 'inspiration and revelation' there as well. It was quite a challenge, and a number of the more personal poems from the movement show a sense of strain and impending disaster, as if the poets feared that the slightest relaxation would leave them to drown in that tide of gore.[4] So it is that many poems from this period ripple and jump with a kind of excessive muscular effort, as if they were attempting to justify a personal or a symbolic vision in such crisis-ridden times by the saving injection of huge doses of creative energy into absolutely every image and every line.

> Now as Street-walker and Fascist mount their sullen guard
> Over my love's face, her cheeks are Athen's seawards
> Tumbling pillars through the error of dissolute rains.
> Dereliction of Duty stands in the Dock of Europe's ruins.
> How can I kiss away convulsions in this Grave?
>
> (J F Hendry, 'Fifes')

The Apocalyptics were not a popular nor a long-lived movement in modern verse. J F Hendry began to travel abroad as a translator and published little further poetry until the appearance of *Marimarusa* in 1978, and *A World Alien* two years later; Norman MacCaig renounced his early work and has never republished anything from his first two collections; Tom Scott turned to Lallans and then to English again with his 'Polysemous Veritism' (akin to MacDiarmid's 'Poetry of Fact') in *The Tree*, an epic poem from 1977. Nevertheless, a number of the poets who came to maturity during the 1940s and 1950s did have early ground in common with the New Apocalypse (it was an expression of their times, after all), and so the movement was not quite the literary dead-end it is often assumed to have been. At the very least it was part of a wider post-war exploration of what poetry might be and what it was good for. This had particular force in Scotland where the issues involved a host of different factors, from the Romantic obscurities of the Apocalyptics to the case for Lallans; from Gaelic to MacDiarmid's modernism; from nationalism to verse with a socialist conscience.

These issues and their various proponents were well represented in two of the most influential and outward-looking annual publications of the time, namely *Scottish Art and Letters*, edited by R Crombie Saunders, which ran to five issues from 1944 until 1950, and the three excellent *Poetry Scotland* volumes edited by Maurice Lindsay between 1943 and 1946. (A fourth and final volume appeared from Serif Books with MacDiarmid as guest editor in 1949.) Both magazines were produced by William Maclellan of Hope Street, Glasgow, a publisher who made an enormous contribution to Scottish culture during the 1940s and 1950s, not least with books such as *Dain do Eimhir* and 16 volumes of verse by various writers in the 'Poetry Scotland' series.

It is clear from these periodicals that there was a rising and often contradictory debate about what being 'a Scottish poet' might be taken to mean. Maurice Lindsay included Welsh and Irish writers in *Poetry Scotland, 1*, and was criticised for it by Compton Mackenzie. In the same issue MacDiarmid held that the natural language for a Scottish poet is either Scots or Gaelic, and yet Lindsay's 1946 editorial made a plea for excellence in *any* language, including a Scottish 'English with a difference'—as opposed to those Lallans activists who would prefer to employ positive discrimination even for mediocre work in Scots.

Scottish Arts and Letters, 5 (a special number on the 1950 PEN International Congress held in Edinburgh), featured MacDiarmid on 'The Quality of Scots Internationalism', and J F Hendry on 'Dunbar the European'. In the same issue the editor (MacDiarmid again) criticised PEN for being a tool of the UN and insufficiently radical in its understanding of literary freedom. In *Scottish Journal* MacDiarmid recommended Eluard, Montale and Nazhim Hikmet to his fellow Scots, for they 'could be far more profitably read than the English poets who virtually have the field to themselves,' and yet in an earlier review of J F Hendry's poems, he accused the Apocalyptics of being like most new movements in English literature, namely, 'rigged up in the cast-off garments of French and other European experimentalists of some thirty years earlier'.[5] 'Scottishness' and 'internationalism', for MacDiarmid, were inseparably anti-English and left wing.

George Campbell Hay's thoughtful essays on 'Poetry in the World or out of it?',[6] came to the conclusion that high culture is not the prerogative of an intellectual elite, nor a monied class, for it can be shown to thrive among all ordinary people if they are given leisure and sympathetic social conditions. He cited the culture of Lewis and Iceland as examples, without noting that in such cases, the sheer isolation of these islands must have played an equally crucial part in the formula.

Scottish poets have continued to argue about such issues (and variations upon them), to the present day—a daunting enough thought, perhaps. What the debate shows, nevertheless, is that the existence of the Scottish Renaissance as an argued and arguable *programme* has instilled in many writers the conviction that questions of personal, national, and creative identity must be confronted as a matter of theoretical priority. There have been plenty sterile disputes, but a high degree of politico-cultural awareness exists among many Scottish writers, along with a willingness to find common ground with their peers (and most especially, perhaps, with cultural and linguistic minorities), all over the world.

Which brings us to the discussion of particular poets and how some of them have dealt with this inheritance.

As editor, poet and broadcaster, Maurice Lindsay did a great deal to promote the concept of a renaissance in all three of Scotland's languages during the period under discussion. After early experiments with Scots rhyme he has settled for an English voice which is not notably Northern in its inflection or its habits of expression. Like G S Fraser, Lindsay's technically conservative verse-forms are firmly linked to a neo-classical outlook which speaks (less inwardly wry and insecure than Fraser) on behalf of good humoured social satire and cultured common sense. This makes him something of a *rara avis* among Scottish poets—resolutely resistant to the throes of modernism, he walks the fragmented contemporary streets with an eighteenth-century sense of balance.

George Bruce has taken a starker view, more in line with the bleaker coasts of the North East and a Presbyterian upbringing in Fraserburgh. He has noted that it was the war's 'explicit outrage on human dignity' which brought him to the core of his early verse, as he looked to the fishing community around him in the attempt to understand how life can be lived 'on a minimal basis'. While Bruce could not identify with 'an apparently unreasonable belief in a personal God', he still found that the circumstances of his birthplace offered him a correlative for his own philosophical (even theological) sense that 'human life is precariously placed between light and dark'.[7] Bruce acknowledged the technical influence of Ezra Pound (notably *Hugh Selwyn Mauberley*), but the absolute bareness of his own free verse is unmistakeably Scottish. His lines speak for a world made almost entirely static by irreducible statement and inescapable facticity, yet there are also hints of a saving faith, not least in the value of common affection, as his work develops. Bruce's essential vision is general and existential, even if its terms usually derive from a specifically local imagery of place—family history, rain, shells, stones, journeys and remembered deaths.In one sense or another, he believes that we have always been coastal dwellers:

> Of Balbec and Finistère Proust wrote—
> The oldest bone in the earth's skeleton,
> The land's end of France, Europe, of the Old World,
> The ultimate encampment of fishermen
> Who since the beginning faced
> The everlasting kingdom of fog,
> Of shadows of the night.
> ('Sea Talk')

Among Scottish poets it is George Mackay Brown who has most consistently used the details of his domestic scene as a metaphorical language of universal import. The principle was early identified by Edwin Muir, remembering his own boyhood on the little island of Wyre, which became 'a universal landscape over which Abraham and Moses and Achilles and Ulysses and Tristram and all sorts of pilgrims passed; and Troy was associated with the Castle, a mere green mound, beside my father's house', (*An Autobiography*, Chapter 8). Mackay Brown's view is less mythopoeic and more closely tied to the specifics of Orkney's social history. His poems, nevertheless, still move towards ideal and undoubtedly metaphysical conclusions. This is particularly marked in the first major collection from the mid 1950s, in which many of his poems seem to offer a modified apocalyptic intensity—'an undersong of terrible holy joy'—on themes of 'Bread and Breath', 'the salty cobbles of a grief' and that 'funnel of darkness, roaring with stars.' ('The Old Women' and 'The Shining Ones'.) Thus 'Hamnavoe' irradiates the little town of its title in the kind of universal celebratory light so often evoked by Dylan Thomas: 'Blessings and soup plates circled. Euclidian light/Ruled the town in segments of blue and gray.' The poem 'December Day, Hoy Sound' offers us the sea, who 'grinds his salt behind a riot of masks'; or the wave who 'will weep like a widow on the rock,/Or howl like Lear, or laugh like a green child.' There are many such lines in *Loaves and Fishes*, and they are characteristic of the apocalyptic impulse to animate the world by sheer effort of imagination, as if the renewal of our sensibilities by such image-making power might lead to the redemption of everything else as well.

Given the Orkney poet's distrust of modernism and of all things to do with the contemporary world, it is ironic that his early work should share millenarian and visionary impulses with a group such as the Apocalyptics. Yet both begin with a sense of dread at modern times, and both hold that impending social and personal disintegration can only be overcome through a revolution from within. For a short-lived and hectic period the Apocalyptics had sought an answer in the forcing house of the imagination and its surreal connections; Mackay Brown's humbler and less grandiose nature, on the other hand, was to lead him towards religious conversion and the Catholic church.

The diction of Brown's next collection was closer to statement (rather like George Bruce's lines, except less stark), as he made witty and timeless music out of the ordinary names and doings of his islanders: 'Rognvald who stalks round Corse with his stick/I do not love./His dog has a loud sharp mouth./The wood of his door is very hard.' ('Ikey on the People of Hellya'.) By now the everyday rituals of island farming and fishing had come to have a sacramental force for Mackay Brown—deeply associated with his own Catholicism—and he expressed his vision of this simple life in bare and poised language, as if the stability of Christian symbology has come to offer a calmer and less frenetic assurance to the creative self.

Norman MacCaig made the same shift towards a quieter and less energised diction. Even so, his disclaimed Apocalyptic work still shows evidence of the poet to come, with a special delight in the given world of landscape and animals, and an awareness of his complex relationship to them as creator/ observer: 'The Graces and the planets and everything/that goes lucky and beautiful in numbers/have a high feather and a bold song./And there's a song here fluttered in rivers/that never halts on a weary foot/or flags in courage or wants wit.' ('Quadrilles–Jig Time'.) In MacCaig's case the Romantically affirmative and potentially religious impulse of such celebration was soon under the control of a sceptical, practical and classically inclined sensibility. Nevertheless, a 'metaphysical' habit of mind survived the gulf which lies between *The Inward Eye* and *Riding Lights* from nine years later. The verses in the latter collection speak more plainly of MacCaig's everyday experience between the streets of Edinburgh and his beloved Western Highlands, but they are always 'poems *in* a landscape', rather than 'landscape poems'.

Ruthven Todd accepted that he could not 'return to scythe the corn or build a stack', because although 'the islands stay the same', 'the difference has grown in me'. (As Lewismen, exiled in effect from the society in which they were raised, Iain Crichton Smith and Derick Thomson have felt the pains of such separation with literal force.) George Mackay Brown, on the other hand, opted to stay with 'scythe' and 'stack', and committed his work to the re-creation of his belief in an original prelapsarian unity between 'me' and 'the islands'. Norman MacCaig's point of view was more philosophical from the start, and much of his work stems from a witty and chary recognition of the epistemological 'difference' that must *always* be present between the world and those who write about it: 'Trees and stars and stones/Are falsely these and true comparisons/Whose likeness are the observer. He/Stares, in the end, at his own face . . .' ('By Comparison'.) Yet MacCaig is no solipsist, for although his best work has been consistently reflective, it is still bound in an unsentimentally life-affirming way to the minutiae of the everyday world. The move towards free verse (which was completed with *Surroundings* in 1966), has led to some remarkably powerful later poems whose terseness has given a new edge to this writer's darker insights into human pain and loss.

MacCaig's 'metaphysical' vein became the chief territory of W S Graham's mature work, although the poet's first two collections embraced an apocalyptic mode of obscure but rhapsodic celebration—full of synaesthesia and transferred epithets—which was more than reminiscent of Dylan Thomas or Gerard Manley Hopkins. With *The White Threshold* (1949) and *The Nightfishing* (1955), however, Graham's style began to clarify, perhaps under the influence of his admired Joyce, a writer less prone to visionary ferment. In these volumes the prevailing images were chosen from coast and sea, as if 'nightfishing' were symbolic of what all writers must pursue, expressed in an extended allegory of hard graft with the herring fleet. Graham had found his most consistent theme, as he came to explore how his art and his own sense of self are inextricably linked and 'named . . . to the bone'—created and re-created—from no more than an assemblage of autobiographical images and the mysteriously autonomous marks of pen on paper.

Living many years in Cornwall and an admirer of Joyce, Beckett, Pound, Eliot and Marianne Moore, Graham did not consider his work to be 'characteristic of Scots poetry', although he did 'recognise a Scots timbre in [his] 'voice''. A tone of intellectual density and passionate incantation may well relate to this timbre, along with an admitted 'fondness for Anglo-Saxon and Scandinavian roots, also for translations of early Jewish and Scottish Gaelic verse.'[8]

> Burned in this element
> To the bare bone, I am
> Trusted on the language.
> I am to walk to you
> Through the night and through
> Each word you make between
> Each word I burn bright in
> On this wide reach . . .
>
> Younger in the towered
> Tenement of night he heard
> The shipyards with nightshifts
> Of lathes turning their shafts . . .

Then in a welding flash
He found his poetry arm
And turned the coat of his trade.
From where I am I hear
Clearly his heart beat over
Clydeside's far hammers
And the nightshipping firth.
What's he to me? Only
Myself I died from into
These present words that move.

('Letter II')

In fact a number of such pieces from the 1949 volume, including 'Three Letters', 'The Children of Greenock' and 'The Children of Lanarkshire', show a direct concern with his Scottish origins. Twenty-eight years later, the same autobiographical impulse led to fine poems such as 'Loch Thom', 'Greenock at Night I Find You' and an outstandingly moving elegy for his father, 'To Alexander Graham'.

Graham's rather abstruse voice must have seemed out of phase with the prevailing urbanity of 'the Movement' and other English poetry of the 1950s, and it was to be 15 years before he produced another collection. His style became barer and still clearer as he moved towards what I believe to be his finest work. With the appearance of *Malcolm Mooney's Land* (1970) and *Implements in their Places* (1977), it is as if a general awareness of structuralist theory among British readers had at last prepared them for what had always fascinated Graham, just as the evolution of such concepts may have helped the poet himself towards a new clarity.

These two collections contain some of modern literature in English's most engaging explorations of the elusive nature of saying, making, and meaning. Poems such as 'Malcolm Mooney's Land', 'The Constructed Space', 'Approaches to How They Behave' and 'What is the Language Using Us for?' meditate on how words are spun out of darkness (or the arctic-white page) as we go along—a fascination shared by Joyce, Beckett, Wallace Stevens, John Ashbery and other writers whose imaginations have been in tune with contemporary insights into how language works and significances accumulate: 'Speaking is difficult and one tries/To be exact and yet not to/Exact the prime intention to death./On the other hand the appearance of things/Must not be made to mean another/Thing. It is a kind of triumph/To see them and put them down/As what they are.' ('Approaches to How They Behave'.) In fact the poet does speak more plainly of his life and friends and everyday moments in many of these verses, often with great poignancy–an effect which the effortfulness of the earlier work could not achieve.

Graham's creative awareness of poetics is to be valued among Scottish writers, for he sometimes seems to have been under-rated and rather neglected. Among his near contemporaries, only Edwin Morgan, Ian Hamilton Finlay and Iain Crichton Smith have shown a similar sensitivity to postmodernist changes in poetic theory and resources.

Edwin Morgan's first three collections might well be said to share Graham's fondness for Anglo-Saxon roots (Morgan has made a number of Old English translations, after all), as well as his fascination with sea imagery, linguistic density, and a highly rhetorical tone:

> Lands end, seas are unloosed, O my leviathan
> Libertinism, armoured sea-shoulderer, how you broke
> Out over foam and boulder! Break ascetic man
> Like seas to cringing crag-hang home. Mainward
> My freedom looks, towards everything that is nature alone.
>
> ('The Cape of Good Hope')

Like so many of the poets in this discussion, Morgan seems to have moved from a compressed and energy-bound diction in his early work (*Dies Irae*, and *The Cape of Good Hope*), towards the more colloquial and relaxed utterance of *The Second Life* from 1968:

> And a white mist rolled out of the Pacific
> and crept over the sand, stirring nothing—
> cold, cold as nothing is cold
> on those living highways, moved in
> over the early morning trucks . . .
>
> ('The Old Man and the Sea')

Morgan has noted that he feels more in common with European and American poets than he does with English writers,[9] and his extensive work in translation speaks for itself. The direct address in many of his own poems is certainly much closer to Whitman, Hart Crane, Ginsberg, Voznesensky or Mayakovsky, than it is to the urbane and ironic understatement so common in English letters during the fifties and sixties.

> What innocence? Whose Guilt? What eyes? Whose breast?
> Crumpled orphan, nembutal bed,
> White hearse, Los Angeles,
> DiMaggio! Los Angeles! Miller! Los Angeles! America!
>
> ('The Death of Marilyn Monroe')

Such lines may not be overtly Scottish in subject matter or diction, but they are even less likely to have been written by any contemporary south of the Border. In fact, in this respect it seems to me that Morgan owes a specific debt to a Scottish penchant for the formal sermon. Certainly this would explain his tendency to make sudden shifts from the everyday scene into abstract disquisition and metaphysical contexts. Consider, for example, the apocalyptic (once again) fervour at the end of 'Stanzas of the Jeopardy'; the biblical diction used throughout 'The Cape of Good Hope'; and the extraordinary, exhilarating shift from sleazy urban realism to measured homily in 'Glasgow Green': 'Do you think there is not a seed of the thorn/as there is also a harvest of the thorn?/Man take in that harvest!/Help that tree to bear its fruit!/Water the wilderness, walk there, reclaim it!' ('Glasgow Green'.)

Of course Morgan has written a number of justly admired 'Glasgow poems' whose feet are firmly rooted in the grimy everyday, but even here, ('Trio', 'In the Snackbar', 'King Billy', 'Death in Duke Street', 'Christmas Eve'), there remain hints and more than hints of a spiritual dimension, or an aching sense of its lack.

Widely read in modern literature and literary theory, Morgan is at home with the concept of defamiliarisation as proposed by the Russian formalists,[10] and he has gone on to pursue his own vision of verbal estrangement in many evocative and disturbing poems. These include the relatively simple narrative poems in which the writer adopts a persona, as in 'Hyena', for example, in which the animal's sensibility offers us a sudden insight into the true strangeness of the world: 'I howl my song to the moon—up it goes./Would you meet me there in the waste places?' His science fiction poems often create a similar effect, in that the reader can only slowly decipher their contexts in some supposed future and the assumptions which underlie it. In similar style he has written other pieces which operate through what Jonathan Culler calls 'deictic confusion',[11] in that it is not at all obvious who is speaking to whom and about what. We can follow the *sense* of poems such as 'Frontier Story' and 'The Barrow' alright, but because the *context* is not clear, their meaning becomes tantalisingly elusive.

Morgan is fascinated by how language breaks down and makes itself together again, especially in the case of messages which have been somehow garbled or mutated in the telling. Hence 'Boxers' offers us a dialogue at cross purposes across a very bad telephone connection. Its true sense can (just about) be decoded, but the point is that the misheard conversations create a new reality much more intriguing and imaginatively satisfying than whatever the literal truth might have been. There is a whole genre of 'computer print-out' poems—comic and serious—which also operate on this principle, as in 'The Computer's First Christmas Card' and 'Message Clear'. Finally, some of his most entertainingly original and 'defamiliarised' poems relate to an exotic tropical locus of his own imagination—somewhere between Conrad, Stevenson and Maugham. Poems such as 'Islands', 'Floating off to Timor', 'Tropic', 'Shantyman', 'Lord Jim's Ghost's Tiger Poem', and 'Shaker Shaken' all relate to what the French Symbolists knew, or to that which Wallace Stevens saw as 'the palm at the end of the mind'.

> There was an old glade of tombs we went to
> every rainy season to renew
> our stock of ghosts, once brought back a rice doll,
> grew into a fine peasant boy, kept our accounts—
> said the old ghost in the Monsoon Club.
>
> ('Lord Jim's Ghost's Tiger Poem')

The strangeness of such lines reminds us of the sheer *fictionality* of all literature, and of how we only have words to make reality anew (or to make new realities) in our heads. Morgan's most extended and serious use of defamiliarisation is to be found in *The New Divan*, a sequence of a hundred

poems of about 15 lines each, reminiscent of a similar collection—a *divan*—
by the great fourteenth-century Persian poet Hafiz. Here the poet's memories
of the middle east, where he served during the war, are inextricably interwoven
with a literary exoticism which uses different voices, with hints of Hafiz,
Fitzgerald, Rilke, Burroughs, all to make a fascinatingly out-of-time and
oblique series of meditations on the many faces of love, romance, idealism,
suffering and decay:

> 39.
> Fairuz is singing. The notes throb and twist
> from some radio across the street. Like wings
> they beat past evening balconies. The lonely see
> them, almost see them, as they lean. Any
> day someone will come, belong, return! She sings (we
> bring the weight of hopes, hung round, hung-up) the final
> flake and loosened quiver, winding down, of love, A plant
> needs more than water, some say. Sunspot,
> green fingers, transistor on a stool—
> or tuneless whistling through teeth
> with love, if love makes two blades three—
> it's the brightest
> of all this
> hurried wandering meskin scene where nothing's right
> and we lie and die many alone uncalled.
>
> (from 'The New Divan')

Morgan has written a number of concrete poems which are comparably
powerful, but his engagement in this field mostly reflects a playful delight in
the witty shaping of words and puns. It is our next poet who has most fully
explored the theoretical and social resonances of concrete poetry, even to a
point well beyond the printed page.

The immediate roots of the concrete poetry movement are notably inter-
national, and they can be traced from Mallarmé's *Un coup de dés . . .*, and
Russian Suprematism, to Eugen Gomringer's *Constellations* (1953) and the
Noigandres group from Brazil. Of course 'shaped' poems go back to George
Herbert in the seventeenth century and even to the Greeks, but modern
concrete theory emerged in the 1950s, and Edwin Morgan, and especially Ian
Hamilton Finlay, have made a considerable contribution to it.

Finlay's first poems from *The Dancers Inherit the Party* (1960), appear
relatively conventional, yet their consciously lucid, minimal lines have charm
and wit. Next came *Glasgow Beasts an a Burd . . .* a set of Zen poems in
Glasgow patois, with paper-cuts by John Picking and Pete McGinn—equally
witty, equally minimal: 'honess/pals/like/no been born/a cleg/s e bess'. This
little book was a pioneer of its kind, pointing to later developments from
Stephen Mulrine, Alan Spence, Tom McGrath and especially Tom Leonard;
but after his next piece, *Concertina*, Finlay's interests turned almost exclusively to concrete poetry and his special vision of what mind and art and
culture and society have to do with each other.

These issues were engaged during the early 1960s through 25 numbers of Finlay's periodical *Poor. Old. Tired. Horse.*, and the manifold productions of his Wild Hawthorn Press. The early material from *Rapel* (1963) and *Telegrams from My Windmill* (1964) is quite in keeping with the general concepts behind 'concrete' verse and Gomringer's work in particular, but Finlay's art has continued to evolve in a philosophically wide-ranging, and (for the late twentieth century) unique way; 'In the context of this time', he has written, 'it is not the job of poetry to "expand consciousness" but to offer a modest example of a decent sort of order.'[12] Thus his spirit is entirely Classical in an age whose poetry has been given over to what he would regard as Romantic egocentricism, with its emphasis on the primacy of personal expression and anguish. In this anti-modernist vein he challenged the vogue for 'confessional' verse, and quarrelled with the influence of MacDiarmid as the *éminence grise* of Scottish letters. It follows that the publication of his own work—hundreds of single cards, folders and poem/prints, realised with the help of many different artists—spoke for art (however 'serious'), as a matter of light-hearted conceptual insight and communal realisation, rather than as an exclusive value-object or autobiographical 'message'.

Such an emphasis sets Finlay rather apart from his Scottish contemporaries, and entirely separate from any who would have poetry as a matter of psychological self-expression. On the other hand, an objectively socialist or nationalist alignment seems equally alien to him. Nevertheless, despite the singularity of his work, Finlay should not be isolated from other Scottish writers. He may have quarrelled with MacDiarmid, but he shares the elder poet's enthusiasm for public controversy over artistic matters, not to mention his fine sense of the value of provocation—as witness the battles of 'Little Sparta' about the rateable status of a garden temple/art gallery at his home at Stonypath. It is equally stimulating to link him with a totally different writer such as George Mackay Brown, in that both men deplore the excesses of modernism while speaking for a humbler and more organic relationship between the artist and his community. Of course, Brown's final assurance is religious, while Finlay's is rooted in aesthetic theory, but a radical critique of current values is still implicit in every line of their work. In the matter of poetic theory, Finlay's interest in how language *works* is shared in different ways by W S Graham, Edwin Morgan and, in some of his poems, Iain Crichton Smith.

Finlay's particular fascination is with how culture manifests itself in relatively selfless and accessible sign-making activities. Ships' names, the port registration letters of fishing boats and a whole series of sundials have all featured in his work. Quotation is very difficult with these pieces, for they depend on typographical design and have an accumulative effect; nevertheless, whether drawn, printed or worked in card, wood, glass or stone, his aim has been to open our eyes to new visual possibilities and their fresh meanings. To the same end he has studied the cultural history of emblems—those popular icons of moral import or implication—ranging from seventeenth-century woodcuts to the names and figures painted on planes and tanks from the second war.

Much given to a semiotic analysis of the confusion and sterility to be found all around us, Finlay would promote a gentle haiku-like attentiveness in our perceptions and responses. Thus in print his concrete poems offer visual or conceptual puns, as, for example, when the morphological or assonantal parallels between 'waves/sheaves', 'net/planet' and 'star/steer' open our minds—very quietly—to new meanings and connections. Such an approach has meant that his work, for all its simplicity, can be analysed in the most abstruse structuralist terms. Indeed, it has evolved still further from words and signs and their contexts, towards sculptures and inscribed stones in a garden which is itself conceived as a living expression of the interpenetration of mind and nature. Examples can be found at the Max-Planck Institute in Stuttgart and, most notably, at the poet's home in Lanark.

The next development in a highly idiosyncratic and widely read sensibility saw Finlay conflating images from the classical and neo-classical past with the most unlikely contemporary symbols. Thus echoes of Poussin and the inscription '*Et in Arcadia Ego*' are brought into juxtaposition with a German Tiger tank, sylvan, but menacing in its dappled leafy camouflage. The many layers of reference, and the comic and dark ambiguities which underlie a statement of this sort, speak for an increasing complexity and sophistication in Finlay's work. Certainly it has come a long way from the early assurances of peace and fruitfulness which he found in the names and lines of homely Scottish fishing boats, or in his preferred images of clouds, waves, stars, seasons, canals and nets.

Replete with revolutionary allusions to totalitarian architecture and Jacobin France, the most recent work relates to the fact that Finlay's prickly integrity has kept him almost permanently embattled with local bureaucracy and the Scottish Arts Council. In fact his 'war' at 'Little Sparta' in 1983 *became* a work of art (something between a 'happening', and an instant archive), dedicated to the illumination of what Finlay sees as all the sterile and compartmentalised habits of mind in modern society. Whatever the reasons, and whether he writes 'poetry' or not anymore, he has not been very widely appreciated in Scotland, yet his vision of the nature and the importance of the arts continues to be uniquely stimulating and controversial.

Iain Crichton Smith's awareness of language is undoubtedly related to his Gaelic roots and the fact that he long considered English, by which he is best known as a writer, to be a 'foreign language'. His early work explored the powerful tensions of love and hate which he felt between his creative self and the social and religious pressures of his upbringing on the Island of Lewis—where 'they have no place for the fine graces/of poetry':

> . . . The great forgiving spirit of the word
> fanning its rainbow wing, like a shot bird
> falls from the windy sky. The sea heaves
> in visionless anger over the cramped graves
> and the early daffodil, purer than a soul,
> is gathered into the terrible mouth of the gale.
>
> ('Poem of Lewis')

Smith has drawn upon his background and his personal fears to find many such expressions of the 'cramped' Calvinist life. Given his admiration for Robert Lowell, it might be thought that this would lead to directly 'confessional' verse. Yet this is not the case—Smith is a very elusive poet—for he uses his own history in order to examine wider questions about the nature of Scotland and the Scottish cultural inheritance. Then again, his poetry moves beyond solely domestic or national themes to pursue what is ultimately a philosophical quest—even if its specific images still derive from a Scottish experience.

Consider, for example, his attraction to the unforgiving intensity which is part of the Puritan ethos he criticises:

> That was great courage to have watched that fire,
> not placing a screen before it as we do
> with pictures, poems, landscapes, a great choir
> of mounting voices which can drown the raw
> hissing and spitting of flame with other fire.
>
> That was great courage to have stayed as true
> to truth as man can stay.
>
> ('A Note on Puritans')

He knows that puritanism has also made men brutish, but he still cannot help admiring the conviction that will tackle the eternal fire and make every living moment into a crucial hinge between gaiety or despair. How then, as an artist, can one find 'pictures' or 'poems' to do justice to such a sense of terrifying immanence?

> To stand so steady that the world is still
> and take your cold blue pen and write it down
> (all that you see) before the thought can kill
> and set on the living grass the heavy stone
> is what you're here for, though the trembling hand
> shake with the terror of that nothing which
> opens its large void mouth as it yawned
> like a drunk man lying in a starless ditch.
>
> (from 'Love Songs of a Puritan')

In fact a great many of Crichton Smith's poems deal with the difficulty of breaking through the screen of words to do justice to his sense of the terror, brightness and mystery at the heart of being. This almost visionary existentialism is especially evident in the imagery of light and fire from his early work, where 'light strikes . . . like a gong', and 'living and dead turn on the one hinge/of a noon intensely white, intensely clear.' ('In Luss Churchyard'.) The same impulse can be found in his sequences of philosophical meditation, such as 'Deer on the High Hills', 'Transparencies' and 'The White Air of March'; or in those character studies or monologues which he imagines from failed or trapped lives ('School Teacher', 'The Widow', 'Statement by a

Responsible Spinster'); or in poems which derive from more literary accounts of isolation and survival such as *Hamlet in Autumn* and *The Notebooks of Robinson Crusoe.*

Little wonder that such a poet should be drawn to the plight of Gaelic in particular, and of language in general. This is the theme of 'Am Faigh a' Ghaidlig Bas?'/'Shall Gaelic Die?', a sequence of impressionistic, fragmented, flippant and desperate reflections on the interconnected instabilities of language and identity, and hence of reason, culture, the nature of art and our grasp of reality. The question is crucial as far as Highland culture is concerned, but Ian Mac a'Ghobainn sees sadly little hope for a Gaelic future.

As far as his own writing is concerned, Crichton Smith has become more conscious of poetry as a literary act, and of how it can offer the intensity which, in his early verse, he seemed to identify in a realm somehow *beyond* language. Thus, rather than seek 'immutable universal' truths in pure gold or the flame of puritan conviction, the poet will now align himself with 'coins that are old and dirty, the notes that are wrinkled like old faces,/they are coping with time; to these I give my allegiance, to these I owe honour, the sweetness.' ('Shall Gaelic Die?'.) 'Dirty' or not, in creative hands even the crumpled currency of words can show a redemptive ability to *speak* new and unpredictable things, and on behalf of the arts this may be the best response to Wittgenstein's challenge—cited in 'Shall Gaelic Die?'—which says: 'That thing about which you cannot speak, be silent about it'. From such an understanding, Smith has created a number of fine pieces which are full of 'defamiliarised' effects and a movingly opaque beauty. Poems such as 'My Child', 'Tears Are Salt', 'Speech for Prospero', 'The Red Horse' and 'Speech for a Woman' are a contemporary interpretation of what MacDiarmid understood Mallarmé to be saying about poetry as 'the reverse of what it is usually thought to be; not an idea gradually shaping itself in words, but deriving entirely from words . . .'. ('Author's Note' in *Lucky Poet.*)

Which brings us back to MacDiarmid's early hopes, and the conclusion that the best of the 'second generation' poets who wrote in English have indeed remained outward-looking and fully aware of 'current tendencies in technique and ideation', without losing a sometimes painful sense of their own cultural inheritance. The last lines of Smith's 'Speech for Prospero' offer the old enchanter's farewell to his magic island, but in an equally cogent context they speak for a Scottish poet looking back to Lewis, and forward to a new and stranger future:

> Goodbye, island, never again shall I see you,
> you are part of my past. Though I may dream of you often
> I know there's a future we must all learn to accept
> music working itself out in the absurd halls and the mirrors
> posturings of men like birds, Art in a torrent of plates,
> the sound of the North wind distant yet close
> as stairs ascend from the sea.

NOTES

1   'The Scottish renaissance was conceived in the First World War, and leapt into lusty life in the Second World War'; Hugh MacDiarmid, 'Scottish Arts and Letters', in *The New Scotland* (London, 1942), p 151.

2   'Esta Selva Selvaggia', in *Scottish Arts and Letters*, 3 (1947), pp 16–18.

3   *The New Apocalypse* (1940) was edited by Hendry alone; *The White Horseman* (1941) and *The Crown and the Sickle* (1944), were joint ventures. The English members included Vernon Watkins and Nicholas Moore, while their surrealistic and iconoclastic drive was also found in early work from Dylan Thomas and David Gascoyne.

4   The vitalism espoused in Lawrence's *Apocalypse* has the same sense of fevered intensity, written as it was, in the knowledge of his own impending death.

5   'The Key to World Literature', *Scottish Journal*, 4 (1952), p 12; and 'Six Scottish Poets of Today and Tomorrow', *Poetry Scotland*, 2 (1945), p 68.

6   In *Scottish Art and Letters*, 2 and 3 (1946, 1947).

7   George Bruce, in *Contemporary Poets*, James Vinson (ed), 3rd edn (London, 1980), p 193.

8   W S Graham, in *Contemporary Poets*, p 582.

9   Edwin Morgan, in Robin Fulton, *Contemporary Scottish Poetry* (Loanhead, 1974), p 18.

10 *See* 'Introduction to *Wi the Haill Voice*' and 'Into the Constellation' in *Essays by Edwin Morgan* (Cheadle, 1974).

11 Jonathan Culler, *Structuralist Poetics* (London, 1975), pp 164–70.

12 Ian Hamilton Finlay, in *Contemporary Poets* p 491.

Chapter 21

Gaelic Prose

DONALD JOHN MacLEOD

Prose is a relative newcomer on the Gaelic literary scene, dating from the early nineteenth century and, in any quantity, from the period at the end of that century and the beginning of the next. With a few notable exceptions, the most that can be said of the Gaelic prose produced in both these periods is that it is of historical significance, establishing prose-writing as a new genre in Gaelic and evolving a standardised Gaelic prose style, after a period of varied experimentation.

The variety of Gaelic prose styles developed in the turn of the century period, in fact, reflects the whole spectrum of intellectual and social trends of the time. The father of Gaelic prose, Dr Norman MacLeod, writing in the early nineteenth century, had based his style on that of the newly translated Gaelic Bible and on the voluminous writings of the Puritan divines. His long latinate sentences and aureate flourishes continued to be a dominant influence on Gaelic prose style for a long time.

Donald Mackinnon, first Professor of Celtic at Edinburgh University, gave MacLeod's fulsomely moralistic, often emotive style a drily academic rigour, while retaining his over-riding seriousness. Mackinnon's philosophical reflections on Gaelic proverbs, written mostly in the 1880s and 1890s are his best remembered work: their formal style verging often on the ponderous, was also an influence on later writers.

If Mackinnon represents the beginnings of serious Gaelic scholarship, Kenneth MacLeod's prose reflects another, quite different form of Celtic consciousness, namely the Celtic Twilight of which Yeats was the most notable literary exponent at the time. MacLeod's essays are based on the great Gaelic oral tale tradition but he added to the traditional motifs which he borrowed a fey *fin de siecle* sensibility and the parlour room polish which he and his collaborator, Marjory Kennedy-Fraser, were later to add to the songs of the Hebrides. MacLeod's prose style is highly mannered and often cloyingly rich.

By the beginning of this century, Gaelic prose was becoming more established and the writers correspondingly more relaxed in their approach, relaxed enough in fact to tolerate humour. Notable examples of this are the delightfully whimsical essays on animal and human nature of Donald Mackechnie and the gently humorous, lightly moralistic contributions of the Rev Donald Lamont, over a 50 year period, to the Church of Scotland's *Life and Work*.

The Gaelic prose of this period also reflects, indirectly, the rise of an important demographic phenomenon in Gaelic life—the growth of large concentrations of Gaelic-speakers in Lowland cities and the consequent formation of a new artistic and entertainment infrastructure. The new Gaelic Societies of the cities, of Glasgow in particular, created, among other things, a demand for Gaelic 'readings', of which several volumes appeared in this period.

These are mostly retellings of traditional oral tales or original imitations of these. They are of little intrinsic literary interest but were important in demonstrating how the oral traditions of Gaelic could be creatively reprocessed to satisfy the new taste for Gaelic written literature.

The most prolific writer by far of those tradition-based short stories was Mull man, John MacCormick, whose tales of adventure or humour, usually set in the Highland past or in exotic locations, were very popular with the new book-reading public.

MacCormick's work also reflects the influence of a major political movement of the time, the rise of Scottish Nationalism: to be precise, he came under the influence of a notable patron and catalyst of Gaelic writing in the person of Ruaraidh Arascainn is Mhairr, a scion of one of Scotland's oldest families and a pioneer of the nationalist movement. An ardent convert to the Gaelic cause, Marr published for over 20 years the influential quarterly, *Guth na Bliadhna* (Voice of the Year), as well as the shorter-lived story magazine, *An Sgeulaiche* (The Storyteller).

Marr was one of those Scottish Nationalists who show an inverted adulation of English culture by using it as a constant basis for comparison. So, for example, he sponsored a competition for a Gaelic play on the life of MacBeth to correct the 'errors' made by Shakespeare (MacCormick won it) and, generally, encouraged his writers to emulate the best of English literature.

It was undoubtedly Marr who encouraged MacCormick to try his hand at a Gaelic novel. When *Dun Aluinn* was published in 1912, it was the first novel to be printed in Gaelic. While that is not an insignificant landmark, the novel itself is, in fact, banal, often lapsing into sheer pathos. MacCormick, a competent writer of adventure yarns, had clearly overreached himself.

Of the relatively substantial body of Gaelic prose produced in this period, in fact, there is only one short story which is indisputably of lasting literary merit, albeit it is not well known at the present time. And it is the only story known to have been produced by its author.

Donald Sinclair was an engineer living in Liverpool who took what some may regard as an incongruous interest in the ancient traditions of his native Barra, to the extent of spending vacations filling notebooks with archaic expressions from the dictation of no doubt bemused old islanders. Sinclair's poetry, for which he is best known, is suffused with Catholic mysticism, sometimes verging on Wordsworthian pantheism, expressed in a richly overlaid poetic diction: it is full of vivid imagery and genuinely poetic inspiration.

Sinclair, however, also came under the influence of Ruaraidh Arascainn is Mhairr. He also overreached himself, dissipating his very real talent on epic poems and three act dramas on such subjects as the Forty-five Rising.

Ironically, Sinclair's most notable literary achievement is probably his very simple account, in the short story *Lughain Lir* (Sea Warriors), of the changing relationship between a young island boy and his fisherman grandfather. It is interesting, if not very productive, to reflect on what Sinclair might have achieved, had he been encouraged to explore simple everyday events in the sensitive, deceptively simple way he does in *Lughain Lir*. As it is, he brought this crucial pioneering phase in the history of Gaelic prose to an end with a fine flourish.

All in all, the period 1880 to 1914 had seen prose established as a literary form in Gaelic; it saw considerable stylistic experimentation leading to the beginning of agreement on a standard Gaelic prose style; and it produced a handful of essays and stories of literary merit.

By 1914, Gaelic Scotland, in common with the rest of Europe, had other, less civilised preoccupations. Gaelic literature generally was to take some time to recover from this violent hiatus but, by the 1930s, it was beginning to stir again, most notably in the form of the brilliant and seminal verse of Sorley MacLean.

By the 1950s, MacLean's poetry had stimulated a general revival of Gaelic literature. By that time also, national educational changes meant that more young people from the Gaelic-speaking heartland were gaining access to higher education and, as a result, a new readership was being created—an essential prerequisite for the development of a healthy prose literature.

In time, the beginnings of a supportive infrastructure began to take shape, through, for example, the setting up of the Gaelic quarterly, *Gairm*, in 1956—it is still running—and the formation of the Gaelic Books Council which, through its grants scheme, has greatly increased the number of books published in Gaelic.

The rich Gaelic oral tradition of tale and wittily told anecdote has continued to be a factor—although not the most important one—in this period.

The science fiction and mystery stories of Colin Mackenzie and the more varied output of Eilidh Watt, for example, reflect the influence of oral tradition in their use of traditional motifs, their often prolix prose style and loose construction.

Suathadh ri Iomadh Rubha (By Many Headlands), the autobiography of Lewis crofter, Angus Campbell, is a remarkable linguistic tour de force. Campbell draws on a large stock of traditional phraseology to richly, if rather indiscriminately, embroider his anecdotes of his early life in Lewis and his experiences in a German prison-of-war camp in Poland.

The most significant effect of Gaelic oral tradition in this period, in fact, has been the vigour and versatility that writers have gained by judiciously blending colloquial dialect usages with the standard Gaelic prose style they had inherited from the early part of the century.

Paul MacInnes and Finlay J MacDonald are particularly fine examples of this. MacInnes, a fine craftsman, has produced a number of interesting short stories. MacDonald's *Air Beulaibh an t-Sluaigh* (In the Public Eye), itself skilfully crafted, has a classic feel to it: it is the story of the psychological pressure suffered by a daughter of the manse when she finds herself pregnant, pressures which comes close to destroying her.

The short story has, in fact, been the dominant form in Gaelic literature in the last two or three decades. The variety of techniques is, in itself, impressive, embracing the satire of Finlay MacLeod, the gentler humour of Norman Campbell, the surrealistic imagination of Donald John MacIver, the austere intellectualism of Iain Crichton Smith and the many-faceted virtuosity of John Murray.

Smith's several volumes of short stories explore a number of important themes, in particular the nature of power and authority, the intricacies of human relationships and, in a distinctive series in his first volume, the relationship of exiles to their roots.

Iain Crichton Smith's overt interest in ideas and his correspondingly spare prose style has lent refreshing variety to Gaelic literature but has not pleased everyone: this is not surprising since Gaelic literature has only recently begun to escape from the diaglossic apartheid which confined it to home-neighbourhood domains in speech and to the expression of humour and sentiment in literature.

Smith's novel, *An t-Aonaran* (The Loner), is the story of a loner, living on the fringes of an island village, who is gifted, but misunderstood and persecuted because he is different. Although the idea is by no means original, the novel's brevity and intensity ensures its impact: it is a poet's novel, the image clearly delineated and centrally situated in the narrative.

John Murray has published only one volume of short stories but in those he has shown himself to be a master of the form, handling a wide range of techniques with consummate ease—stream of consciousness, flashback, the anti-hero, allegory, traditional Gaelic earthy humour, Joycean epiphany.

Murray's prose is simultaneously polished and colloquial, capable of being vigorously racy and delicately sensitive. It is especially distinguished by its blend of seriousness, humour and irony and the subtle chemistry going on within this blend.

The title story of Murray's collection, *An Aghaidh Choimheach* (The Mask), examines the nature of the deceptions and cherished illusions which make life tolerable and which form the grist of human relationships, as well as creating memorable characters in the unmarried brother and sister, who have spent their lives parsimoniously together and who react with unexpected rancour to their brother, returning from exile in Canada after living a full life there. A quietly moving narrative, the tranquil surface of this story hides many layers of insight into human relations. It is typical of this writer's work. While the Gaelic short story has had a productive and distinguished last few decades, the Gaelic novel has been more noticeable for its relative abscence.

This may be, as Mathew Arnold suggested a long time ago, because the Celts really do lack the 'architectonic faculty'—preferring the lyric to the epic, for example. It may be that, as Frank O'Connor has pointed out, the short story form is especially appealing to minorities and the downtrodden, because it takes the individual, often the idiosyncratic individual, as its norm, with society as only a shadowy backdrop: that, he suggests, is how minorities regard themselves in relation to the majority culture.

Of course, there could be much more mundane reasons for the shortage of

Gaelic novels: the newness of prose of any kind as a literary form, the relatively small readership, the fact that so few writers make a living from writing in Gaelic.

In any event, despite the relative paucity of Gaelic novels, there is at least one which is impressive by any yardstick. This is Norman Campbell's *Deireadh an Fhoghair* (The End of Autumn).

Campbell's narrative is earthy, richly eloquent, redolent of character and atmosphere, bringing alive his central characters, their lives and their small community in a most memorable way. This is a novel, not of ideas, nor even of narrative, but an imaginative re-creation of life in a particular rural community, in all its sounds, smells, sights and eccentric characters. No one has ever described Highland life this precisely, not even Neil Gunn. It has a totally Gaelic feel to it.

Deireadh an Fhoghair is an exciting new work by a young writer. A language which could produce it is surely not a dying language. And yet its subject is an aging threesome, the last survivors of a decaying community. Whether that is a truer omen of the fate of Gaelic than the fact that such a work is produced at all is something that time alone will tell.

Chapter 22

Scots, Poets and the City

BARRY WOOD

The purpose of this chapter will be to consider the poetry of the city in Scotland and in particular to look at the ways poets have used Scots in their representation and interpretation of the urban experience. Since MacDiarmid's commitment to the language in the 1920s, the urban Scots voice—crucial to the revival of the language—has grown in both strength and variety. The work of MacDiarmid himself, Robert Garioch, Edwin Morgan and Tom Leonard will be the principal focus of study here although there are several other poets—Sydney Goodsir Smith, Alexander Scott, Tom Scott and Duncan Glen, for example—whose work certainly deserves fuller consideration. 'Urban Scots' is used in this chapter primarily to refer to the development of a language of the city for specific literary purposes and in this respect, it is understood that the language of the poets may be different from, or serve significantly different purposes to, the language of the novelists and playwrights. In so far as the latter aim at 'realism', they are usually concerned with an accurate representation of the way people actually speak and their interest in the language is thus closely related to that of the social linguist. The urban Scots of the poets studied here is not one language but many and involves the cultivation of a number of styles, varied in idiom, vocabularly and accent, but primarily dependent on the demands of individual poets in their response to the complexities of experiences in the culture of the city.

Scots as a modern literary language is an essentially urban invention. This is not to say that the city has been the primary object of Scots poetry or to question the fact that the major survival of Scots in the nineteenth and early twentieth centuries was in the rural dialects. But dialect is one thing and literary Scots another, and the development of the latter has always depended on a highly self-conscious exploitation of the literary tradition and has frequently used as one of its principal tools that epitome of the culture of the cities, the dictionary. Hugh MacDiarmid's repossession of the language in the 1920s was partly a matter of the body (a recovery of the language of the feeling and sense) and of the body politic, but he was always clear about his debt to Jamieson's *Etymological Dictionary* and to Wilson's word-glossary of *Lowland Scotch* and about the extent to which this debt committed him to the idea of Scots recreated for specific literary purposes. In this, Mac-Diarmid was rather modernist than conservationist and vigorously differentiated his own use of Scots not only from that of the kailyard poets of the nineteenth century but also from the revivals of some of his contemporaries who tended to perpetuate in their work an image of Scotland which was largely rural in its way of life and traditional in its forms of expression. MacDiarmid, on the contrary, insisted on Scots as a language containing within it modes of perception and consciousness peculiarly relevant to the discoveries of modern psychology and modern science. It is true that many of MacDiarmid's own early Scots lyrics are themselves predominantly rural in setting and imagery; but it is arguable that in his exploitation and extension of the idiom in such poems as 'The Eemis Stane', 'Empty Vessel' and 'Bombinations of a Chimaera' he was able to demonstrate the possibility of adapting, as he put it in an early essay, 'an essentially rural tongue to the very much more complex requirements of our urban civilisation'.

In this context one of the most interesting poems in MacDiarmid's first two collections of Scots lyrics is 'The Dead Leibknecht'. The poem is a free adaptation of a poem by Rudolf Leonhardt which MacDiarmid probably first encountered in a translation by Jethro Bithell. MacDiarmid's version retains the central theme of the original but changes Leonhardt's free verse patterns to a more emphatic ballad-like metre and, by a sharpening of the visual imagery, makes the hint of apocalypse in the original a more distinct and menacing possibility. As a translation the poem is clearly important to MacDiarmid in affirming the relationship of his own work to that of other contemporary European poets and in fact he developed the use of translation as a form of allusion more fully in *A Drunk Man Looks at the Thistle*. The language of the poem does not exploit the idiomatic and metaphorical possibilities of Scots as fully as 'The Eemis Stane', but it does have the rhythmic and colloquial vigour common to MacDiarmid's best early poems. What is particularly remarkable about the poem however is that it is almost alone in *Sangschaw* and *Penny Wheep* in being directly concerned with the landscape and people of the city:

> The factory horns begin to blaw
> Thro' a' the city, blare on blare,
> The lowsin' time o' workers a',
> Like emmits skailin' everywhere.
>
> And wi' his white teeth shinin' yet
> The corpse lies smilin' underfit.

Although in itself a minor achievement the Liebknecht poem is nonetheless a valuable indication of the direction MacDiarmid was taking in his effort to create an idiom in Scots which would be adequate to express the complexities of contemporary urban thought and sensibility.

A Drunk Man Looks at the Thistle is the fullest and finest enactment of this purpose. The urban style and character of the poem is not a question of overt subject-matter or even specific thematic preoccupations; it is a question of voice rather than imagery, of idiom and perspective rather than landscape and setting. The Scots of the poem is highly eclectic, inventive and in terms of spelling and syntax often inconsistent; but it is a rich and flexible language for the expression of a wide variety of feelings and ideas. The voice of the Drunk Man is the voice of the modern urban poet-intellectual—questing, discontented, rebellious, self-divided and finally trapped in the anguished realisation of the tragi-comedy of his situation and fate. The voice is firmly established in the finely contrived opening lines of the poem and develops through often rapid shifts of feeling and tone to the central psychic and philosophical explorations of the later sections. The conflicts and contradictions of the poem are rather encountered than resolved for the poem as a whole makes a virtue—as Monroe K Spears suggests all modernist poems must do—of the discontinuities and ambiguities of the modern experience. The language of the poem draws on traditional literary, dialect and contemporary colloquial usages and therefore does not directly reproduce the actual speech of the ordinary urban dweller. Writers who attempt to reproduce such speech patterns—usually with a cleaned-up working class accent and vocabulary—were not particularly successful. The work of Charles J Kirk and W D Cocker—collected in Hamish Whyte's *Noise and Smoky Breath*— serves to show that the poetry produced under such conditions was often either a kind of pawky doggerel as in Cocker's 'Glesca' or a weak echo of the suburban London voice impersonated by John Davidson in 'Thirty Bob a Week'. The limited use of Scots in these poems—or perhaps the limited range of feeling, experience and idea which the Scots is expected to express— is far removed from MacDiarmid's purposes and represents a narrower view of the Scottish character than he was prepared to entertain in the 1920s. It is interesting to note however that in letters to William Soutar in the 1930s MacDiarmid speaks of a project to write a collection of urban-industrial poems in Scots which would, he suggests, 'cut out purely intellectualist pyrotechnics' in order to articulate without condescension an authentic urban working-class experience. The project was not developed but in suggesting the need to voice the feelings and experience of the urban dispossessed it could be said to look forward to some of the developments in Glasgow particularly in the 1960s and 1970s.

In *A Drunk Man Looks at the Thistle* MacDiarmid, whilst creating a language which was capable of articulating the essential style and perspective of the urban mind, nonetheless left out of account the particularities of day-to-day experiences and the description of actual landscape. In what Hamish Whyte has called his 'passionate pessimistic poems' of the 1930s and 1940s MacDiarmid writes about the city in almost entirely negative terms. The poems are mostly written in the chopped-up prose style of much of his later work and the departure from Scots seems to break the connection between language and experience. These poems in fact quote extensively from other authors and often read more like extracts from essays on the city by some disillusioned outside observer than like poetic representations of the city mind and experience. MacDiarmid's interests were for the most part elsewhere— in the poetry of exile, silence and cunning—and although such works as *In Memoriam James Joyce* are, in a sense, unimaginable without the technological paraphernalia of a sophisticated urban culture they engage only theoretically with it. It is possible to imagine a Drunk Man at home in the city, even if unhappy and sceptical about its benefits; the poet of 'In the Slums of Glasgow' and 'Talking to Five Thousand People in Edinburgh' is the classic poet of the unreal city, alienated from its people and general life and pessimistic about the possibility of change because it would involve the transformation not only of urban conditions and institutions but also of the consciousness of the city's inhabitants.

The poets who began working in Scots during the 1940s—for example, Sydney Goodsir Smith, Alexander Scott and Tom Scott—have also contributed to the poetry of the city. Sydney Goodsir Smith is the author of a Joycean novel about the city, *Carotid Cornucopius*, as well as a number of Edinburgh poems—'The Grace of God and the Meth-Drinker', 'Slugabed' (the fifth section of *Under the Eildon Tree*), 'Kynd Kittock's Land' and 'Gowdspink in Reekie'—which, despite displaying a certain energy of personal feeling, are flawed by a too easy assumption of modernist technique and a tendency to rhetorical excess and fanciful sub-Joycean neologising. His most disciplined and effective urban poem is *The Twal*, a translation of Blok's famous poem of the 1917 Revolution. Alexander Scott's lengthiest treatment of the urban theme is *Heart of Stone*, a meditative poem on Aberdeen which uses a highly alliterative style to present a personal, often satirical view of the city. The poem does not altogether succeed, partly because its highly-wrought rhetoric whilst occasionally effective in evoking the character of the city 'stanced in stalliard stane' frequently seems over-contrived. Tom Scott has translated Villon and Baudelaire into Scots and has written of the visionary city in *An Ode Til New Jerusalem*; but his most convincing achievement in the urban idiom is his *Brand* sequence which is perhaps rather a portrait of a small town than of the big city mentality.

The most significant poets of the city to emerge during the 1950s and 1960s are Robert Garioch and Edwin Morgan. Garioch representing a kind of enlightened traditionalism in contrast to Morgan's more thoroughgoing pursuit of the new. They are contrasting figures in a number of ways, even apart from the fact that their work relates to the very different urban cultures of Edinburgh and Glasgow. Early in his career, Garioch committed himself to Scots and set about the development of a mainly colloquial style which would enable him to impersonate a variety of Edinburgh characters and to reflect in a characteristically ironical manner on the life and times of the city. The voice heard in Garioch's work is not unlike that heard at the end of MacDiarmid's *A Drunk Man Looks at the Thistle*: the weary and occasionally impatient voice of realism and common sense. Garioch's poetry is, in a phrase used by Robert Conquest to describe the work of the English 'Movement' poets, 'empirical in its attitude to all that comes' and for the most part traditional in its forms and versification. Morgan, on the other hand, apart from the fact that he writes primarily in English rather than Scots, is sympathetic to the experiments of literary modernism and—without loss of moral and intellectual coherence—has demonstrated his versatility in a variety of styles. There is in the work of both poets, however, a common interest in the city and in modern science and a positive sense in their work of the value of translation in the development and enlargement of their poetic styles and subject-matter.

Garioch's series of Edinburgh sonnets in fact are very clearly influenced by his translations of the Roman dialect poems of Giusseppe Belli. The interest and quality of the translations varies considerably; some remain firmly rooted in nineteenth-century social and religious controversy whilst others are only partially successful attempts at 'imitation' to make the originals relevant to the present. The best of them however make their point clearly enough, as in 'The Beasties of the Yirdly Paradise':

> But eftir Adam cam to be their chief,
> in cam the gun, the pole-aix and the whup,
> dauds on the heid, and ilka cause for grief.

> And syne, for the first time yon man of micht
> reiv'd frae the beasts their word, garr'd them shut up,
> sae he alane cuid speak, and aye be right.

The real value of the Belli translations is that they provided the model—in form, tone and in the use of colloquial urban speech—for some of the best of Garioch's own poems. The sequence of Edinburgh sonnets are mainly satirical in their reflection on the life of the city but are, nonetheless, remarkably varied in the range of voice they entertain and in the possibilities of irony they exploit. Some of the sonnets are primarily comic, like the slyly outrageous 'Ane Offering For Easter' or 'I Was Fair Beat', both of which use the sonnet form to good effect. 'I Was Fair Beat', for example, rhymes 'juicy' with 'Debussy' and 'randy pussy' and contains the lines:

> Kurt Schwitters' Ur-sonata that gaes 'Grimm
> glim gnimm bimmbimm,' it fairly wad hae sent ye

> daft, if ye'd been there . . .

The mocking, exasperated tone is nicely pointed up by the verse lines and the poem demonstrates Garioch's skill in playing off the rhythms of speech against the constraints of the form. Some of the sonnets are clearly impersonations: the amiable drunk in 'Heard in the Cougate', the somewhat uncertain academic snob in 'Did Ye See Me?' and the aggrieved workingman in 'Heard in the Gairdens'. But there is enough correspondence between the language of those poems which are in the poet's own voice and those which are not to make it clear that he is not condescending in his impersonations. The language establishes a sympathetic understanding if not an identity of feeling and perception between the ventriloquising author and his other selves. The comedy of these poems is inseparable from the particular forms of the language: the transcription of slurred drunken speech—'inaidie' for 'in aid of'—in 'Heard in the Cougate' and the use of an ornate poetic diction to expose through parody the pompous speaker in 'Did Ye See Me?' Edinburgh clearly provides a fertile ground for Garioch's satirical imagination but his attacks are largely genial and forgiving, even when their object is the civic pretension of 'the seenil City Faithers' in 'Festival 1962' or the foreign and domestic follies of the Festival in 'Embro to the Ploy'. Garioch's poetry is very much that of a city-dweller who, however critical, delights in the city itself and sees little of interest or comfort outside it. His 'muir' after all is almost as forbidding and hostile to the merely human as MacDiarmid's 'raised beach': 'A plewman warslin in a warld of glaur/som weit back-end . . ./kens something of the stuff that maks our warld/and plouters owre it, cursing'.

The city is his human universe and in the long verse epistle 'To Robert Fergusson' he expresses with a characteristic irony and wit the ambivalence of his feelings towards the city and his own life within it. Fergusson's influence on Garioch's development of a distinctive urban idiom is perhaps more profound than that of Belli. Fergusson was a poet who was rescued from neglect by the writers of the Scottish renaissance in the 1940s and 1950s. MacDiarmid was one of his early champions and clearly saw him as a more valuable model for the twentieth-century poet than Burns. Garioch's poem is a kind of homage to the eighteenth-century poet and, as part of its tribute, borrows not only its form but a good measure of its vocabulary and idiom from his work. The poem measures the modern city—with its 'hauf-inch marble peel' on shop-fronts in Princes Street—against the image of the city celebrated in Fergusson and laments in particular the fact that the city now speaks two languages: 'ane coorse and grittie,/heard in the Cougait,/the tither copied, mair's the pitie,/frae Wast of Newgate'. The division was, of course, already apparent in Fergusson's own day (Burns himself suffered its consequences); but the basic point for Garioch is that it leaves the poet who writes in Scots uncertain of his audience and more isolated than his eighteenth-century predecessors. The poem embodies a paradox in that, in its use of Scots, it gestures towards a period when the language could be believed in as a shared and common property whilst at the same time it reinforces the idea that the modern poet is constantly compelled to invent a language which is only partially relevant to himself and others who live in 'some suburb new and bare' in the twentieth-century city. It may be precisely Garioch's awareness of the penalties of his situation which permits him to create such a powerful and authentic verse. In his other fine poem to Fergusson, 'At Robert Fergusson's Grave: October 1962', he transforms the urban idiom into a new eloquence, permitting it to recover its lost urbanity to become the epitome of a civilised speech—measured, self-aware and authoritative.

'At Robert Fergusson's Grave' is the triumph of Garioch's personal reaction of the tradition. His experiments with more modern modes of expression—in his translations of Apollinaire, for example—are less characteristic of his talents although they have clearly contributed to the writing of 'Brither Worm' and 'Sisyphus' with their macabre vision of human alienation and absurdity.

Garioch's encounters with the modern are wary, partial and provisional. By contrast, Edwin Morgan's modernism is apparent not only in the fact that he writes about the city but also in his experiment with a variety of poetic means to represent the realities of urban experience. Morgan's pluralistic exploration of the city includes poems of direct, personal witness like 'Trio' and 'Christmas Eve', the Instamatic 'found' poems, longer reflective free verse poems like 'The Starlings in George Square', 'Glasgow Green' and 'For Bonfires', the surrealistic 'Rider', the graphically realistic sequence of monologues 'Stobhill' and the ten 'Glasgow Sonnets'. Morgan writes mainly in English but his use of Scots is more extensive, interesting and integral to his purposes than is generally allowed for. In his representations of Glasgow speech in 'Good Friday', for example, in his use of certain words—'shilpit', 'greeting', 'gallus', etc—for particular expressive purposes in 'Glasgow Sonnets' and in his Scots translations of Mayakovsky, Morgan has engaged in a varied exploration of the potentialities of the language.

His translations into Scots of some of the poems of the Russian Futurist poet Mayakovsky—written during the 1960s and published as *Wi the Haill Voice* in 1972—are of special significance in that they were specifically intended to demonstrate the way that the distinctive modernist qualifies of Mayakovsky's work could be matched by Scots. As Morgan puts it in his introduction to *Wi the Haill Voice*, the experiment seemed justified because Scots rather than English could more readily accommodate the 'racy colloquialism and linguistic inventiveness' of the originals and was therefore a more accurate reflection of their 'abrupt changes of tone, . . . fantasy, lyricism, and direct civic and moral concern'. Morgan draws on a wider range of spoken and literary Scots than he uses elsewhere in his work and for this reason the translations—for all their energy and vividness—can be thought of as a kind of pastiche or virtuoso performance. But as an exploration and testing of the linguistic resources of Scots, the translations are clearly important. Morgan's interest in the Russian poet is not solely linguistic; it is related to the value Morgan places in Mayakovsky's work as 'an attempt to incorporate into verse something of the urban, industrial and technological dynamism of the modern world.' It is interesting in this connection that Morgan frequently links Mayakovsky with the American poet, Hart Crane, whose work he admires for similar reasons: for its linguistic energy and as a positive response to twentieth-century urban culture. Like some of Morgan's other linguistic experiments, the Mayakovsky translations have influenced his work elsewhere and contributed to the development in his work of a more direct representation of city life.

Although there are some brief references to Glasgow scenes and characters in Morgan's earlier work, it is only in the 1960s and early 1970s that he begins to write about the people, places and environment of the city out of his immediate experience. Some of his early Glasgow poems are simply records of a personal experience in encounters in a style which gives more prominence to the incident itself than to the language it is expressed in. 'Good Friday,' 'At the Snack Bar' and 'Christmas Eve' are representative poems in this style. 'Trio' is another example, although in this poem the incident described is virtually sacramentalised as the group of Christmas shoppers take on an aura of more traditional figures bearing gifts. 'Glasgow Green' is one of the longer poems which offers a more general view of urban life, although here, too, the documentary character of the poem is clearly subject to the poet's own structuring of our perception of the 'real' even at the moment when he is insisting that it is not:

> This is not the delicate nightmare
> you carry to the point of fear
> and wake from, it is life, the sweat
> is real, the wrestling under a bush
> is real, the dirty starless river
> is the real Clyde, with a dishrag dawn
> it rinses the horrors of the night
> but cannot make them clean,
> though washing blows
>   where the women watch
> by day
>   and children run,
>   on Glasgow Green.

The sense of a problematical relationship between language and reality is central to much of what Morgan writes about the city and consistent with his view that, as he puts it in 'A Jar Revisited,' 'spaec . . ./is fictitious'. A number of his other urban poems such as the 'instamatic' series and the surrealistic 'Rider' raise the issue directly: in a sense, the image 'captured' photographically in 'Glasgow 5 March 1971' is as surreal as the ironic juxtapositions and bizarre images of 'Rider'. The dividing line between conventional and experimental modes of expression in Morgan's work is not absolute, and the range of his work reinforces the idea that the 'urban' in modern poetry is as much a way of seeing and construing as of the view itself. 'Pictures Floating from the World' and the concrete poems are as integral to his urban perspective as the naturalistic 'Death on Duke Street'. Openness to experience and to different ways of representing it is a key feature of Morgan's work and it is interesting that the development of the urban idiom coincides with the more explicit expression of the vulnerabilities of personal feeling and relationship.

Within the plurality of styles in Morgan's work—and considering his commitment to 'openness'—it is perhaps surprising to find that he also uses the closed form of the sonnet. If the challenge of the Mayakovsky translations was to match the exuberance of the Russian with the bizarre and unusual in Scots, the challenge in the ten 'Glasgow Sonnets' is clearly to incorporate the complex materials of the modern city within the tight form of the sonnet. Placed at the end of the collection, *From Glasgow to Saturn*, the sonnets mark a return to earth. They contain much detailed imagery of a largely derelict or disappearing urban landscape and, apart from some occasional awkwardness, they do so with notable success:

> A shilpit dog fucks grimly by the close.
> Late shadows lengthen slowly, slogans fade.
> The YY PARTICK TOI grins from its shade

like the last strains of some lost *libera nos
a malo*. No deliverer ever rose
from these stone tombs to get the hell they made
unmade . . .

But the poems clearly aim at more than a documentary realism. Throughout the sequence the contrasts, conflicts and contradictions of the modern city are acted out: between the deprived slum tenement dwellers and the agents of 'filthy lucre'; between the conservationists whose aim is to 'prop up' images of the past and those who see motorway flyovers 'breed loops of light/in curves . . . clean and unpompous'; between a vernacular language which suggests some familiarity and involvement and a formal rhetoric which establishes distance and implies judgement; between the poet's vision of the city as 'a feast/ of reason' and the harsh realities of the 'wrecker's ball'; between political and industrial struggle and the 'stalled lives' of trapped individuals. In outline as hard and distinctive as the tenement blocks and monolithic high-rise flats on Red Road, the sonnets are the response of the poet as humanist with a clear sense of the classic moral and social configurations of the city. The burden and tension which the ideal and the real place upon each other is paralleled by the tension between the sonnet form (with its echoes of the ideal city) and the subject matter. The ten Glasgow sonnets are by no means Morgan's final word on the city (see 'Tarkovsky in Glasgow' and *Sonnets from Scotland*) but they are a kind of summation of his attitude and point of view which is made no less complex by his awareness that 'The images are ageless, but the thing/ is now.'

Morgan's creation of his own complex urban idiom was part of a broad development of Scottish urban literature in the 1960s and 1970s which was particularly related to Glasgow and included novels, short stories and plays as well as poetry. Novelists as varied in style as Alasdair Gray, William McIlvanney and James Kelman and playwrights such as Tom McGrath, John Byrne, Liz Lochhead and Marcella Evaristi all show an increased confidence in the use of urban materials. At the same time, a number of poets began to exploit the possibilities of urban Scots dialect and, again particularly in Glasgow, the short urban Scots lyric developed into a sub-genre of Scottish poetry. Ian Hamilton Finlay in *Glasgow Beasts* (1961) initiated the mode but there are further notable examples in the work of Duncan Glen, Stephen Mulrine and Alan Spence. The most radical and extensive experiment in this style, however, is by Tom Leonard.

Leonard's use of urban dialect is more complicated and varied than that of most of the other poets who have tended to use it for only occasional purposes. His view of language is contained most succinctly in the poster-poem—also printed on the cover of *Intimate Voices* 1965–1983—which works variations on the text 'in the beginning was the word' and concludes 'nthibiginnin wuzthiwurd/ nthibiginninwuzthiwurd/ in the beginning was the sound'. The authority invested in 'the word'—the reverence, respect and compliance we are expected to show it—is precisely what Leonard challenges by his insistence on the 'sound', the shaping of language by the human voice, the subtleties of communication in what Tom Paulin calls 'the living, but fragmented speech' of the modern city.

As Philip Hosbaum has noted, Leonard has a good ear for speech and part of the subtlety of his 'urban dialect' poems is that they create a strong sense of the exact gesture, pause, accent and idiom of the speaking voice. Leonard seems to respond with particular relish to the terse understatement of urban speech, exploiting it sometimes for epigrammatic wit: 'nuthnlik disperr/ keepsyi gawn' or for its idiomatic humour, as in 'The Dropout': speylt useless yi urr/. . ./cawz rows inan empty hooss'. In 'A Summer's Day' he writes a parody of conventional love poetry which also reflects on the inadequacies of contemporary articulacy: 'yir eyes ur/ eh/ a mean yir/ pirrit this wey/ ah a thingk yir/ byewtifl . . .'. Language used in this way is also the source of the humour in 'hangup' with its hilarious parody of literary minimalism and in 'Moral Philosophy' which reflects on modern philosophical relativism and self-doubt. 'The Good Thief', however, whilst continuing to satisfy expectations of comedy, enlarges the possibilities of meaning by having the thief speak to Christ in the idiom of a Glasgow Celtic football supporter:

> heh jimmy
> ma right insane yirra pape
> ma right insane yirwanny us jimmy
> see it nyir eyes
> wanny us

With its pauses, phrasing, run-on-words, parallels and repetitions, the language and versification create exactly the effect of a voice which is at once truculent, confiding and perplexed. Skilful, witty and concise, the poem is a *tour-de-force* of macabre and ironic insight.

Many of the best poems in Glasgow speech are a form of impersonation; the succinct dramatisations of the resentment and reproaches of the parent for her educated son in 'The Qualification' and 'The Dropout', for example. In 'The Hardmen' he questions the attitudes and myths about the Glasgow male and in 'No Light' he exploits the starkness of the urban idiom in order to reflect and expose a harsh and brutalised social environment: '. . . a liftid/ ma boot right back n/ smashdit rightniz mouth'. 'Tea Time' is a small comedy of marital anxiety and 'treat me izza sexual objict' acts out in violent images in fantasy of sexual frustration. In these poems the mimetic manipulation of language is used to reveal both the emotional and behavioural gesture of the speaker. The close relationship between language, action and feeling is demonstrated in 'Fireworks', a poem in which the speaker's excitement and admiration in watching a soccer-player score a goal is exactly traced in the poem's form.

In using the sounds of speech as the basis of his poetry Leonard is able to notate—often from an ironic viewpoint, as the poems mentioned make clear—particular feelings, attitudes and individual experience. But he also takes stock of the adequacy of the 'urban dialect' as a mode of expression and explores the nature of its relationship to English, which, in its 'received pronunciation', is the language of power. In 'Unrelated Incidents,' for example, he presents a series of comic-satirical reflections on 'English' as an instrument of social and political control and moral authority. But Leonard's interest is in subverting rather than replacing English as 'thi langwij/ a thi/ intillect', and in this his purpose is quite distinct from that of the Lallans poets. As the speaker in 'Paroakial' puts it, though with a double-edged irony, 'goahty learna new langwij/ sumhm ihnturnashnl/ Noah Glasgow hangup.' Leonard's own use of English in poems like 'A Priest Came on at Merkland Street' (his longest and perhaps least understood poem on the urban theme) and in such superbly subtle studies of feeling and relationship as 'Storm Damage' and 'The Appetite' indicates that his use of the Glasgow urban dialect is only one part of his revaluation of poetic and linguistic resources. As an urban poet, he expresses through his Glasgow speech a solidarity with the linguistically (and thereby, he implies, socially and economically) dispossessed of the city. But, as the ironies of a number of the poems indicate, his attitude towards the language is ambiguous, and the conflict between background and education—which is a recurrent theme in his work—is unresolved.

Leonard's poetry represents one of the most acute and disturbing accounts of the urban experience and—taken together with the work of MacDiarmid, Garioch and Morgan gives a good indication of the diversity of response which Scottish poets have made to the challenge of the modern city.

FURTHER READING

Garioch, Robert, *Collected Poems* (1977)
—— *Complete Poetical Works* (1983)
Leonard, Tom, *Intimate Voices: Selected Work 1965–1983* (1984)
—— *Situations Theoretical and Contemporary* (1986)
Lindsay, Maurice (ed), *Modern Scottish Poetry: an Anthology of the Scottish Renaissance 1925–1975* (1976)
MacDiarmid, Hugh, *Complete Poems* (1982)
Morgan, Edwin, *Wi the Haill Voice* (1972)
—— *Poems of Thirty Years* (1982)
—— *Sonnets from Scotland* (1984)
Scott, Alexander (ed), *Modern Scots Verse 1922–1977* (1978)
Whyte, Hamish (ed), *Noise and Smoky Breath: An Illustrated Anthology of Glasgow Poets 1900–1983* (1983)

Chapter 23

Scottish Theatre 1950–1980

RANDALL STEVENSON

'Here be deserts and wild beastes' wrote medieval cartographers: and so, crypt-
ically, would I write Scotland's name upon any Theatre chart . . . dra-
maturgically speaking, Scotland is in the bronze age, still.[1]

Playwright George Munro's pessimistic assessment of the situation in the
early 1950s can be seen as largely justified by Scottish theatre's slow, often
disappointing development in the first half of the twentieth century and by
particular setbacks which occurred around 1950. The outstanding Scottish
playwright of the time, James Bridie, died in 1951. Glasgow Unity, a company
which had developed a politically-committed, popular form of theatre
throughout the 1940s, ceased operations, for financial reasons, in the same
year. Theatre Workshop—which might have settled in Glasgow after successful visits to Scotland with plays such as Ewan McColl's *Uranium 235*
(1946) and *Johnny Noble* (1946)—moved away in 1952 to a permanent base
at Stratford East in London. Despite such losses, however, Scotland in the
early 1950s was not altogether so barren theatrically as Munro's comment
suggests. Founded by James Bridie in 1943, Glasgow Citizens' Theatre
continued to provide a platform for some Scottish plays for many years after
Bridie's death; while from its beginnings in 1947 the Edinburgh Festival
contributed to widening Scottish interest in drama. This was particularly
focused by Tyrone Guthrie's famous festival production of Sir David
Lindsay's *Ane Satire of the Thrie Estaitis* in 1948, which alerted a whole
generation of audiences and writers to particular possibilities for the Scottish
stage. The early 1950s also possessed a group of writers whose work—despite
its limitations—opened up several areas of interest successfully extended by
later playwrights: exploitation of the vitality of Scottish speech; use of Scottish
history as a source of subjects and themes; and development for the stage of
some of the forceful, disturbing realities of Lowland urban life.

The writer most concerned with the last of these areas was George Munro
himself. The title of his one-act play 'From Scenes Like These' provides a
bitter motto for drama which generally presents 'From Falls of Clyde to Tail
o' the Bank . . . Destruction. Dirt. Despair.' Characters in *Gold in his Boots*
(Glasgow Unity, 1947) and *Mark but this Flea* (Glasgow University, 1970)
also use Burns's phrase 'From scenes like these old Scotia's grandeur springs'
to refer ironically to dilapidated, oppressive urban environments further

sullied by the drunkenness or violence of their inhabitants. The darkness of their lives is relieved only rarely by romance or realisation of dreams of football glory, and is often deepened by religious conflict between Protestant and Catholic, another repeated feature of Munro's concern with Scottish urban life. A character in *Gold in his Boots* remarks 'I hate and detest this religious bigotry. People are so busy fighting for mansions in the sky they're content with middens on earth' (I, ii). Prepared by his career as a journalist for detailed, persuasive portrayal of 'middens' in West of Scotland cities, an upbringing in the Brethren also equipped Munro as an acute observer of the narrow, divisive religious outlooks presented in *Vineyard Street* (Citizens', 1949) as well as *Gold in his Boots* and *Mark but this Flea*. These are also an element in the family tensions explored in Munro's best play, *Gay Landscape* (Citizens', 1958). This shows the expanding influence of 'Destruction. Dirt. Despair.' (II) over three generations of a family whose memories of an earlier Highland home are gradually, foully eroded by the grimness of Glasgow. *Gay Landscape* offers in this way a paradigm for developments in Scottish theatre since the war; the rural, sometimes idealised settings of the first half of the century giving way to a starker urban realism. *Gay Landscape*, however, is also moved some way beyond the realism of its setting by the extraordinary intensity of the family feuds it portrays, and by the overwhelming greyness of Munro's city vision. His strangely rhythmic, alliterative language adds to this movement beyond the naturalism of his other work, his occasional faults of melodrama and disjointed construction generally avoided in a play whose exceptional power should not be lost to the Scottish repertoire.

Robert Kemp was much less concerned than Munro with urban life, or with the contemporary world in general. His prolific output includes only three rather insubstantial plays with contemporary settings: *Festival Fever* (1956), *The Penny Wedding*, (1957), and *The Perfect Gent* (1962). Kemp was mostly occupied with opening up areas of Scotland's history for the stage, and with adapting or translating into Scots. It was his shortened, modernised, version of *Ane Satire of the Thrie Estaitis* which Guthrie used at the Edinburgh Festival in 1948, and he also successfully adapted some of Henryson's fables for radio, where he worked as a producer. His excellent Scots translations of *L'Ecole des Femmes* (*Let Wives Tak Tent* (1948)) and *L'Avare* (1958) find in Molière's portrayals of a hypocritical society some of the relevance Tom Gallacher and others later discovered in bringing Ibsen to the Scottish stage. Another of Kemp's important contributions at the time was his role in founding and administering the Gateway Theatre, which included many Scottish plays in its productions between 1953 and 1965.

Kemp's own historical drama suffers at times from a lack of the vision and depth which his adaptations derive from their originals. This is especially apparent in his play about Robert the Bruce, *The King of Scots* (Dunfermline Abbey, 1951), and in *Master John Knox* (Gateway, 1960). These are chronicles or pageants, insufficiently developed in dramatic conflict or characterisation. Tension is also slackened by Kemp's bland, pseudo-Shakespearean English: possibly under the influence of contemporaries such as Eliot or Christopher Fry, verse is used almost throughout, but the rhyming couplet form chosen for *The King of Scots*, for example, tends to undermine rather than contribute to the seriousness of the action. *The Saxon Saint* (Dunfermline Abbey, 1949) is more successful, using the relationship of King Malcolm and Queen Margaret to bring to dramatic focus conflicts between native Scots and imported English language and manners. Some conflict between Kemp's own religious and nationalist feelings may, however, account for a central confusion in the play, which presents Margaret as an admirably pious figure despite attitudes which are pacifying and civilising but also ultimately Anglicising. Such attitudes and the tensions they engender are more clearly presented in Kemp's best play, *The Other Dear Charmer* (Citizens', 1951). Contrasts between a rough Scots authenticity and English gentility are dramatised in the relationship between Robert Burns and an Edinburgh admirer, Nancy Maclehose, who is deeply disturbed by Burns's scorn for 'polite English.' Burns himself is aware that

> there have always been two forces in my life . . . like two horses pulling different roads . . . the Scotch horse and the English horse. (I)

Burns's eventual preference for Jean Armour over Nancy Maclehose, for passion over gentility, and for Scots over English, substantiates the suggestion in some of Kemp's work of a specific strength for Scottish drama latent in the nation's language as well as its history.

Robert McLellan (whose career is examined in David Hutchison's essay) is probably the most influential of mid-century dramatists who revived interest in Scots history and language, though his concern with the latter area at least is strongly supported by other writers. Alexander Reid, for example, remarks in an introduction to his *Two Scots Plays* (1958)

> The return to Scots is a return to meaning and sincerity. We can only grow from our own roots and our roots are not English . . . If we are to fulfil our hope that Scotland may some day make a contribution to World Drama . . . we can only do so by cherishing, not repressing our national peculiarities (including our language), though whether a Scottish National Drama, if it comes to birth, will be written in Braid Scots or the speech, redeemed for literary purposes, of Argyle Street, Glasgow, or the Kirkgate, Leith, is anyone's guess.

Reid's remarks might be taken as a manifesto for the development of Scottish drama since the war: unfortunately, his own plays do not match the commitment of this introduction. *The Lass wi' the Muckle Mou'* (Citizens', 1950), and *The Warld's Wonder* (Citizens', 1953), do demonstrate a flexible, funny use of braid Scots, and commute with typically Scottish ease between earthly and supernatural domains. Each, however, is set in the Borders in the Middle Ages, 'where Elfland touches the world'—the sort of benign, distant, half-magical setting beloved of Kailyard writers. The result is a slight, often sentimental quality, altogether too far from 'Argyle Street, Glasgow, or the Kirkgate, Leith.'

Some of Reid's views were extended in the verse plays of Alexander Scott in the 1950s: they were also vigorously realised in Sydney Goodsir Smith's *The Wallace* (Edinburgh Festival, 1960), distinguished by the rhetorical power of its use of Scots. This contributes greatly to the celebratory, rousing qualities in the play which were well developed in its Festival revival in 1985. Like much of Kemp's drama, however, *The Wallace* is celebratory and pageant-like rather than imaginative or analytic in terms of either character or action. Smith's presentation of Wallace's relations with the nobles illustrates some perennial conflicts in Scottish history and politics, but much of the rest lacks focus, concision, or effective staging: a narrator, rather than dramatic action, is used to communicate many of the major events of the play.

Development of the themes and interests established by mid-century playwrights did not take place immediately: Goodsir Smith's *The Wallace* is one of very few plays in the late 1950s or early 1960s to follow in the promising directions set out by the work of Kemp, Reid, Munro or McLellan, or indeed to contribute much to the Scottish stage in any other way. As Edwin Morgan suggested at the time, Scottish drama by the mid 1960s still had 'a long way to go . . . Huge areas of Scottish life fly past uncommented on'.[2] This apparent gap in Scottish writing for the stage might be explained by the continuing tendency among dramatists at the time to follow in the footsteps of James Barrie towards the remunerative theatres in London's West End. Roger MacDougall, for example, began his career with *Macadam and Eve* (1950) which moves between physical and spiritual in a Scottish manner and context, recalling Bridie's *Mr Bolfry* (London, 1943), especially in its concern with a sort of devil-figure. MacDougall's second play, however, *To Dorothy a Son* (London, 1951) adopts a manner of vacuous West-End comedy which he sustained until illness overtook his career. Even Robert Kemp, with *Off a Duck's Back* (Windsor, 1960), showed a tendency to move in the direction of well-crafted comedy, while William Douglas Home, brother of the Conservative Prime Minister, made a more predictable departure from Scotland to a lucrative career in the commercial theatre. James Forsyth has been a similarly permanent exile from the Scottish stage, although as Tyrone Guthrie suggested in 1956, his plays have been debarred from commercial success, and sometimes from critical acclaim, perhaps on account of their heightened language and the odd, inward quality of some of their characterisation. Of playwrights emerging at the time, only Ronald Mavor remained much interested in Scottish settings, as in *The Keys of Paradise* (Gateway, 1959), or Scottish characters, such as the young man initiated into a Hemingway-like Paris in *Aurelie* (Byre Theatre, St Andrews, 1961). Though often confined, like his father James Bridie, within middle-class concerns and the box sets usually used for their portrayal, Mavor moves beyond these in his most ambitious play, *Muir of Huntershill* (Pitlochry Festival Theatre, 1962). This takes up a subject of interest to several later playwrights, attempting to trace the whole adventurous career of the radical advocate Thomas Muir, founder of the Society of the Friends of the People in late eighteenth-century Edinburgh.

Developments in any nation's drama require a strong theatre to sustain them: in the Irish context, for example, Yeats, Synge and O'Casey might never have written for the stage without the opportunities offered by the Abbey Theatre in Dublin. If Scottish authors were still tempted to leave for London in the 1950s, and the native scene quiescent, it was at least partly as a result of the absence of sufficient encouragement of new writing from within Scottish theatres. The Gateway did support the work of Kemp, McLellan, Reid and others such as Ada F Kay and James Scotland, but the Citizens' was still complaining in 1966 that 'there aren't enough Scottish plays'.[3] Largely as a result of initiatives at the Traverse Theatre Club (founded in 1963), and later, at the Royal Lyceum, the situation in the mid-1960s began to change in favour of new Scottish writing, helping to establish the new generation of Scottish playwrights whose work is considered below.

Jim Haynes, one of the founders of the Traverse, felt that even by 1966 it had discovered enough new talent to suggest that a 'second Golden Age' was at hand.[4] Though his optimism about Scottish theatre has yet to be fully vindicated, the Traverse was immediately successful in establishing two playwrights whose work occupied a central place in Scottish theatre throughout the next two decades—Stanley Eveling and C P Taylor. Born in Newcastle, Eveling has been since 1955 a philosophy lecturer in Edinburgh University: although many of his plays later transferred to London, almost all were first produced by the Traverse. Some of his work has encouraged critics to see him as a sort of modern moralist: *Come and be Killed* (Traverse, 1967), for example, seems chiefly concerned with the issue of abortion. Eveling's theatre, however, is abstract and philosophical rather than only moral. *Come and be Killed* considers the question of abortion not so much for itself, but rather as a context for a wider examination of how responsibility or the nature of good and evil may be determined in a world no longer ethically secured or made meaningful by religious faith. Eveling has suggested.

> Human action acquires a meaning beyond the social and beyond the social and human there is only the Divine. With the destruction of this conceptual possibility, the demystification of life and existence which science achieves, the ultimate stance of human beings, their last and desperate position is evacuated of meaning.

This sense of an 'evacuation of meaning', along with the existential views of the hero of *Come and be Killed*, ally Eveling with dramatists such as Samuel Beckett whom Martin Esslin has categorised as belonging to a Theatre of the Absurd. Eveling recalls of his first experience of Beckett's drama

> It wasn't until *Waiting for Godot* came along that I really felt excited by the idea of writing plays. As soon as I read it, I said, 'That's it. Home. That's what I'm going to do . . . All mysterious and full of possibility'.

Like the dramatists of the Absurd, Eveling developed a style based on his rejection of the 'self-deception', in a problematic world, of the 'well ordered rational play where solutions are achieved'.[5] Some of his plays do offer fairly transparent meanings, even solutions, as in the allegory of the rise of the Nazis in *The Strange Case of Martin Richter* (Close Theatre, Glasgow, 1967), or the wry, self-reflexive examination of writing and imagination in *Dear Janet Rosenberg, Dear Mr Kooning* (Traverse, 1969). Other works such as *Mister* (Lyceum, 1970) are concerned with attempts to connect an obsessive or dream-ridden world with a more everyday one. Eveling's first play, *The Balachites* (Traverse, 1963), however, is generally representative of the later development of his theatre, moving from a more or less recognisably real world into a strange, abstract dimension, 'mysterious and full of possibility.' The puzzling quality which results has often caused Eveling to be criticised for an 'evacuation of meaning' which has been seen as repetitive or gratuitous. As such criticisms suggest, there is at times an element of *avant garde* flirtation with the easily transcendental, the vaguely profound, which marks some of Eveling's plays as too easily indulgent of the psychedelic mood of the late 1960s and early 1970s. At its best, however, as in *Vibrations* (Edinburgh University, 1968), Eveling's drama shows bizarre events unfolding not gratuitously but as realisations or metaphors for the uncertain minds of the protagonists, much in the manner of Kafka, or, on the stage, of Pinter. *Vibrations* communicates very directly the sense of dislocation and disconnection of consciousness in a world without absolute sense, described by one of the characters as 'obdurate, hostile, inimical . . . our enemy.' *Vibrations* also has the merit, typical of Eveling's plays, of remaining funny and entertaining even while puzzling and profound. Despite the incomprehension which initially surrounded his work, as it did Pinter's, such qualities have encouraged evaluation of Eveling as one of the most original voices in British theatre in the 1960s and 1970s; one able to direct new freedoms of expression within the theatre towards an examination of uncertainties which accompanied new freedoms, moral and metaphysical, in a post-religious age. His work greatly extended the range of Scottish theatre, allowing for an incorporation within it of some of the new forms and interests widespread in European drama at the time.

C P Taylor's long, prolific career—he wrote around 60 plays, for television and radio as well as the stage—took him in an almost opposite direction to Stanley Eveling, geographically at least. Born in Glasgow, Taylor spent his later years largely in Northumbria, and many of his plays were set and performed in Eveling's home town, Newcastle. These include some of Taylor's extensive work for children. *Live Theatre: Four Plays for Young People* (1983), for example, shows a colourful, sympathetic vision of children or young adults working out by means of fantasy or imagination a place for themselves in the real world. Elsewhere in his work, Taylor takes a less optimistic view of distractions from reality in the form of fantasy or extremes of ideals. *The Ballachulish Beat* (1966), for example, is partly a slight satire on the contemporary popular music industry, but also a strange parable about violence and corruption created by acting out any political programme, however idealistic in conception. One of Taylor's best plays, *Bread and Butter* (London, 1966) more subtly incorporates tensions between ideal and actual in a conflict between two characters, Morris and Alex, summed up by the latter as follows:

> I just take it for granted the world moves slow. But forward, forward, all the time. I think people like to live tomorrow as near the same as they live today . . . So, changes come slow, Morris. Not fast enough for people like you, Morris. Because you see how things could be, how good they *could* be, if everybody had your picture of the future and carried it out. (II, iv)

Though *Bread and Butter* shows some sympathy for Morris's tortured, rather vain ideals, Taylor in the end seems to favour Alex's simpler love of open spaces, birds, and the equanimity of a bread-and-butter style of life. Set in the Gorbals from the 1930s to the 1960s, the play also locates in Morris's and Alex's family life a very wide range of historical changes and issues of socialist reform.

Bread and Butter establishes some of Taylor's characteristic themes: later plays show an increasing sophistication in dramatic techniques for their expression. *And a Nightingale Sang* (Newcastle, 1977) continues Taylor's incorporation within working-class family life of a sense of the wider movements of contemporary history, in this case, during the Second World War. But the play's suggestion that events such as a girl's engagement may be as important as the declaration of war is now supported by a style of dialogue particularly adapted to emphasis of mundane rather than exalted, domestic rather than historic. Speeches are chaotically inconsequential and entangled throughout, creating an intricate, funny communication of the muddled conversation and emotion of family life; its warm, disorderly vitality more than sufficient to absorb the huge threats of the time. This disconnected dialogue is extended in some of Taylor's later plays into an oblique manner of general construction which diminishes narrative or logical connection between individual scenes. In *Good* (London, 1981), for example, this makes disturbingly plausible the progress of a 'good' man towards Nazism. Opportunities for moral choice never emerge from the confused texture of daily life with sufficient clarity to allow protagonist or audience a firm grasp of the malevolence which eventually leads to work in the concentration camps. A complex approach to history, personal and national, is also a feature of one of Taylor's best plays with a Scottish setting, *Walter* (Traverse, 1977). This follows unpredictable movements in the mind of a dying Jewish entertainer, who confuses with present experience recollections of an impoverished Glasgow childhood, and of the hopes held out at that time by the great socialist, John MacLean. The juxtapositions which result focus a long view of working-class history, showing the place within it of ideals, and their difficult relation to ordinary life. The warmth and breadth of vision in Taylor's dramatisation of this life in *Walter* is typical of his work as a whole. This vision, and the particular dramatic tactics he creates for its communication, give him a good claim to being the best Scottish dramatist to emerge since the war. Following the success of *Good* in London, and Taylor's early death in 1981, this claim is at present probably most recognised outwith Scotland.

Another prolific playwright to emerge during the 1960s, Tom Gallacher, was initially less fortunate than Taylor or Eveling in finding Scottish venues for his work, though restitution was made in the 1970s by Pitlochry Festival Theatre, where he was writer in residence for a time. Premiered at the Citizens in 1969, and later revived at Pitlochry, Gallacher's first Scottish production, *Our Kindness to Five Persons*, introduces a repeated interest of his writing. The play depicts—sometimes rather melodramatically—emotional relations within a small, tight group, a 'magic circle' of family and friends, concentrated around two brothers who have shown unequal ability in escaping from their wretched city childhood. *The Only Street* (Dublin, 1973) examines a similar predicament. Both plays also show how present experience has come to be clouded by past events, in ways which demonstrate Gallacher's 'passionate admiration' for Ibsen, whose plays *A Doll's House* and *An Enemy of the People* he has adapted for performance at the Royal Lyceum.

Gallacher's interest in relations between brothers, and between past and present, reappears in one of his best plays, *Mr Joyce is leaving Paris* (Dublin, 1971), which opens with Joyce, drunk and irresponsible, arguing with his brother Stanislaus in Trieste in 1908. The second act illustrates Gallacher's ability to move beyond naturalistic action: dreams, songs and flashbacks are used to show Joyce in 1939, haunted by various voices, Stanislaus's included, which examine the worth of his earlier life and artistic career. Essentially a playwright of ideas, Gallacher uses this career as a basis for a self-reflective questioning of the role and responsibilities of the artist, and of the relationship of drama and imagination to truth and life. These questions are further developed in plays such as *Schellenbrack* (London, 1973); and *Revival* (Dublin, 1972), which investigates in a specifically theatrical context conflicts of art and reality connected to a production of Ibsen's *The Master Builder*.

Gallacher's concern with the role of the artist and the 'magic circle' of close family relations also extends into his reworking of *The Tempest, The Sea Change* (Traverse, 1976). Not one of his most successful plays, *The Sea Change* is nevertheless significant for its title and, above all, its setting on an oil rig. Gallacher later remarked of Scotland in the early 1970s that 'the burgeoning riches of oil off the Scottish coast accomplished a sea change in the Arts as well . . . Scottishness was an asset, not a liability'.[6] As Gallacher's comment suggests, this sense of potential affluence for Scotland established for much of the 1970s a sense of possibility for financial and political autonomy which greatly added to the credibility of the Scottish Nationalist party: it also generally renewed interest in the 'asset' of Scottish identity and culture. This was developed by a number of playwrights who investigated Scotland's history, speech and state of mind more directly than had Eveling, Gallacher, or even C P Taylor in the 1960s. For a time, they found an ideal venue for their work not at the Traverse, centre of developments in the previous decade, but at the Royal Lyceum theatre in Edinburgh.

Set up under Tom Fleming's directorship in 1965, the Edinburgh Civic Theatre Trust inherited at the Lyceum some of the role, and some of the audience, developed by Robert Kemp and Fleming himself at the Gateway Theatre. In the early 1970s, under the control of Richard Eyre, Clive Perry and his associate Bill Bryden, it went on to realise much of Fleming's ambition for a theatre of 'national significance.' Impressed by a Festival production of *Ane Satire of the Thrie Estaitis* and its huge cast of Scottish actors, Bryden came to believe in 'a truly Scottish theatre . . . expressing Scotland for the people of Scotland', and in 'new plays, new writers' as a means towards achieving this ideal.[7] The first of the Scottish authors whose work Bryden introduced to the Lyceum was Stewart Conn, not exactly a 'new writer', however. Though Conn considers his early plays as only 'apprentice work', at least one of them, *I Didn't Always Live Here*, had enjoyed popular success when first performed at the Citizens' in 1967, appealing directly to Glasgow audiences through its grimly realistic setting in the city. *I Didn't Always Live Here* also established an area Conn returned to in some of his Lyceum plays. *The Aquarium* (1973), for example, examines what one of its characters calls 'the middle-class Glaswegian: a study in decay' (I, i). As in *I Didn't Always Live Here*, this decay is accelerated by the dreary impoverishment of the characters' lives and environment: it is particularly sharply focused in this play, however, especially in its later stages, by dream-like and symbolic sections which perhaps reflect something of Conn's admiration for Stanley Eveling. The effect of a depressing urban environment is further examined in *Play Donkey* (Lyceum, 1977), which traces the condemned mercenary Tommy's upbringing through various scenes which show his grieving parents in their Scottish home. Tommy also rather grimly suggests the connection between possible oil revenues and Scotland's new nationalism when he remarks

> Bonnie Prince Charlie . . . I mean, he didn't make it, did he. And we've been trying ever since. That's where I should've been. Back there. Marching on the bloody English . . . I mean there'd have been some point in that, eh? Fighting for wur freedom, after all these centuries. Might even have been a chance of me getting paid for it, now there's all that oil. (II, xiii)

Tommy's position as a victim caught between forces—poverty, diplomatic indifference, foreign hostility—is emphasised by his mother's recollection that even as a child, 'when they played Donkey or that . . . our Tommy always seemed to be the one in the middle' (I, ix). This idea reappears in *The Aquarium*, whose characters feel they are 'the ones to suffer, time and time again. The pigs in the middle' (I, ii). It is also central to the play which opened Bryden's campaign for Scottish theatre at the Lyceum, *The Burning*. Like Robert McLellan's *Jamie the Saxt* (1937), *The Burning* shows the struggle between James and the Earl of Bothwell, generating (like Arthur Miller's *The Crucible*) stage excitement from the witches whom Bothwell enlists to help his cause. Even witches, however, are eventually victims, along with the common people of Scotland, of a power struggle in which the king and Bothwell are 'the upper and nether millstones . . . one way or another, it is those trappt in the middle, must pay the price' (II, iv). Directions followed by later Scottish playwrights were firmly established by this vision of the common people oppressed by an unjust history: its expression in *The Burning* is greatly enhanced, like McLellan's in *Jamie the Saxt*, by the vigour of the Scots language Conn creates for his characters. A poet as well as a dramatist, Conn's speech, verse and song are the most consistently successful aspects of his staging, perhaps as a result of his long involvement with radio drama. His work as a drama producer for Radio Scotland has helped to sustain an important outlet for Scottish play writing. Radio has been perhaps particularly successful in presenting the work of authors like Conn who are poets as well as dramatists—for example, George Mackay Brown's *A Spell for Green Corn* (1967).

One genuinely new writer to emerge at the Lyceum in the 1970s was Bill Bryden himself. His drama helped to develop for the stage the working life and speech of the West of Scotland: his home town, Greenock, is the setting for his first play, *Willie Rough* (1972), an account of a shipyard strike during the Red Clydeside period of John MacLean—'like a fever up an doun this river' (II, xiii). *Willie Rough* benefits from a Brechtian clarity and economy of scenic construction: Bryden's second play, *Benny Lynch* (1974) is similarly structured, but around a better-developed central narrative. In the story of the brilliant Glasgow boxer, at first successful but eventualy drink-sodden and pathetically abandoned, Bryden finds a paradigm for the corrosive effects of Glaswegian poverty and the capacity for self-defeat and self-destruction even in those talented enough to escape them for a time.

Bryden's successful treatment of West Coast speech and manners was helped by another figure influential at the Lyceum in the early seventies, Roddy McMillan, an outstanding actor whose performance as the foreman in *Willie Rough* exemplified his talent for portraying dour, resilient Scottish characters. His long career included appearances in Alexander Reid's plays in the early 1950s, and even a part in Robert McLeish's *The Gorbals Story*, produced with great popular success by Glasgow Unity in 1946. *The Gorbals Story* probably influenced McMillan's own first play, *All in Good Faith* (Citizens', 1954), which uses a similar crowded tenement setting for its portrayal of a family so firmly entrapped by the desperate conditions of city life that even sudden riches cannot save them. Starkly authentic in setting and dialogue, the play's bleak view of Glasgow provoked what McMillan felt to be a hostile reaction among some early audiences and critics, deterring him from writing again for the stage for nearly 20 years. His second play, *The Bevellers* (Lyceum, 1973), is set in a glassworks during a young apprentice's first day at work, and extends the strong dialogue and tough, claustrophobic environment of *All in Good Faith*. At one level, it is simply a painfully accurate portrayal of some of the realities of working life—the humour and dignity of shared toil as well as its numbing arduousness. *The Bevellers* also has a more metaphoric level, however: the basement setting represents the depths of wage slavery which traps characters beneath the idle feet of passers by, while the vividly-presented grinding and bevelling work is emblematic of some of the harsh, habitual cruelties of Scottish working life, illustrated with particular clarity in their devastating effect on the young boy. This unusual depth in portraying a working community suggests that Roddy McMillan's long silence deprived the Scottish stage of a talent which might have been able to sustain the committed strengths of the Glasgow Unity company into the fifties and beyond.

Another playwright influenced by Unity, Edward Boyd, records a great admiration for Roddy McMillan, and has extended some of his tough treatment of urban life into his own work, most of the best of which has been for television. Along with several other commentators, Boyd has also suggested that ' "The Bevellers" made possible the success of a *soufflé* like "The Slab Boys" '.[8] Set in the dye-mixing room of a carpet factory, John Byrne's play does share with *The Bevellers* the unusual quality of portraying working life sustainedly and in detail, and appears, as Boyd suggests, to be in an altogether lighter and more frivolous style. Brilliantly inventive comic dialogue is the greatest strength of *The Slab Boys*: its humour, however, is highlighted by darker aspects of the play, particularly the veiled desperation of a central character frustrated by his family and his sense of artistic failure. *The Slab Boys* (1978) and its sequels, *Threads* (1979) and *Still Life* (1982), contain too much pain to be only 'soufflé': they are instead highly entertaining developments for the stage of the Glasgow area's distinctive humour, which often originates in experience so bitter as to make some laughter peculiarly essential.

Even after the departures of Bill Bryden and Clive Perry in the mid 1970s, the Lyceum continued to produce promising new Scottish plays, such as Ian Brown's inventive view of Mary Queen of Scots, *Mary* (1977). In an earlier play, *Carnegie* (Lyceum, 1973), Brown had considered the complex character of the 'two-faced philanthropist' and 'three-faced bugger' Andrew Carnegie. In *Mary*, the even more multifaceted figure of the queen is appropriately dramatised through a multiplicity of styles, tones, and historical points of view. Their variety communicates unusually successfully the extent of the problem Mary's much-dramatised life has posed for Scottish history and the Scottish imagination.

Towards the end of the 1970s, however, the excitement and initiative at the Lyceum in the earlier part of the decade had begun to fade, and the Traverse, venue for Byrne's *Slab Boys* trilogy, was once again the centre of new developments. Another of its successes was *The Hard Man* (1977), one of the most controversial plays of the decade. Written by a former editor of *Peace News* and *International Times*, Tom McGrath, in collaboration with Jimmy Boyle, it presented the latter's career as one of Scotland's most wanted criminals and violent prisoners. The sensational quality of this subject matter partly distracted attention from the unusualness of the play's technique, employing a percussionist on stage to accentuate bursts of choreographed violence, 'calculated to release energy in the audience', according to McGrath. Such tactics reflect his involvement in experimental theatre in Glasgow in the 1960s, and his admiration for the 'sculptural theatre . . . wonderfully creative use of space' established by Polish directors such as Grotowski and Kantor. Such interests are extended in Tom McGrath's later experimentation with a variety of subjects and genres; perhaps most strikingly in the almost wordless tribal ritual *Animal* (Traverse, 1979), which developed for the Scottish stage some of the more exciting movements in recent Continental theatre, Poland's in particular.

The Traverse was also the venue for Donald Campbell's first play, *The Jesuit* (1976), which shows its author's admiration for Robert McLellan, and his own central concern with what he calls 'exploration of the complexities and potential of the idioms of Scottish speech'.[9] This potential is employed in *The Jesuit* to highlight and further isolate the Jesuit martyr Robert Ogilvie, the only figure in the play to speak standard English throughout, and to bring more warmly to life, partly by contrast, the common soldiery through whose experience the play's bitter religious conflicts are mostly presented. Rather like Stewart Conn, Campbell shows the common people as resilient victims of the conflicts and machinations of higher powers:

> it's aye the same—the meenisters and the priests and the high-heid anes'll dae the argyin and the stirrin up—but when it comes tae the killin and the deein . . . (II, iv).

Campbell's presentation of ordinary figures trapped in historical conflicts continues in *Somerville the Soldier* (Traverse, 1978), concerned with a soldier who refuses to allow his personal reputation to be appropriated by forces either of radicalism or reaction during the Chartist period of the 1830s. Heroic resilience of ordinary people also figures in *The Widows of Clyth* (Traverse, 1979) which uses the speech and landscape of Campbell's native Caithness as a background for a story of survival by women deprived of support by their husbands' drowning.

Like *The Jesuit*, Hector MacMillan's *The Rising* (Dundee Rep, 1973) uses Scots to differentiate a wide cast of characters: like Campbell, or Conn, MacMillan envisages historical forces as a threat or trap for the common people. Described by MacMillan in his preface as an attempt 'to recreate on stage the essence of a part of our history', *The Rising* depicts the rebellions which spontaneously broke out throughout the Scottish lowlands in 1820. It presents a bitter picture of justified radicalism destroyed by English influence and the complicity of the Scottish upper class. Like Sydney Goodsir Smith, and several of the Scottish playwrights of the 1970s, MacMillan uses choruses of Burns's 'bought and sold for English gold' to emphasise his view of Scottish history. Folk song, vivid dialect and stark portrayal of conflict are also among the strengths of MacMillan's most successful play, *The Sash* (Pool Theatre, Edinburgh, 1974). Like George Munro's *Mark but this Flea*, the play examines religious hatred, opening to the sound of 'The Sash' being played and sung in the streets of Glasgow on 12 July. Violent in mood and action, some of the effectiveness of *The Sash* is compromised by the stage energy generated by the play's central figure, a bigoted but immensely vital orangeman. Like *Mark but this Flea*, however, *The Sash* locates some sympathy and some hope for the future in characters from a younger generation. Like Munro, MacMillan also presents religious bigotry—'fighting for mansions in the sky'—as a distraction from political commitment to improving 'middens on earth': *The Sash* concludes with the chorus

Tell them to Hell with Orange and Green!

Our banner like our common blood
Should be Red!—not Orange, not Green!

This conclusion and the general tone of *The Sash* and *The Rising* help to indicate that the 1970s were buoyant years not only for nationalist sentiments but for socialism in Scotland. Scottish participation in the miners' strike, and, particularly, the prolonged occupation of the Upper Clyde Shipbuilders' Yard in 1971 demonstrated the power of labour action in Scotland, and its successful results were widely celebrated on the stage. Though concerned with an earlier phase of Clydeside radicalism, Bryden's *Willie Rough* had an obvious relevance to contemporary events at UCS which heightened its popular appeal at the time. The story of the occupation of Upper Clyde Shipbuilders (thinly disguised as a boot factory) was also presented in another very popular performance in Glasgow in 1972, *The Great Northern Welly Boot Show*. Though its mixture of songs and sketches seemed only light satiric entertainment, the production was significant at least as a focus for a range of talents later to develop in several directions on the Scottish stage. The designer was the artist and playwright John Byrne, author of *The Slab Boys*. Some of the music was by playwright Tom McGrath, and the songs were by Billy Connolly, who later added to his success as a stand-up comedian by writing plays of hard-worded stairheid naturalism such as *An me wi' a Bad Leg Tae* (Borderline, Ayrshire, 1976). The script as a whole was by Tom Buchan, who had earlier practised some of its style in a 'satirical liberation romp' *Tell Charlie Thanks for the Truss* (Traverse, 1971) and went on to write more muted, naturalistic 'party political broadcasts on behalf of the human race' such as *Over the Top* (Traverse, 1979).

Another very useful legacy of *The Great Northern Welly Boot Show* was the lessons it offered performers who went on to found with John McGrath a Scottish branch of the 7:84 Theatre Company. McGrath had begun his career writing for the English stage (as well as for films and television), plays such as *Events while Guarding the Bofors Gun* (London, 1966) and *Bakke's Night of Fame* (London, 1968) showing his talent for crisp dialogue and concise scenes, moved briskly forward, in these two plays, by the death wish of the protagonist. Though still partly psychological in interest, and broadly naturalistic in style, *Random Happenings in the Hebrides* (Lyceum, 1970), indicates a transition in McGrath's interests towards Scottish affairs and political subjects. In England in 1971 he helped found the 7:84 company, dedicated to the proposition that 7 per cent of the nation's population should not possess 84 per cent of its wealth, and in general to challenging audiences with the sort of questions raised by the character in *Yobbo Nowt* (7:84 England, 1975) who explains

The capitalist system—that's my subject, right? It makes people cheat and rob each other, turns men and countries against each other, and it's unjust, corrupt and evil: how come you . . . put up with it? (11)

Fish in the Sea (Liverpool, 1972) shows the beginnings of the broad, didactic style McGrath developed for the communication of such issues. He later described this as

> An emergent mode of theatre . . . which speaks the language of working class entertainment and tries to develop that language to make critical, progressive theatre primarily for popular audiences.[10]

Performers from *The Great Northern Welly Boot Show* already knew this 'language', having learned for themselves that traditional forms of Scottish entertainment, pantomime or music hall, could be adapted into enjoyable political and satiric theatre. With John McGrath they developed 7:84 Scotland's first production, *The Cheviot, the Stag and the Black, Black Oil* (1973), which used songs, recitations, caricatured characters, and direct address to an audience also involved in singing and dancing. The overall format corresponded to another type of popular entertainment, the ceilidh, giving the show immediate popular appeal to audiences throughout the company's extended Highland tour. Its success also derived from the urgent topicality of the issues it analysed. Analogies with the Highland clearances—and the subsequent conversion of Scotland into a game park for absentee landlords—made the current exploitation of Scotland by the oil industry comprehensible in terms of the nation's bitter past. By dramatising a series of successful acts of resistance, McGrath also shows what can and must be done about Scotland's continuing history of expropriation and exploitation. This commitment to contemporary issues, along with a broad popularity of appeal in examining them, allowed 7:84 to reach the heart of Scottish life and interests in a way which had not been seen on the stage since the demise of Glasgow Unity at the start of the 1950s. Though 7:84 has never altogether repeated the success of *The Cheviot, the Stag and the Black, Black Oil*, it established a newly extended theatre audience which remained for subsequent projects in the 1970s such as *The Game's a Bogey* (1974), which presents the life of John MacLean; *Little Red Hen* (1975), tracing Scottish labour history throughout the twentieth century; and *Joe's Drum* (1979), a response to the fact that a majority of the Scottish population voted for devolution in the 1979 referendum, and were denied it, while a majority voted against a Conservative government, which was inflicted upon the country nonetheless.

Joe's Drum is in this way something of an epitaph for the seventies in Scotland, and for the theatrical revival which occurred in the decade. Tom Gallacher similarly summed up contemporary events by remarking 'the Referendum was most unfairly lost; an anti-Art Government came to power again'.[11] Each event had adverse consequences for Scotland and its theatre. Failure of the referendum curtailed nationalist sentiments which had lain behind renewed theatrical interest in Scotland and its identity: Scottishness no longer seemed so much of an asset. The reappearance of a Conservative government likewise curtailed socialist optimism: *Blood Red Roses* (7:84, 1980), one of John McGrath's 'Two Plays for the Eighties', shows the labour movement mostly as a rearguard action, while the other, *Swings and Roundabouts* (7:84, 1980), abandons the broad, bold didactic style of the

1970s in favour of naturalism and farce. More generally, the new government's further fierce retrenchment in public spending damaged the operation of many theatres: the situation has deteriorated since 1977, when the Scottish Arts Council's annual report warned that 'tightening of belts, cut backs in casts, shorter seasons, and a lot of make do and mend . . . cannot continue for long without seriously affecting standards' (p 15).

One of the groups to suffer in this way has been the Scottish Theatre Company, set up in 1980 partly as a result of a long period of hopes and agitation for a Scottish National Theatre. Neil Gunn suggested the need for one in 1938; it was further recommended by an Arts Council report in 1970; and Bill Bryden claimed it as 'the right of the people of Scotland' in the course of his work at the Lyceum in the early 1970s. During this promising period, Roddy McMillan and several others at the Lyceum and elsewhere believed that 'a national theatre was beginning to loom through the mist',[12] but it faded from sight again after Bryden's departure—ironically for the National Theatre of London—and the failure to build an opera house complex as its permanent home. Lacking a permanent base and generally short of funds, Scottish Theatre Company has yet to establish itself as a likely means of creating a Scottish National Theatre.

Even without such an institution, however, and despite recent restrictions in funding, a comparison of the 1970s with the early 1950s shows Scotland relatively well provided with theatrical resources. Opened by James Bridie in 1950, the Royal Scottish Academy of Music and Drama continues to provide a specific training for Scottish performers, and some element of drama teaching is now included in the work of most Scottish schools and universities. Founded in 1974, the Scottish Society of Playwrights has supported writers in various ways, publishing the work of good dramatists such as Joan Ure, little known apart from her work for radio. 7:84's extensive tours with *The Cheviot, the Stag, and the Black Black Oil*, and with subsequent productions, have created in village halls and working men's clubs throughout Scotland a new audience for drama, often far from the mainstream lowland theatres. Other Scottish and visiting companies, Scottish Theatre Company included, have been encouraged to adopt a touring strategy, helped by the increased availability of stage spaces in arts and leisure centres around the country. One new touring company, Fir Chlis, founded in 1979, briefly suggested (before financial problems overtook them in 1981) the possibility of a professional theatre as an outlet for Gaelic drama, which continues to be written by authors such as Ian Crichton Smith. Even in terms of permanent bases, progress has been made since the 1950s: most of the auditoria of that time remain more or less functional, while new theatre buildings have been established at Pitlochry and Dundee. Throughout the period considered, the Edinburgh Festival has continued to stimulate audiences, writers and performers with the best in world drama, while the Festival Fringe has particularly contributed to interest in the experimental and *avant garde*. The Traverse theatre was created fairly directly out of energies generated by the Fringe: as Stanley Eveling has suggested, the unusualness of its playing area has been a continuing stimulus to playwrights' experimentation and innovation.

Another outstanding theatrical asset has been the Citizens' Theatre in Glasgow, often described, since the arrival of Giles Havergal as director in 1969, as the most exciting repertory theatre in Britain. Critics sceptical of its contribution specifically to Scottish theatre overlook the work of another director, Robert David MacDonald, a Scottish writer of exceptional range and intelligence. His personal knowledge of the work of German authors and directors such as Piscator and Hocchuth, and his talent as an adapter and translator from several European languages, have contributed greatly to the Citizens' many productive forays into the Continental repertoire, and to the formation of its own characteristic style. Some of this is expressed in one of MacDonald's rarer original plays, *Chinchilla* (Citizens', 1977). Its tracing, even through strange or decadent circumstances, of 'passion for beauty, a thirst to show, a lust to tell' (I) might be taken as representative of the work of the Citizens' itself; the flamboyant, self-conscious artifice of its productions arising incongruously from among the rubble of Glasgow's decaying city centre. Extraordinary projects such as MacDonald's adaptation of Proust, *Waste of Time* (1979), have brought the best of European literature, imagination and theatre to Gorbals Cross for many years. Such an achievement cannot fail to be of use in helping to form a new generation of Scottish playwrights.

In the work of Peter Arnott, John Clifford, Marcella Evaristi, George Gunn, Chris Hannan, Liz Lochhead, and Stuart Paterson, there is at any rate evidence that a promising new generation is beginning to establish itself. Many of the playwrights discussed above are also still active. Their work over the past three decades offers at least a firm basis for future developments, despite limitations critics have rightly diagnosed as accompanying its strengths. Some of these shortcomings are summarised by David Hutchison, for example, when he remarks at the end of his valuable survey *The Modern Scottish Theatre* (1977) that 'few Scottish dramatists have shown the capacity to move from documentation to metaphor' (p 149). Hutchison's specific criticism of Stewart Conn's *The Burning*—that it 'tells a story at the expense of exploring fully its implications' (p 139)—might also be more widely applied to other recent plays of historical interest: *The Rising*, *The Wallace*, *The Jesuit*, *Willie Rough*, or many of the plays of Kemp or McLellan. Two defences of such writing must nevertheless be suggested. The almost embarrassing frequency with which *Ane Satire of the Thrie Estaitis* has been revived indicates the paucity of further models for Scottish playwrights: in general, the absence of a Scottish dramatic tradition which might have established tactics for assimilating in the theatre Scotland's turbulent flux of public life and affairs. Recent excursions into Scotland's past have as a result almost the status of first attempts 'to recreate on the stage the essence of a part of our history', in Hector MacMillan's phrase. So it is perhaps not surprising that some playwrights have not always progressed beyond mere narratives of events to provide a broader vision of their relevance to human nature or political organisation in general. In examining the latter area, John McGrath has in any case remained consistently 'Plugged into History' (one of his titles) in analysing both causes and cures for political oppression.

A second defence of recent drama is that what appears to be mere 'documentation' of certain phases of Scotland's past may be suggestive enough to be metaphoric in itself. Characters in *The Rising*, for example, who are persecuted for their wish to 'set up a Scottish assembly, or Parliament, in Edinburgh' can obviously 'appeal wi confidence tae posterity' if the posterity concerned is a Scottish theatre audience in 1973. Other histories of oppression, in which the Scottish people are 'the ones to suffer . . . pigs in the middle', carried a relevance to nationalist sentiment or socialist views in the 1970s obvious enough not to require explicit statement. Rather like W B Yeats in Ireland, some recent Scottish writers have used past histories, or heroes, as contexts which comment implicitly upon, or help to develop, national identity or political understanding in the present. This is particularly demonstrated by the extent of recent interest in the Clydeside Marxist John MacLean, who figures in plays such as *Willie Rough*, *The Game's a Bogey*, *Little Red Hen*, and *Walter*. Retelling of John MacLean's story is obviously relevant to a country which has consistently supported socialism throughout recent decades, helping to create for Scottish radicalism a confident sense of appropriateness and historical continuity.

History has been one centre of interest in recent Scottish drama: plays such as *Willie Rough* also belong to its other dominant mode, realistic treatment of the conditions of Lowland city life, seldom presented on the Scottish stage before the nineteen-forties. Development of this area has at times been inhibited by what Hutchison calls a 'naturalistic portrayal of circumstances' which fails to 'seek to relate that portrayal to wider social and indeed spiritual concerns'.[13] As in recent treatments of history, however, there may be virtue even in apparently modest aims and styles. Alasdair Gray's novel *Lanark* (1980) describes Glasgow as

> the sort of industrial city where most people live nowadays but nobody imagines living . . . if a city hasn't been used by an artist not even the inhabitants live there imaginatively. (Chapters 11, 22)

Though often omitting 'wider spiritual concerns', plays such as *The Sash*, *Willie Rough*, *I Didn't Always Live Here*, *An Me wi' a Bad Leg Tae* generate a simple but powerful excitement through the immediacy of rapport between urban life on stage and the experience of an audience rarely granted by earlier playwrights any imaginative vision of the cities in which most of its members are likely to live. This excitement is much enhanced by the development of a language which lets the stage speak to spectators in the tones and terms they might use to speak to themselves or to each other. In this way, recent dramatic exploitation not so much of Braid Scots but of the language of 'Argyle Street, Glasgow, or the Kirkgate, Leith' has greatly added to the theatre's ability to communicate Scottish issues to the Scottish people with direct, compelling clarity.

In thus developing the language and themes of a specifically Scottish theatre, the drama has at last begun to extend some of the initiatives apparent in Scottish fiction and poetry in the earlier part of the century. Tardiness in doing so may be attributed to many factors. It might, for example, be compared to the relative slowness of development of twentieth-century English theatre, apparently unable to move beyond bourgeois naturalism until the late 1950s. Or it might be seen as a further example of what Edwin Morgan has described as 'the slow, broken, and disturbed development of drama which Scotland owes to a complex of historical circumstances'[14]—perhaps including some dwindling legacy of Knox or Calvin which makes Scots uneasy enthusiasts for theatre in general. At any rate, the drama's progress in the period surveyed has been faster, and less disturbed, at least until 1979, than at any time earlier in Scotland's history. More imagination within and beyond the naturalist domain; more width and depth of vision are still required, but the work of the writers discussed has ensured that fewer areas of Scottish life 'fly past uncommented on', and that there are now, tentatively established, styles and techniques adapted to the communication of Scottish experience, past and present. Jim Haynes's 'Golden Age' still seems rather distant, but by the end of the seventies Scottish drama had at least moved some way beyond the bronze age which George Munro discerned around him 30 years earlier.

NOTES

1 George Munro, 'The Adventures of a Playwright,' unpublished typescript, Mitchell Library, pp 5, 7.
2 Edwin Morgan, 'Scottish Writing Today II: The Novel and the Drama,' *English*, Autumn 1967, pp 228, 229.
3 David Williams, director of the Citizens', interviewed by Frank Cox, 'The Scots and the Theatre,' *Plays and Players*, March 1966, p 60.
4 Jim Haynes, interviewed by Frank Cox, 'Life at the Traverse,' *Plays and Players*, May 1966, p 69.
5 Stanley Eveling, *The Total Theatre* (Edinburgh, 1972), pp 10, 11; and interviewed in *Scottish Theatre News*, September 1983, p 21.
6 Tom Gallacher, 'To Succeed at Home,' *Chapman 43–4: On Scottish Theatre*, Spring 1986, p 89.
7 Tom Fleming, quoted by Frank Cox, 'The Scots and the Theatre,' *Plays and Players*, April 1966, p 62. Bill Bryden, 'Bricks on our Shoulders,' *Theatre 74*, Sheridan Morley (ed) (London, 1974), p 127.
8 Edward Boyd, Introduction to Roddy McMillan *All in Good Faith* (Glasgow, 1979).
9 Gavin Selerie (ed), *The Riverside Interviews, 6: Tom McGrath* (London, 1983), pp 188, 238. Donald Campbell, 'A Focus of Discontent,' *New Edinburgh Review*, Spring 1979, p 4.
10 John McGrath, *A Good Night Out* (London, 1981), p 100.
11 Tom Gallacher, op. cit. (note 6).
12 Bryden's opinion appears in 'Bricks on our Shoulders' (*see* note 7), p 130; Roddy McMillan's view is mentioned by Edward Boyd (*see* note 8).
13 David Hutchison, 'Roddy McMillan and the Scottish Theatre,' *Cencrastus*, Spring 1980, p 7.
14 Edwin Morgan, op. cit. (note 2).

FURTHER READING

BOOKS

Campbell, Donald, *A Brighter Sunshine: A Hundred Years of the Edinburgh Royal Lyceum Theatre* (Edinburgh, 1983)

Hutchison, David, *The Modern Scottish Theatre* (Glasgow, 1977)

JOURNALS

Chapman 43–4: On Scottish Theatre (Spring 1986)

Scotish Theatre (1969–73)

Scottish Theatre News

The Mitchell Library in Glasgow holds a good collection of unpublished Scottish drama in typescript, as well as published plays and other material relating to Scottish theatre. Some of this has also been collected by Linda Mackenney for the Scottish Theatre Archive, now established in Glasgow University Library.

INDEX

The index is arranged word-by-word.
Authors are indexed under their own name; their works appear twice, under title,
and listed with the author.